Deleuze and Literature

Thanks to Trevor Pull for technical assistance,
and to Alex Edwards for her help and support.

For Courtney Anne Buchanan
and David Dennis Marks.

Deleuze and Literature

Edited by Ian Buchanan and John Marks

Edinburgh University Press

Edinburgh University Press Ltd
22 George Square, Edinburgh

Reprinted 2003
Transferred to digital printing 2006

Typeset in 10.5 on 13 Sabon
by Hewer Text Ltd, Edinburgh, and
printed and bound in Great Britain by
CPI Antony Rowe, Eastbourne

A CIP record for this book is
available from the British Library

ISBN 10 0 7486 1207 6 (paperback)
ISBN 13 978 0 7486 1207 9 (paperback)

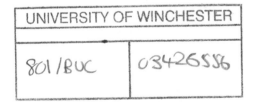

Contents

Deleuze and Literature

Ian Buchanan and John Marks

It would be impossible to overestimate the importance of literature to Gilles Deleuze. In 1964 he published the first French edition of *Proust and Signs* (1972), and in 1967 a study of the work of Sacher-Masoch, *Masochism: An Introduction to Coldness and Cruelty* (1989). *The Logic of Sense* (1990), published in French in 1969, was a philosophical work which included material on Artaud, Lewis Carroll, Fitzgerald, Klossowski, Lowry, Tournier and Zola. Together with Félix Guattari he published *Kafka: Toward a Minor Literature* (1986) in 1975, and the two volumes of the *Capitalism and Schizophrenia* project, *Anti-Oedipus* (1984) and *A Thousand Plateaus* (1987), contain important material on literature, including a long section on the concept of 'becoming' in *A Thousand Plateaus*, which offers a reading of Melville's *Moby Dick*. It was not, however, until Deleuze's last published book, *Essays Critical and Clinical* (1997), that he produced a series of essays on the subject of literature and writing in general.

There, Deleuze argues that while it is true that the essential problem of writing is indeed a matter of language, it is not a textual problem. Rather it is a matter of creating what he likes to call (borrowing from Proust) a 'foreign language' within language. He draws on the work of Maurice Blanchot in order to draw a distinction between a limit which is outside language, and the particular limit that he wishes to explore, which is 'outside of language' (Deleuze 1997: lv). This 'outside' is made up of blocs of seeing and hearing – 'visions and auditions' – which are not made up of language, but which language makes possible. Literature must attempt, to borrow Beckett's phrase, to drill holes in language in order to see and hear what lies behind, and to release new colours and sonorities (Deleuze 1997: iv). For Deleuze and Guattari, it is significant that Kafka's work frequently makes use of animal sounds and cries of pain. Deleuze and Guattari refer to Kafka's diaries, in which he says metaphor makes him 'despair of literature' (Deleuze and Guattari 1986: 22). Instead, Kafka seeks to turn language away from signification and representation towards the expression of intensities.

For Deleuze, it is a matter of record that what is interesting takes place 'in the middle'. And literature, more surely than any other form of discourse, has the potential to explore the middle.[1] In this way, literature can explore the 'event'. A commonsense narrative conceives of events in a conventional way: an event, like a battle, has a locatable beginning and an end, and is constructed by a series of actors. However, considered in terms of impersonal becomings – what Nietzsche calls the untimely – events, even great events like battles, are much more enigmatic: 'Any event is a fog of a million droplets' (Deleuze and Parnet 1987: 65). An event is necessarily effected in bodies, as they collide and interpenetrate, but there is also the 'metaphysical event', which is on the surface like a mist over the prairie. A battle is a collision of bodies, but there is also 'an impassive, incorporeal, impenetrable battle' (Deleuze and Parnet 1987: 64). The Stoics make a line of separation pass between things and events, and this allows them to explore the 'it', the impersonal aspect, of the event (Deleuze and Parnet 1987: 63). We may think that, as active agents, we are at the heart of events, but the event tends to dissolve the self. Stoic philosophy responds to this problem by seeking to embrace the impersonality of the event. Literature can plunge into the 'middle' and exhaust the possibilities of the event, laying them out on a plane of immanence.

In so doing, the writer eschews the *ressentiment* and the tendency towards judgement of the priest. The priest is a 'trickster', who avoids becoming in favour of imitation and taking possession of fixed properties, and, worst of all, judgement. The French literary scene, on Deleuze's view produces a dreary sort of 'nationalism in letters', a mania for judging (Deleuze and Parnet 1987: 50). Greek tragedy inaugurates a mode of judgement which becomes an essential element of the Judeo-Christian tradition. Spinoza is the first to break with this tradition, followed by four great disciples: Nietzsche, D. H. Lawrence, Kafka and Artaud.[2] Nietzsche shows that the system of cruelty is opposed to the 'bookish doctrine' of judgement. Judgement implies an organisation of bodies, whereas the body of the physical system is 'an affective, intensive, anarchist body that consists solely of poles, zones, thresholds, and gradients' (Deleuze 1997: 131). Combat, and in particular 'combat-between', also replaces judgement. Combat is opposed to the sicknesses of war, the lowest degree of the will to power, and fascism. For Deleuze, it is a question of bringing into existence rather than judging: 'What expert judgement, in art, could ever bear on the work to come?' (1997: 135). Of course, to 'have done with' judgement does not imply a relativist position according to which everything is of equal value. It is rather a question of being flexible enough in one's thinking to allow something new to enter into existence:

> If it is so disgusting to judge, it is not because everything is of equal value, but on the contrary because what has value can be made or distinguished only by defying judgement. What expert judgement, in art, could ever bear on the work to come? It is not a question of judging other existing beings, but of sensing whether they agree or disagree with us, that is, whether they bring forces to us, or whether they return us to the miseries of war, to the poverty of the dream, to the rigors of organization. (Deleuze 1997: 135)

If the critical vocation of literature is derived from Deleuze's reading of Spinoza – literature as a means of suspending judgement and establishing affects – the clinical vocation of literature as a means of constructing percepts is derived from Deleuze's reading of Bergson. Deleuze's seminars at Vincennes dealt frequently with Bergson in the early 1980s, laying the groundwork for his work on cinema, but also making references to literature which are briefly alluded to in the cinema books. Bergson allows Deleuze to think of cinema in terms of a machinic universe of a-centred perception: a world without centre in which the 'kino-eye' has been liberated from its conventional human form. Under these conditions, perception takes off on a line of flight to become a form of *délire*. Deleuze speaks admiringly of Scorsese's *Taxi Driver*, in which Travis Bickle experiences a form of *délire*, a purely optical situation in which the conventional articulation of perception-action is interrupted, permitting a 'blooming' ['éclosion'] of *délire*. This leads Deleuze to draw a series of parallels between the *nouveau roman* and a particular form of cinematic consciousness. (In fact, Robbe-Grillet's *For a New Novel* (1989) constitutes something of a 'missing link' in Deleuze's reading of literature.) The *nouveau roman* privileges a purely 'optical' mode, seeking to divest language of the dead weight of memories, metaphors and associations. However, this formal commitment to description aims not at objectivity, but at a sort of pure *subjectivity*. Again, it is a question of thinking in terms of the middle, of suspending judgement and thinking in terms of packets of sensation rather than 'characters'.[3]

It is obvious, then, that Deleuze's approach to literature cannot be distinguished from his innovative work on cinema. He admires all art which aspires to a genuinely 'fictional' purity (in the sense of 'pure subjectivity' discussed above), which seeks to 'break things open', as he says of Foucault, in order to explore the middle. Literature can bore holes in language to achieve this effect, and cinema can also 'make holes' in order to go beyond the cliché. Sometimes it is necessary to restore the lost parts, to rediscover everything that cannot be seen in the image, everything that has been removed to make it 'interesting'. But sometimes, on the contrary, it is necessary to make holes, to introduce voids and white spaces, to rarify the image, by suppressing many things that have been added to make us believe that we were seeing everything. It is necessary to make a division or make emptiness in order to find the whole again (Deleuze 1997: 21). Similarly, Deleuze claims that literature also has a political function, but a function which is collective, since writing itself is essentially a collective activity (Deleuze and Parnet 1987: 51).

Ultimately, the political task of writing consists in 'inventing' a people who do not yet exist. In the same way that writers do not write with their ego, so they do not write on behalf of a people. The collective emerges, in this way, from the writer's creation of pre-individual singularities. The 'collective', in Deleuzian terms, is a form of 'delirium', speaking *with*, writing *with* (see Deleuze 1997: 4). According to Deleuze and Guattari, a minor literature does not come from a 'minor' language, but rather a 'deterritorialised' variation of a major language, such as Prague German, the 'paper language' that Kafka uses. They are here inspired by Kafka's comments on minority literature, and in *Kafka: Toward a Minor Literature* (1986) Deleuze and Guattari outline the essentially 'political' function of 'minor literature'. It is a form of literature in which the delirium of language creates a sort of free indirect discourse whereby there is no private history that is not immediately public (see also Deleuze 1997: 57).

Questions of style and politics lead us to areas which can usefully be developed out of Deleuze's work on literature. Deleuze restricts himself, as we have already seen, to a largely modernist canon. Of course, in one way, writers such as Kafka and Beckett are thematically close to Deleuze. It is possible, however, to produce readings of other forms of literature which are inspired by Deleuze. For example, Deleuze and Guattari talk of 'Balzac's greatness' in terms of his ability to create percepts which give characters 'giant dimensions' (1994: 171). In this way, Deleuze avoids the 'ideological double bind', whereby Balzac stands for either unenlightened representationality or readerly experimentation, depending upon one's historical vantage point (Jameson 1981: 18). Despite occasional appearances to the contrary, Deleuze avoids the pitfalls of writing a literary manifesto. Essentially, Deleuze offers a literary aesthetics, or, in more general terms, an aesthetics of writing. The depth and intensity of Deleuze's interest in literature can be measured in some part by the fact that this volume, as substantial and searching as it is, in no way exhausts all the avenues one might pursue in engaging with Deleuze's writing about literature. In fact, our suspicion is that no one volume could do justice to it. What we have tried to do is assemble a range of articles that, to use an older form of literary critical expression that Deleuze seems especially to have favoured, offers both a way in and a way out of Deleuze.

We open with a chapter entitled 'Deleuze and Signs', in which André Pierre Colombat argues that Deleuze's entire work rebukes the notion of sign as it has been defined by the principle semiological tradition that stretches from St Augustine to Saussure. This tradition, he argues, culminated (somewhat disastrously for critical thinking, as it tuns out) in the supremacy of the signifier witnessed in contemporary thought today. And although Deleuze would himself want to challenge this supremacy, he didn't do so by abandoning the notion of the sign itself. Characteristically, his challenge came in the form of a profound redefinition of the term itself. From *Proust et les signes* (1964) to *Critique et clinique* (1993) Deleuze used the word 'sign' with different and sometimes discordant meanings. Contrary to many of his structuralist peers, Deleuze rejected any conception of the sign which limited it to a linguistic model. In place of the Saussure-derived semiology his contemporaries advocated, Deleuze substituted his own newly fashioned system which he based in part on Peirce's 'semeiotics', but also on the work of Hjelmslev, Austin and Searle. Colombat argues, however, that his main inspiration came not from these sources, but rather from his lifelong study of Spinoza. The founding principles of Deleuze's (and Guattari's) semiotics, he suggests, can already be found in Deleuze's *Spinoza et le problème de l'expression* (1968). From there, Deleuze incorporated the question of signs into much larger problems of expression and of expressivity.

In 'How Deleuze can help us make Literature work' Bruce Baugh picks up the thread of two of Deleuze's crucial questions and wonders how they might be used to explicate his theory of literary analysis: 'Given a certain effect, what machine is capable of producing it? And given a certain machine, what can it be used for?' (Deleuze and Guattari 1984: 3). What Baugh finds here is the basis for a set of principles that if we were to follow them would enable us to do something like a Deleuzian analysis of a text. He suggests that we could call Deleuze's implicit literary theory a revolutionary pragmatics of reading. He shows that the theory has two main mechanisms: on the one hand, there is a mechanics of reading itself; on the other hand, there is an experimentalist pragmatics. The first part of the theory is entirely objective, interested only in whether a work is capable of producing a certain effect. Baugh suggests that we think of this as the Spinozist moment of the theory. The second part of the theory, which is also objective, he notes, since it deals with the question of whether a given effect furthers the objectives of an individual or group, is more properly thought of as evaluative. It considers whether effects are helpful or harmful, which presupposes a determination of what can count as being 'good for' the person or group. Baugh suggests we think of this as the diagnostic or Nietzschean moment of the theory. Both aspects of theory are necessary to determine whether and how a literary work can 'work' for someone. More importantly, Baugh demonstrates that a consideration of both at the same time is possible, without falling into the kind of dialectical reading Deleuze famously loathed.

In 'The *Paterson* Plateau: Deleuze, Guattari and William Carlos Williams', Hugh Crawford opens with the assertion that Deleuze's famed 'toolbox' does not equip us with a hammer to crack open the closed and privileged system of novels or poems to reveal hidden gems of truth. It is, he notes, naive to think of literary analysis as simply the search for some hidden meaning or other. Even so, he adds, it cannot be ignored that the prospect of a fresh new vocabulary is usually felt as an invitation to reread canonical texts in its light in the hope of discovering something previously missed. In other words, however anti-interpretative critics may proclaim themselves to be, the literary critical enterprise remains, perhaps in spite of itself, bound to interpretation. This is of course something Deleuze refused to accept. And as Crawford puts it, he dashes the hopes of fashion-conscious literary scholars looking to ride the latest critical wave in a stroke. Interpretation, Deleuze says, in his customarily vehement manner, is a disease of the earth. In this respect, Crawford argues, Deleuze appears to share the central concerns of one major American writer who never actually features in his work, namely William Carlos Williams. A fact which Crawford shows is surprising because much of his work, in its thinking and in its strategies, particularly in the case of the long poem *Paterson*, is remarkably similar to Deleuze's. Crawford's implication is that while it is true Deleuze's work cannot provide a new reading of *Paterson* – in the sense of a new interpretation of it – reading the two authors side by side can nonetheless produce an illuminating juxtaposition, particularly with respect to the different ways they confront the rejection of traditional meaning.

Philosophy is, as Deleuze says, a question of what is going to happen and what has happened, 'like a novel': 'Except the characters are concepts, and the settings, the scenes, are space-times. One's always writing to bring something to life, to free life from where it's trapped, to trace lines of flight' (Deleuze 1995: 140–1). In '*Underworld*: The People are

Missing' John Marks uses Don DeLillo's master work as the occasion to argue that Deleuze's approach to literature can be adumbrated by Maurice Blanchot's term, '*entretien*'. It literally means 'conversation', but also indicates that which is perpetually 'in-between'. The aim of this chapter is to intensify tendencies already evident in the novel so as to explore the impersonal forces it releases. Ultimately, it is a question of exploring what Deleuze calls 'style' (the point at which writing becomes 'gaseous'), with the hope of providing new ways of activating and evaluating Deleuzian concepts. Here, it is the concept of the 'event' which comes to the fore and suggests itself as a form of *entretien*. The event is the 'middle' which literature inhabits as a site in which to create fiction. Fiction in this sense is not opposed to the true, but rather depends upon the 'powers of the false'.[4] Like Blanchot, Deleuze is interested in those enigmatic 'in-between' spaces which condition the conventional components of literary texts – characters, events, dialogue and so on – but which are frequently elided.

His interest in the 'in-between' seems to have been reason why Deleuze was so drawn to modernist authors like Beckett and Joyce since they were the first to explore it self-consciously. His allegiance to these authors, and their contemporaries in the other arts, Mahler, Debussy, Cézanne, Klee, Kandinsky and so on, raises the interesting question of whether or not he should be thought of as a modernist (we know he refused the label postmodernist). Now, according to Claire Colebrook, in the 'Inhuman Irony: The Event of the Postmodern', it is possible to regard Deleuze's work as exemplary of our time and so, in spite of his rejection of the label, provide a theoretical rubric for our sense of the postmodern. But, this encloses Deleuze *within* history or postmodernity and consequently diminishes the (perhaps utopian) promise of the eternal return in his work. And this, as Colebrook explains, would be to deprive us of what is ultimately the most refreshing aspect of Deleuze's uptake of Nietzsche. For what Deleuze takes from Nietzsche is not just an attempt to free thought from the constraints of the past as a dead weight, but a ceaseless and remorseless striving for a form of the new that will be self-renewing. It is this concern for the new that above all raises the suspicion that Deleuze might be better thought of as a modernist, however anachronistic that might be. The new, Deleuze argues, is not just what supersedes the old, it is 'untimely'. This, as Colebrook illustrates with respect to contemporary fiction, is the temporal form of the 'in-between' discussed by Marks.

This 'untimely' aspect of great literature is what enables it to indict history, as Gregg Lambert explains in 'On the Uses and Abuses of

Literature for Life'. His title is of course an allusion to Nietzsche's treatise 'On the Uses and Abuses of History for Life'. Lambert takes up this question in a parallel manner by asking what are the uses and abuses of literature for life? Or to put it another way, what kind of health does literature promote for 'an individual, a people, a culture' (1997: 63)? With these questions in mind, Lambert suggests that Deleuze's 'clinical' conception of literature, if taken on board, will radically alter the conditions of literary criticism. From a literary historical perspective, Deleuze's notion of the health of literature clearly functions as a kind of 'war machine' against the dominance of institutional criticism in the modern period. This again raises the question, which is so insistent throughout this volume, of whether or not we could imagine something like a 'Deleuzian school of literary theory'. For any student of Deleuze's writings, and especially those works written in collaboration with Guattari, the response to this question might seem all too obvious. However, as Lambert cautions, in today's academy where Deleuze's worst fears seem to have come true and 'marketing' has become an efficient cause in its own right determining the use of theory, we must remain on our guard against the possibility that Deleuze's work, too, can be perverted against its own nature. Even so, were it not possible to discern at least a set of principles that could count as Deleuzian, then this discussion would be moot. Balanced 'in-between' the undesirable molar recuperation (perversion) of Deleuze's work into the basis of a canon and the free-form anarchy of a *laissez-faire* approach, Lambert attempts to provoke creative dialogue around the very conditions that would make a Deleuzian pragmatics distinct from other hermeneutic models.

Kenneth Surin, in ' "A Question of an Axiomatic of Desires": The Deleuzian Imagination of Geoliterature', takes us a step further in this direction by inquiring whether Deleuze's transcendental empiricist, philosophical counter-tradition gives rise to, or informs, his literary counter-tradition, namely minor-writing. Surin delineates Deleuze's position by distinguishing it quite sharply from its main competitor in today's critical arena, deconstruction. Although he is not often mentioned by Deleuze, the target of much of his polemic on the issue of the centrality of the 'outside' of the text has to be Derrida, Surin argues. While Deleuze is clearly not against the idea of a text having its organising principles controverted or dismantled, his objection to structuralism, that it is ultimately just a system of points and positions, similarly applies to Derrida, who for all his insistence on the irremediable 'instability' and 'decentredness' of any system nevertheless has to retain them in order to make exactly this critique. Contrary to this, Surin argues that for Deleuze, the instability of the text is not so much a function of the absence of some kind of centring or Archimedean point which could guarantee or establish a determinate or monocentric meaning, but from the Bergsonian notion of the 'power of the false'. The Deleuzian book, as Surin conceives it, is always a series of effects generated by the 'power of the false', a power that in his view functions as the book's 'outside' in such a way as to overwhelm any fantasy it might entertain of being fixed and rigidly hierarchical. If in fact Deleuze is a 'poststructuralist' (a term whose provenance, as Surin helpfully reminds us, is American, not French!), then it must be recognised as a poststructuralism of a distinctly Bergsonian tint, and not merely Nietzschean. The point is, as Surin argues, it is Deleuze's Bergsonism, with its unquenchable vitalism, that sets him apart from Derrida most.

While it is true that Deleuze's conception of literature explicitly rules out interpretation insofar as that is taken to be the search for some kind of hidden or deeper meaning, that does not mean his concepts cannot be used to construct new kinds of hermeneutic apparatuses. As Marlene Goldman demonstrates in 'Transvestism, Drag, and Becomings: A Deleuzian Analysis of the Fictions of Timothy Findley' this is precisely the reason why literary critics of all stripes should be interested in Deleuze. But, by the same token, such interest need not be slavish, nor travel only one way. Goldman adopts Deleuze's 'problematological' method both to develop a reading of Canadanian writer Timothy Findley's fiction and to challenge what she sees as an oversight in Deleuze and Guattari's writing on the complicated topic of the nature of the relationship between transvestism and becomings. She takes issues with Deleuze and Guattari's brief, but very ambiguous pronouncements in *A Thousand Plateaus*, on the distinction between what they see as authentic instances of deterritorialisation and the imitative practices of transvestites and drag queens (Deleuze and Guattari 1987: 275). As Goldman argues, their comments suggest that the path to true or proper deterritorialisation lies elsewhere than transvestism: it is suspect in their view because it appears to be too closely aligned with mere imitation to unleash true becomings. However, this position is not consistently maintained by Deleuze and Guattari, and this, as Goldman points out, is the real problem. In describing the rites of transvestism in primitive societies, they appear ready to accept, contrary to their position on drag queens in the west, that such rites *can* instigate a becoming of sorts. Goldman demonstrates that something essential in Deleuze's thinking has been left out. To begin with, Deleuze and Guattari do not make a practical distinction between transvestism and drag; moreover, while they do indeed discuss transvestism, they do not acknowledge drag's potential to instigate becomings. Thus a Deleuzian analysis of Findley becomes the occasion for Goldman to redeem drag and transvestism in Deleuze's thinking, a move which is undoubtedly long overdue.

Timothy S. Murphy, too, in 'Only Intensities Subsist: Samuel Beckett's *Nohow On*', makes use of Deleuze's hermeneutic model to extend Deleuze's suggestive, but never fully fleshed-out reading of the prose writings of Samuel Beckett. As Murphy points out, Beckett's work is consistently privileged by Deleuze – usually as a ready source of exemplification for certain of his philosophical arguments – yet he never produced an extensive reading or exegesis of it (as he did for his other literary touchstones, Proust and Kafka). The two essays on Beckett he did produce, 'The Greatest Irish Film (Beckett's *Film*)' and 'The Exhausted'[5], examine only the smallest subset of Beckett's dramatic work, namely his film and television projects. Even so, Deleuze nevertheless offers a significant number of what Murphy will call 'intensive' readings of Beckett's prose, that is to say, brief, allusive references, which assume familiarity. Murphy argues that these 'intensive' readings are evidence that Beckett's prose works are called upon by Deleuze to perform a peculiarly illustrative function: they are used to exemplify the role and the power of what Deleuze referred to as 'pure intensity'. That is to say, these allusions to Beckett that Deleuze is evidently so fond of making are not merely tactical, they have a hermeneutic value of their own which is yet to be explored fully. Murphy's highly provocative, but also extremely compelling argument is that Beckett's last prose works, the three novellas collected as *Nohow On*, can be used to better grasp the implications of what is easily the most radical and difficult aspect of his concept of intensity: the anti-Kantian differential theory of the faculties that forms the core of Deleuze's 'transcendental empiricism' in *Difference and Repetition*. Here, then, an understanding of the way Deleuze uses literature becomes a shortcut, or, at any rate, a guide, to understanding his philosophy.

In 'Nizan's Diagnosis of Existentialism and the Perversion of Death', Eugene W. Holland interrogates Deleuze's idea that, instead of being either expressive or reflexive, literature is diagnostic. He sharpens our understanding of this claim by contrasting it with the idealistic position taken by contemporary psychoanalytic critics that at the end of the day literature understands psychoanalysis at least as well as psychoanalysis understands literature. Of course, Freud himself made no bones about his debt to literature. He was prepared to concede that the best poets discovered the unconscious long before he did; only they weren't aware of it. Likewise, Marx allegedy said he learned more about class struggle from Balzac than from all the non-fiction he read. But Deleuze effectively goes further than this. He does not merely acknowledge a debt to authors of fiction, thus admitting they have something to say, but retaining the right to say it better, as both Freud and Marx ultimately do, however much they might protest their deference, he treats them as full-blown cultural and historical diagnosticians in their own right. According to Holland, then, this means a Deleuzian approach to reading literature implies a two-fold transformation of standard psychoanalytic approaches: on the one hand, it treats the text as diagnostic not expressive; and on the other hand, it diagnoses collective not individual ills. Using this as his template, Holland outlines the ways in which Nizan's novels can be read as diagnoses of Heideggerian and Sartrean existentialism. As Holland shows, the central question Nizan raises is compatible with the Nietzschean ethic implicit in Deleuze's use of the notion of diagnosis: for Nizan, the crucial issue not so much whether existentialism is an instance of petty-bourgeois ideology, but rather, *who it is* that thinks and feels this way?

In 'I and My Deleuze' Tom Conley undertakes a Deleuzian analysis of a short story by Melville that is so intricate and so – one wants to say – loving, of detail (the filigree of Deleuze's work equally as much as the minutae of Melville's story), that it defies either summary or circumscription. Conley argues that even to think of Deleuze *and* literature together is already to engage with his concepts of difference and repetition, intercession, spiritual automata, minoritarian practices, sensation and, above all, style. This is because even if one were to succeed, for instance, in defining how Deleuze reads Proust on the basis of his analyses of Bergson, the topic of Deleuze *and* literature would amount to an exercise in difference itself and elude one's grasp. The conjunction of Deleuze *and* literature recalls what Deleuze called the 'method of AND', and in so doing repudiates in advance any impression that his work can be about literature. And it shows that his work is driven by the same creative tactics he identifies in his favourite authors and calls upon so often to exemplify and, even, embody his concepts. For Conley, there is no escaping the fact that to consider Deleuze's corpus in light of literature means that it has to be read as literature. His implication, for which his own essay stands as both argument and demonstration, is that the reader must work through the writing with the eye and ear of an artist or a poet.

Notes

1. See *Dialogues* (Deleuze and Parnet 1987: 39). Deleuze and Parnet claim that the French think too much in terms of 'trees', always wanting to start again from a beginning which is a tabula rasa, whereas the 'English' start in the middle, thinking in terms of grass rather than trees.
2. See 'To Have Done with Judgement' (Deleuze 1997: 126–36). Deleuze argues that Spinoza, rather than Kant, carried out a true critique of judgement.
3. See Deleuze and Parnet 1987: 41–2. For Deleuze and Parnet, Thomas Hardy's characters are 'packets' of variable sensations. In this way, Hardy combines a strange respect for the individual with an understanding of the unique chance of an empiricist experimental world which constitutes the individual as such a collection of sensations.
4. See Gilles Deleuze, *Cinema 2: The Time-Image*, translated by Hugh Tomlison and Robert Galeta (London: Athlone, 1989), Ch. 6 'The Powers of the False'.
5. Both essays are included in Deleuze 1997.

Bibliography

Deleuze, Gilles (1972 [1970]), *Proust and Signs*, trans. Richard Howard, New York: George Braziller. Originally published in France in 1964.

Deleuze, Gilles (1986 [1983]), *Cinema 1: The Movement-Image*, trans. Hugh Tomlinson and Barbara Habberjam, London: Athlone and Minneapolis: University of Minnesota Press.

Deleuze, Gilles (1988 [1966]), *Bergsonism*, trans. Hugh Tomlinson and Barbara Habberjam, New York: Zone Books.

Deleuze, Gilles (1989 [1985]), *Cinema 2: The Time-Image*, trans. Hugh Tomlinson and Robert Galeta, Minneapolis: University of Minnesota Press.

Deleuze, Gilles (1989 [1967]), *Masochism: An Introduction to Coldness and Cruelty*, trans. Jean McNeil, New York: Zone Books.

Deleuze, Gilles (1990 [1968]), *Expressionism in Philosophy: Spinoza*, trans. Martin Joughin, New York: Zone Books.

Deleuze, Gilles (1990 [1969]), *The Logic of Sense*, trans. Mark Lester with Charles Stivale, ed. Constantin V. Boundas, New York: Columbia University Press.

Deleuze, Gilles (1994 [1968]), *Difference and Repetition*, trans. Paul Patton, New York: Columbia University Press.

Deleuze, Gilles (1995 [1992]), *Negotiations*, trans. Martin Joughlin, New York: Columbia University Press.

Deleuze, Gilles (1997 [1993]), *Essays Critical and Clinical*, trans. Daniel W. Smith and Michael Greco, Minneapolis: University of Minnesota Press.

Deleuze, Gilles and Guattari, Felix (1984 [1972]), *Anti-Oedipus: Capitalism and Schizophrenia*, trans. Robert Hurley, Mark Seem, and Helen R. Lane, Minneapolis: University of Minnesota Press.

Deleuze, Gilles (1986 [1975]), *Kafka: Toward a Minor Literature*, trans. Dana Polan, Minneapolis: University of Minnesota Press.

Deleuze, Gilles (1987 [1980]), *A Thousand Plateaus: Capitalism and Schizophrenia*, trans. Brian Massumi, Minneapolis: University of Minnesota Press.

Deleuze, Gilles (1994 [1992]), *What is Philosophy?*, trans. Hugh Tomlinson and Graham Burchell, New York: Columbia University Press.

Deleuze, Gilles and Parnet, Claire (1987 [1977]), *Dialogues*, trans. Hugh Tomlinson and Barbara Habberjam, New York: Columbia University Press.

Jameson, Fredric (1981), *The Political Unconscious: Narrative as a Socially Symbolic Act*, London: Methuen.

Robbe-Grillet, Alain (1989), *For a New Novel: Essays on Fiction*, trans. Richard Howard, Evanston: Northwestern University Press.

Chapter 1

Deleuze and Signs

André Pierre Colombat

Deleuze's entire work rebukes the notion of sign as it was defined by theologians (St Augustine) and by linguists (Saussure). That tradition led to the supremacy of the Signifier in contemporary thought. However, from *Proust et les signes* (1964) to *Critique et clinique* (1993) Deleuze used the word 'sign' with different and sometimes discordant meanings. Contrary to many of his structuralist contemporaries, Deleuze rejected any conception of signs limited to the linguistic model, largely dominated in France by the work of Saussure. This led him, along with Guattari, to progressively reject Lacanism and its Hegelian foundation.[1] In place of semiology Deleuze substituted his own system of signs, which is based in part on Peirce's 'semeiotics', but also on the works of Hjelmslev, Austin and Searle. I will argue however that his main inspiration comes from his lifelong study of Spinoza. The founding principles of Deleuze's and Guattari's semiotics can already be found in Deleuze's *Spinoza et le problème de l'expression* (1968). From his first essays, Deleuze incorporated the question of signs into much larger problems of expression and of expressivity.

But the concept of 'expression' carries here a definition that differs radically from any form of essentialist, or Platonic, imagery. It announces already the Deleuzo-Guattarian concept of 'becoming'. This 'expression' is inseparable from the differentiating process that unfolds it. It never resembles what it expresses, the power that it 'explains'. The French infinitive '*expliquer*' from the latin '*plicare*' means here '*déplier, dérouler,*' to 'unfold' in different series, or modes, the powers of a substance or a specific arrangement:

> But such synonyms (of the verb 'to express') are less significant than the correlates that accompany and further specify the idea of expression: '*explicare*' and '*involvere*'. Thus definition is said not only to express the

nature of what is defined, but to involve ['envelopper'] and to explicate it ['expliquer']. Attributes not only express the essence of substance: here they explicate it, there they involve it. Modes involve the concept of God as well as expressing it, so the ideas that correspond to them involve, in their turn, God's eternal essence. To explicate is to evolve, to involve is to implicate. (Deleuze 1990a: 15–16)

Contrary to the power of expressions, the power of signs is based on an illusion, on the pious belief in a distinct order of the Signifier – the transcendental law, the Word of God, the Phallus, the castration complex and so on from which every part of the Creation (or any form of 'creation') emanates. As Deleuze pointed out, Spinoza criticised the discourse of revelation and the Scriptures themselves because they present us with only 'variable "signs"', extrinsic denominations that guarantee a divine commandment [. . .] Because the goal of the Scriptures is to make us submit to certain lifestyles, to make us obey and to ground us in obedience' (1990: 56). In *Mille Plateaux* (1980), Deleuze and Guattari extended this criticism to linguistics and language in general because their essence is to carry a fundamental kind of commandment that they call an 'order-word' (*mot d'ordre*).

The paths I propose to follow in this essay will first lead us from Deleuze's criticism of linguistic signs and natural languages to his concept of expression that characterises in great part the semiotics he developed with Guattari. Their criticism of semiology promotes a new kind of semiotics based on a new pragmatics. It cannot be disconnected from a new clinical gaze put upon the unfolding of expressions of life itself. In Deleuze's thought, the redefinition of the 'critical' is inseparable from a redefinition of the 'clinical' as it frees itself from images of death and negativity, which were central to most of French thought since the first World War (mostly through the influence of Freudism since the 1920s and of Hegelianism since the 1930s). These redistributions and redefinitions of the 'critical' and of the 'clinical' are also directly dependent on a diffuse new regimen of light that makes them possible. From the beginning to the end of this research, from the inadequacies of signs to the characterisation of pure light in the univocal expression of Life, Deleuze remains fundamentally a Spinozist at heart.

Deleuze's and Guattari's criticism of linguistic signs is well summarised by their concept of 'order-word'. The French expression '*mot d'ordre*' is commonly used to refer to a command for action given by both a symbolic and concrete power structure to a large and indeterminate group of individuals. In the first sense, the power structure designates that of an army. However, by extension, it also refers to the power of the leaders of a political party or union. For example, the common expression *'un mot d'ordre de grève'* designates a call or command for a strike ordered by the heads of a union. Deleuze and Guattari refer to Austin's work to explain that in a natural language, the illocutionary subtends the locutionary. Command and performance are at the heart of information, grammar and communication. For Deleuze and Guattari, as for Austin and Searle, the illocutionary – that is, the enunciation of a statement considered as an act that modifies the relationship between two interlocutors – is constitutive of the perlocutionary. It can be paraphrased in the form of an order-word. For Deleuze and Guattari: 'Linguistics is nothing without pragmatics (semiotic or political) to define the effectuation of the *condition of possibility* and the usage of the linguistic elements' (1987: 85). This statement is also directly indebted to the maxim through which Charles Sanders Peirce defined pragmatism. Peirce's maxim stated that:

> In order to ascertain the meaning of an intellectual conception one should consider what practical consequences might conceivably result by necessity from the truth of that conception; and the sum of these consequences will constitute the entire meaning of the conception. (Peirce 1960, V: 6)

Consequently, there is no language independent of the generalised pragmatics that *A Thousand Plateaus* attempts to theorise (Deleuze and Guattari 1987: 75–110).

One then has to distinguish between a sign and something else that Deleuze, after Spinoza and a long tradition before him,[2] calls an 'expression'. On one side we find the signs of the prophet, the theologian, the priest, the psychoanalyst, the linguist: the signs of representation, negation, judgement and revelation. The expression is inseparable from the powers of the heterogeneous world, or arrangement, that it expresses. It 'unfolds' and 'involves' but it has nothing to 'unveil'. On the other side the philosopher must unfold the affirmative 'expression' of the Spinozist, or better said, the 'expression' of the 'expressed' that constitutes adequate knowledge (Deleuze 1990: 151–2). A sign is the impure image of a pure meaning, of a pure abstraction, that has to be extracted or unveiled in order to ground language and its order-words. In Deleuze's own words:

> Revelation and expression: never was the effort to distinguish two domains pushed further. Or to distinguish two heterogeneous relations: that of sign and signified, that of expression and expressed. *A sign always attaches to a propium*; it always signifies a commandment, and it grounds our obedience. (1990: 56, 181–2)

Knowledge attained through signs is always inadequate. Signs are always equivocal as they separate life and thought and make of thought the tribunal of life. Only knowledge through expression can be adequate. Expressions are univocal and only they can express the Spinozist univocity of Being (1990: 329–30). They express the unique substance, the same Nature, as it 'unfolds', 'develops', 'expresses'[3] itself in different viewpoints or attributes, such as thought and extension, just as two different names and their different manifestations (complicatio) can express or 'envelop' the same individual.

But this example of the two names does not explain the main opposition between signs and expression. Their opposition lies in opposite concepts of difference that Deleuze characterised in *Difference and Repetition*:

> In one case [that of the signs], the difference is taken to be only external to the concept; it is a difference between objects represented by the same concept, falling into the indifference of space and time. In the other case [that of expression], the difference is internal to the Idea; it unfolds as pure movement, creative of a dynamic space and time which correspond to the Idea. (1994: 23–4)

This parallel assumes that what Deleuze calls an Idea in *Difference and Repetition* is similar to what Spinoza calls an 'essence' according to *Expressionism in Philosophy: Spinoza*. This parallelism is corroborated by the way that Deleuze uses the concepts of Idea and essence as synonymous in *Proust and Signs*. It explains the qualitative and fundamental difference that Proust and Deleuze delineate between the material signs of the world of sensations and the immaterial signs of Art: 'The Essence is precisely this unity of sign and meaning (*sens* in French) as it is revealed in a work of art. Essences or Ideas, that is what each sign of [Vinteuil's] little phrase reveals' (1972: 41). Here, a sign reveals an essence that is no longer an abstraction of the mind but the active power of a world that only a musical phrase, an intensive, pre-signifying expression, can unfold. Deleuze reinforced this parallelism as he himself defined any idea as 'it incarnates a natural or spiritual power' (1990: 23). In a Deleuzian context this 'power' is that of expressivity, the unfolding or expression of a univocal Being that is Life itself (1997: 1–6). Deleuze then concluded in his first book on Spinoza: 'The opposition of expressions and signs is one of the fundamental principles of Spinozism' (1990: 182).

The entire schizoanalytical project of the two volumes of *Capitalism and Schizophrenia* clearly followed in the same orientation. The signs of the Freudian family theatre of the unconscious can be subsumed under the revelation of the same Signifier, the Phallus and the submission of the subject to the terrifying commandments of the castration complex. To this signifying representation the *Anti-Oedipus* and *A Thousand Plateaus* oppose asignifying lines of flight, machinistic arrangements, concrete connections, developments or 'expressions' of matters and fluxes. Where Freud, and even Lacan, saw signs, signifier and signified – a language and a syntax – Deleuze and Guattari describe connections, transformations, arrangements and productions (see Joel Birman). Questions such as: 'What does such a sign mean?', 'What does it stand for?' are replaced with questions such as: 'How does such a sign affect me?', 'How does it work?', 'To which concrete social, political, or erotic arrangements is it connected?' In this manner, the problem of the expression replaces that of the designation and of the signification. It becomes clear that Deleuze reads in Spinoza a special kind of empiricism that will inspire the core of his work: 'One of the paradoxes in Spinoza [. . .] is to have rediscovered the concrete force of empiricism in applying it in support of a new rationalism, one of the most rigorous versions ever conceived' (1990: 149).

We are now clearly dealing with a new kind of sign, with signs considered as expressions, with 'asignifying signs' connected with Deleuze's transcendental empiricism and Guattari's machinistic unconscious. An 'asignifying' sign, such as the notes in Vinteuil's little phrase, does not find its ultimate condition of possibility in the necessary abstraction of a Signified. It belongs to other regimens of signs such as the 'pre-signifying', the 'counter signifying' of the 'post-signifying' semiotics characterised in *A Thousand Plateaus* (1987: 118–26). These signs are not to be characterised by their infinite and circular connection to other signs, nor by their connection to the abstract theatre of the Spirit. They are to be considered as intensive and immanent signals expressing, marking and unfolding the powers of a given milieu or heterogeneous arrangement. Consequently, for Deleuze, Artaud's work always remained far more important than that of Carroll. Such an empiricism and its expressions are inseparable from a thought of the immanent.

Deleuze's thought has often been characterised, both by himself and by his commentators, as an immanent thought of the multiple. In this framework, according to Alain Badiou, only one critical method seems possible:

> Immanence demands that one start from where thought has already begun, as close as possible to a singular case, to its movement. Something

is thinking in our back and one is always already being thought and forced to think. Such is the virtue of the case. (1997: 25; my translation)

It is also in this sense that Deleuze claimed that his philosophy was a very concrete thought, a transcendental empiricism, a philosophy that exposes the empirical conditions of possibility of thought. Indeed, Deleuze's thought on signs could be presented as a long succession of a special kind of 'case studies' largely based on the concept of affect and on his readings of Spinoza and Nietzsche. In each 'case' Deleuze replaces the problem of signs, designation, signification and representation with that of the expressed and the expression. What am I affected by? What do I affect? What creates in me great joy or great sadness? What forces me to think? What kind of political, social, sentimental arrangements am I connected to, associated with? What are my, your, our desiring machines? To the founding oppositions of Saussure and the linguistic model of French structuralism, Deleuze opposes the 'complicatio', the dynamic combination of heterogeneous series expressing, 'unfolding', the power of the virtual. Such a method has direct implications for Deleuze's various non-linguistic definitions of a sign.

A Deleuzian 'sign' always appears in the context of an encounter or an invention, in a space in-between, not as a discovery. It has become a truism to say that one 'discovers' only what was already in a position to be discovered or, better said, as Bergson put it in a text quoted by Deleuze:

The truth is that in philosophy and even elsewhere, the point is to find the problem and subsequently to characterize it, rather than to solve it. Indeed, a speculative problem is resolved as soon as it is well characterized [. . .] But stating the problem is not simply uncovering, it is inventing. (1988: 15)

The task of any researcher is not merely to find answers but to invent and define his or her problem and his or her problematic. Regarding signs, this implies that we are or become sensitive to certain linguistic or non-linguistic signs depending on our receptivity, on the arrangements and haecceities we become part of. One way we define an individual is through the characterisation of the signs to which this individual responds.

As Deleuze often noticed, a cabinet maker must first become sensitive to the 'signs' of wood before he can work with it, transform it. Such signs are expressions of what one can do with a specific piece of wood within a specific arrangement. They are expressions of a battle between active and reactive forces that the cabinet maker has to evaluate and connect to other forces and arrangements. They 'mean' nothing. Reading an author implies that we first become sensitive to his or her own worlds, signs and style; as Deleuze insisted throughout his reading of Proust: intelligence always comes after experience. Or, as he also explained to his students on the very first day of his seminar of Foucault: 'You must trust the author you are studying. Grope your way through. You must ruminate, gather notions again and again. You must silence in you the voices of objection. You must let him speak' (Tuesday, 22 October 1985, Université de Vincennes à St Denis).

In the very last chapter of his last book, Deleuze explained in what way this progression develops a clear Spinozist perspective.

> But when one asks *how* we manage to form a concept, or how we rise from effects to causes, it is clear that at least certain signs must serve as a springboard for us, and that certain affects must give us the necessary vitality (book V of the *Ethics*). From a random encounter of bodies, we can select the idea of those bodies that agree with our own and give us joy, that is, that increase our power. And it is only when our power has sufficiently increased, to a point that undoubtedly varies with each case, that we come in possession of this power and become capable of forming a concept. (1997: 144)

Thinking is inseparable from such a selective process, from an evaluation of the forces enveloped in the 'signs' we encounter. The selection and combination of these signs and forces constitute an experimentation that can allow us to create or invent a problematic, an arrangement. This dynamic arrangement, or 'complicatio', characterises best our thought, our actions in the world at a given time. It expresses, explains or unfolds our active 'viewpoint'.

Deleuze's *Proust and Signs* showed that all the characters of *A la recherche du temps perdu* are receptive to different kinds of signs or to the same signs in very different manners. Sensations, such as the taste of the famous *madeleine*, seem to work as intensive signs that do not need any signification to conjure up entire worlds and vital 'truths' that couldn't have been attained otherwise. It appears, once again, that Deleuze's readers are confronted with different meanings and uses of the word 'sign' that sometimes seem incompatible and need to be clarified.

Deleuze's first study of signs in a literary context was developed in the now-classical essay *Proust and Signs*. It is to be noticed that in this book, Deleuze is not interested in linguistic signs or codes, as Barthes would be for example, but rather in Proustian semiotics in general. *Proust and Signs* proposes that for Proust there are four kinds of signs that are accessible in four different worlds defined by four different aspects of time. They are, first, the empty signs of the world of social life (*mondanité*). These replace action in a time we waste and 'lose'. Second, the signs of love that always lie because they always imply in the beloved the existence of a world from which the lover is excluded. They develop in a time that escapes us, that we lose and which will never return. Third, sensitive signs in the sensitive world can bring real joy in a past time found again but which quickly vanishes. Only the fourth kind of sign, that of art, can bring long-lasting joy, as it metamorphoses all other signs and leads us to the revelation of the Essence, of pure time or Time itself.

The first two categories of time lost seem to be remnants of Peirce's Thirdness, the sensitive world of his Secondness and the world of art of his Firstness that it would transmute into the 'immaterial signs' of Art characterised in *Proust and Signs* (see Table 1.1 and Deleuze 1972: 39–50). However, Deleuze never alludes to Peirce in this book, written twenty-one years before *Cinema 2*.

Table 1.1 The different types of signs in *Proust et les signes*

Time Found Again/pure Time	Time Recovered by the body or by memory	Time Lost, that we will never find again	Time Lost, wasted
World of the Arts	Sensitive world	The World of Love (passions)	Social Life (*mondanité*)
Signs of art: ductile and immaterial, they metamorphose all the others	Sensitive signs	Signs that lie	Empty signs

In the Deleuzian neo-Spinozist critical system, different kinds of signs appear in different 'worlds', in different 'modes' of thought or of extension, to each of which corresponds a different aspect of time and a different regimen of light. It is clearly the case in *Proust and Signs*, but also in every book by Deleuze. In each one of his 'case studies' the philosopher characterises heterogeneous series, the laws of formation and proliferation of these series, their 'problematics' or their 'process', how they relate 'transversely' to one another while remaining heterogeneous, how each one of them expresses different modalities of the same attribute and beyond that of the same intensive and virtual 'stuff', the univocal Spinozist substance.

Thus, Deleuze's semiotics first consists in freeing the concept of sign and expression from linguistics, from their reduction to the dualism signifier/signified, to the syntagmatic, to a narration and ultimately to the reign of the Signifier, the judgement of God and that of the interpreter. Deleuze scarcely used the word 'sign', except in his two books on cinema, probably because that reduction or oversimplification was quite common in the structuralist and poststructuralist years. Consequently, Deleuze's two books on cinema shed a new light on his criticism of linguistic signs. They also exemplify his radical opposition to any form of structuralism based on linguistics or even to the most brilliant and subtle word games played by Derrida's Deconstruction. The point is not to unveil a Signifier nor a paradoxical founding trace but to evaluate forces, arrangements and an entire battlefield; to map thinking as a vital process.

As it is often the case with Deleuze and Guattari, the two philosophers started by touching up a theory, that of Freud in the *Anti-Oedipus* for example, and ended by upsetting it completely. Deleuze's other emblematic strategy, as is the case in his Nietzschean criticism of Platonism, is to bring a theory to its limits, inverting its premises and overthrowing its conclusions. In the case of his two books on cinema, the rival system is that of Christian Metz and its very influential semiology of film. Deleuze begins with praising Metz because he asked the most important question: 'Instead of asking "In what ways is the cinema a language (the famous universal language of humanity)?", he poses the question "Under what conditions should cinema be considered as a language?"' (1989: 25). Unfortunately, according to Deleuze, Metz didn't follow up on his own lead and fell into the traps of linguistics:

> And his reply is a double one, since it points first to a fact, and then to an approximation. The historical fact is that cinema was constituted as such by becoming narrative, by presenting a story, and by rejecting its other possible directions. The approximation which follows is that, from that point, the sequences of images and even each image, a single shot, are assimilated to propositions or rather to oral utterances: the shot will be considered as the smallest narrative utterance. (1989: 25)

Then the trap door is shut and Metz's work falls in a 'typically Kantian vicious circle' according to which:

> Syntagmatics applies because the image is an utterance, but the image is an utterance because it is subject to syntagmatics. The double of utterances and grand syntagmatics has been substituted for that of images and signs, to the point that the very notion of sign tends to disappear from this semiology. It obviously disappears, clearly, to the benefit of the signifier. (1989: 26)

Kristeva's and Eco's works, according to Deleuze, fell into similar traps. For Deleuze, as for Pasolini and Eisenstein, cinema is much more than a language. If it is to be compared to a language at all, it is very different from anything we usually call a language. In the case of cinema, narration and signification are only a consequence of an image, of an analogy between an image and language. They are not given as such. The analogy between an image and language misses the specificity of the image itself and of the non-linguistic signs that compose it before it eventually becomes a narration (1989: 29).

Rejecting Metz's semiologic model, Deleuze turns to the work of Charles Sanders Peirce as it was translated and interpreted in French by Gérard Deledalle. For Deleuze 'Peirce's strength, when he invented semeiotics, was to conceive of signs on the basis of images and their combinations, not as a function of determinants which were already linguistic' (1989: 30). For Peirce, as read by Deleuze through Deladalle's translation, a sign is characterised by three different ways of combining three different kinds of images, leading to the distinction between nine elements of signs and ten different signs (1989: 30). But, in Peirce's system, the function of these signs is to add a new knowledge to their object, depending on their interpretation or Interpretant. Then, for Deleuze these signs reintroduce the function of linguistic signs in Peirce's work. For Deleuze their function is 'to absorb and reabsorb the whole content of the image as consciousness or appearance ("*apparition*")' (1989: 31). Ultimately, Peirce's Interpretant – understood by Deleuze as a 'consciousness, an apparition' (see Figure 1.1) – left no room for a matter that would be irreducible to enunciation. Deleuze then concludes that Peirce did not go far enough: 'it seems that Peirce became as much of a linguist as the semiologists'. For Deleuze, Peirce did not 'maintain his initial orientation long enough, he renounced constituting a semiotics as a "descriptive science of reality"' (1989: 31).

Figure 1.1 The triadic relation according to Peirce (*Collected Papers* V. 1–2, § 242, 141–2).

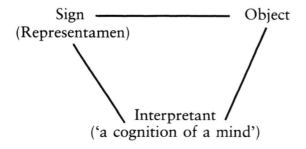

Table 1.2 Peirce's three trichotomies (after Deledalle, quoted by Deleuze, 1989: 45; in English 30, which can be compared to Peirce's *Collected Papers* II. 2, § 264, 150)

	Firstness	Secondness	Thirdness
Representamen	Qualisign (1.1)	Synsign (1.2)	Legisign (1.3)
Object	Icon (2.1)	Index (2.2)	Symbol (2.3)
Interpretant	Rheme (3.1)	Dicisign (3.2)	Argument (3.3)

Table 1.3 Peirce's second trichotomy (as it was summarised by Todorov and Ducrot corresponding to the line of the 'object' in Deledalle's schema, 2.b.)

Firstness felt qualities	Secondness experience of an effort	Thirdness (signs/representamen)
Icon: determined by its dynamic object through its internal nature (the same quality as the object: a black stain/ the colour black, an onomatopoeia, the diagram of relations between different properties)	Index: determined by its dynamic object through the relation it has with it (in continuity with the denoted object; a symptom/a disease)	Symbol: determined by its dynamic object only in the sense in which it is to be interpreted (refers through the force of a law: the words or signs of a language)

Peirce's main fault was, according to Deleuze, to have missed the fact that the three kinds of images he characterised (Firstness, Secondness, Thirdness and which Deleuze rebaptised 'image-affection', 'image-action' and 'image-relation') are not a given. They cannot be reduced to the form of an Interpretant's consciousness. They can be deduced from what Deleuze calls the Image-Movement and its signs which are themselves perceivable only through the becomings of the Image-Time and its own opsigns, soundsigns and hyalosigns between which one eventually finds pure Time. These specific signs were derived by Deleuze from his analysis of cinema and they cannot be applied directly to literature. Deleuze often insisted on the fact that each form of art transforms and creates its own tools and its own matter. However, three of Deleuze's basic assumptions and redefinitions regarding signs and semiotics can help us understand what he calls a 'sign', and also an 'affect', in a literary context.

After his rejection of Metz's theory and his analysis of the limits of Peirce's trichotomies, Deleuze presented his own definition of a sign as 'a particular image that refers to a type of image, whether from the point of view of its bipolar composition, or from the point of view of its genesis' (1989: 32). Then, if 'the movement-image is matter [*matière*] itself' but a 'matter that is not linguistically formed', 'signs themselves are features of expression (*traits of expression* [my emphasis]) that compose and combine these images, and constantly re-create them, borne or carted along by a matter in movement' (1989: 33). From all this we shall retain the enigmatic phrase '*traits d'expression*' and draw some conclusions that will take us directly to literature and its use of signs within and beyond linguistic signs.

These '*traits d'expression*' seem to be very similar to the 'singularities' of *The Logic of Sense*. They could be characterised as intensive points, marks of affects from the encounters of various intensities – of light in the case of cinema – on and with receptive surfaces: the screen, the eye and, most importantly, the brain. As vibrations from these points affect other singularities, regular curves can appear shaping progressively intensive zones, affecting matters, creating forms, objects, concepts, linguistic signs, in which these intensive relations are 'enveloped', 'folded'. *The Logic of Sense* describes in a similar manner the birth of sexuality and that of language (1990: 186–233). One task of the critic will be to unfold linguistic signs to reach this intensive level of non-linguistic signs, of 'traits of expression', of the expression and of the expressed. In this endeavour, Deleuze often refers to the work of Hjelmslev:

> The linguist Hjelmslev calls 'content' [*matière*] precisely this element which is not linguistically formed, although it is perfectly formed from other points of view. He says 'not semiotically formed' because he identifies the semiotic function with the linguistic one [. . .]. But its specificity as a signaletic material is none the less presupposed by a language. (1989: 21; note 9 p. 287)

Deleuze and Guattari used Hjelmslev's theory in their book on Kafka. Once again they started by borrowing concepts and transforming them until they abandoned them completely in order to create their own theory.

They began by distinguishing in Kafka's work between a form of content – inclined head/raised head – and a form of expression – photography and sound (Deleuze and Guattari 1986: 3–8). However, what matters is not the structural relations between these two planes but, in their own words, how they constitute 'an *expression machine* capable of disorganizing its own forms, and of disorganizing its forms of content, in order to liberate pure contents that mix with expressions in a single intense matter' (1986: 28). The rest of their essay then characterises how Kafka's writing, mostly through its use of sounds, ousts representation. It also devalues Hjelmslev's theory itself by using writing as a process to multiply series, contiguous blocks of images, to trace transversal lines between them. Thus it creates many 'arrangements' that will release entire 'asignifying' series of becomings (or 'lines of flight') and enable them to proliferate and access the intensive, pre-philosophical and pre-linguistic world of expression itself. In this respect, writers have to create processes to turn forms of representation into elements of experimentation (1986: 49), to replace the transcendence of the law with the immanence of desire (1986: 49, 50–1). This dynamic process is precisely what differentiates a minor from a major literature.

In Deleuze's essays on cinema, a 'sign' refers to specific and serial relations between different elements, different 'traits of expression' within one single image or between different images. Each sign envelops a specific combination of an expressive matter in becoming, in a specific aspect of time that constitutes a continuous exchange between the actual and the virtual within pure time. These 'traits of expression' are active before the appearance of any formed matter, of any language, narration or signifier. They are the condition of possibility of experience and thought itself in a space that Deleuze and Guattari also called the pre-philosophical, which is at the foundation of Deleuze's so-called 'transcendental empiricism'. They have direct implications for Deleuze's and Guattari's approaches to literary texts in general.

For Deleuze, as for Peirce, heterogeneity is at the heart of what makes a sign possible at all (1989: 30). This precision appeared as early as in *Difference and Repetition*:

> Signs involve heterogeneity in at least three ways: first, in the object which bears or emits them, and it is necessarily on a different level, as though there were two orders of size or disparate realities between which the sign flashes (*fulgure*); secondly, in themselves, since a sign envelops another 'object' within the limits of the object which bears it, and incarnates a natural or spiritual power (an Idea); finally, in the response they elicit, since the movement of the response does not 'resemble' that of the sign. The movement of the swimmer does not resemble that of the wave, in particular, the movements of the swimming instructor which we reproduce on the sand bear no relation to the movements of the wave, which we learn to deal with only by grasping the former in practice as signs. That is why it is so difficult to say how someone learns: there is an innate or acquired practical familiarity with signs, which means that there is something amorous – but also something fatal – about all education. We learn nothing from those who say: 'Do as I do'. Our only teachers are those who tell us to 'do with me', and are able to emit signs to be developed in heterogeneity rather than propose gestures for us to reproduce. (1994: 22–3)

Deleuze continues using the word 'sign' here but it is clear that his 'signs' have nothing to do with those of the linguist or those of the theologian.

They are not equivocal but univocal, they are not analogical but expressive. According to this quote, a 'sign' can appear, or rather 'fulgurates' only in between 'two different orders of size or disparate realities'.

As in a comparison used several times by Deleuze, in *Difference and Repetition*, a sign appears like lightning between two different intensities. A sign is a special kind of image, a sensitive phenomenon but 'intensity is the form of difference in so far as this is the reason for the sensible (*sensible*). Every intensity is differential, by itself a difference' (1994: 222). We now have to consider a sign within its own world, within its own aspect of time but also within a differential and intensive system constituted by its own heterogeneous series. A sign is part of a very special kind of phenomenon, of a system, in the sense a weather forecaster talks about a 'weather system':

> Every phenomenon flashes (*fulgure*) in a signal-sign system. In so far as a system is constituted or bounded by at least two heterogeneous series, two disparate orders capable of entering into communication, we call it a signal. The phenomenon that flashes across this system, bringing about the communication between disparate series, is a 'sign' ['*signe*' appears between quotation marks in the original text]. (1994: 222)

Linguistic signs are only one kind of sign among others, as for Pasolini cinema was a kind of language entirely different from so-called 'natural-language' (1989: 287). At this point, Deleuzian asignifying signs are 'traits of expression' that characterise the 'expressed'. But the 'expressed' is inseparable from the notion of sense (1994: 311). In *The Logic of Sense*, the fulguration of the sign, the *continuum mobile* of 'sense' itself, or the smile of the Cheshire cat with its paradoxes, are constitutive of the 'structure' of language itself. *A Thousand Plateaus* also summarises this criticism of the linguistic sign (Deleuze and Guattari 1987: 11–118) and goes beyond to characterise other, pre-linguistic and counter-linguistic, 'regimens of sign' all based on the concept of expression (1987: 118–48).

The differentiating power of expression is what makes life, thought and language possible at all. This power of thought and language is the intensive difference, the 'event' that differentiates, that separates propositions from states of affairs and creates successively a sexual surface, a physical surface and a metaphysical surface (1990b: 237–8, 239–49). Going back and forth between the works of Artaud, Carroll, Spinoza and these three surfaces, we can better conceive Deleuze's and Guattari's own theory of pre-linguistic and asignifying signs as it relates to the birth of the fragile surface of sense and language. From the 'chaosmos' of Nature or Life where pure intensities and unshaped matters reign, from the actions and the passions of bodies, the Deleuzian concept of Event separates and organises series that make possible the unfolding of expression and language:

> What renders language possible is that which separates sounds from bodies and organizes them into propositions, freeing them for the expressive function. It is always a mouth which speaks; but the sound is no longer the noise of a body which eats – a pure orality – in order to become the manifestation of a subject expressing itself. (1990b: 181)

The Logic of Sense retraces this genesis thanks to a redefinition of the concept of event:

> What separates speaking from eating renders speech possible; what separates propositions from things renders propositions possible. The surface and that which takes place at the surface is what 'renders possible' – in other words, the event as that which is expressed. The expressed makes possible the expression. But in this case, we find ouselves confronted with a final task: to retrace the history which liberates sounds and makes them independent of bodies. (1990b: 186)

This is precisely how the logic of sense will explain the fundamental difference between the work of Artaud and that of Carroll. While Artaud desperately struggled with intense suffering, with the monsters of the depths of the body, to extract an intensive language, Carroll kept on playing much safer word games at the still-fragile surface of language. This is best exemplified by Deleuze's opposition between Carroll's and Artaud's Jabberwockies (1990b: 82–6).

In those pages, Deleuze calls the 'expressed' an 'event'. In other pages of the same book, always referring to ancient Stoicism as taught at the Sorbonne by his professor, Emile Bréhier, he also characterises an event as a verb in the infinitive such as 'to cut' or 'to eat' or 'to run'. Then we understand that an event has close connections with what was called earlier a 'viewpoint' or what will be called in later books by Deleuze a 'continuous variation'. 'To run', for example, can be thought of as an event that combines (or 'complicates') in a unique way the forces of my body with that of the wind, of the sun, of the resisting ground, of my thoughts, of my desire at that moment and so on. But each time it is a new event, a new cast of the dice. It is also in that sense that events express, develop, complicate and thus create haecceities.

The event, the 'expressed', is for Deleuze the in-between tension, the fulguration and movement that are inseparable from the confrontation of two forces or of two intensities. The movement of this confrontation develops two series on the side of an intensive fault in which the event, the 'expressed', which appears as a 'continuum mobile' that Deleuze also calls 'sense'. This *continuum mobile* characterises the 'logic of sense' and eventually gives birth to language itself. This basic movement defines the serial thought of Deleuze, his reading of Spinozist 'explication', 'development', 'unfolding' or 'expression' of Life in its various attributes and modes. As elements, 'traits' of the problematic of expression, signs 'envelop' the logic of sense and sense is thereby folded in it ('implied') like a thing in another. This is clearly expressed throughout *Proust and Signs*.

Deleuze's transcendental empiricism is not interested in language as such but rather in what makes it possible, what confrontations, what relations of forces, what viewpoints, what events are folded in, enveloped in signs. It is therefore not surprising that Deleuze never discusses literary texts from the perspective of a linguist. What interests him in a text are the processes, the resisting strategies writers invent in order to demystify language itself, to experiment with it, to 'complicate' signs, to confront the Outside or Life itself, to survive this confrontation and to create their own work their own events, milestones or shelters for a new 'life in the folds'. Such processes or strategies are also analysed in *A Thousand Plateaus* (Deleuze and Guattari 1987: 118–48). In this regard, philosophy and literature are inseparable.

All these remarks characterise the problematic of expression with regard to the conditions of possibility of linguistic signs and that of signs in general. This problematic defines what Deleuze also called the '*sayable*', what can be said (*le dicible*). But what can be said is inseparable from what can be seen. The '*sayable*' cannot be separated from the '*visible*' (*le régime d'énonciation* from *le régime de visibilité*). Hence, Deleuze's system of signs and problematic of expression, particularly in literature, lead him to a very characteristic neo-Spinozist theory of Light.

Deleuze's last book, *Essays Critical and Clinical*, was entirely dedicated to the study of literature. Considering what I have said so far, it is not surprising that the very last chapter of *Essays Critical and Clinical* was dedicated to a detailed analysis of the general structure of Spinoza's *Ethics*. Unfortunately, the English translators of this book chose not to respect the crucial order of composition chosen in parallel with that of *A Thousand Plateaus* and that of Spinoza's *Ethics*. The last essay of the original edition of *Essays Critical and Clinical*, 'Spinoza and the three *Ethics*', characterises both the fundamental differences and the necessary intertwining of the three worlds of the Ethics: those of Signs (also called affects), Concepts and Percepts (also called Essences). These worlds are analysed in connection with what are, according to Deleuze, the three constituents of the text of the *Ethics*: the scholia, the propositions and the demonstrations, and the Fifth book. To each world and aspect of Spinoza's text correspond different regimens of light: the Sombre (*le Sombre*)[4] for the logic of signs, Colour for the logic of concepts and Pure Light for the logic of the percept. Nowhere in this essay does Deleuze mention literature. However, it constitutes a perfect conclusion to his life-long study of the 'disjunctive synthesis' or 'complicatio' between literature, signs and philosophy.

Table 1.4 The three planes of the *Ethics*

Light	Colour	Sombre
Percepts	Concepts	Signs
Essences, Singularities, pure figures of light	Common Notions, optical figures	Affects, values of the chiaroscuro

Literature selects, develops and confronts signs in different worlds, along different aspects of time according to differing processes of continuous variation or transversals that Deleuze calls a writer's 'style'. In that respect, like Sade and Masoch, a writer is a very special kind of clinician who selects and organises signs into symptoms, images as on diagrams, to create his or her own symptomatology (1989a: 15–16). But the perception and organisation of these signs into symptoms are directly dependent on a specific regimen of visibility and enunciability, on a regimen of Light, that will define the clinical at a specific time.

For Michel Foucault, the birth of the clinic was inseparable from the observation of death. For the clinician, signs appear from an obscure depth that is necessarily connected to death. In that respect, Foucault's thought, like the thought of many of his contemporaries, could be compared to Leibniz's baroque thought about which Deleuze writes: '[Leibniz] saw the Dark[5] (*le Sombre*) ("fuscum subnigrum") as a matrix or premise, from which chiaroscuro, colors and even light will emerge' (1997: 141). Indeed, Foucault characterised the birth of the clinic in the following terms:

> It will certainly be decisive for our culture that the first scientific discourse it held on the individual had to pass through this moment of death. Western man could constitute himself as an object of science to his very own eyes [. . .] only in reference to his own destruction. (quoted by Dreyfus/Rabinow 1984: 33; my translation)

From 'klinê,' the Greek word for 'bed', clinical observation characterises the empirical observations made by the physician at the bed of a sick and dying patient. For Deleuze, in a Spinozist perspective, the clinical is first characterised by an evaluation and a selection of signs operated by the writer and the philosopher. But again, these Deleuzo-Spinozist 'signs' are of a very particular kind: 'Signs *do not have objects as their direct referents*. They are states of bodies (affections) and variations of power (affects), each of which refers to the other' (Deleuze 1997: 141).

As a clinician or a Nietzschean physician of civilisation, a writer will first evaluate signs depending on whether they express an increase or a decrease of his or her powers of living. Are they sources of joy or of sadness? Are they adequate or inadequate to the structure (*fabrica*) (1993: 176, in English: 141) of his or her life? The cries (*les cris*) of the language of signs are the mark of this battle of the passions, of joys and sadnesses, of increases and decreases of power (1997: 145). The Sombre is only a consequence of these confrontations, not an originating background:

> Signs are *effects of light* in a space filled with things colliding into each other at random [. . .]. In Spinoza, on the contrary (to Leibniz), everything is light, and *the Dark* (*le Sombre*) is only a shadow, a simple effect of light, a limit of light on the bodies that reflect it (affection) or absorb it (affect). Spinoza is much closer to Byzantium than to the Baroque. (1997: 141)

Very similar remarks were made throughout Deleuze's work to repudiate Hegelian negation and its offshoots (see for example Deleuze 1994: 205–6; Colombat 1991: 587). Because it deals with signs, with the evaluation and selection of affects, of passions, in different regimes of light, the writer's work can be seen as preparatory to that of the philosopher who deals with concepts: 'Signs or affects are inadequate ideas and passions; common notions or concepts are adequate ideas from which true actions ensue' (Deleuze 1997: 143).

But beyond or rather in-between the conceptual characters of the Writer working with affects or Deleuze's neo-Spinozist signs, and that of the Philosopher working with concepts, appears the image of a kind of Spinozist, an anonymous, imperceptible Overman, maybe a pure Artist, made of Percepts and pure Light. This is the kind of 'man' who wrote the fifth book of the *Ethics*:

> This is the third element of Spinoza's logic: no more signs or affects, nor concepts, but Essences or Singularities, Percepts. It is the third state of light. No longer signs of shadow (*le Sombre*), nor of light as color, but light in itself and for itself. (1997: 148)

These three aspects of light corresponding to Spinoza's three kinds of knowledge are inseparable from each other. Their relationship and proportion will of course vary tremendously with every individual and every intellectual production. If literature is largely connected to the first kind of knowledge, it is however inseparable from the others that it 'envelops' and 'unfolds', that it 'explains', 'implies' and 'complicates' in multiple ways.

Notes

1. Regarding this last point, see Joel Birman (1998: 484).
2. See A. Koyré (1929), quoted by Deleuze (1990: 112).
3. On these notions, see also *Proust and Signs* (1972: 103–6).
4. I would prefer to translate '*le Sombre*' by the 'Sombre' rather than the Dark, preferred by the English translation of this essay in order to avoid the neo-romantic dialectic that opposes Light to Dark/Darkness, which is avoided by the French text.
5. See note 4 above.

Bibliography

Austin, John L. (1975), *How to Do Things with Words*, 2nd edn., Oxford: Oxford University Press.
Badiou, Alain (1997), *Deleuze La Clameur de l'être*, Paris: Hachette.
Birman, Joel (1998), 'Les signes et leurs excès. La clinique chez Deleuze', in Gilles Deleuze, *Une vie philosophique*, edited by Eric Alliez, Institut Le Plessis-Robinson: Synthélabo, pp. 476–94.
Colombat, André P. (1991), *Deleuze et la littérature*, Bern: Peter Lang.
Deleuze, Gilles (1972) [1964], *Proust and Signs*, trans. Richard Howard, New York: George Braziller.
Deleuze, Gilles (1986 [1983]), *Cinema 1: The Movement-Image*, trans. Hugh Tomlinson and Barbara Habberjam, London: Athlone and Minneapolis: University of Minnesota Press.
Deleuze, Gilles (1988 [1966]), *Bergsonism*, trans. Hugh Tomlinson and Barbara Habberjam, New York: Zone Books.
Deleuze, Gilles (1989a [1985]), *Cinema 2: The Time-Image*, trans. Hugh Tomlinson and Barbara Habberjam, London: Athlone and Minneapolis: University of Minnesota Press.
Deleuze, Gilles (1989b [1967]), *Masochism: An Introduction to Coldness and Cruelty*, trans. Jean McNeil, New York: George Braziller, Reprinted 1971 by Zone Books, New York.
Deleuze, Gilles (1990a [1968]), *Expressionism in Philosophy: Spinoza*, trans. Martin Joughin, New York: Zone Books.
Deleuze, Gilles (1990b [1968]), *The Logic of Sense*, trans. Mark Lester with Charles Stivale, edited by Constantin Boundas, New York: Columbia University Press and London: Athlone.
Deleuze, Gilles (1994 [1968]), *Difference and Repetition*, trans. Paul Patton, London: Athlone and New York: Columbia University Press.
Deleuze, Gilles (1997 [1993]), *Essays Critical and Clinical*, trans. Daniel W. Smith and Michael A. Greco, Minneapolis: University of Minnesota Press.
Deleuze, Gilles and Guattari, Félix (1984 [1972]), *Anti-Oedipus: Capitalism and Schizophrenia*, trans. Robert Huley, Mark Seem and Helen R. Lane, New York: Viking Press, 1977, and London: Athlone.

Deleuze, Gilles (1986 [1975]), *Kafka: Toward a Minor Literature*, trans. Dana Polan, Minneapolis: University of Minnesota Press.

Deleuze, Gilles (1987 [1980]), *A Thousand Plateaus: Capitalism and Schizophrenia*, trans. Brian Massumi, Minneapolis: University of Minnesota Press.

Deleuze, Gilles (1994 [1991]), *What is Philosophy?*, trans. Hugh Tomlinson and Graham Burchell, Columbia: New York University Press.

Dreyfus, Hubert and Rabinow, Paul (1984) *Michel Foucault: Un parcours philosophique*, Paris: Gallimard.

Eco, Umberto (1995), *The Search for The Perfect Language*, Oxford: Blackwell.

Hjelmslev, Louis (1968–71), *Prolégomènes à une théorie du language*, Paris: Editions de Minuit.

Koyré, A (1929), *La Philosophie de Jacob Boehme*, Paris: Vrin.

Koyré, A (1947), *Mystiques, spirituels: alchimistes du XVIe siècle allemand*, Paris: Armand Colin.

Metz, Christian (1968, 1972), *Essai sur la signification au cinéma*, vols I and II, Paris: Klinsieck.

Peirce, Charles Sanders (1960), *Collected Papers of Charles Sanders Peirce*, vol. I–VI, Cambridge, MA: Harvard University Press.

Searle, John R. (1969), *Speech Acts: An Essay in the Philosophy of Language*, Cambridge: Cambridge University Press.

Todorov, Ducros (1972), *Dictionnaire encyclopédique des sciences du langage*, Paris: Seuil.

Chapter 2

How Deleuze can help us make Literature work

Bruce Baugh

In *Anti-Oedipus*, Gilles Deleuze and Félix Guattari pose the question: 'Given a certain effect, what machine is capable of producing it? And given a certain machine, what can it be used for?' (Deleuze and Guattari 1983: 3). Their conception of 'machine' is very broad, and includes literary texts, which they wish to analyse in terms of the effects a text is capable of producing. Likewise, their notion of 'effect' is also broad, and includes not only a work's effects on the ideas and feelings of the reader during the course of reading, but changes in the reader's dispositions, attitudes and behaviours that may link up with other forces affecting the reader, particularly social and political forces, and in such way that, in the best instances, readers are able to put these forces to work to overcome the inhibiting and restrictive effects of the dominant social forces. Hence, for them 'reading a text is never a scholarly exercise in search of what is signified, still less a highly textual exercise in search of a signifier. Rather, it is a productive use of the literary machine . . . that extracts from the text its revolutionary force' (Deleuze and Guattari 1983: 106).

We could call this theory a revolutionary pragmatics of reading. The theory comprises two parts: a mechanics of reading, or an analysis of how a literary work produces certain effects, and hence of the work as a machinic assemblage; an experimentalist pragmatics, or the experimental production of effects that are then evaluated in terms of the reader's goals and values. The first part of the theory is entirely objective, since it considers whether a work is in fact capable of producing certain effects, and in determining the nature of those effects; we might think of this as the Spinozist moment of the theory. The latter part, however, is also objective, since it is a question of fact whether a given effect furthers the objectives of an individual or group (whether the effect is helpful, harmful or indifferent). Nevertheless, the second part of the theory is also evaluative: effects are evaluated in terms of whether they are beneficial or harmful (good or bad), and this presupposes a determination of what is 'good for' the person or group. We might think of this as the diagnostic or Nietzschean moment of the theory: an evaluation of forces in terms of whether they increase or decrease a power of acting. Both moments are necessary to determine whether and how a literary work can 'work' for someone.

In short, instead of asking what a work of literature *means*, Deleuze and Guattari suggest, we might gain more by asking: *what can it do?* Nor need the question be 'what is the work *supposed* to do, what effect was it *intended* to have?', or 'what was it made for?' Things made for one purpose can work quite well to serve another: we can all be *bricoleurs*, using the materials and methods at hand in new and different ways, either aiming at a specific result, or freely experimenting just to see what happens. Readers have their own purposes and desires, both as individuals ('does it work for me?') and as members of a larger group ('does it work for us'?). Deleuze and Guattari claim that 'the greatest force of language was discovered once a *work* was viewed as a machine, producing certain effects, amenable to a certain use', and quote Malcolm Lowry concerning his own work: 'it's anything you want it to be, so long as it works' (Deleuze and Guattari 1983: 109). The claim, then, is that considering the use of literary works maximises the powers of both works and readers, rather than subordinating one to the other.

Experimental Reading

Deleuze and Guattari describe their approach to texts as 'experimental'. For some of us, that may call up associations with 'experimental art', or 'experimental film', which is 'avant-garde' and breaks with conventional practices, and this association isn't altogether off the mark: 'experimentation' does involve improvising, creating, trying new things. The other side of 'experiment' is 'experience': when we try new things, we also see how they work, we observe, and our observations and experiences are an essential part of testing a new tool, technique or method (see Deleuze and Guattari 1986: 7). Improvisation, innovation and experience are linked in experimentation. We experiment with something 'in the making' so that we can 'make something of it': 'what we experience, experiment with, is always . . . what's coming into being, what's new, what's taking shape', not something 'over and done with' that has nothing more to teach us (Deleuze 1995: 106). An experimental approach is thus innovative, results-oriented (pragmatic) and experiential (empirical), although the most salient feature of the results is that they are new in ways that could not have been predicted or determined in advance (Deleuze and Guattari 1983: 370–1). In short, a truly experimental approach does not aim at a pre-determined result, but experiments in order to *discover* what effects can be produced.

This is how Deleuze and Guattari approach reading. They want to treat literary works as machines capable of producing effects, and they want to take apart and analyse these machines to see how the effects are produced; they even want to tinker with the mechanism to see whether the machine can produce other effects than the usual or traditional ones, much as a mechanic might tinker with a car engine.

> What we're interested in is how something works, functions – finding the machine. (Deleuze 1995: 21–2)
>
> The issue was not – at least, not *only* – to try to interpret [the work], but, above all, to practice it as an experimental machine, a machine for effects, as in physics. (Bensmaïa 1986: xi).

Or, as Deleuze and Guattari say with respect to their analysis of Franz Kafka's works:

> We believe in one or more Kafka *machines* that are neither structure nor phantasm. We believe only in a Kafka *experimentation* that is without interpretation or significance and rests only on tests of experience. (Deleuze and Guattari 1986: 7)

The point is to discover what works for the reader:

> You see the book as a little non-signifying machine, and the only question is, 'Does it work, and how does it work?,' How does it work for you? If it doesn't work, if nothing comes through, you try another book. (Deleuze 1995: 8)

Reading is then 'a series of experiments for each reader in the midst of events that have nothing to do with books . . . getting the book to interact with other things, absolutely anything' (Deleuze 1995: 8–9). A literary work *works* when the reader is able to make use of the work's effects in other areas of life: personally, socially, politically, depending on the reader's desires, needs and objectives. 'It is a question of seeing what use a text is in the extra-textual practice that prolongs the text' (Schrift 1995: 63), of making use of the text to accomplish goals other than those of simply reading and interpreting it.

It's worth emphasising that the experimental discovery or production of effects is not the same as determining what a text means. It's clear that an experimental reading doesn't search for a single meaning (what the author really meant): such a reading subordinates the reader's objectives to that of the author (or perhaps the text), when this 'intended meaning' can only be a matter of conjecture in any case. By restricting the goal of reading to the imaginative attempt to identify and duplicate a prior intention, interpretation rules out questions of use and efficacy in favour of meaning-exegesis (Deleuze and Guattari 1983: 206), and in two ways. First, knowing the meaning of something (a symbol, word, image) gives us no clue as to what it does or what is done with it, its operative use or its positional functioning within an functional assemblage (Deleuze and Guattari 1983: 181). Second, interpretation is a process of identification: 'this means that'. This holds whether interpretation proceeds via analogy, representation or symbolism. In every case, the aim is to assign an identifiable meaning or set of meanings that correspond to a signifier, thereby excluding others ('this means *that*, but *not this other*'). Deleuze and Guattari regard this as a 'flattening out' of the polyvocal nature of the real. But more importantly, hermeneutic interpretation belongs to a 'imperial-despotic system', where written signifiers are expressions of a hidden voice (of the emperor, of a god), requiring the priest's interpretation. This effective alliance of priest and despot substitutes a fiction of revealed 'truth' for efficacy, and subjugates creative production to the reproduction of meaning, under the rule of the despot-priest who claims privileged access to the truth (see Deleuze and Guattari 1983: 206–8, 240; Deleuze and Guattari 1987: 114–17). The model for this system may be the ancient priest (Aaron, the priest of Apollo at Delphi), but the model is perpetuated in all those practices that regulate and restrict the possible uses of texts to the search for 'what it means', whether the priest determining the meaning assumes the role of a literary critic, a scholar, a psychoanalyst, or a teacher. Readers take on this role even if their concern is what it means *for them*: personalising or subjectivising interpretation in no way alters its basic nature.

By the same token, pluralising meaning, or making meaning indefinite, does not circumvent any of these difficulties. Experimentation is not the discovery that the same work means different things to different people, or that it has a meaning that is ambiguous or undecidable. When the concern for 'identifying' meaning ceases, then the difficulties of doing so because of ambiguity or undecidability become uninteresting. From this standpoint, it doesn't matter whether interpretation seeks a signified meaning or a 'transcendent signifier' supporting a 'chain of signification' in which each signifier signifies another signifier, endlessly (Deleuze and Guattari 1983: 208). The recent interpretative turn to 'scientificity', 'pure textuality' and the like merely puts the signifier in the place formerly occupied by the signified: it is now the signifier that unlocks the 'truth' of

the text, and the question of 'truth' still assumes primacy over that of use. Moreover, the signifying system retains 'a minimal identity' for signifiers through the systematic differences between them, which are considered as oppositions; every signifier, however 'mobile' it is in virtue of the play of signification that runs through the chain, is assigned a recognisable and determinate function through the 'coded gaps' between signifiers, so that the oppositions and exclusive disjunctions between signifiers confer an 'identity' on each signifier (Deleuze and Guattari 1983: 242). The upshot is that exegetical methods based on the Saussurian sign (signifier-signified) merely subordinate the signified to the signifier, since differences among signifieds are determined by differences among signifiers, and retain interpretation's logic of identity through exclusion or opposition.

As for what the text means to different people, this is one of the effects of the text, but mere consciousness of an effect and opinions based on such consciousness (interpretation) do not constitute a genuine understanding of the nature of the effect or how it was produced. Even if the question is how a text produces an effect on *you*, that question can't be answered by reference to your subjective opinions, or even the 'association of ideas' based on your personal experiences, any more than you can explain the experience of the colour 'green' just by reference to your consciousness of it and the associations of green (plants, spring, life, youth and so on). As Marx says, 'We cannot tell from the mere taste of wheat who grew it; the [consumption of the] product gives us no hint as to the system and relations of production' (Deleuze and Guattari 1983: 24). To explain 'green' you'd have to do the physics of light and the neurophysiology that explained how the sensation of 'green' is produced; to explain wheat's existence as a commodity, you'd have to analyse the relations of production and techniques that produced it. The same is true of texts: to really understand their effects, you have to know how the effects are produced, how the text works. Such is the work of literary analysis that is subsequent to experimentation.

Experimentation, however, comes first, and involves playing and working with the text in order to see what effects it is capable of producing, without being constrained by what someone or something else (author or text) intended. It is to attempt to produce something new, rather than reproduce an already constituted meaning or set of meanings, 'an attempt to put the text to work, to bring its theoretical and practical concerns into play . . . through a kind of repetition freed from the phantoms of identity and productive of differences' (Macherey 1996: 148). This is why Deleuze and Guattari state that they 'aren't even trying to interpret, to say this means that' (Deleuze and Guattari 1986: 7):

We will never ask what a book means, as signified or signifier; we will not look for anything to understand in it. We will ask what it functions with, in connection with what other things it does or does not transmit intensities, in which other multiplicities its own are inserted and meta-morphosed. (Deleuze and Guattari 1987: 4)

Experiment, never interpret. (Deleuze and Parnet 1987: 48)

Despite experimentation's freedom from subordination to 'truth' and 'meaning', it is far more objective than interpretation. Interpretation involves an *opinion* concerning what a work or author 'really meant', even if this concerns the question of whether there is a key signifier that determines the functions of all the rest; by contrast, whether something produces an effect, and what the effect is, is an *objective* matter. Either something really does produce a desired effect, or it fails to do so; and when it fails, it was either because it wasn't right for the circumstances, or because it was intrinsically incapable of doing the job, or just because someone didn't know how to make it work. Effectiveness is not a matter of opinion or interpretation. What something is capable of doing, and the actual effects it produces, doesn't depend on what we think about it, or how we feel about it, and that's true even if we're talking about some-thing's effect *on* your feelings and beliefs. The pain-reliever may really dull the pain or not, the beer may quench your thirst or not, your friend's fingers may find and scratch that itchy spot, or not, a political tract may change your political convictions, or not. That the effect happened, how it was produced (the processes leading up to it), whether it was beneficial or harmful, whether it enabled or prevented other effects from being produced: these are all questions of what really happened. Obviously, then, experimentation cannot arbitrarily assign to a work effects of which it is incapable, any more than we can force a Toyota Tercel to out-race a Porsche 911, whatever we might wish or imagine. Nor do our opinions or beliefs concerning the work's capabilities determine the effects it pro-duces; rather, we observe and experience the effect after the fact. By experimenting and finding what a work is really capable of, we at the same time discover both what the work cannot do and the extent to which our estimates of the work's capabilities differ from the observed results. But experimentation, insist Deleuze and Guattari, always deals with the real, not with subjective impressions (see Deleuze and Guattari 1986: 70). Experimentation alone reveals what a work can do, and for whom.

Perhaps the point could be made clearer through an example. Music critic Greil Marcus always takes an experimental approach, whether writing about Elvis Presley or Bob Dylan. In his book, *Invisible Republic:*

Bob Dylan's Basement Tapes, Marcus quotes from another critic, Howard Hampton, on one of the songs recorded by Bob Dylan and the Band back in 1967, as these musicians conducted some basement experiments with the tradition of American popular music:

> It's no more than a ragged, unfinished rehearsal, stopping and starting, Dylan calling out the chord changes to the Band and then fumbling them ('D . . . wait, uh, no, not D, E . . .'). Yet it has a floating melody like no other he has found, sung in a voice of rapture and enigma he has sought ever since. The music-box piano . . . and the frontier-church organ lift [the song] out of time: the words are like some bootleg gospel of Christ, ellipsis as parable. It's a vision of transmutation: Christ returned both as supplicant and unbeliever, as in folk legends where he escaped with Mary Magdalene to exile in France or assumed the form of King Arthur . . . 'When I come back, when I don't make my return,' he proclaims as his first (or last) dispensation, 'A heart shall rise and a man shall burn.' (Marcus 1997: 85–6)

Marcus comments that 'this is not an interpretation', since Hampton isn't trying to define or decode what Dylan sang, but is responding to a provocation (Marcus 1997: 86). Just as Dylan and the Band are experimenting with chords, different sounds (music-box, church organ) and traditions (musical, social, religious), so Hampton connects this performance with the Gospel, with heretical folk traditions of Christ, with Arthurian legend, in order to achieve his own transmutation. Marcus merely takes the experiment a step further by using Hampton's text to further his own project of transmuting America through the 'provocation' of the unrealised promises of 'the old, weird America' that Marcus hears in Harry Smith's *Anthology of American Folk Music* (itself an astonishing experiment of conjunctive synthesis that brought together in one four-record set African-American and hillbilly blues singers, folk balladeers, Appalachian banjo players, gospel choirs, and more, without reducing this multiplicity to a dialectical unity or an essence): a promise that Marcus hears revived in Dylan's basement tapes.

An exemplary reading, then: not because Marcus achieves a correct or true interpretation of Dylan's music, but because he shows us what the music can do (or what Marcus can do with it). This example also shows that experimenters (Dylan and the Band) in search of one thing (here, the voice of tradition) may discover something entirely different, with uses they hadn't dreamed of (a counter-tradition): an unpredictable and truly new effect. This sort of 'accidental discovery' has been the source of many important scientific and technical developments (such as vulcanised rubber and penicillin) The same process can occur with literary works. Even if you think you know which of the text's effects might prove useful, in the course of looking for these you may find other effects that answer to an entirely different problem than the one you were trying to solve. Perhaps in the course of using Émile Zola's *Germinal* in order to gain insight into how economic class shapes individual character you discover instead a thematic of the beast-machine (the devouring and voracious mine, the miners as beast-machines, the capitalist system) that connects to the feral computers of the films *Matrix* and *2001: A Space Odyssey*, the human-beast-machine synthesis of fighter-bombers, and to all the possibilities of a transmutation that is simultaneously a becoming-animal and a becoming-machine. Whether this discovery matters depends on what you're able to do with it, or what you make of it: that is, it depends on whether it increases your power of acting, not simply by furthering your goals (many of our goals, according to Deleuze and Guattari, promote powerlessness), but by helping you evaluate your goals in terms of whether they promote or inhibit what you can do. A discovery of a textual becoming-animal-machine might help you to think about the synthesis of the organic-inorganic being you become when you use a computer to hook up to the World Wide Web or send e-mail, the computer (and the Internet) being extensions of your faculties of perception and communication, and in turn modifying what you do, perceive and think, turning your 'subjectivity' into functions of the 'informational' exchanges essential to capitalist production/consumption under 'globalisation'. That is, it's a discovery that may enable a critical evaluation of the effects of 'plugging in' to computer technology. The point is that it's up to *you* to experiment and determine how to make use of texts in achieving a critical understanding of the forces at work in texts and in society, in order to resist some of these by making use of others; experimenting with texts is always also 'living experimentally' (see Nietzsche 1986: 8; Deleuze 1988: 40; Deleuze and Parnet 1987; 47).

Pragmatic concerns do indeed guide the experimental analysis of literature to the extent that a text, like anything else, can produce a vast number of effects, and this forces us to be selective, and focus on those effects which matter to us. That will be a function of what we want to do, not just in our reading, but in our lives. Are you searching for ways to advance a political struggle? Are you trying to connect with historical forces and forge connections with a cultural heritage? Are you looking for ways to redefine and reconstitute yourself, ways that would unblock energies previously channelled into socially prescribed activities? Whatever our focus, however, we will get nowhere unless we determine how a work produces its effects, or give an account of the causes of those effects. Those causes are by no means restricted to the text itself, but extend to the social, linguistic and cultural forces at work in the text and in the reader. What these forces are, how they function both inside and outside the text, how they come together to form elements of the text: these are determined through what Deleuze and Guattari term an 'active dismantling' of the text.

Finding how it works: Active Dismantling

Think of the literary work as a machine, say Deleuze and Guattari, and figure out what are the different pieces and how they fit together, and this will explain how a text produces effects. 'This functioning of an assemblage [*agencement*] can be explained only if one takes it apart to examine both the elements that make it up and the nature of its linkages' (Deleuze and Guattari 1986: 53).[1]

On the face of it, taking apart a work and analysing its structure is standard literary interpretation. What are the elements of a work of literature? The standard reply, the one we're all taught, would refer to such things as 'characters', 'plot', 'theme', 'symbols', 'metaphors', 'genre', 'period', all of which together determine what the work 'means'. So, Shakespeare's *King Lear* is an Elizabethan tragedy, the story of a king who foolishly leaves his kingdom to the wrong two daughters and so meets his downfall; Lear's foolish pride and Goneril and Regan's selfish envy drive the plot; its themes are love and loyalty (and their opposites), bastardy and legitimacy, trust and mistrust; the storm on the heath symbolises Lear's growing madness, the 'raging' of his mind; its meaning is, variously, that humans are playthings of the gods ('they kill us for their sport'), or that our vulnerabilities make it difficult to genuinely express or accept love.[2] Not only are all these elements identifiable, but they are all organically related to the whole and to each other: each element has a function defined in relation to the whole.

This is all very familiar, only it's not at all what Deleuze and Guattari are after. A more careful 'active dismantling' of the work would analyse its elements into more minute components (words, images, actions, spatial arrangements), allowing these components to come into different relations than the standard interpretation would allow, not to provide a better interpretation, but to see what the work is capable of doing (Deleuze and Guattari 1986: 7, 48). Configurations of images and words can constitute non-figurative 'figures' that do not represent or mean anything, but which produce determinate effects, especially at the level of affect or feeling (see Deleuze and Guattari 1983: 243–4; Lyotard 1971). In addition, the work's components are also analysed in relation to forces that exist outside the text (desires, potentialities, structures), of which the work's components are effects, and which determine how the work's components combine and the effects of these combinations. Finally, the whole work is a totality *of* its parts, but not a unifying and totalising synthesis: the whole is another aspect of the work, its functional unity, but this is a new part added to the other parts and relations that constitute the work (Deleuze and Guattari 1983: 42).

Let's look, for example, at character. Character is not something unified and self-contained, a 'subject', but a condensation of forces and relations, 'a functioning of a polyvalent assemblage of which the solitary individual is only a part' (Deleuze and Guattari 1986: 85), and which involves not only psychic forces, but also social ones. It's a commonplace that Lear's character is constituted by a desire for love and for recognition of his authority, as well as by a fear of his desire being recognised, and so the forces that compose him also bring about his destruction. Yet these same forces pass through others (Regan, Goneril, Cordelia, Edmund, Gloucester), and take on different configurations and enter into different relations, for example, composing Lear's authority and pride in Regan and Goneril's obsequiousness, decomposing it through their ambition, both the subservience and ambition being constituted by Lear's desire and his daughters' responses to it. Lear's desire is thus not a 'property' of Lear the solitary individual, since it is nothing outside his relations with others, and involves those others as much as him, even though it doesn't belong to the others either; it is a force connecting the characters without being confined to any of them, a 'between' rather than a point. Moreover, this force is connected to social forces: the institutions of property, kingship, marriage and primogeniture under feudalism, together with its codes of personal loyalty (to king, to spouse, to parent). All these social forces are factors of 'social production', the production of society through the investment of desire in the social field (Deleuze and Guattari 1983: 29). Just as in modern society bureaucracy is desire, 'the exercise of a certain number of powers' (Deleuze and Guattari 1986: 56–7), so too for the feudal administrative apparatus in *King Lear*; in general, 'social investments are themselves erotic, and inversely . . . the most erotic of desires brings about a fully political social investment, engages with the entire social field' (Deleuze and Guattari 1986: 64). *King Lear* is a veritable experimental laboratory, investigating precisely this interpenetration of social and personal forces, the diffusion of desire through persons and institutions in ways that are mostly unconscious. Since the forces that compose and decompose characters are both social and psychic, we can only conclude that these forces are impersonal, even when they connect persons. At the same time, however, those forces are as singular or unique as the relationships that manifest and express them, and so are 'impersonal singularities'. They cannot be summarised in a *Zeitgeist*, but are determinable only through an analysis of the particular effects and interactions they involve.

Deleuze and Guattari's own literary analyses of Proust, Kafka and others involve a patient and careful analysis of the nature of the forces at work within a text. But even this brief consideration of *King Lear* gives us some indication of how character, rather than being a fundamental term, is a global effect of forces and relations, of 'proliferating fluid ensembles' in 'perpetual transformation' from one set of relations to another (Deleuze and Guattari 1986: 12, 84–5). The 'individual', divisible into a singular constellation of forces, may indeed be 'an irreducible multiplicity' (Deleuze 1989: 133). But since they are nothing outside the forces and relations that constitute them, characters need not be coherent (although the forces that constitute them can achieve a certain provisional stability and consistency), and it would be pointless to look for a decisive moment of 'recognition' where the true nature and fate of an individual is revealed.[3] It is not the 'truth' or 'meaning' of a character we are after, but an understanding of the forces at work in that character.

From that point of view, character doesn't 'represent' anything, it expresses forces in the way in which the speed of a car 'expresses' the state of its engine, its transmission and its relation to the road. What a character, theme or image is capable of doing is a function of its ability to enter multiple relationships with other elements of the work, and the effects produced will vary with the relationships, so that the component is nothing outside of those relations (Deleuze and Guattari 1986: 60). Instead of being a unified subject possessing a 'truth', character is something like a 'general function' that passes through different series, and in doing so takes on different specific functions: the daughter in *King Lear* functions differently in the triangle 'father/daughter/husband' than in the double 'sister/sister'. Nor, by the way, need we confine ourselves to groups of threes and twos: unlike in some structuralist literary criticism, there is no set schema or pattern, no formal 'structure', that we have to apply to all works. Rather, we experiment. If we find that a grouping of three functions to produce an effect (in *Lear*, having to do with love, desire and statements of claim), and if we can make use of this for our own purposes (say, as part of an analysis and critique of proprietary love and the system of social relations in which this sort of love has its place), then that's an experiment that has brought in *prima facie* 'good results'.

Obviously, we will learn nothing of what the work can do if we attribute to it capacities it does not have; we are not after an alchemical and symbolic interpretation of the work, but a physical-chemical analysis of its elements. Even a careful experiment may go awry: the structures or schemata we apply may fail to yield any good result, and this may force us to go back and rethink not only our schemata, but the questions we put to the work that gave rise to them. In determining the nature and function of a work's elements, however, we don't have to treat the literary work as an organism, each part of which has a specific, well-defined function, so that the critic's job is to perform an 'anatomy' of the text according to a fixed structural pattern.[4] An experimental reading realises that parts of the work can perform functions other than those assigned by the author, and that they function differently in conjunction with different elements. Like the experimental scientist, then, the experimental reader does not assume that the nature of what is under investigation is already known or can be understood through some already given schema, but takes the standpoint that its nature can only be discovered through experiment: through trying new things, and observing the results, we may eventually produce an effective schema.

Hence, there are no pre-determined limits to experimentation and questioning. Suppose our experiment brings in some useful results; we can always experiment further, seeking different patterns and configurations in the text that might have different effects and uses.[5] Again, in *King Lear*, Edmund is the 'natural' but 'illegitimate' son who, naturally, seeks his rightful (legitimate) claim to recognition as a son and so treats his father and brother unnaturally; Regan and Goneril, 'got between the lawful sheets', are 'unnatural hags', treating Lear with unnatural contempt, after he, contrary to both law and the natural order, made his daughters his parents by giving them authority over him; so the function of 'natural/ unnatural', 'bastard/legitimate' keeps shifting through different contexts, involving the different characters in different ways, in Edgar's case passing through convention as law (which disinherits him), in Goneril and Regan's, through law (Lear's royal decree) contrary to convention, in both through heridity (and nature), although heriditary nature produces more 'natural' (that is, conventional) effects in Cordelia and Edgar. One effect of *King Lear* might then enable us to dismantle the 'nature/convention' dichotomy, which can be useful when trying to overcome conventions that pass themselves off as natural, or which classify certain relations as 'unnatural', most obviously in the case of family relations.

None of this amounts to considering *King Lear* a treatise on primogeniture, or on legitimacy and bastardy, or love and betrayal. It's not a question of what the work is about, but about what it *can do*, and particularly, what it can do for us. In fact, Deleuze and Guattari reject the search for overarching themes and archetypes because this would involve grouping together into a single category too many diverse phenomena, which may take on different functions in different contexts, and may express forces that can combine in different ways (Deleuze and Guattari 1986: 7). There is no point in asking about a character, theme, signifier or symbol 'if one hasn't asked exactly what its importance is in the work – that is, *how it functions* (and not what its "meaning" is)' (Deleuze and Guattari 1986: 45).

Nevertheless, we don't need to confine our investigation to how an element functions within a single work, or even the *oeuvre* of a single author. We can also combine elements extracted from one work with those of another. To continue with the *King Lear* example, it's not at all difficult to relate the characters and plot elements of *King Lear* to Jane Smiley's novel, *A Thousand Acres*, (1991); after all, Smiley has deliberately set Shakespeare's tale in the US Midwest in the early 1980s. This displacement produces a number of new relations and effects, in particular with respect to 'the land'. In *King Lear*, the land is both an inheritance, and so the focus of passions of greed and ambition, and (on the heath) a place of exposure to the harshness of nature. In *A Thousand Acres*, the flat, American farm prairie is all of these things, but it is also much more: it is the coefficient of machinery, such a tractor or a car (each being the effect of a large and prosperous holding, the speed of each being the measure of the land's vastness). Its flatness produces effects of perspective (vastness that reduces individuals to insignificance, the difficulty of finding a 'middle distance' in which to put individuals in their proper perspective) and of visibility (everyone sees everyone else), which in turn produce effects of hiding and dissimulation (secrecy, hypocrisy). It is the agent of cooperation and antagonism, as it is in *King Lear*, but it is also an agent in a secret, subterranean way, in the water's transmission of molecules and particles through the water table and the process of evaporation and condensation, with toxic effects on the people who live and work on land; it is an agent of life and death, and the passive victim of human designs. It is, in the end, a series of forces that enter into a cycle connecting it with the being of the characters ('Lodged in my every cell, along with the DNA, are molecules of topsoil and atrazine and paraquat and anhydrous ammonia and diesel fuel and plant dust, and also molecules of memory . . . All of it is present now, here; each particle weighs some fraction of the hundred and thirty-six pounds that attaches me to the earth, perhaps as much as the print weighs in other sorts of histories' (Smiley 1991: 369)). Not only does Smiley's portrayal of her characters subvert their Shakespearean parallels, but her portrayal of the land gives us a clearer understanding of how character is produced by relations with unconscious and impersonal forces, such as those of the land.[6]

There are no *a priori* limits on which work may be combined with which other; only the results of such experimental combinations can tell us which of them might prove useful. Smiley's objective was to make use of *King Lear* as part of a critique of the patriarchal American farm family, not to interpret Shakespeare; our objective is to make use of Smiley's novel in ways that we find useful, by forging yet other connections, and not necessarily in keeping with Smiley's intentions. We are not constrained to reproduce a 'meaning' that the novel or the author has already constituted; we are free to take up the forces the work has expressed and made manifest, allowing those forces to reverberate in us, and seeing where they can take us. When we do that, it becomes indeterminate where the work's effects leave off and our use of them begins: the result is as much an effect of our response as it is of the work. This is true, for example, of Deleuze's own use of the texts of other philosophers, such as Nietzsche, Spinoza, Bergson, Hume and Leibniz, to the extent that the authors considered by Deleuze become so integrated in Deleuze's own projects that one can refer to the result as a hybrid: Deleuze–Nietzsche, Deleuze–Spinoza, and so on. Asking whether Deleuze's uses of these philosophers constitutes a correct interpretation of their thought seems completely beside the point; what is interesting is what Deleuze is able to do with their thoughts, and what we in turn are able to do with Deleuze's.

Powers of Language

Realising that characters, incidents, plots and themes are the global effect of countless minute forces helps us to take those forces out of their conventional configurations and make use of them in different ways. But there are lots of other forces at work in literature, particularly at the level of language.

Deleuze and Guattari are especially concerned with the use of different usages or idioms: making a language 'stammer' by writing in an idiom other than the dominant one (in 'black English' rather than standard American English; in the German of a Czech Jew rather than that of a Berlin bourgeois). This contestation of a language from within, the setting

of 'minoritarian' forces of the language over against the majority consensus, can resist the constraints of convention, Law and the state; being
'a foreigner in one's own language' involves 'placing all linguistic, and
even non-linguistic, elements in variation', freeing them from their conventional roles (Deleuze and Guattari 1987: 98). For language always
functions within the wider social apparatus, so that resisting the 'major'
use of a language amounts to resisting how the dominant consensus
defines reality and assigns roles and functions within it. This resistance is
more than merely 'symbolic', then; it gives writers and readers, speakers
and hearers, a way of understanding society according to their own
desires and interests, and a different way of affecting one another through
speech (to understand this, we may consider the different effect of the
word 'nigger' when uttered by a socially dominant 'white' to a subservient
'black', or when uttered by one African-American to another, for example, in the context of a rap song).

Minoritarian usage depends on how differing usages produce different
effects, and how these effects are linked to social contexts and social
forces. So, for example, we should not try to translate or decode what
James Brown means when he sings, 'Papa's got a brand new bag', or even
try to determine what African-Americans would understand him to *mean*:
to understand how this phrase works, we would have to know what
effects it produces among a certain group of people, in what contexts it
would likely be uttered, to whom it would usually be addressed, and so
on. It would be futile and beside the point to try to determine whether
'bag' is a metaphor for something else, that is, whether it really means
what some other word designates (some other word in the majoritarian
use of the language), since that in effect would transpose 'bag' from one
context to an entirely different one, and substitute the question 'what
effect would an ostensibly synonymous word have on a white audience?'
for the original question ('what effect did this phrase have on African-
Americans in 1965?'). Treating Brown's phrase as 'metaphorical' will not
give us an understanding of its minoritarian usage of English or the effects
of this usage (among which we'd have to include its distillation of various
African-American usages in order to summon or convoke an African-
American 'community' more or less coextensive with those African-
Americans who hear this summons as addressed to *them*.).[7] Nor is this
a matter of 'interpreting' what Brown's phrase 'meant' to the African-
American community; it is rather a question of analysing the phrase's
effect, through an analysis of the social-linguistic forces with which the
phrase intersected and of its socio-political results (including the fact that
after Martin Luther King's assassination in 1968, a James Brown concert

was broadcast live on radio, which turned out to be a pivotal moment: from soul to funk, from King's dream to Malcolm X's pragmatic 'by any means necessary' for many African-Americans). Only through this analytical understanding of how the phrase works would we be able to make effective use of it for our own purposes.

The focus on effectiveness and use is quite distinct from an analysis of metaphor and meaning. Metaphor is inseparable from meaning (metaphor is when one word 'represents' another), and designating a phrase or word a metaphor thus limits its possible functions and effects to those of meaning and representation (Deleuze and Guattari 1987: 77). Deleuze and Guattari argue that 'sense' (especially 'good sense' and 'the correct meaning') function to limit what language can do by ruling out some effects as impermissible, and this restrictiveness both belongs to 'the hierarchic and imperative system of language as a transmission of orders', and masks the 'social factors, relations of force, [and] diverse centers of power' at work in language (Deleuze and Guattari 1986: 20–3). Language can achieve effects quite apart from the representation of ideas and things, even when symbolic or metaphorical representation was the author's aim.

For words can have direct effects, on listeners, or on states of affairs in the world. Think of the effect of a police officer hollering 'stop!', or a baseball umpire signalling 'safe!': the first affects the listener's behaviour; the second affects a state of affairs by rendering the runner 'safe' (see Deleuze and Guattari 1987: 76–83). This is obviously true in the case of imperatives (commands, orders, injunctions), entreaties and requests, or what some linguists and philosophers of language call 'performatives', which is when a certain speech act, uttered by the right person in the right circumstances, brings about or alters a state of affairs (a justice of the peace saying 'I now pronounce you husband and wife' has the effect of making a couple legally married, for example). It can even occur in simple declarative and descriptive sentences, with different effects depending on the position of the speaker: 'This pie is mouldy' can be a simple observation, usually leading to the speaker or someone else throwing it out; it can, however, be a statement of complaint (when uttered in a restaurant, by a customer to a server), or even of condemnation ('You served this mouldy pie to a customer; you're fired!'). Even when it is merely a representation of a state of affairs, it often carries with it the force of trying to gain the hearer's agreement ('Yes, it is mouldy') by affecting the hearer's perception ('I hadn't noticed, but now that you mention it, yes, I see that it is mouldy'). For Deleuze and Guattari, the primary function of language is to affect others: 'In speaking, I do not simply indicate things and actions; I also commit acts that assure a relation with the interlocutor, in keeping with our respective situations: I command, I interrogate, I promise, I ask, I emit "speech acts" ' (Deleuze 1997: 73).

The direct production of effects can also be a result of the words and images of a literary work. Some words and linguistic images, says Deleuze, are 'signs' that express forces in the text, and which have a direct effect on the reader (Deleuze 1972: 93–157). For example, an image can compress different moments of time into one, creating a temporal density rather than a chronological flow from past to present to future. For Deleuze, and for many others, Marcel Proust is the master of this technique, but he is far from the only one. Consider the sequence of images in the opening pages of Anne Michaels' *Fugitive Pieces* (1996): bog-boy, Tollund Man, Grauballe Man, a well-preserved stone-age child with cockleshells around his neck dug up during a road excavation, a golem; a wooden city submerged in water and clay, glass beads and clay bowls dug up by archaeologists and smashed by soldiers, a wooden door burst off its frame, buttons in a chipped saucer smashed to the ground, 'little white teeth'. Here we pass rapidly from a forest in eastern Europe in the 1940s to that forest 2500 years ago, from the narrator emerging from mud to the stone-age child, from the necklace to beads to buttons to teeth, from the narrator (as a boy) emerging from mud to the resurrection of the dead, to birth and rebirth ('Afterbirth of earth'), and the creation of life from clay (a golem, Frankenstein's monster, Pygmalion, the book of Genesis).

There is a compression of moments of time (past and present), of the narrator and others (the stone-age child, the 'bog-men'), of teeth and buttons. There is also a series of what Deleuze would call 'becomings' that proceed in divergent directions: the narrator becoming the dead child, the dead child becoming the narrator (and so resurrected when he emerges from the mud), the narrator becoming a mole digging into the ground, the ground becoming the womb that hides and shelters the narrator, who becomes a foetus and an afterbirth, a golem and a sorcerer. Past and present remain distinct, but they don't follow one another in linear succession, they move back and forth through the equivalent of cinematic 'jump cuts', so that past and present interpenetrate, while yet retaining their differences. This, and not any great richness of language and metaphor, is what gives these pages their considerable density and force. The scene manifests all the force of a trauma: sudden jumps in time, sudden connections, a past that underlies the present (in more ways than one) and breaks through the surface of the present to emerge not (as in

Proust) as a personal memory or recollection, but as a collective and prehistoric past, connected to the present in fact, not just in thought. To borrow the words Deleuze uses to talk about film, here.

> [T]he elements themselves are constantly changing with the relations of time into which they enter, and the terms with their connections. Narration is constantly being modified in each of its episodes, not according to subjective variations, but as a consequence of disconnected spaces and de-chronologized moments. (Deleuze 1989: 133)

The effect of such images and the transitions they produce is thus to release us from the linear chronology of narrative, which runs from past to present to future, or beginning to middle to end, and which constitutes the 'plot'. A plot or narrative, according to Aristotle's classic formulation in his *Poetics*, is a sequence of incidents having the unity of a single 'action' and its consequences, and so having a distinct beginning, middle and end. It's the ending (or climax) that gives meaning to the events leading up to it, and that give the first events in the narrative the status of a beginning (for example, is Oedipus' recognition of his having murdered his father and committed incest with his mother that determines which events belong to the narrative, and where it begins). That is why in classical narratives, such as tragedy, the end always appears inevitable: the events narrated are precisely those that led to the ending. Narrative time is then an inexorable march towards an inevitable future. When we narrate our own lives, time becomes the bending back of our inevitable future death on to the incidents of our life, the finality of death and the finitude of life being what gives life a meaning, and that meaning is, from that point of view, inevitably 'tragic'.[8]

But when literature fractures this order, it allows moments to be related to each other in multiple and non-linear ways; instead of a straight line from past to present to future, there are many curved lines that can pass through points on the line in an order other than linear succession. Time is de-chronologised: like Billy Pilgrim, the hero of Kurt Vonnegut's *Slaughter-house Five*, the reader becomes 'unstuck in time', moving between various moments. Not that the beginning and the end cease to exist, but they take on a different role, serving to mark the limits between which the time-voyager can travel, and that you can take an infinite number of trips within these limits. In that sense, within the finitude of life (bounded by birth and death) there lies an infinity, since moments are not traversed only once and in only one direction, but an infinite number of times, from innumerable directions. Life, then, or what lies 'in the middle', is raised to an infinite power for the reader of literature who undergoes its effect of de-chronologisation. 'Everything grows from the middle' (Deleuze and Parnet 1987: 12, 23), middles that are not defined by their place in a linear sequence with a beginning and an end, but by the infinite number of connections that can be made between the events they contain (see Deleuze and Guattari 1987: 293).

Perhaps this is the greatest thing that literature can do: release us from tragic and finite linear time, and raise life to an infinite power, at least for a moment. Literature at its most 'forceful' can be defined by this power of getting unstuck in time, rather than by any specific use of images or metaphors (images and metaphors are merely means for realising the destruction of linear time). In great works, all moments of time are virtually present *at once*, and can be actualised in infinite ways, in any order; this potentially infinite becoming-actual thus constitutes a different order of time than chronology or history (Deleuze 1995: 59, 123, 152–3). For Deleuze, the greatest writers (and film-makers) are the ones who experiment with time and whose works produce effects of de-chronologisation. Great works intensify life, and life is intensified in us when we encounter them. No matter what your specific aims and purposes, an intensification of *power* and of a feeling of life will better equip you to accomplish them, for power is a matter of 'being able', a capacity for doing things.

Will it Work for me?
Or, Why not Everyone Loves Proust

Whether a work increases the reader's power of acting, and in what way, depends on the work, the reader, and the manner of their encounter. Both the reader and the work are bodies, or extensive parts in a configuration that expresses a 'system of relations' or essence (Deleuze 1990: 201–2, 209–10; Deleuze 1988: 95, 98), the essence being 'a power of existing or acting' (Deleuze 1990: 89–90), a degree or power of intensity (Deleuze 1990: 183, 191, 196–9; Deleuze 1988: 98) or a capacity for affecting and being affected that is as actual and dynamic as the body that expresses it (see Deleuze 1990: 194, 304, 313; Deleuze 1988: 65). When two bodies whose relations of parts agree with each other encounter and affect one another, this results in an increase in both bodies' powers of acting, and this increase is experienced affectively, through a feeling of power, or 'joy'. Whether the encounter is 'good' depends not just on the nature or essence of the two bodies, but also on how they bodies are disposed at the moment they encounter each other: bodies actualise their power of acting in different degrees at different times, depending on their relations to other bodies that may agree with their nature, increasing their power, or disagree with it, decreasing their power (Deleuze 1988: 40, 63–5): because every body is affected by numerous bodies at any given time, the state of any two bodies depends on more than those two bodies alone (ultimately, Spinoza and Deleuze argue, it depends on the relations that obtain between all bodies in the universe at that moment). The encounter between reader and literary work thus depends on the reader's sex, gender, class position, language, level of education, historical situation and so on, but also on how these aspects of the reader are being affected by other circumstances. Consequently, a work may work for a reader at some times and not others, and whether and how a work works depends on the forces and resources the reader brings to the encounter. (It must be noted in passing that in his own essays in literary criticism, Deleuze is not always alive to this point, assuming that certain works will have the same effects on everyone, at least when they work properly; this assumption, however, is profoundly at odds with his basic ontology.)

Since not every literary work intensifies the feeling of life in everyone, the point is to find the one that does for you, and this can only be done through tests of experience. For the nature of the forces at work in both work and reader can be determined only through their encounters with each other and with others. In general, 'Existence itself is . . . a kind of test . . . a physical or chemical test, like that whereby workmen test the quality of some material' (Deleuze 1990: 317; see Deleuze 1988: 40), the powers and capacities of a thing being revealed only through its inter-action with other things, and reading is thus a test of the powers of both the reader and the work at the moment of their encounter. The much bally-hooed epiphany occasioned by the narrator of *In Search of Lost Time* eating a madeleine and drinking herbal tea has always left me standing outside, like an observer; throughout the whole novel, I feel like a tourist in a foreign country, observing the strange and rather quaint customs and manners of the locals, and never fully understanding them. It's not clear whether this is a failure on my part or the work's; it's more on the order of a relationship or encounter with someone that doesn't work because of some incompatibility between two people. For when I read Anne Michaels, or Michael Ondaatje's *The English Patient* (1993), or Rohinton Mistry's *Such a Long Journey* (1991), the destruction of chronological time does make me feel like a stranger in my own country, and in my own language, and the effect of this is energising: I become unstuck in time; my feeling of life intensifies. This does not mean that Ondaatje's and Mistry's novels are superior to Proust's; they work better for me, but might not for someone else.

What accounts for the difference in effect? It's not because Proust is French and hence foreign that his work doesn't resonate in me: Ondaatje's and Mistry's novels likewise take me to times and places I didn't live through, and are written from the standpoint of authors who are 'foreign' (Indian, Sri Lankan), despite their Canadian citizenship. Perhaps in all these writers, I experience in a most vivid way the 'deterritorialisation' of people who live on the margins of empires (British or American), people displaced and on the move, and that their novels invoke or 'summon' a minority of which I feel myself to be a part. The effectiveness of the work is always, in one way or another, a political question (a question of groups, minorities and majorities, minor and major usages). In the case of the novels of Mistry, Michaels and Ondaatje, theirs is an agreement between their nature and mine, although it would take considerable analysis to determine why this is.

The question then is never simply 'What can a work do?', but always 'What can it do for you/me/us?' Does the work invoke a minority, and am I a part of it? Answering this question determines not whether the work is 'good' in some objective sense or according to recognised literary 'values', but whether it is good 'for me'. By 'good for me', Deleuze (following Spinoza and Nietzsche) means something that increases my power of action (Deleuze 1990: 254–7; Deleuze 1988: 41–3). The only way to discover which works, and which readings of them, can do this is to experiment. When reading mobilises the forces active in the work so that these increase the power of the forces in you, then the work works for you. When that doesn't happen, says Deleuze, put that book aside and look for one that does. For 'The ultimate aim of literature is to set free . . . this creation of a health or this invention of a people, that is, a possibility of life' (Deleuze 1997: 4).

Notes

1. *Agencement*, for which the standard translation is 'assemblage', carries the connotation of 'agency', not in the sense of individuals having intentions, but in the sense of 'a cleaning agent', i.e. something capable of doing something, of producing an effect. See Deleuze and Guattari 1986: 55.
2. This is the interpretation of Stanley Cavell, in his essay, 'The Avoidance of Love: A reading of *King Lear*', in Cavell 1976: 267–353.
3. This view of character, and the importance of the moment of 'recognition', are central elements of Aristotle's theory of tragedy in his Poetics. In many ways, Deleuze and Guattari's literary theory could be called an *Anti-Poetics*.
4. This is the approach made famous by Northrop Frye's *Anatomy of Criticism* (1957).
5. See Deleuze and Guattari 1986:76: 'Why have we aligned *the faraway and the continuous* [. . .], on the one hand, with *the distant and the close* [. . .], on the

other? It has nothing to do with the words; we could have chosen others: it is a question of experimentation and concepts'. It is a question, that is, of experimenting with concepts and treating concepts 'heuristically', not as giving us the 'essence of a thing, but as giving us certain possibilities of knowing and understanding, or of organizing our experience in a useful way, or giving us certain possibilities of acting.'

6. See François Zourabichvili, in Patton 1996: 196: 'From now on, the relation to the landscape is no longer that of an autonomous and pre-existent inner life and an independent external reality supposed to reflect this life. The landscape is an inner experience rather than the occasion of an echo . . . The landscape does not return me to myself: it involves me in a becoming where the subject is no longer coextensive with itself, where the subjective form is inadequate . . . I no longer contain myself, nor can I recover myself in the coherence of a Self or Ego . . . To live a landscape: one is no longer in front of it, but in it, one passes into the landscape.'

7. On minoritarian usage and how it can function to invoke a 'people' or a minority, see Daniel W. Smith 1997: xli–li. A more obvious James Brown number exemplifying this would, of course, be '(Say It Loud) I'm Black and I'm Proud'.

8. This is an aspect of Martin Heidegger's theory of time in *Being and Time* (1927), where he conceives of 'temporality' in terms of our 'being-towards-death'.

Bibliography

Aristotle (1987), *Poetics*, trans. Richard Janko, Indianapolis/Cambridge: Hackett Publishing Company.

Bensmaïa, Réda (1986), 'Foreword', in Deleuze and Guattari, *Kafka: Toward a Minor Literature*, Minneapolis: University of Minnesota Press.

Cavell, Stanley (1976), *Must We Mean What We Say?*, New York: Cambridge University Press.

Deleuze, Gilles (1972), *Proust and Signs*, trans. R. Howard, New York: George Braziller.

Deleuze, Gilles (1988), *Spinoza: Practical Philosophy*, trans. Robert Hurley, San Francisco: City Light Books.

Deleuze, Gilles (1989 [1985]), *Cinema 2: The Time-Image*, trans. Hugh Tomlinson and Barbara Habberjam, London: Athlone and Minneapolis: University of Minnesota Press.

Deleuze, Gilles (1990 [1968]), *Expressionism in Philosophy: Spinoza*, trans. Martin Joughin, New York: Zone Books.

Deleuze, Gilles (1995), *Negotiations*, trans. Martin Joughin, New York: Columbia University Press.

Deleuze, Gilles (1997 [1993]), *Essays Critical and Clinical*, trans. Daniel W. Smith and Michael A. Greco, Minneapolis: University of Minnesota Press.

Deleuze, Gilles and Guattari, Félix (1983 [1972]), *Anti-Oedipus: Capitalism and Schizophrenia*, trans.

Robert Huley, Mark Seem and Helen R. Lane, Minneapolis: University of Minnesota Press.

Robert Huley, Mark Seem and Helen R. Lane (1986 [1975]), *Kafka: Toward a Minor Literature*, trans. Dana Polan, Minneapolis: University of Minnesota Press.

Robert Huley, Mark Seem and Helen R. Lane (1987 [1980]), *A Thousand Plateaus: Capitalism and Schizophrenia*, trans. Brian Massumi Minneapolis: University of Minnesota Press.

Robert Huley, Mark Seem and Helen R. Lane.
Gilles Deleuze and Claire Parnet (1987), *Dialogues*, trans. Hugh Tomlinson and Barbara Habberjam, Minneapolis: University of Minnesota Press.
Frye, Northrop, (1957), *The Anatomy of Criticism*, Princeton, NJ: Princeton University Press.
Heidegger, Martin (1927), *Sein und Zeit*, Marburg: Max Niemayer Verlag.
Lyotard, Jean-François (1971), *Discours, Figure*, Paris: Klincksieck.
Macherey, Pierre (1996), 'The Encounter with Spinoza', in Patton (ed.), *Deleuze: A Critical Reader*, Oxford: Blackwell, pp. 139–61.
Marcus, Greil (1997), *Invisible Republic: Bob Dylan's Basement Tapes*, New York: Henry Holt and Company.
Michaels, Anne (1996), *Fugitive Pieces*, Toronto: McClelland and Stewart.
Mistry, Rohinton (1991), *Such a Long Journey*, Toronto: McClelland and Stewart.
Nietzsche, Friedrich (1986), *Human, All Too Human*, trans. R.J. Hollingdale, Cambridge: Cambridge University Press.
Ondaatje, Michael (1993), *The English Patient*, Toronto: Vintage Books.
Patton Paul (1996), *Deleuze: A Critical Reader*, Oxford: Blackwell.
Schrift, Alan D. (1995), *Nietzsche's French Legacy*, New York and London: Routledge.
Shakespeare, William (1998), *King Lear*, ed. Russell Fraser, New York: Signet Classic.
Smiley, Jane (1991), *A Thousand Acres*, New York: Ballantine Books.
Smith, Daniel W. (1997), 'Introduction: "A Life of Pure Immanence": Deleuze's "Critique et Clinique" Project', in Deleuze, *Essays Critical and Clinical*, Minneapolis: University of Minnesota Press, pp. xi–liii.
Vonnegut, Kurt (1969), *Slaughter-house Five: or, The children's crusade: a duty-dance with death*, New York: Dell.
Zola, Émile (1968 [1885]), *Germinal*, trans. L. W. Tancock, Harmondsworth: Penguin.
Zourabichvili, François (1996) 'Six Notes on the Percept', in Patton (ed.), *Deleuze: A Critical Reader*, Oxford: Blackwell, pp. 188–216.

Chapter 3

The *Paterson* Plateau: Deleuze, Guattari and William Carlos Williams

T. Hugh Crawford

> Geeze, Doc, I guess it's all right
> but what the hell does it mean?
> (*Paterson*: 114)

There is good reason to hope that the philosophy of Gilles Deleuze (and his sometime collaborator Félix Guattari) will provide a new and productive way to do literary criticism. After all, from his first major philosophical statements in *Difference and Repetition* and *The Logic of Sense* all the way to his last book with Guattari (*What is Philosophy?*) and his own *Essays Critical and Clinical*, Deleuze showed a keen interest in literature and a sharp critical (and clinical) acumen. Indeed, for Anglo-American literary scholars, these hopes are raised higher by his frequent reference to Lawrence, Miller, Woolf and Melville (to name but a few of his literary touchstones). However such hopes are misplaced. Deleuze does not make frequent reference to literature because his arguments in some way give him special access into the meaning (psychological, social, ideological) of those texts. Instead, literature is a source for his philosophical concepts and mode of argumentation. Literature is a particular machinic assemblage that can in part be distinguished from some philosophy machines, but maintaining such distinctions is completely outside Deleuze's project. For him, philosophy does not provide a way to read literature, but, without doubt, literature functions with and plugs into the larger desiring machine he calls philosophy.

In other words, Deleuze's famed 'toolbox' does not include a hammer to break open the closed and privileged system of a novel or poem to reveal the hidden gleams of truth contained within. Of course it is naive to characterise literary practice as the search for the elusive deep-hidden meaning embodied in individual generic structures, but the prospect of invoking a new and somewhat fresh vocabulary in critical practice is usually an invitation to reread canonical texts in light of this new 'approach'. Whether it is traditional explication or the subtle revelation of hidden hegemonic tendencies, the literary critical enterprise remains bound to interpretation. In a stroke, Deleuze dashes the hopes of literary scholars looking to ride the latest critical wave: 'Significance and inter-pretosis are the two diseases of the earth, the pair of despot and priest' (Deleuze and Parnet 1987: 47). His work calls for writing outside the despotic world of stratified meaning, a place where work is concerned not with identity or equivalence (the verb 'to be') but instead with the conjunction 'and' (see Deleuze and Parnet 1987: 56–9). Meaning there is the product of repetition, linkage and accumulation.

In this (and a number of other instances), he shares the concerns of an American writer who never appears in his work: William Carlos Wil-liams. There is no clear reason why Deleuze never discovered or did not respond to Williams, a writer working out of Whitman's tradition who exerted a profound influence on Allen Ginsberg and most of America's post-Second World War poets. Much of his work, particularly his long poem *Paterson* (composed and published in the years just following the Second World War), shows a remarkably similar set of ideas and strategies, a shared philosophy if you will, with Deleuze. While Deleuze's work cannot provide a new reading of *Paterson*, reading the two in tandem – folding these texts together – produces striking and useful juxtapositions, particularly regarding the different ways these writers confront the rejection of traditional meaning (as hierarchy or identity), the problem of immanence in a machinic assemblage, the notion of multiplicity in the construction of a speaking self (particularly selves speaking minor languages), and the various lines of escape produced by ambulant mechanisms. Following the strategies articulated by Deleuze, Guattari and Williams, the approach of this chapter is to avoid using the verb 'to be' to confer identity and meaning, and instead to use the conjunction 'and' to link together two markedly different but usefully similar socio-technical-cultural assemblages.

The Double Articulation

In 1944 (the years when he was composing the first books of *Paterson*), Williams set out the problems he was pondering as the result of the formalist experiments of high modernism (work that he contributed to himself and held in great admiration). As a physician, Williams was acutely aware of the inadequacy of representational systems when faced with the complex materiality of disease. At the same time, he recognised the importance of discursive systems in recognising and articulating those very illnesses (see, in particular, the medical stories in *The Farmers' Daughters* which explore in minute detail the moment of diagnosis). The composition of his long poem raises problems regarding both form (how to sustain a long poem in the absence of traditional meter and plot) and the insistent presence of the material world. The final stanza of 'A Sort of a Song' articulates this problematic:

> —through metaphor to reconcile
> the people and the stones.
> Compose. (No ideas
> but in things) Invent!
> Saxifrage is my flower that splits
> the rocks.
>   (Williams 1988: 55)

Williams describes multiple divisions and strategies: people, stones, words; the agency of the flower, of metaphor, composition, and voice. He settles (uneasily) on what becomes the motto of *Paterson:* 'No ideas but in things', a claim that has wonderful resonance with his perhaps most famous gnomic poem:

> So much depends
> upon
> a red wheel
> barrow
> glazed with rain
> water
> beside the white
> chickens.
>   (Williams 1986: 224)

Similar to Deleuze and Guattari, who, as philosophers of the next generation, had to resist the formalism of high structuralism, Williams distances himself from the formalist exercise of modernism with an insistent materialism foregrounding the function of the 'thing' in the production of knowledge. In the poem above, the simple, insistent materiality of the wheel barrow carries the meaning of the poem: a meaning that does not point beyond or beneath the straightforward objective quality of the thing in itself. One must emphasise this is not a simplistic materialism, nor a naive denial of depth. The phrase 'So much depends' clearly points to discursive systems that are (obviously) not contained by the wheel barrow itself, and the rain-water glaze emphasises the mediated quality of vision and, by implication, discourse. As in 'A

Sort of a Song', composition, metaphor, words, invention and things form a complex hybrid, but, as Williams recognised long before the efflorescence of structuralism, it is a hybrid that cannot be reduced to discursive systems or semiology.

This by no means makes *Paterson* a simple or direct presentation of the thing. He may exhort himself to 'say it' but it is never easy to understand the ideas in the things. His readers might respond like the unnamed respondent in *Paterson*: 'Geeze, Doc, I guess it's all right/but what the hell does it mean?' (Williams 1992: 114) or like Mike Wallace in Book IV, who calls one of Williams' poems a 'fashionable grocery list' (Williams 1992: 222). The notion of a simple thing (or a thing-in-itself) is ultimately the product of facile dualisms and a failure to recognise the complex circumstances the nodes of intensity where things appear as *events*, not discrete entities. This is a point Williams often demonstrates in his ongoing search for the 'beautiful thing': 'I was permitted by my medical badge to follow the poor, defeated body into those gulfs and grottoes. And the astonishing thing is that at such times and in such places – foul as they may be with the stinking ischio-rectal abscesses of our comings and goings – just there, the thing, in all its greatest beauty, may for a moment be freed to fly for a moment guiltily about the room' (Williams 1951: 288–9). It must be emphasised here that the glimpse of the beautiful thing is not a moment of transcendence, nor a point of absolute stoppage. It is a moment of intensity that owes its coalescence to a complex assemblage, here of disease, infection, filth, the medical industry, and the teeming city of Paterson that let him into those 'grottoes'.

Perhaps confronted with comments similar to those Williams encountered ('Geeze Gilles, what the hell does it mean?'), Deleuze and Guattari introduce their own long poem, *A Thousand Plateaus*, with a rejection of traditional notions of meaning production, and, at the same time, introduce a term that Williams also found useful in exploring the socio-material-semiological assemblage:

> We will never ask what a book means, as signified or signifier; we will not look for anything to understand in it. We will ask what it functions with, in connection with what other things it does or does not transmit intensities, in which other multiplicities its own are inserted and metamorphosed, and with what bodies without organs it makes its own converge. A book exists only through the outside and on the outside. A book itself is a little machine; what is the relation (also measurable) of this literary machine to a war machine, love machine, revolutionary machine, etc. – and an *abstract machine* that sweeps them along? (Deleuze and Guattari 1987: 4)

Successful or at least happy readers of *A Thousand Plateaus* take seriously this disclaimer (which should perhaps be included in future prefaces to *Paterson*). Their work is an antidote to interpretosis – the reduction of the machine to meaning as identity, to strata of determination – in favour of meaning as connection, folding together the inside and outside of the various planes (discourse, consistency, affect).

Guattari explains in *Chaosmosis* that the abstract machine described above is rigorously anti-Platonic. Such a machine does not provide a passage to pure universals, abstracted from the detritus of the material world ('the stinking ischio-rectal abscesses of our comings and goings'), but instead is a drawing together of the strata so strenuously divided by rational thought: 'When we speak of abstract machines, by "abstract" we can also understand "extract" in the sense of extracting. They are montages capable of relating all the heterogeneous levels that they traverse' (Guattari 1995: 35). In his own way, Williams makes precisely the same point in the passage from his autobiography quoted above. The thing of beauty that momentarily flies about the room – the same beautiful thing he pursues with such abandon in *Paterson* Book III – is not an ideal form. It/she is extracted from fragrant circumstances. His abstract machine leaves those circumstances intact, always resisting the movement to generalisation. After all, this was the poet who celebrated the quiet dignity of the man who gathered dog shit from the gutter (Williams 1986: 42), and who insisted that the universal was only to be found in the local. His work was in the invention of abstract machines – socio-technical assemblages – that enabled him to perform that extraction, and he always made sure to call attention to the 'outside' of the book, to the simple fact that such texts necessarily participate in assemblages larger than closed discursive formations: the function served by his 'medical badge', his automobile, his typewriter, the modern poetic movements (his long, personal relationship with such writers as H.D., Marianne Moore, Ezra Pound, and Wallace Stevens to name but a few of his many literary friendships) and the complex circumstances of the people and things that inhabit his poems and fiction, that inhabit Paterson and *Paterson*. Williams even shares the same vocabulary as his French philosophical brethren, defining the poem as a 'small (or large) machine made of words' (Williams 1988: 54). Although he was given to flip comments, this assertion should be taken seriously not simply because it is a handy metaphor to think through poetic form (words are interchangeable parts and so on), but also because it marks an essentially pragmatic concept of poetic form and purpose. For Williams a poem is a machinic assemblage that cuts across a broad range of enunciative and non-enunciative planes *in order to* produce a conjunction and an intensity.[1]

The philosophical concept of the abstract machine calls attention to both the practice of *extraction* and, at the same time, Deleuze and Guattari's own version of pragmatism, which emphasises the *process* of abstraction, the necessarily ongoing and always unfinished construction of universality. As Deleuze acknowledges in an interview, 'Abstractions explain nothing, they themselves have to be explained: there are no such things as universals, there's nothing transcendent, no Unity, subject (or object), Reason; there are only processes, sometimes unifying, subjectifying, rationalising, but just processes all the same' (Deleuze 1995: 145).[2] This is fundamental to the notion of the abstract machine, and at the same time, a remarkable description of the practice of *Paterson*. The unity of the subject (Dr Paterson, the titular narrator of the poem) and of the object (the city and its environs) is never taken as a given, and is only constructed as process (never as completed entity). Locating the universal only in local circumstances denies any movement towards arborescence that makes meaning via identity and hierarchical movement (the verb 'to be'). Instead meaning is the product of conjunction, an ambulatory, nomadic coordination: AND, AND, AND.

Abstract machines (indeed, all machines) operate in assemblages that, depending on their size, extension, and durability, create the possibility of semi-determinate meaning, and, consequently, the closing-off of lines of flight. Such assemblages can become part of arborescent systems that promote a determinate sense of reality or the illusion of hegemony. Guattari explains the irreducible character of machinic assemblages, how they necessarily bring in heterogeneous materials that destabilise clearly demarcated meaning. His discussion, similar to Bruno Latour's critique of the Enlightenment purification impulse in *We Have Never Been Modern*, makes problematic the facile invocation of such notions as hegemony:

> Contemporary machinic assemblages have even less standard univocal referent than the subjectivity of archaic societies. But we are far less accustomed to the irreducible heterogeneity, or even the heterogenetic character, of their referential components. Capital, Energy, Information, the Signifier are so many categories which would have us believe in the ontological homogeneity of referents. (Guattari 1995: 46)

In their discussion of the war machine and nomad science which they set up against the state and royal science, Deleuze and Guattari denounce the hierarchies and striations that result from believing in the 'ontological homogeneity of referents'. In their formula, the hydraulic model of royal science is derived from mathematically calculable laminar flows, the production of strata or striations on smooth space (Deleuze and Guattari 1987: 361–3). Royal science sets boundaries, divides, defines and restricts. In linguistics, the division of form from content is another such micro-assemblage that Williams and Deleuze and Guattari reject in favour of a more fluid and turbulent model (nomadic hydraulics). Deleuze and Guattari argue for a monism that rejects the imperialism of systems of signification at the expense of the immanence of the world and the materiality of informatics itself:

> All of this culminates in a language stratum that installs an abstract machine on the level of expression and takes the abstraction of content even further, tending to strip it of any form of its own (the imperialism of language, the pretensions to a general semiology). In short, the strata substantialize diagrammatic matters and separate a formed plane of content from a formed plane of expression. They hold expressions and contents, separately substantialized and formalized, in the pincers of a double articulation assuring their independence and real distinction and enthroning a dualism that endlessly reproduces and redivides. They shatter the continuums of intensity, introducing breaks between different strata and within each stratum. They prevent conjunctions of flight from forming and crush the cutting edges of deterritorialization [. . .]. (Deleuze and Guattari 1987: 143)

According to Deleuze and Guattari, the double articulation of linguistics – form of expression and form of content – proves an excellent method for consistently reinscribing dualism at the point of connection and the moment of intensity. Such a strategy enables the bracketing out of, for example, non-enunciative systems and such absurdities as the more naive versions of 'everything is a text' so popular among literary scholars in the 1980s. Structuralism (and some versions of deconstruction) takes as its mainspring the absence of 'things' except as they participate in a closed system of signification, except as they stand in and point towards some scientific, literary or philosophical abstraction. The bracketing out of 'things' as actors which can produce specific local effects given certain configurations of socio-technical-discursive assemblages ignores the multiplicity that necessarily inheres in the singular event.

In *A Novelette*, Williams expresses a similar attitude with his critique of science (or, one might say, 'royal science'): 'When these things were first noted categories were ready for them so that they got fast in corners of understanding. By this process, reinforced by tradition, every common thing has been nailed down, stripped of freedom of action and taken away from use' (Williams 1970: 295–6). The reterritorialisation of the 'thing' (here, the object of science) by a stratifying abstract machine crushes its production of local, singular event or haeceity. One should also note here Williams' continued pragmatic position: the 'common thing' not only loses freedom, but is also 'taken away from use'. It can only function as an element in a static, territorialized structure, instead of participating in a machinic assemblage to produce conjunction and intensity, turbulence on smooth space.

Nevertheless, literary and philosophical texts are necessarily linguistic constructions. The presence of the thing is always and only marked by its absence. Its representation links it to the narrow strata of language, the double articulation. Even though he does not discuss them directly in his literature or criticism, these are points that Williams grappled with, dealing with them in two ways. First, in his texts, he consistently insists that his readers confront the thing as a thing (even if it is a thing expressed). This is not to say he was so naive as to presuppose an unmediated representation of the thing, but rather he offers description after description of simple 'objective' details without comment. He refuses to make the thing stand in for some other, more abstract idea or concept. The 'no ideas but in things' dictum does not point 'up' to ideas; instead, it points 'down' to things. His descriptions of the material world do not form an arborescent system, but instead, like the leaves of grass described by Walt Whitman (his fellow poet from New Jersey), his things accrete meaning and produce through coordination, not subordination: 'The bridge tender wore spectacles and used a cane. And the rotary movements of the bridge was a good example of simple machinery. Write, said he to himself taking up the yellow pad from the seat of the car and beginning to scratch with –' (Williams 1970: 284–85). In *Paterson*, he even takes on the science of stratification – a geological survey – in the service of his own machinic heterogenesis. On a single page (139), he reproduces the results of a well bored in 1879–80 to a depth of 2100 feet. The page, appearing in the middle of his long poem, simply enumerates the substratum of Paterson – red sandstone, sandy shale, selenite, quicksand and so on – without comment. Of course one may generalise that such a survey is of the bedrock on which the city and the poem are based (a disheartening and almost nauseating explication), but even so, it remains a wonderfully local symbol. Its details do not rise to the 'level' of traditionally poetic utterances. Instead, the reader gets simple juxtaposition. These strata, unlike the language stratum ('the imperialism of language, the pretensions to a general semiology'), are not linear or arborescent: his geology is rhizomatic.

His other response to the absence of the material object represented in the text is his insistence on the materiality of informatics itself. Much has been made of Williams' use of the typewriter as his primary mode of composition. As noted in the quotation in the previous paragraph, he would write down his impressions of a particular scene or event on a stray piece of paper (often on his prescription pads), but he assembled his poetry on the typewriter. This helps to account for the look of the poems on the page, the most obvious example being the close connection between his famous stepped-down triadic line and the typewriter's tab key. Williams' poetry is of the machine age and is clearly formed by the machines used to compose it.[3] What is often lost in such observations regarding his work is the symmetrical point: that his poems – their material presentation – also produce the machinic assemblage of their composition. The look of the poems on the page emphasises the poem as a material thing, as the product of a complex socio-technical *dispositif*. Words in Williams are material. In *The Great American Novel*, he asks, 'can you not see, can you not taste, can you not smell, can you not hear, can you not touch – words?' (Williams 1970: 159). The answer is a resounding yes, as he produces in *Paterson*, Book III, the language of the people on the street chaotically tumbling down the page, breaking all rules of typesetting. This is not a simple dada gimmick. Williams is calling attention to the simple but often ignored idea that words *are* things.

From the Mouths of Polish Mothers

Resisting the striations of the double articulation is never simply a matter of *which* words and *which* things, but also *whose* words, *whose* things. The primary impulse, a significant cog in Deleuze and Guattari's desiring machine, is their constant search for points of instability, where material irrupts into the plane of discourse or where discursive planes collide, crumple and heave up on to each other like so many icebergs, producing fresh fractures and associations. A key concept they develop regarding such points of instability is the 'minor language', examined in their book on Kafka:

> How many people today live in a language that is not their own? Or no longer, or not yet, even know their own and know poorly the major language that they are forced to serve? This is the problem of immigrants, and especially of their children, the problem of minorities, the problem of a minor literature, but also a problem for all of us: how to tear a minor literature away from its own language, allowing it to challenge the language and making it follow a sober revolutionary path? How to

become a nomad and an immigrant and a gypsy in relation to one's own language? (Deleuze and Guattari 1986: 19)

For them, a minor language is an enunciative assemblage that necessarily carries with it the possibility of deterritorialising the biunivocal meaning determined by official discourse. In this position, Deleuze acknowledges a debt to Foucault (who was also a great archaeologist of the minor voice): 'What's influenced me most is his theory of utterance, because it involves conceiving language as a heterogeneous and unstable aggregate and allows one to think about how new types of utterance come to be formed in all fields' (Deleuze 1990: 150). Springing from this notion of language as an unstable aggregate, Deleuze and Guattari's minor language is a virus that, upon inoculation, proliferates uncontrollably, producing chaotic multiples and spontaneous growths upon the rigid segmentarity of determinate meaning.

Williams, firmly rooted in his New Jersey suburban medical practice where his patients were primarily poor, immigrant factory workers, knew both the power and the disruptive capacity of a minor language and literature. Even as he acknowledged his appropriation of the words and stories of this officially voiceless and illiterate populace, Williams clearly revelled in their subversive quality. He famously claimed that the words for his poetry came directly 'from the mouths of Polish mothers', and, in *Paterson*, he freely interpellates the language of numerous sources: newspaper articles, history books, signed and unsigned letters. Some of the more notorious of these texts are the letters of a young poet, Marcia Nardi, which excoriate Williams for his failure to provide her with adequate emotional support.[4] There also appear in the latter books letters which are early publications of Allen Ginsberg and Gilbert Sorrentino (then representatives of a minor literature that only later began to attain majority status).

Examples of minor voices abound throughout Williams' work, and their status is always problematic. He clearly leaves himself open to charges of appropriation and exploitation; nevertheless, those voices tend towards the subversive. They undercut the magisterial voice of literary modernism (the ironic detachment of, for example, T. S. Eliot or Wallace Stevens), and open the door for disruptions completely beyond the control of the author or narrator. Williams clearly takes pleasure in the construction of an assemblage that is potentially as chaotic or turbulent as the world he describes. Deleuze was also stung by the accusation that he appropriated the experiences of minor groups (see 'Letter to a Harsh Critic' in *Negotiations*), a point he addresses obliquely in *Dialogues*:

You might say that writing by itself, when it is not official, necessarily comes into contact with 'minorities' who do not necessarily write on their own account, about whom no one writes either, in the sense that they would be taken as object, but on the contrary, in which one is caught up willy-nilly, from the fact that one is writing. A minority never exists ready-made, it is only formed on lines of flight, which are also ways of advancing and attacking. (Deleuze and Parnet 1987: 43)

Williams daily encountered those who do not write and, like Deleuze's point in this quotation, does not so much take them up as objects,[5] as, by writing, he constructs an enunciative assemblage through that minority (even as he constructs that minority) which can potentially disrupt 'official' writing, and form a line of flight – a way of 'advancing and attacking'. For Williams, even memory can open the door to an internalised minor speech, and to the multitudes contained there:

> since the spaces it opens are new
> > places
> > > inhabited by hordes
> > > > heretofore unrealized
> > > > (Williams 1992: 78)

From the beginning of his long poem, Williams takes up the topic of minor languages, asking many of the same questions as Deleuze and Guattari. Dr Paterson wanders, listening to the thunder of the falls, wondering:

> (What common language to unravel?
> ..combed into straight lines
> from that rafter of a rock's
> lip.)
> > (Williams 1992: 7)

He takes as his problem the location of a common language, but his solution to commonality remains in heterogeneity, the multiplicity of the speakers and the spoken. This does not mean that he wholeheartedly embraces such multiplicity. Soon after the above quotation, language appears again as a topic, here lamenting those who cannot speak:

> The language, the language
> > fails them
> They do not know the words
> > or have not
> the courage to use them.
> > (Williams 1992: 11)

It is of some significance that Williams does not presume to speak for these wordless people (although he sometimes cannot resist a bit of criticism). Instead he searches for scraps of speech, rags of words to piece together not in a cohesive reconstruction of another how-the-other-half-lives, but instead as a fleeting glimpse (a beautiful thing flitting about the room) which becomes part of *Paterson*.

So Dr Paterson seeks a 'common language' (Williams 1992: 7) and hears,

> Voices!
> multiple and inarticulate. voices
> clattering loudly to the sun, to
> the clouds. Voices
> assaulting the air gaily from all sides.
>
> —among which the ear strains to catch
> the movement of one voice among the rest
> (Williams 1992: 54)

As readers of *Paterson* know, one only momentarily catches the movement of one voice. This marks another element of the disruptive capacities of certain enunciative assemblages. For Williams and Deleuze and Guattari, minor *speech* is a revolutionary resource, a way of undoing the biunivocality of official or arborescent discourse, but Deleuze also places great value on a physiological discourse disrupter – the stutter:

> Is it possible to make language stutter without confusing it with speech? Everything depends on the way we consider language. If we extract it like a homogeneous system in equilibrium, or close to equilibrium, defined by constant terms and relations, it is obvious that the disequilibriums and variations can only affect speech (nonpertinent variations of the intonation type). But if the system appears in perpetual disequilibrium or bifurcation, if each of its terms in turn passes through a zone of continuous variation, then the language itself will begin to vibrate and stutter, but without being confused with speech, which never assumes more than one variable position among others, or moves in more than one direction. (Deleuze 1997: 108)

Deleuze sets out a multiplicitous stuttering. Language can stutter on the vocal level, like Williams' chattering falls – the halting speech of the mass of voices in the poem – or the language itself can be made to stutter, to tremble as it becomes other. The old, official phrases can be broken up. In his essay on Melville's Bartleby, Deleuze explains how the main character's agrammatical utterance, 'I prefer not', unleashes both a multiplicity of meaning and a cascade of events that overwhelm the characters and circumstances in the story and the reader of the story as well. This agrammatical speech is a form of language stuttering. Unlike another of Melville's heroes, Billy Budd, Bartleby does not himself suffer from a physiological stutter, but he breaks apart the language of the law office and the story.

In 'How to Write' Williams describes another form of stuttering, his way to deterritorialise biunivocal discourse: 'all this is the birth of a new language. It is a new allotment of significance. It is the cracking up of phrases which have stopped the mind' (Williams 1976: 100). The critique here is not on the level of the word (the problem of identity and biunivocality) but on the phrase. It is a repudiation of the simple clichés that make the world comfortable for their unthinking users. To accomplish this Williams adopts several strategies. He often writes short vignettes, scenes where he can incorporate minor language – found phrases – as fresh or destabilising forces. 'Hi, open up a dozen, make/ it two dozen! Easy girl!/ You wanna blow a fuse?' (Williams 1992: 137). He would also use measure – his often bizarre line breaks – to make his phrases and sentences stutter. 'The Red Wheelbarrow' is a classic example where the compound words 'wheelbarrow' and 'rainwater' are divided and set on separate lines. This strategy makes many of his poems impossible to read as straightforward sentences. Instead, they result in a halting, a stuttering that produces precisely the vibration Deleuze describes. Such line breaks – Williams' obsessive quest for a new measure – are designed primarily to break up old associations and to help to form a new mind. Williams was well aware of the role of language in fabricating both the world and the mind, and he saw his stuttering as a form of liberation, a point raised explicitly, though plaintively, in *Paterson*:

> Without invention nothing is well spaced,
> unless the mind change, unless
> the stars are new measured, according
> to their relative positions, the
> line will not change, the necessity
> will not matriculate: unless there is
> a new mind there cannot be a new
> line
>
> (Williams 1992: 50)

When compared with much of his other writing on measure, it becomes obvious that Williams is making a symmetrical argument: new line = new mind; new mind = new line. What cannot be ignored in reading the lines

Williams produces is their halting nature. It is a poetics of fracture, cutting across many discursive strata and confounding the double articulation that becomes a source of new knowledge and new modes of knowing.

Williams also takes up the violence inherent in this fracturing: 'Kill the explicit sentence, don't you think? And expand our meaning – by verbal sequences. Sentences, but not grammatical sentences: dead-falls set by schoolmen' (Williams 1992: 188). This is the point where his sense of language and composition could be described as most fully Deleuzian. Clearly they share a disdain for the boundaries produced by the schoolmen, for whom language must be a 'homogeneous system in equilibrium, or close to equilibrium'. Killing the explicit sentence upsets this equilibrium and, rather than creating nonsense, opens up vertiginous possibilities for the production of sense, for the becoming of meaning. What is key in this passage, and emblematic of the entire poem, is the middle phrase: 'by verbal sequences'. This is the AND, AND, AND of Deleuzian discourse. The explicit sentence has a point. It anchors meaning. The accretion of verbal sequences creates both a zone of indiscernibility and a proliferation of paths; it is a stuttering of language as a whole.

While *Paterson* is replete with simple, direct, and generally grammatical sentences, they fail to cohere into a grand unity. The poem proceeds in fits and starts, slowly building through repetition and proliferation but achieves no resolution. It never snaps into the clarity of identity; it never answers the question, 'Geez, Doc, what does it mean?' but instead opens itself up to one vast stutter. In the preface to *Kora in Hell*, Williams quotes Wallace Stevens' critique of his work: 'to fidget with points of view leads always to new beginnings and incessant new beginnings lead to sterility' (Williams 1970: 15). Deleuze and Williams take the opposite viewpoint. Fidgeting with speakers, with fresh beginnings, particularly on the macrolevel leads to a language that shivers into a thousand tiny fragments, each of which bears the seed for striking configurations of new knowledge.

An American Nomadology

Discussing the work of Williams' poetic forebear, Deleuze sets out the problem he sees Whitman as facing: 'The object of American literature is to establish relations between the most diverse aspects of the United States' geography . . . as well as its history, struggles, loves, and evolution' (Deleuze 1997: 59). On first reading, this seems an obvious assertion to make about Whitman and much of American literature, which has often been characterised as an embrace of a large and sprawling multiplicity. However, one must recognise the special place geography holds in

Deleuze's thought. The spatialisation of thought – its deployment across heterogeneous planes or plateaus – makes geography and its sibling sciences, cartography and nomadology, both fundamental and problematic. The geographical is never a given, but instead is always constructed through the establishment of relations. Geography and nomadology work in virtual spaces where the philosopher charts zones of intensity and lines of flight.

This point in Deleuze's work is further complicated by his (and Guattari's) notion of the nomad, which is linked to abstract machines and virtual lines of flight. Deleuze is fond of invoking Toynbee's claim that the 'nomads are the ones who don't move on, they become nomads because they refuse to disappear' (Deleuze 1995: 138).[6] While this claim seems counterintuitive – the traditional western notion of the nomad is of those who are always moving on – it ties in well with a number of Deleuzian concepts, including the notion of minor language and minor or nomad science (Deleuze and Guattari 1987: 361–74). It is precisely because they do not move on and yet do not become (literally) territorialised, that the nomads provide a model for minor disruption. They become the clinamen on which a turbulent cascade begins (the falls at Paterson). Deleuze and Guattari are careful to distinguish the nomad from the immigrant. The latter moves with a purpose: from point A to point B. On the other hand, the nomad moves (physically, spatially, intellectually) *as* purpose. The territorialised immigrants establish new boundaries (and maintain links to distant territories); they make their home in striated space. The nomad explores (and constructs) smooth space by becoming ambulatory, and, conversely, through ambulatory becoming.

It is perhaps not surprising that a major theme of *Paterson* is this very ambulatory becoming. As discussed earlier, Williams confronted a range of immigrant populations throughout his career as a physician. At the same time, he emphasised his own immigrant status, commenting frequently on his 'mixed' parentage, which included an English father and a mother who was a combination of Basque, French, Puerto Rican and Jew. Also, of course, he celebrated the Americanness of just such multiplicity. As an immigrant, he and his family had already arrived at point B. Indeed, Williams lived his entire adult life in a house just around the corner from the one where he was born. His literary friends (Ezra Pound, Robert MacAlmon and so on) frequently exhorted him to come to Europe in order to expand his seemingly limited horizons. But Williams, like Toynbee/Deleuze, soon recognised that, as an intellectual nomad, he needed to not go away. Instead, he had to construct his own virtual lines of escape:

> Escape from it – but not by running
> away. Not by 'composition.' Embrace the
> foulness.
>
> (Williams 1992: 103)

In Deleuze, a line of escape is never a 'running away', but instead is a fleeing to. Williams also resists 'composition' as a territorialisation (the sentences of schoolmen), emphasising instead writing as expressive possibility. His line of escape (and his poetic line) is through foulness, the 'stinking ischio-rectal abscesses' of his medical practice and his nomadic life, his life as a poetic artisan: 'The artisan is *the itinerant, the ambulant*. To follow the flow of matter is to itinerate, to ambulate. It is intuition in action' (Deleuze and Guattari 1987: 409). Rather than composing a segmentary space, the ambulant moves in smooth space, and his or her goal is in the perambulation, in becoming-nomad.

Deleuze and Guattari open *The Anti-Oedipus* by invoking the stroll of the schizophrenic and the perambulations of Beckett's characters. Near the beginning of 'Sunday in the Park' (*Paterson*, Book II), Williams offers his own description (cribbed from the *Journal of the American Medical Association*):

> The body is tilted slightly forward from the basic standing position and the weight thrown on the ball of the foot, while the other thigh is lifted and the leg and opposite arm are swung forward (fig. 6B). Various muscles, aided. (45)

Of course this is straight physiology, but in many ways it sounds no less absurd than Beckett's descriptions. Indeed, it raises pointedly the sheer complexity of embodiment. No single discursive description can accurately represent an action most people have internalised by the end of their first year. Here the plane of corporeality juts into the plane of discourse, disrupting all notions of adequate mimesis. It is of some consequence that Williams quotes the *Journal of the American Medical Association*, the representative of State medical science, in a text that, contra-State-sanctioned discourse, remains insistently nomadic. Deleuze and Guattari make a similar point regarding another State-sanctioned discourse, the Law: 'with the legal model, one is constantly reterritorializing around a point of view, on a domain according to a set of constant relations; but with the ambulant model, the process of deterritorialization constitutes and extends the territory itself' (Deleuze and Guattari 1987: 372). The ambulant model predominates in 'Sunday in the Park', where Williams does (in the words of Wallace Stevens) 'fidget with points of view' with an eye towards extending the territory he traverses, and traversing makes.

In some ways, 'Sunday in the Park' represents Williams' most consistent effort to maintain a singular point of view. Ostensibly Dr Paterson is walking through the park, registering his impressions. But Williams, as usual, does not offer a consistent or linear narration. Instead he registers the stray fragments of speech he hears and the things he sees, breaking the narrative enough to avoid arborescence. A stable point of view cannot coalesce, in part because Dr Paterson/Williams is charting a geography of percepts where the process is his becoming imperceptible. The book opens with these lines:

> Outside
>
>   outside myself
>
>   there is a world,
>
> he rumbled, subject to my incursions
> —a world
>
>   (to me) at rest,
>
>   which I approach
>
>   concretely—
>
>   (43)

One could read this as a reinscription of the subject/object dichotomy, but Williams has little truck with solipsistic maundering. Instead, what he invokes as the world is a milieu of action, a space for the conjunction of forces: the vital force of the speaker/narrator and the equally vital force of the non-organic life called the park. Stevens' critique of multiple points of view depends on privileging the thinking/speaking subject over this non-organic milieu. Williams' response to such biunivocal reduction is the becoming imperceptible of the speaking subject: 'Why even speak of "I," he dreams, which/interests me almost not at all?' (Williams 1992: 18).[7] The 'outside' is subject to the speaker's incursions not so much through his crossing a boundary, but by following the fold that only provisionally and temporarily creates the effect of an inside that is opposed to an outside.

For Williams, as for Deleuze,

> The minimum real unity is not the word, the idea, the concept or the signifier, but the *assemblage*. It is always an assemblage which produces utterances. Utterances do not have as their cause a subject which would act as a subject of enunciation any more than they are related to subjects as subjects of utterance. The utterance is the product of an assemblage – which is always collective, which brings into play within us and outside us

populations, multiplicities, territories, becomings, affects, events. (Deleuze and Parnet 1987: 51)

'Sunday in the Park' is just such a contraption, a machine of enunciation, but it is also a percept machine, and it is on this point of perception that Williams' non-subjective assemblage becomes further complicated. Williams always celebrated the precisely registered detail, and indeed was one of the first poets to let that impulse carry the weight of his poetry. Many of the shorter poems are simply descriptive, literal without a hint of figuration. Such an impulse demands an observer with a stable point of view equipped with a simple, straightforward vocabulary. As we have seen, in his long poem this stable perceiver is replaced by a speaker in the process of becoming imperceptible. Deleuze calls this the movement from perception to the percept. A perception requires a perceiver in some form of Cartesian space, whereas a percept is an assemblage that interpellates perceivers in their becoming. François Zourabichvili explains it this way in relation to the landscape (or the park in Paterson, New Jersey):

> [T]he relation to the landscape is no longer that of an autonomous and pre-existent inner life and an independent external reality supposed to reflect this life. The landscape is an inner experience rather than the occasion of an echo; not the redundancy of lived experience, but the very element of a 'passage of life'. The landscape does not return me to myself: it involves me in a becoming where the subject is no longer coextensive with itself, where the subjective form is inadequate when faced with the unformedness of becoming. I no longer contain myself, nor can I recover myself in the coherence of a Self or Ego. (1996: 196).

It is somewhat ironic that the percept, which is at least provisionally linked to perception, marks the moment when the self becomes *imperceptible*, when coherence is lost in the flux of nomadic life, and the ego becomes the effect of a folding of inside and outside, or, more specifically, the inside is revealed as a momentary invagination of the outside.[8] The poem itself, when taken as a complete entity of five books (originally only four were projected) also folds on to itself. The last book has often been read as a metacommentary on the previous four, so the text becomes vortical. Williams or Dr Paterson as self basically disappears from the poem, folded in among a multitude of voices, organic and non-organic enuciative machines. In addition, the possibility of having knowledge is framed in the occupation of a milieu in the process of becoming. The final lines of Book V:

> We know nothing and can know nothing.
> >   but
> >   the dance, to dance to a measure
> >   contrapuntally,
> >   Satyrically, the tragic foot.
> >   (236)

Knowledge requires a *relative* measure (nomadic and not state science) and the becoming-animal of the poet. His dance is a satyr's dance; his measure is a crippled or hooved foot; his dance is a physical stutter.

Dr Paterson's Clinic

One of the most famous of Williams' early poems is the opening of *Spring and All* where the narrator, an early version of Dr Paterson, is driving to the 'contagious hospital' and describes what he sees:

>   All along the road the reddish
>   purplish, forked, upstanding, twiggy
>   stuff of bushes and small trees
>   with dead, brown leaves under them
>   leafless vines—
> >   (Williams 1988: 183)

Three forces are in conjunction here that warrant some scrutiny: birth, disease, and anthropomorphism. The poem is an abstract machine that produces a complex notion of health. Clearly, as the title notes, this is a poem about the coming of spring; these bushes and small trees are beginning to bud (a frequent theme in Williams' work). But at the same time, the poem opens with reference to contagion, to pathology, and there is something frightening or sinister about this reddish, purplish material. It marks overabundance, proliferation, the chaos of rank overgrowth which is also signalled by last year's dead vines. The meadows and woods of Williams' world are rarely cultivated, and the vegetation erupts obscenely into the scenes he describes. Later these same plants are described as entering 'the new world naked', which is as close as Williams will get to a metaphor – here of his own paediatric practice.

The relationship between Williams' medical practice and his poetry, prompted by his own comments, has been the source of much speculation and discussion. The criticism generally works across two registers (which correspond to the double articulation): how the medical practice provides material for the poems and fiction; and how his literary practice is framed by the material and discursive concerns of medical practice.[9] The assemblage in *Spring and All* and the later *Paterson* points towards another plane: health. Following Nietzsche (with his usual twists), Deleuze also raises the question of health and literature. In the opening to *Essays Critical and Clinical*, he defines the writer as 'the physician of himself and the world. The world is the set of symptoms whose illness merges with man. Literature then appears as an enterprise of health' (Deleuze 1997: 3). Poet as physician, literature as a practice of world health: these notions coalesce in the poem above, and are clearly part of the conjunction of forces in *Paterson*, where 'Health as literature, as writing, consists in inventing a people who are missing' (Deleuze 1997: 4). Williams' medical practice extends to his literature in the production of health through a two-stage process: symptomatology and nomadology.

These stages loosely correspond to the distinction Deleuze makes between the critical and the clinical:

> *Criticism* and *the clinic* ought strictly to be identical: but criticism would be, as it were, the outlining of the plane of consistence of a work, a sieve which would extract the particles emitted or picked up, the fluxes combined, the becomings in play; the clinic, in accordance with its precise meaning, would be the outline of lines on this plane or the way in which the lines outline the plane, which of them are dead-ended or blocked, which cross voids, which continue, and most importantly the line of steepest gradient, how it draws in the rest, toward what destination. (Deleuze and Parnet 1987: 119–20)

At this point, Deleuze is discussing literary criticism, so the plane of consistence would be formed by the specific literary text: its form, content, mode of enunciation. When criticism is turned on to the world as a whole by the physician/poet, the plane of consistence consists of diagnostics: the symptomatology of the detail or the event, patiently articulated particle by particle. Such a diagnostics concerns not just the 'objective' details of a material world, but also the place of the observer, other human observers, non-human actors, and language; and, more important, the fluxes and combinations of those particles. It is an assemblage (*agencement*) as agencing.

However, for Williams (and Deleuze), criticism by itself is only the first stage in the production of health. In *Kora in Hell*, Williams comments negatively on a simplistic or positivistic symptomatology: 'Although it is a quality of the imagination that it seeks to place together those things which have a common relationship, yet the coining of similes is a pastime of very low order, depending as it does on a nearly vegetable coincidence. Much more keen is that power which discovers in things those inimitable particles of dissimilarity to all other things which are the peculiar perfections of the thing in question' (Williams 1970: 18). In this quotation emerges an important distinction between traditional (non-Deleuzian) criticism and the clinical impulse. In establishing common relationships, the 'imagination' is part of the 'language stratum that installs an abstract machine on the level of expression and takes the abstraction of content even further, tending to strip it of any form of its own (the imperialism of language, the pretensions to a general semiology)' (Deleuze and Guattari 1987: 143). Williams' critique of first-stage symptomatology is that it is a form of identification which is necessarily linked to a movement to generalisation, and, ultimately, to judgement.

His alternative, which marks the movement to the clinical or (in a related way) the nomadic, is to focus on the particles of dissimilarity: points of difference, places and spaces of non-identity. This is clearly linked to the notion of the poet/physician whose diagnosis of the world must necessarily focus on the anomaly: the detail that marks the object *as* different. The movement to the clinical then is not the eradication of this anomaly (as in traditional medicine or much literary criticism for that matter), but in linking these details, the 'perfections of the thing in question' into a dynamic assemblage: *not to judge but to assemble* is the route to health.

The critical/clinical impulse takes the writer outside literature and outside (or at least to the edge) of language. It is a form of practice and a mode of existence, and, like the nomadological principle of Dr Paterson's stroll, marks a becoming imperceptible: '*Criticism and the clinic*: life and work are the same thing, when they have adapted the line of flight which makes them the components of the same war-machine. In these conditions life has for a long time ceased to be personal and the work has ceased to be literary or textual' (Deleuze and Parnet 1987: 141). Deleuze clearly demands a different form of criticism ('A clinic without psychoanalysis or interpretation, a criticism without linguistics or significance' Deleuze and Parnet 1987: 120); one without universals, without judgement, without identity. But this desire is not a product of negation (no absolutes). Instead it is a form of conjunction, a nexus of multiplicity which is the only sure road to health. *Paterson* requires (and creates) just such a critical/clinical war machine. It is both a symptomatology (enumeration of the particles of dissimilarity) and a nomadology: Williams the physician/poet assembles a non-identical, anti-judgement machine that works its rhizomatic magic through proliferation, the overabundant and multiplicitous production of AND . . . AND . . . AND.

Notes

1. In a different context, Guattari makes a similar claim: '[The structuralists] have postulated a general signifying translatability for all forms of discursivity. But in doing so, have they not misunderstood the essential dimension of machinic autopoiesis? The continual emergence of sense and effects does not concern the redundancy of mimesis but rather the production of an effect of singular sense, even though infinitely reproducible' (Guattari 1995: 37).
2. Williams' version of this sentiment appears in one of his letters: 'Order is what is discovered after the fact, not a little piss pot for us all to urinate into – and call ourselves satisfied' (Williams 1984: 214).
3. For discussions of Williams and the machine age, see Anne Janowitz (1983), 'Paterson: An American Contraption'; Henry M. Sayre (1989), 'American Vernacular: Objectivism, Precisionism, and the Aesthetics of the Machine'; Lisa M. Steinman (1987), Made in America; and Cecelia Tichi (1987), Shifting Gears: Technology, Literature and Culture in Modernist America.
4. For a feminist interpretation of the 'appropriation' of Nardi's letters, see Gilbert (1985), 'Purloined Letters: William Carlos Williams and "Cress"'. An alternate perspective can be found in Crawford (1996), 'Paterson, Memex and Hypertex'.
5. On Williams' treatment of his patients as objects, see Crawford (1993), Modernism, Medicine, and William Carlos Williams, Chapter 3, and 'The Politics of Literary Form.'
6. See also Deleuze and Parnet 1987: 37.
7. Deleuze notes that the final enterprise of writing is 'becoming imperceptible' (Deleuze and Parnet 1987: 45) and goes on to claim that 'In reality writing does not have its end in itself, precisely because life is not something personal. Or rather, the aim of writing is to carry life to the state of a non-personal power' (Deleuze and Parnet 1987: 50).
8. On the relation of the self to folding, see Deleuze 1986: 94–123.
9. For Williams' own comments, see Chapter 43, 'Of Medicine and Poetry' in The Autobiography (1951). On the medical content of the literature, see Mariani (1981) William Carlos Williams. A New World Naked. On medicine as a form of expression, see Crawford (1993), Modernism, Medicine, and William Carlos Williams.

Bibliography

Crawford, T. H. (1992), 'The Politics of Literary Form'. Literature and Medicine 11, pp. 147–62.

Crawford, T. H. (1993), Modernism, Medicine, and William Carlos Williams, Norman, OK: University of Oklahoma Press.

Crawford, T. H. (1996), 'Paterson, Memex and Hypertext', American Literary History, 8.4, pp. 665–82.

Deleuze, Gilles (1986), Foucault, trans. S. Hand, Minneapolis: University of Minnesota Press.

Deleuze, Gilles (1995), Negotiations, trans. M. Joughlin, New York: Columbia University Press.

Deleuze, Gilles (1997), Essays Critical and Clinical, trans. Daniel W. Smith and Michael A. Greco, Minneapolis: University of Minnesota Press.

Deleuze, Gilles and Guattari, Félix (1983), Anti-Oedipus: Capitalism and Schizophrenia, trans. Robert Hurley, Mark Seem and Helen R. Lane, Minneapolis: University of Minnesota.

Deleuze, Gilles and Guattari, Félix (1986), *Kafka: Toward a Minor Literature*, trans. Dana Polan, Minneapolis: University of Minnesota Press.

Deleuze, Gilles and Guattari, Félix (1987), *A Thousand Plateaus*, trans. Brian Massumi, Minneaplis: University of Minnesota.

Deleuze, Gilles and Guattari, Félix (1994), *What is Philosophy?* trans. Hugh Tomlinson and Graham Burchell, New York: Columbia University Press.

Deleuze, Gilles and Parnet, Claire (1987), *Dialogues*, trans. Hugh Tomlinson and Barbara Habberjam, New York: Columbia University Press.

Gilbert, S. (1985), 'Purloined Letters: William Carlos Williams and "Cress" ', *Williams Carlos Williams Review*, 11.2.

Guattari, Félix (1995), *Chaosmosis: An Ethico-Aesthetic Paradigm*, trans. Paul Bains and Julian Pefanis, Indianapolis: Indiana University Press.

Janowitz, A. (1983), '*Paterson*: An American Contraption', *William Carlos Williams: Man and Poet*, ed. Carroll Terrell, Orono: National Poetry Foundation.

Latour, B. (1993), *We Have Never Been Modern*, trans. Catherine Porter, Cambridge, MA: Harvard University Press.

Mariani, P. (1981), *William Carlos Williams: A New World Naked*, New York: McGraw Hill.

Sayre, H. M. (1989), 'American Vernacular: Objectivisim, Precisionism, and the Aesthetics of the Machine', *Twentieth Century Literature*, 35.3, pp. 310–42.

Steinman, L. M. (1987), *Made in America*, New Haven: Yale University Press.

Tichi, C. (1987), *Shifting Gears: Technology, Literature and Culture in Modernist America*, Chapel Hill: University of North Carolina Press.

Williams, W. C. (1951), *The Autobiography of William Carlos Williams*, New York: New Directions.

Williams, W. C. (1961), *The Farmer's Daughters*, New York: New Directions.

Williams, W. C. (1968), *Selected Essays of Williams Carlos Williams*, New York: New Directions.

Williams, W. C. (1970), *Imaginations*, ed. W. Schott, New York: New Directions.

Williams, W. C. (1976), *Interviews with William Carlos Williams*, ed. L. Wagner, New York: New Directions.

Williams, W. C. (1984), *The Selected Letters of William Carlos Williams*, ed. J. C. Thirlwall, New York: New Directions.

Williams, W. C. (1986), *The Collected Poems of Williams Carlos Williams*, vol. 1, 1909–39, eds A. W. Litz and C. MacGwan, New York: New Directions.

Williams, W. C. (1988), *The Collected Poems of William Carlos Williams*, vol. II, 1939–62, ed. C. MacGowan, New York: New Directions.

Williams, W. C. (1992), *Paterson*, revised edition, ed. C. MacGowan. New York: New Directions.

Zourabichvili, F. (1996), 'Six Notes on the Percept', *Deleuze: A Critical Reader*, ed. Paul Patton, Oxford: Blackwell, pp. 188–216.

Chapter 4

Underworld: The People are Missing

John Marks

> History is inseparable from the earth [*terre*], struggle is underground [*sous terre*], and, if we want to grasp an event, we must not show it, we must not pass along the event, but plunge into it, go through all the geological layers that are its internal history (and not simply a more or less distant past). I do not believe in great resounding events, Nietzsche said. To grasp an event is to connect it to the silent layers of earth which make up its true continuity, or which inscribe it in the class struggle. There is something peasant in history.
>
> (Deleuze, *Cinema 2: The Time-Image*)

Deleuze and Literature: *un entretien*

Deleuze's approach to literature might be summarised by the term favoured by Maurice Blanchot, *entretien*, which literally means 'conversation' or 'discussion' but also indicates that which is 'between', an interrelational space, the pause which is the necessary interruption in discourse (Blanchot 1993: 75–6). Like Blanchot, Deleuze is interested in the enigmatic 'in-between' spaces, which make possible the conventional categories of the literary texts, such as characters, events, dialogue, but which are frequently elided. Philosophy, politics, sport, literature all need 'mediators', instigators of movement which operate in-between the 'solid, geometric' abstractions of opinion and normal perception (see Deleuze 1995: 123–4). Rather than characters, for example, Deleuze is interested in the forces that compose a character, and the 'percepts' and 'affects' which operate independently from individuals. Similarly, rather than thinking in conventional terms of the event as a discrete and significant historical occurrence, he opens up a new, *untimely* space for the event, and, rather than reporting real conversations, the novelist brings out 'the madness of all conversation and of all dialogue' (Deleuze and Guattari

1994: 188). Literature is, then, not simply an object upon which Deleuze focuses his philosophical gaze, but rather a tool with which to explore the fictionality which is inherent in his philosophy. Gregg Lambert has emphasised the importance of 'fiction' in Deleuze's work in a paper on Deleuze's 'critique' of pure fiction:

> [F]iction (though not all of it) is pure speculation, which means it is false in a very special way. It constitutes a 'point de deterritorialization' that bifurcates words and releases incompossible and indiscernible elements that enter into new variations around the position of the actual. (Lambert 1997: 141)

Fiction is the act of prising apart conventional modes of perception and representation in order to release impersonal forces. Some works of fiction demonstrate a particular capacity to explore the in-between spaces, and in this way to release philosophical forces. Borges, for example, creates fictions which explore incompossible worlds, and Beckett sets out a plane of 'exhaustion', in which any order of preference or organisation in relation to a final goal is renounced (Deleuze 1997: 153). Jean-Clet Martin reads Deleuze alongside Foucault and Melville, and locates at the heart of their work a 'transversal eye' which is capable of both ranging across forked, incompossible perspectives and breaking apart 'closed ensembles' in order to release 'new surfaces and new visions' (1998: 107). This transversal eye allows the interstice to achieve a degree of independence, surveying a 'Sahara', a desert which grows from the middle (1998: 110). It is a question of exploring what Deleuze calls 'style', the point at which writing becomes 'gaseous', where it becomes possible to 'open up words, break things open, to free earth's vectors' (1995: 134). Philosophy is, similarly, not interested in historical events, individuals and conversations, but rather untimely becomings, forces and free indirect discourse. Philosophy is, as Deleuze says, a question of what is going to happen and what has happened, 'like a novel': 'Except the characters are concepts, and the settings, the scenes, are space-times. One's always writing to bring something to life, to free life from where it's trapped, to trace lines of flight' (1995: 140–1).

This chapter aims to use concepts elaborated by Deleuze in order to create an *entretien* with Don DeLillo's *Underworld* (1997), to take tendencies which are already in the novel a little further in order to explore the impersonal forces which are released in the in-between, or the 'middle'. A literary reading of this sort should also aim to provide new ways of activating and evaluating concepts used by Deleuze, to put these concepts into a new kind of motion. In the case of *Underworld* it is particularly the concept of the 'event' which comes to the fore and suggests itself as a form of *entretien*. The event is the 'middle' which literature inhabits as a site in which to create fiction. Fiction in this sense is not opposed to the true, but rather depends upon the 'powers of the false'.[1] Fiction takes the virtual and makes it consistent. In this way, concepts which are essential to understand the literary component of Deleuze's work – haecceity, percept, affect, free indirect discourse, polyphony, counterpoint, point of view – appear as a cluster around the central concept of the event.

Before looking at *Underworld*, it is useful to understand Deleuze's allusions to the event in cinema and literature must be read in the context of aesthetic innovation in postwar Europe, particularly the so-called *nouveau roman*, and the films of Antonioni. Deleuze suggests at the beginning of *The Time-Image* that the formal innovation of much immediate postwar art was a way of responding to the moral, political and existential questions posed by the Second World War. The formal impersonality, for example, of the *nouveau roman* is not an act of turning away from the 'chaos' of moral ambiguity, but rather the attempt to create a new, immanent form which entails a maturity of perspective, the possibility of having done with 'judgement'. Judgement depends upon pre-existing, fixed values, and precludes the invention of the new:

> It is not a question of judging other existing beings, but of sensing whether they agree or disagree with us, that is, whether they bring forces to us, or whether they return us to the miseries of war, to the poverty of the dream, to the rigors of organization. (Deleuze 1997: 135)

Antonioni, for example, writing about Marcel Carné in the late 1940s, admires the commitment to 'technique' which sets him apart from the 'committed', 'content-orientated' cinema of René Clair and the Popular Front era. According to Antonioni, Carné never allowed himself to be forced into giving expression to a theme which precedes matters of style. Carné's stylistic adherence to the particular allows him to suspend judgement. What matters is the force with which he re-creates reality: 'No act is refused, no consequence shunned, everything is illuminated and interpreted with a precise intuition of the particular.'[2]

War as an 'event' tends to reveal the inadequacies of conventional realism.[3] Moments of conflict are inextricably linked with an immense network of effects, long-term causes and consequences, experiences of horror *and* liberation in civilian populations, complex feelings of shame, fear and dislocation. The event of war becomes associated with other, enigmatic 'events' such as the 'phoney war', and the Cold War introduces a new war of waiting and displaced conflict. The landscape before and after the battle tells us as much as the battle itself. The empty space, the tiredness of the human body, that which comes before and after, the story that can only be told *in filigree*, all find expression in the films of Antonioni:

> an astonishing development of the idle periods of everyday banality; then, starting with *The Eclipse*, a treatment of limit-situations which pushes them to the point of dehumanized landscapes, of emptied spaces that might be seen as having absorbed characters and actions, retaining only a geophysical description, an abstract inventory of them. (Deleuze 1989: 5)

Antonioni talks himself in terms of removing the 'actual' event from his films. In a piece entitled 'The Event and the Image' he writes of an incident one morning in Nice, at the beginning of the Second World War, when he sees a drowned man dragged up on to the beach. He begins:

> The sky is white; the sea-front deserted; the sea cold and empty; the hotels white and half-shuttered. On one of the white seats of the Promenade des Anglais the bathing attendant is seated, a negro in a white singlet. It is early. The sun labours to emerge from a fine layer of mist, the same as every day. There is nobody on the beach except a single bather floating inert a few yards from the shore. (1963–4: 14)

He then goes on to describe the conventional 'event' which takes place when the bather is seen to be drowned, and pulled from the sea, the scene being observed by two children. However, if Antonioni were to make a film on this event, which takes place during the so-called 'drôle de guerre' (phoney war), he would remove the 'actual event':

> It was wartime. I was at Nice, waiting for a visa to go to Paris to join Marcel Carné, with whom I was going to work as an assistant. They were days full of impatience and boredom, and of news about a war which stood still on an absurd thing called the Maginot Line. Suppose one had to construct a bit of film, based on this event and on this state of mind. I would try first to remove the actual event from the scene, and leave only the image described in the first four lines. In that white sea-front, that lonely figure, that silence, there seems to me to be an extraordinary strength of impact. The event here adds nothing: it is superfluous. I remember very well that I was interested, when it happened. The dead man acted as a distraction to a state of tension. (1963–4: 14)

The actual event, the incident that occurred, can be dispensed with, in favour of a sort of immanent event which is contained in the waiting, the boredom, the emptiness of the landscape. Antonioni creates a bloc of percepts and affects:

> But the true emptiness, the *malaise*, the anxiety, the nausea, the atrophy of all normal feelings and desires, the fear, the anger – all these I felt then, coming out of the Negresco, I found myself in that whiteness, in that nothingness, which took shape around a black point. (1963–4: 14)

This imaginary film sequence is a time-image, a shot which contains and seeks to convey the pressure of time. The time-image responds to the problem of *seeing* which is crucial to the film-director. This problem of seeing is intimately connected to the enigmatic nature of the event, since 'the problem is to catch a reality which is never static, is always moving towards or away from a moment of crystallisation' (1963–4: 14).

American Literature: An Affair of the People

Don DeLillo's *Underworld*, published in America in 1997, deals with the postwar period in America. The novel opens with a novella-length description of the legendary 1951 baseball game between the Giants and the Dodgers, and employs a large cast of characters, several of whom are connected to Nick Shay, born in the 1930s in the Bronx. DeLillo also creates fictional versions of Lenny Bruce, J. Edgar Hoover, Frank Sinatra and Jackie Gleason. Geographically, the novel moves between a number of locations, including the Bronx, the American Southwest, and Kazakhstan in the present day. It is possible to extract a fairly conventional narrative context from the episodic and fragmentary sprawl of the novel, which would run as follows: Nick Shay grows up in deprived conditions believing his father has been murdered by the Mafia, and his troubled adolescence culminates in the accidental murder of a friend. He spends three years in a juvenile correctional facility, after which he works in waste-recycling, gradually establishing a successful career and a quiet middle-class life in Phoenix, Arizona. The trajectory, perhaps imaginary, of the baseball from the Giants-Dodgers game as it changes hands over the years runs in counterpoint to this narrative. However, this conventional narrative exists within a formally complex and even experimental framework. First, Shay can only loosely be described as a 'central' character, located as he is among a cast which includes Klara Sax, an artist with whom he has an affair in his youth; her husband, Albert Bronzini, a science teacher and chess tutor of Nick's brother Matt Shay, who works in the 1970s as a physicist at nuclear bases in New Mexico; Nick Shay's colleague Brian Glassic, who has an affair with Nick's wife

Marian; and Sister Edgar, who works in the current-day Bronx. Second, it is only in the most general sense that the novel moves chronologically from 3 October 1951 to the present day. The novel also moves backwards in time, with a series of narrative clusters which move from 1992 back through to 1951, and, crucially, these general narrative dynamics are played out as an accumulation of fragments, ranging back and forth in time and place, from character to character. All of this has the effect of breaking down notions of character, narrative and event.

In some fairly obvious ways, then, *Underworld* can be identified as a work which might well merit inclusion in the Deleuzian canon, demonstrating the virtues of 'American' literature. For Deleuze, American literature is a minor literature *par excellence*, since private history is immediately 'public, political, and popular', and America itself is ideally a federation of diverse minorities (1997: 57). The opening sentence of *Underworld* announces these themes, introducing the black schoolboy Cotter on his way to the baseball game: 'He speaks in your voice, American, and there's a shine in his eye that's halfway hopeful.' (Dehillo 1997: 11) Deleuze finds in Whitman an American tradition of the 'spontaneous' fragment (1997: 56). The fragment, or the 'sample', what DeLillo calls in the context of *Underworld* the 'sand-grain manyness of things' – a phrase which chimes nicely with Whitman's term 'granulations' – is a part of an infinite patchwork, a fragment of a world which is a collection of heterogeneous parts. In this way, American literature conforms to the philosophical principle that Deleuze traces back to Hume: relations are external to their terms:

> Relations are not internal to a Whole; rather, the Whole is derived from the external relations of a given moment, and varies with them. Relations of counterpoint must be invented everywhere, and are the very condition of evolution. (Deleuze 1997: 59)

An extreme form of these relations of counterpoint would be the sort of fragmentary writing which seeks to liberate 'an infinite *asyntactic* sentence': 'It is an almost mad sentence, which changes in direction, its bifurcations, its ruptures and leaps, its prolongations, its sproutings, its parentheses' (Deleuze 1997: 58). In *Underworld*, DeLillo's fictional Lenny Bruce produces his own 'mad sentences', in the form of fragmentary, jazz-inflected 'bits', a dialogic 'rap mosaic':

> Lenny switched abruptly to ad lib bits. Whatever zoomed across his brainpan. He did bits he got bored with five seconds in. He did psychoanalysis, personal reminiscence, he did voices and accents, grandmotherly groans, scenes from prison movies, and he finally closed the show with a

monologue that had a kind of abridged syntax, a thing without connectives, he was cooking free-form, closer to music than speech, doing a spoken jazz in which a slang term generates a matching argot, like musicians trading fours, the road band, the sideman's inner riff, and when the crowd dispersed they took this rap mosaic with them into the strip joints and bars and late-night diners, the places where the nighthawks congregate, and it was Lenny's own hard bop, his speeches to the people that rode the broad Chicago night. (1997: 586)

DeLillo's own style lends itself to the construction of such 'mad' sentences, which create verbs ('Time-magazined') from proper names, curious adjectives ('bomb-shadowed') and which sweeps across the imaginary mental topography of 'beat' philosophy:

> The whole beat landscape was bomb-shadowed. It always had been. The beats didn't need a missile crisis to make them think about the bomb. The bomb was their handiest reference to the moral squalor of America, the guilty place of smokestacks and robot corporations, Time-magazined and J. Edgar Hoovered, where people sat hunched over cups of coffee in a thousand rainswept truck stops on the jazz prairie, secret Trotskyites and sad nymphomaniacs with Buddhist pussies – things Lenny made fun of. (545–6)

Fragmentary writing entails an art of counterpoint which joins planes together. Counterpoint in literature explores the 'contrapuntal, polyphonic, and plurivocal compounds' (Deleuze and Guattari 1994: 188). Rather than considering the opinions and social types of the characters, it is a question of the relations into which they enter. Similarly, counterpoint is the expression, not of conversation, but of 'the madness of all conversation and of all dialogue, even interior dialogue' (Deleuze and Guattari 1994: 188). Techniques of counterpoint also give the novel a cinematic quality, and *Underworld* employs in fairly obvious ways a range of cinematic techniques, which help to give the novel its polyphonic texture. The opening description of the baseball game, for example, combines a movement between three main viewpoints – the schoolboy Cotter Martin, the radio commentator Russ Hodges and J. Edgar Hoover – with a montage of shots which can be attributed to the roving camera-eye of the narrator:

> Men running, the sprint from first to third, the man who scores coming in backwards so he can check the action on the base paths. All the Giants up at the front of the dugout. The crowd is up, heads weaving for better views. Men running through a slide of noise that comes heaving down on them. (36)

Point of View

Counterpoint and polyphony are linked to the concept of 'point of view', which Deleuze elaborates in his book on Leibniz (Deleuze 1993). Concentrating on harmonic developments in the history of music, he shows how the harmonic closure of baroque opens out into the potentially dissonant polytonality of the neo-baroque, a polytonality which Boulez describes as a 'polyphony of polyphonies' (Deleuze 1993: 82). As far as Deleuze is concerned, the baroque is essentially a transition from Leibniz's solution of ultimate harmony between incompossible worlds towards a new dissonance. The neo-baroque sets out divergent series on the same stage, 'where Fang kills, is killed, and neither kills nor is killed' (Deleuze 1993: 82). Fiction responds to this transition, as does philosophy: 'In a same chaotic world divergent series are endlessly tracing bifurcating paths. It is a "chaosmos" of the type found in Joyce, but also in Maurice Leblanc, Borges, or Gombrowicz' (Deleuze 1993: 81). That is to say, fictions which are 'crazy' enough to attempt to include the multiplicity of incompossible worlds. The most obvious example of the bifurcating paths in *Underworld* is the story of the baseball which Cotter snatches at the stadium. Initially, Cotter's father, Manx Martin, sells the ball to a fan at Yankee Stadium who is waiting to buy World Series tickets. However, from this point on, the ownership of the ball is harder to trace. It is possible that the ball is passed on to Chuckie Wainwright, the son of the adman who buys the ball from Manx Martin. Chuckie, who flies B-52 bombing raids during the Vietnam war, *may* become a post-Vietnam drifter who *may* have sold the ball to a baseball memorabilia collector, from whom Nick Shay *may* have bought the ball.

Polyphonic effects are also achieved in the novel by the use of a technique which is close to what Deleuze calls 'point of view'. In his discussions of Leibniz, Deleuze emphasises the importance of 'point of view' as a perspectivism which goes beyond banal relativism. By relativism, Deleuze means the idea that knowledge and perception is relative to the subject. Instead, perspectivism means that the subject *is* a point of view; the subject is constituted by the point of view rather than the point of view being constituted by the subject. In *The Fold* Deleuze disinguishes Leibniz's perspectivist conception of folded matter from a Cartesian geography of the world in which the self is a centre. For Leibniz, the self is not a centre but a modulation located within folded matter, and in Leibniz's baroque grammar the predicate is a relation and an event, rather than an attribute: 'Thought is not a constant attribute, but a predicate passing endlessly from one thought to another' (Deleuze 1993: 53). Point of view is, therefore, defined as the region of the world that the individual expresses clearly in relation to the totality of the world which is expressed in a confused and obscure manner. The baseball game in *Underworld* is itself an event which is constructed from a series of perspectives, and each perspective expresses a small zone of clarity. Take for example the commentator Russ Hodges: 'He is hunched over the mike. The field seems to open outward into nouns and verbs. All he has to do is talk' (36). The characters in the novel do not have relative perspectives on the game, but rather the game is constituted as an event by a multiplicity of perspectives.

The Event: The Game and its Extensions

Much of Deleuze's philosophical work has been concerned with discovering the nature of events,[4] and the 'event' is a crucial component in Deleuze's rigorously impersonal aesthetics. The concept is discussed at length in *The Logic of Sense* in the perhaps unlikely contexts of Stoic philosophy (particularly in Stoic paradoxes), English and American *nonsense* (Lewis Carroll), and literature (Fitzgerald, Bousquet, Zola). Deleuze opposes a philosophical understanding of the event to a conventional commonsense or historical notion, emphasising the radical impersonality of the event and its elusiveness. In *What is Philosophy* Deleuze and Guattari show that the event is actualised in a state of affairs, in a body or a 'lived', but it also has 'a shadowy and secret part' which is separate from the actualisation of the event (Deleuze and Guattari 1994: 156). Similarly, in *The Fold* Deleuze claims that, for Leibniz, the event has a 'silent and shaded part' (1993: 106). Literature, like film, can create time-images by setting out a plane of immanence, exploring what Antonioni call the 'horizon of events', to create virtual events, an immanent 'passage of Life' which goes beyond the lived and the livable (Deleuze 1997: 1).

Considering the historical event, Deleuze and Guattari refer to Péguy, who approaches the event in two ways. On the one hand, it can be recorded in terms of historical effectuation and conditioning. However, there is another way, which 'consists in reassembling the event, installing oneself in it as in a becoming, becoming young again and aging in it, both at the same time, going through all its components and similarities' (Deleuze and Guattari 1994: 111). They also talk of this second conception of the event in terms of a 'vapour' – a sort of mist over the prairie – which the event releases from everything that a subject lives (1994: 159). This is what Deleuze calls the 'pure event', a concept which he illustrates in the opening paragraph of *The Logic of Sense* by means of an innovative reading of Lewis Carroll's work in terms of a sort of Stoic paradox. Alice becomes larger than she was and smaller than she becomes. This is the paradox of becoming, eluding the present and affirming both directions [*sens*] at the same time (1990: 1). The pure event is in this way 'pure immanence', and is the impersonal movement to which art must aspire. Deleuze returns to Lewis Carroll in *Essays Critical and Clinical*, admiring the 'surface nonsense' of Carroll's *Sylvie and Bruno*:

> Surface nonsense is like the 'Radiance' of pure events, entities that never finish either happening or withdrawing. Pure events without mixture shine above the mixed bodies, above their embroiled actions and passions. They let an incorporeal rise to the surface like a mist over the earth, a pure 'expressed' from the depths: not the sword, but the flash of the sword, a flash without a sword like the smile without a cat. (1997: 22)

The secret part of the event, which is distinguished from both realisation and actualisation is the *Eventum tantum* that is always awaiting the event: 'a pure virtuality and possibility, the world in the fashion of a Stoic Incorporeal, the pure predicate' (Deleuze 1993: 106). For Deleuze, Leibniz introduces the second great logic of the event. In the first place, the Stoics make the event the incorporeal predicate of a subject ('the tree greens', rather than 'the tree is green'). Leibniz implements the second logic of the event by thinking of the world itself as event. The subject is what goes from one predicate to another, which is to say one aspect of the world to another (Deleuze 1993: 53).

As we have already seen, the 'pure' fictional event is inevitably linked to the desire 'to have done with judgement'. Literature which incorporates such pure events might serve to open up multiple variations. As Gregg Lambert shows, Deleuze approaches the 'secret part' of the event by the use of new concepts, such as the Leibnizian baroque, and the time-image in cinema, as it emerges from a crisis of the movement-image.[5] The concepts of the event and pure fiction suggest radical additional dimension to the use of polyphony, as Deleuze and Guattari indicate when referring to Dos Passos:

> Dos Passos achieves an extraordinary art of counterpoint in the compounds he forms with characters, current events, biographies, and camera eyes, at the same time as a plane of composition is expanded to infinity so as to sweep everything up into Life, into Death, the town cosmos. (Deleuze and Guattari 1994: 188)

Fiction allows the writer to extrapolate the event to infinity, to create virtual events, and in a recent essay Don DeLillo talks of the status of writing in similar terms:

> Fiction is true to a thousand things but rarely to clinical lived experience. Ultimately it obeys the mysterious mandates of the self (the writer's) and of all the people and things that have surrounded him all his life, and all the styles he has tried out, and all the fiction (of other writers) he has read and not read. At its root level, fiction is a kind of religious fanaticism, with elements of obsession, superstition and awe. (1998: 4)

DeLillo has consistently tackled the question of the event in the novel, attempting to release a 'vapour' from the lived, and locating the 'shadowy and secret part' of the event, or, in DeLillo's own terms, the 'game and its extensions'. He has been particularly preoccupied with the status of the Kennedy assassination as event, and in fact, talking about *Libra* argues that the novel has a particular role to play in exploring what he calls 'variations we might take on an actual event' (DeLillo quoted in DeCurtis 1991: 59). *Underworld* is an attempt to reassemble the dual event of the 'The Shot Heard Round the World' – as Bobby Thompson's winning run came to be known – and the first Soviet nuclear test in Kazakhstan which took place on the same day.

> There's a man on 12th Street in Brooklyn who has attached a tape machine to his radio so he can record the voice of Russ Hodges broadcasting the game. The man doesn't know why he's doing this. It is just an impulse, a fancy, it is like hearing the game twice, it is like being young and being old, and this will turn out to be the only known recording of Russ' famous account of the final moments of the game. The game and its extensions. The woman cooking cabbage. The man who wishes he could be done with drink. They are the game's remoter soul. (32)

Counterhistory

DeLillo uses the fractured and episodic narrative style of the novel to install himself in the event in terms of immanence and becoming. Fictionality, style and rhetoric are the tools at his disposal as a novelist. In order to explore the event in this way DeLillo seeks to make language 'stutter', seeking to 'open up the sentence, to loosen the screws of punctuation and syntax' (DeLillo 1998: 4). DeLillo emphasises the role of the novel as a kind of 'counterhistory', a dialogic form which undermines the 'monotone of the state'. The novelist sets 'the small crushed pearl of his anger' against the constraints of history, and releases a current of Life. As DeLillo puts it: 'The writer sets his pleasure, his Eros, his creative delight in language and his sense of self-preservation against the vast and uniform Death that history tends to fashion as its most enduring work' (1998: 4). This counterhistory will attempt to release what Deleuze and Guattari call the 'unhistorical vapor' of the event, which is becoming. Language will help DeLillo to reassemble the event and release this unhistorical vapour:

> The writer wants to construct a language that will be the book's life-giving force. He wants to submit to it. Let language shape the world. Let it break the faith of conventional re-creation. Language lives in everything it touches and can be an element of re-creation, the thing that delivers us, paradoxically, from history's flat, thin, tight and relentless designs, its arrangement of stark pages, and that allows us to find an unconstrained otherness, a free veer from time and place and fate. (DeLillo 1998: 4)

The writer wants to find a way of being inserted in the becomings which accompany the actualised historical event, to locate, as DeLillo puts it, 'dreams and routine rambling thoughts', to reinvent the 'neural strands' that link the writer to the individuals who are historical actors (1998: 3). For DeLillo, the writer of fiction has in this way a vocation that Deleuze and Guattari call 'untimely':

> He will engineer a swerve from the usual arrangements that bind a figure in history to what has been reported, rumoured, confirmed or solemnly chanted. It is fiction's role to imagine deeply, to follow obscure urges into unreliable regions of existence – child-memoried, existential and outside time. (DeLillo 1998: 4)

In this way, DeLillo takes historical characters, such as J. Edgar Hoover and particularly Lee Harvey Oswald, and creates conceptual personae rather than what Deleuze and Guattari call 'psychosocial' types (Deleuze and Guattari 1994: 110). These conceptual personae are enlisted by DeLillo, in a writing project which is not unlike Nietzsche's conception of the philosopher as 'physician' of civilisation, diagnosing the becomings which pertain to the historical moment.

In short, *Underworld* fulfills the clinical role that Deleuze admires in literature, painstakingly rereading the symptoms of the event. As mentioned before, *Underworld* begins with a chapter devoted to a description of a legendary baseball game between the New York Giants and the Brooklyn Dodgers in October 1951. The chapter focuses on several characters. Cotter, the schoolboy who manages to leave the stadium with the ball used in the match; Bill Waterson, the spectator who strikes up a conversation with Cotter; the commentator Russ Hodges, 'the voice of the Giants'; and Jackie Gleason, Frank Sinatra and J. Edgar Hoover, who were all actually present at the game. The game is a bloc of sensations, a collection of 'haecceities', of events, which have a 'non-personal individuality'. For example, at the end of the chapter these events seem to cluster around the movement of the drunken fan who, in the empty stadium after the drama of the Giants' victory, slides into second base: 'All the fragments of the afternoon collect around his airborne form. Shouts, bat-cracks, full bladders and stray yawns, the sand-grain manyness of things that can't be counted' (60). A haecceity reminds us that our individuality is an individuality of events, the 'dusty hum of who you are', as DeLillo puts it (21).

DeLillo uses the game, which took place on the same day as the first Soviet nuclear test, as a starting point for an investigation of how this 'dusty hum of who you are' might be articulated within a framework of more conventional 'historical' events. How do these non-personal in-vidualities, which can frequently be 'modest and microscopic' (Deleuze 1995: 141) – the 'stray tumble of thoughts' (11) of the spectators, the game itself, the 'love-of-team that runs across the boroughs' (15), the banter between Gleason and Sinatra, the rhythmic applause of the crowd, the pack of spectators scrambling for the ball after the winning run – constitute a sort of immanent, proliferating event? Hoover, when he is informed of the Soviet nuclear test, makes a point of remembering the date: 'October 3, 1951. He registers the date. He stamps the date' (23). Similarly, jubilant spectators make a point of remembering the precise time at which the winning shot was hit (47). However, as we have seen above, although the event is actualised in a state of affairs, there is always a vapour, a shadowy and secret part. For example, Hoover recognises in the Soviet nuclear test a quasi-linguistic event, the free indirect discourse of secrets and conspiracy theory:

> This is what he knows, that the genius of the bomb is printed not only in its physics of particles and rays but in the occasion it creates for new secrets. For every atmospheric blast, every glimpse we get of the bared force of nature, that weird peeled eyeball exploding over the desert – for every one of these he reckons a hundred plots go underground, to spawn and skein. (51)

Cinema and the Event: The Time-Image

The concept of the event, understood in terms of Deleuze's development of the concepts of the *virtual* and the *actual*, is developed in some length in his work on cinema, but also constitutes a useful analytical tool for literature. If the event is conceived of within an actual system, time must take place between a series of instants, and the event must take place at these instances, or in the time between these instances. However, if the event is conceived of within a virtual system, 'we discover a completely different reality where we no longer have to search for what takes place from one point to another, from one instant to another' (Deleuze and Guattari 1994: 157). The event is the virtual that has become consistent: 'it neither begins nor ends but has gained or kept the infinite movement to which it gives consistency' (Deleuze and Guattari 1994: 156).

By taking time 'off its hinges', philosophy and cinema can create an 'indirect' image of time which allows access to a space which can contain what Deleuze calls the 'powers of the false'. The real here means a conventional conception of reality which is governed by 'the ongoing linkage of actualities', whereas unreality is that which appears discontinuously to consciousness (Deleuze 1995: 65). According to a representational image of thought, time is conceived of as a series of segments or instants. The 'event', however, is a little time in the pure state which occurs 'in-between'. This is a 'meanwhile' (*un entre-temps*): 'The meanwhile, the event, is always a dead time; it is there where nothing takes place, an infinite awaiting that is already infinitely past, awaiting and reserve' (Deleuze and Guattari 1994: 158). Times succeed one another segment by segment, but meanwhiles are superimposed, and every event contains heterogeneous, simultaneous components, which communicate with each other. Modern cinema – Renoir, Fellini, Visconti, Tarkovsky and Zanussi are mentioned as examples – works to create images at the point of indiscernibility of the real and the unreal, the exchange of the virtual and the actual. These are 'imaginary' or 'crystal' images (Deleuze 1995: 66). Modern cinema, particularly the films of Antonioni and Ozu, produces images in which the pressure of time is felt, and at its most innovative constructs the event as a little time in the pure state. Antonioni creates images of idle periods, everyday situations, empty spaces, which mark the indiscernibility of the real and the unreal, the virtual and the actual. These banal or everyday situations can release accumulated 'dead forces' (Deleuze 1989: 7). In the films of Antonioni, Godard and Ozu the potential exists for both the character and the viewer to become visionaries. A new kind of character emerges for a new cinema, which is in its own way, a politically committed cinema. This new character, the seer, releases the vapour of the event:

It is because what happens to them does not belong to them and only half concerns them, because they know how to extract from the event the part that cannot be reduced to what happens: that part of inexhaustible possibility that constitutes the unbearable, the intolerable, the visionary's part. (Deleuze 1989: 19–20)

Time-images in *Underworld*: Dead Time and Lenny Bruce

As Deleuze shows when discussing the geography of Italian neo-realism, empty urban spaces, such as warehouses, building sites and so on create a backdrop for time-images. They are backdrops which reinforce the idea that the event is not an instant, the isolation of a variable at this or that point, but a 'meanwhile', the dead time, or the 'immensity of empty time in which we see it as still to come and as having already happened' (Deleuze and Guattari 1994: 158). The baseball game in *Underworld* DeLillo provides a description of this dead time which operates as a sort of literary time-image, a pressure of time which coexists with the extremes of the game itself:

> Men passing in and out of the toilets, men zipping their flies as they turn from the trough and other men approaching the long receptacle, thinking where they want to stand and next to whom and not next to whom, and the old ballpark's reek and mold are consolidated here, generational tides of beer and shit and cigarettes and peanut shells and disinfectants and pisses in the untold millions, and they are thinking in the ordinary way that helps a person glide through a life, thinking thoughts unconnected to events, the dusty hum of who you are, men shouldering through the traffic in the men's room as the game goes on, the coming and the going, the lifting out of dicks and the meditative pissing. (21)

In a perceptive review of *Underworld* Luc Sante goes some way to showing how DeLillo's fictional Lenny Bruce routines from the time of the Cuban Missile Crisis might function as a slightly different sort of literary time-image. In a section of the novel entitled 'Better Things for Better Living Through Chemistry: Selected Fragments Public and Private in the 1950s and 1960s' DeLillo moves back and forth in time across the two decades, and these 'fragments' are punctuated by Lenny Bruce's fictional club dates which begin on 22 October, running through to 29 October, 1962. As Sante shows, the routines appear in chronological order, like a conventional 'process shot' in cinema – what is in many ways cinema's most crude time-image – where the passing of time is indicated by the leaves of a calendar flipping rapidly. However, he also indicates that they have a sort of literary 'depth of field', in that Bruce's improvisatory genius enables him to articulate the immediate worries of his audience and then move to a virtual future. In this way, he articulates 'a rapid swerve from immediacy to distance' (Sante 1997: 6). For example, Bruce exposes his audience to the strange and unapproachable fictionality of the actual:

> And they all needed Lenny to help them make the transition to the total global thing that's going on out there with SAC bombers rumbling over the tarmac and Solaris subs putting to sea, like *dive dive dive*, it's dialogue from every submarine movie ever made and it's all factually happening but at the same time they find it remarkably unreal – Titans and Atlases being readied for firing. (504)

In *The Logic of Sense* Deleuze talks of the event in terms of humour and death (1990: 151). Every event has a 'double structure', which consists of the embodiment in a state of affairs, but also the event which is 'free from the limitations of a state of affairs, impersonal and pre-individual, neutral, neither general nor particular' (1990: 151). Maurice Blanchot shows that this double structure of the event is characterised by the ambiguity of death, in that death is literally embodied in the individual, but is at the same time impersonal and incorporeal, and Deleuze argues that humour tends to select the pure event, the impersonal and incorporeal part. Lenny Bruce returns several times to a line which particularly pleases him, shouting '*We're all gonna die!*' The effect of the line upon the audience, and Bruce's pleasure in delivering the line, derives from what we might call an affect of impersonality:

> Lenny loves the postexistential bent of this line. In his giddy shriek the audience can hear the obliteration of the idea of uniqueness and free choice. They can hear the replacement of human isolation by massive and unvaried ruin. (507)

Bruce extracts further humour by adding the line 'And you're beginning to take it personally', reminding the audience of the impersonality of war as pure event: 'How can they justify the inconvenience of a war that's gonna break out over the weekend?' (584)

Free Indirect Discourse: Fabulation

In *Gilles Deleuze's Time Machine* D. N. Rodowick forges a series of useful connections between the Deleuzian concepts of fabulation, free indirect discourse and minor literature as collective enunciation (1997).[6] As Rodowick suggests, the concept of *fabulation* depends upon Deleuze's conviction that the function of language is essentially the process of 'opening onto' rather than the construction of a unifying communicative society. In this way, language creates a 'free indirect' oscillation between the individual and the collective. *Fabulation* is the construction of a *récit* which gravitates between documentary and fiction (Rodowick 1997: 157). Fabulation is, in this way, the necessary mode for a minor literature which is written for a people which are 'yet to come'. In *The Time-Image* Deleuze draws a sharp distinction between the belief in 'classical' – American and Soviet – cinema that the masses, the 'people', are a real entity, and a cinema in which 'the people are missing' (Deleuze 1989: 216). The 'people' are present in Eisenstein's *Ivan the Terrible* as a sort of avant-garde, and American cinema before and during the Second World War is characterised by a certain 'unanimity'. In contrast to this, certain forms of postwar cinema invent a minor people, who do not yet exist, except in a state of becoming. In Deleuze's terms, it seems that *Underworld* reinvents Eisenstein as such a 'minor' film-maker, by creating a fictional film by Eisenstein, precisely in which the people are missing, and which stands at some indiscernible point between Soviet realism and pre-war Hollywood. In the mid-1970s section of the novel Klara Sax attends a rare showing of *Unterwelt* in New York:

> The plot was hard to follow. There was no plot. Just loneliness, barrenness, men hunted and ray-gunned, all happening in some netherland crevice. There was none of the cross-class solidarity of the Soviet tradition. No crowd scenes or sense of social motive – the masses as hero, colossal crowd movements painstakingly organized and framed, and this was disappointing to Klara. She loved the martial architecture of huge moving bodies, the armies and mobs in other Eisenstein films, and she felt she was in some ambiguous filmscape somewhere between the Soviet model and Hollywood's vaulted heaven of love, sex crime and individual heroism, of scenery and luxury and gorgeous toilets. (431)

Klara Sax speculates that this 'murky' film, with its 'strange dark draggy set of images', shot possibly in Mexico or Kazakhstan (the site of the 1951 Soviet nuclear test), might be a direct protest, a deliberate rejection of the notion of the 'people' in socialist realism:

> These deformed faces, these were people who existed outside nationality and strict historical context. Eisenstein's method of immediate characterization, called typage, seemed self-parodied and shattered here, intentionally. Because the external features of the men and women did not tell you

about class or social mission. They were people persecuted and altered, this was their typology – they were an inconvenient secret of the society around them. (443)

After the screening, Klara Sax finds that the 'film was printed on her mind in jits and weaves' (445). In Deleuzian terms, it has created a new 'cerebral circuit', which is the measure of innovation in art. Ultimately, Eisenstein's fictional film *Unterwelt* shares much in common with Deleuze's brief discussion of the films of Straub and Huillet (1998: 14–19; see also 1989: 244–7). Deleuze claims that Straub and Huillet are able to create a genuinely cinematic idea, a 'sight-sound dissociation' which makes cinema 'resonate with a qualitative physics of elements'. A voice rises while that which the voice speaks of moves underground (1998: 16–17). The 'event' occurs in the space between the sight and sound. Like the mist over the prairie, what Deleuze calls the 'ethereal speech act' is placed over 'tectonic visual layers': 'It creates the event, but in a space empty of events' (Deleuze 1989: 247). In *Underworld*, the sight-sound dissociation is provided by the conditions in which the film is screened; a silent film with subtitles which are indecipherable to most of the audience, and which is shown in gala presentation at Radio City Music Hall, New York, 1974, becomes for Klara Sax a 'readable' set of images:

All Eisenstein wants you to see, in the end, are the contradictions of being. You look at the faces on the screen and you see the mutilated yearning, the inner divisions of people and systems, and how forces will clash and fasten, compelling the swerve from evenness that marks a thing lastingly. (444)

In conclusion, in *Underworld* the 'people are missing', or rather an underground people are only glimpsed in the form of the ghoulish 'Museum of the Misshapen' at the Kazakh test site that Nick Shay visits in the 1990s, the clinic that he visits near the same site, and the wretched mutants of Eisenstein's *Unterwelt*. The final shot of the film is of a face which loses its 'goiters and gnarls' as it dissolves into the landscape (444–5). The sense of a people that are missing becomes an 'affect' which recurs throughout the novel. That is to say, there is a sense of melancholy, a nostalgia for the people that are missing, which is initially associated with individuals but eventually dissolves into the landscape itself. At first, it is associated with the commentator Russ Hodges:

He hears the solitary wailing, he hears his statistician reciting numbers in fake French. It is all apart of the same thing, the feeling of some collapsible fact that's folded up and put away, and the school gloom that traces back for decades – the last laden day of summer vacation when the range of play tapers to a screwturn. This is the day he has never shaken off, the final Sunday before the first Monday of school. It carried some queer deep shadow out to the western edge of the afternoon. (34)

In the closing pages of the book Nick walks out of the clinic in Kazakhstan and watches children playing follow the leader in the courtyard:

> Something about the juxtaposition deepened the moment, faces against the landscape, the enormous openness, the breadth of sheepland and divided sky that contains everything outside us, unbearably. I watched the boy in his bundled squat, arms folded above his knees. All the banned worlds, the secrets kept in white-washed vaults, the half-forgotten plots – they're all out there now, seeping invisibly into the land and air, into the marrowed folds of the bone. (802–3)

This is what Deleuze calls a 'purely optical and sound situation' which makes us grasp 'something intolerable and unbearable' (Deleuze 1989: 18). In such a situation, the viewer becomes a visionary, perceiving the people who are missing. This is one of the *critical* vocations of literature, namely to invite the reader to look 'in-between'.

Notes

1. See *Cinema 2: The Time-Image*, Chapter 6, 'The Powers of the False' (1989). Here, Deleuze offers a Nietzschean reading of the films of Orson Welles.
2. See Antonioni (1948) Cited in Sam Rohdie 1990: 36. Rohdie regards this article as a general outline for the aesthetic that Antonioni would refine throughout his career, emphasising the fact that the expression of such views was extraordinary for the time, the high point of Italian neo-realism's celebration of populism and humanism.
3. See Ascherson 1998: 7. Ascherson's piece, written in response to Spielberg's *Saving Private Ryan* and David Leland's ostensibly slighter *Land Girls*, offers a lucid critique of Spielberg's realist approach:
   > Nobody spoke about human rights in the war I remember as a child, but only about fear, pity, loss and sometimes joy. And the war is also the day after the war, when the noise stops. It's the day when what looks like a bald old beggar is helped down from the train returning from the prison camps and the small boy asks his mother: 'Is that my dad? Does he have to live with us?' The landscape after the battle, when the soldiers have been buried or sent home – that is also a combat worth many films.
4. See Deleuze 1995: 141: 'I've tried in all my books to discover the nature of events; it's a philosophical concept. The only one capable of ousting the verb "to be" and attributes.'
5. In 'The Deleuzian Critique of Pure Fiction', Gregg Lambert shows that, for Deleuze, the 'concept' corresponds to the differential calculus of partial solutions, and the 'event' becomes a 'tangled tale' — 'a story with several episodes' (1997: 130).
6. See in particular Chapter 6 'Series and Fabulation: Minor Cinema' (Rodowick 1997).

Bibliography

Antonioni, Michelangelo (1948), 'Marcel Carné, parigino', *Bianco e Nero*, December, pp. 17–47.

Antonioni, Michelangelo (1963–4), 'The Event and the Image', *Sight and Sound*, Winter, p. 14.

Ascherson, Neal (1998), 'Missing in Action', *The Observer*, 6 September, p. 7.

Blanchot, Maurice (1993), *The Infinite Conversation*, trans. Susan Hanson, Minneapolis: University of Minnesota Press.

DeCurtis, Anthony (1991), ' "An Outsider in this Society": An Interview with Don DeLillo', in Frank Lentricchia (ed.), *Introducing Don DeLillo*, London: Duke University Press, pp. 43–66.

Deleuze, Gilles (1989 [1985]), *Cinema 2: The Time-Image*, trans. Hugh Tomlinson and Robert Galeta, Minneapolis: University of Minnesota Press.

Deleuze, Gilles (1990 [1969]), *The Logic of Sense*, trans. Constantin Boundas, Charles Stivale and Mark Lester, New York: Columbia University Press.

Deleuze, Gilles (1993 [1987]), *The Fold: Leibniz and the Baroque*, trans. Tom Conley, Minneapolis: University of Minnesota Press.

Deleuze, Gilles (1995 [1992]), *Negotiations*, trans. Martin Joughin, New York: Columbia University Press.

Deleuze, Gilles (1997 [1994]), *Essays Critical and Clinical*, trans. Daniel W. Smith and Michael Greco, Minneapolis: University of Minnesota Press.

Deleuze, Gilles (1998), 'Having an Idea in Cinema', in Kaufmann and Heller (eds), *Deleuze and Guattari: New Mappings in Politics, Philosophy and Culture*, Minneapolis: University of Minnesota Press, pp. 244–7.

Deleuze, Gilles and Guattari, Félix (1986 [1975]), *Kafka: Toward a Minor Literature*, trans. Dana Polan, Minneapolis: University of Minnesota Press.

Deleuze, Gilles and Guattari, Félix (1987 [1980]), *A Thousand Plateaus: Capitalism and Schizophrenia*, trans. Brian Massumi, Minneapolis: University of Minnesota Press.

Deleuze, Gilles and Guattari, Félix (1994 [1992]), *What is Philosophy?*, trans. Hugh Tomlinson and Graham Burchell, New York: Columbia University Press.

Deleuze, Gilles and Parnet, Claire (1987 [1977]), *Dialogues*, trans. Hugh Tomlinson and Barbara Habberjam, New York: Columbia University Press.

DeLillo, Don (1997), *Underworld*, New York: Simon and Schuster.

DeLillo, Don (1998), 'The Moment the Cold War Began', *The Observer*, 4 January, pp. 3–4.

Lambert, Gregg (1997), 'The Deleuzian Critique of Pure Fiction', *Sub-Stance*, vol. 26, no. 3, pp. 128–52.

Martin, Jean-Clet (1998), 'L'Oeil du dehors', in Eric Alliez (ed.), *Gilles Deleuze: Une Vie Philosophique*, Le Plessis-Robinson: Insitut Synthélabo, pp. 103–14.

Rodowick, David Norman (1997), *Gilles Deleuze's Time Machine*, Durham, NC: Duke University Press.

Rohdie, Sam (1990), *Antonioni*, London: British, Film Institute.

Sante, Luc (1997), 'Between Hell and History', *The New York Review of Books*, 6 November, pp. 4–7.

Chapter 5

Inhuman Irony: The Event of the Postmodern

Claire Colebrook

> The actor is not like a god, but is rather like an anti-god (contre-dieu).
> Gilles Deleuze, *The Logic of Sense*

> An author in his book must be like God in the universe, present everywhere and visible nowhere. Art being a second nature, the creator of that Nature must behave similarly. In all its atoms, in all its aspects, let there be sensed a hidden, infinite impassivity.
> Gustave Flaubert, *Letters*

> The observer ought to be an amorist; he must not be indifferent to any feature, any factor. But on the other hand he ought to have a sense of his own predominance – but should use it only to help the phenomenon obtain its full disclosure.
> (Sören Kierkegaard, *The Concept of Irony*)

The Postmodern Epoch

It's possible to regard Deleuze's work as exemplary of our time and so provide a theoretical rubric for our sense of the postmodern. However, to do this – to enclose Deleuze *within* history or postmodernity – would be to diminish the promise of eternal return in his work. What Deleuze takes from Nietzsche is not just an attempt to free thought from the burden of the past, but a striving for a form of the new that will be self-renewing, eternally dislocating itself not only from its own time but from time in general. What is new, Deleuze argues, is not just what supersedes the old; the truly new is eternally new, tearing itself away from all narratives of historical recuperation. Nietzsche's 'untimely' philosophy would be exemplary of this mode: write in such a way that the very figures of time can no longer be recognised within a coherent history. From as early as *The Birth of Tragedy* Nietzsche took the form of nineteenth-century philology and created a way of writing that disrupted complacent historicism. Picture the Greeks, he urged, as a culture strong enough to invent its own origins, capable of creating gods and divine births. When we turn back to the Greeks we should not be viewing our origin, passively enslaving ourselves to a timeless moment of the past. We should view the Greeks the way the Greeks viewed the gods, as invented origins that will ennoble our sense of the present. Similarly, when Nietzsche traced the origins of morality in *The Genealogy of Morals* he found a thoroughly monstrous birth. In the beginning is an act of 'festive cruelty'. Morality is formed when we become too weak to inflict pain for the sheer event of force, but try to *justify* that pain as in accord with some high ideal or law. Nietzsche's genealogy traced morality back to cruelty, and celebrated the 'birth' of tragedy in an age that ignored all questions of birth and origin. But these works only make sense if read as *ironic*. Nietzsche's narrations use the very style of philology and historicism to produce ideas that exceed all history: ideas such as eternal return, that ever-renewing force that *gives* history but that cannot be enclosed or comprehended within history; or the idea of a radical perspectivism. Just as Nietzsche challenged the notion of a continuous history within which 'we' are located, he also challenged the notion of an actual world that is then viewed from perspectives. History is not a unity from which we can discern disparate moments; in the beginning is the chaos or disparity, and it is from these disparate points that various continuous histories are then imagined. In the beginning is the act or event of the moment, while the order of history is a reaction. Similarly, in the beginning is the look or point of view, from which we (reactively) assume some present world that is there *to be seen* (some 'x', as Nietzsche put it, that lies behind our appearances). Both eternal return and perspective in Deleuze and Nietzsche begin as temporal concepts, but then go on to short-circuit the very logic of time. The eternal return is just that power that affirms the events that become time; but this means that the eternal is not just the extension of temporal points *ad infinitum*. To think the 'eternal' adequately is to think it beyond the point of the present. Perspective, or point of view, traditionally suggests some undifferentiated continuity within which each point of experience is located; but for Nietzsche and Deleuze there is only the genesis or internal difference of singularities. This means that we need to rethink point of view beyond its location within history, within experience or within the world. It is not that there is a world, which we only grasp *through* perspectives or points of view. Nor is it that there is no world or real – this would be nihilism. Rather, each point of view is the affirmation of its own infinite world: not a point *within* the real, but the real itself.

If it is impossible to adopt a God-like view from nowhere, then we can at least write from a perspective that displays the very paradox of perspective and point of view. For no matter how much we assert the relativity of our perspectives or viewpoints, the very idea of perspective or viewpoint entails a position *within* some field. Just what are our relative viewpoints relative *to*? We can either remain within a happy and complacent relativity (and this is one of the ways that Nietzsche has been read, as a philosopher of personal styles and perspectives (Nehamas 1985). Or, we can play up the impossibility of this relativity: the very thought of relativism is itself historically relative, and the very immanence of point of view is itself always articulated from point of view (Deleuze 1990: 260). It's this second path from Nietzsche – of a perpetually decentred perspectivism – that Deleuze pursues (Deleuze 1990: 174). The first path is an irony generated from a sense of history and a sense of the concept. The second path is described by Deleuze as a 'superior irony' (1994: 182): an irony that attempts to create a style that is not just historically new, but that troubles all sense of history. This is an irony that does more than work from the limits of a particular concept or epoch; it is an attempt to think the eternally recurrent emergence of concepts in general. For there are some styles that manage to open their epoch.

The irony of eternal return is just such a style. If a style can be created that exposes itself *as style*, then style is no longer the ornamental overlay of a timeless concept. The concept is affirmed in its full temporal becoming. Such an irony would be aligned with the project outlined in *What is Philosophy?*: not only must we avoid locating our concepts within some transcendent plane (such as God, Being or the Subject) we must also attempt to think 'THE plane of immanence' as such (Deleuze and Guattari 1994: 59). Style can work in just this way: not as the style *of* some prior expressing subject or being, but as the fullness of expression itself.

To think this way would reverse Husserl's description of the relation between style and epoch. According to Husserl, the concept of the transcendental subject enables us to think of a being that is not within this or that historical moment; the subject is that point from which all history emerges (1975: 5). The subject might be described from within the style of a certain philosophy; but this style then enables the thought of the origin of all philosophy and all style. The concept of the subject enables us to think the ground of all concepts. Nietzsche's eternal return, by contrast, affirms a style that would preclude any concept from operating as a ground. What is willed in eternal return is not this or that style, or this or that concept, but the very force that over and over again constructs new styles and concepts (Deleuze 1994: 7–8).

This gives us two ways of thinking about style: either as the particular way in which concepts are articulated or as a force that disrupts the generality of concepts. This also gives us two ways, then, for thinking of postmodernity (and postmodern irony). The first would be to see postmodernism as a movement that 'quotes', 'mentions' or repeats styles, but without any sense of a proper or privileged style, and with a sense that one set of concepts is no more 'proper' or grounded than another (Hutcheon 1996; Rorty 1989).[1] The second form of irony would do more than accept the provisional status of our concepts or language games; it would think the very emergence or birth of sense. Such a birth would be *monstrous*: not concepts emerging from a thinking subject or language game, but the chaotic production of sounds, nonsense and voices that subsequently become recognised as forms of sense or concepts. The first form of irony would include all those modes of postmodern literature and interpretation that repeat our language games in an empty, provisional or pastiche-like manner, such that 'we' would now recognise our position as particular and located. Thomas Pynchon's *The Crying of Lot 49*, for example, employs all the devices of a detective novel, but with clues that lead nowhere, signs that remain uncoded and a conclusion that maximises, rather than dissolves, mystery. The novel is written in the first person, from the point of view of a character with a located history and political background. The second form of postmodern irony would preclude recognition, such that the postmodern would be more than the shock of the new and more than the retracing of the present. It would problematise not just a specific style, genre or meaning of the present but the problem of meaning or sense in general. When we 'read' Pynchon's *Mason & Dixon* it is this second or 'superior' form of irony that we encounter. The 'style' of the novel is not that of a character or person; it is the style of a typeface or form of newsprint. The novel opens with the capital letters and punctuation of the broadsheets of its time, but the syntax is not that of newspaper reporting. Written in the present tense, but disrupted by noun phrases in the past tense and use of the passive voice, there is an absence of narrating and narrated subject. Rather, we are given actions and objects: not located within a viewing consciousness so much as 'listed'. These events are described through a combination of idiomatic phrases set alongside tongue-twister, epic epithets that resist being spoken at all ('a stocking'd foot Descent' . . . 'a long scarr'd sawbuck table'). What is being described is the very opening of the narrative scene, the home from which the story of Mason and Dixon will be narrated. It is as though the voice of the novel emerges from a collection of found objects, objects that already impersonate or interpret another style ('some Second-Street Chippendale, including an interpretation of the fam'd Chinese Sofa'):

> Snow-Balls have flown their Arcs, starr'd the Sides of Outbuildings, as of Cousins, carried Hats away into the Wind off Delaware, – the Sleds are brought in and their Runners carefully dried and greased. Shoes deposited in the back Hall, a stocking'd foot Descent made upon the great Kitchen, in a purposeful Dither since Morning, punctuated by the ringing Lids of various Boilers and Stewing-Pots, fragrant with Pie-Spices, peel'd Fruits, Suet, heated Sugar, – the Children, having all upon the Fly, among rhythmic slaps of Batter and Spoon, coax'd and stolen what they might, proceed as upon each afternoon all this snowy Advent, to a comfortable Room at the rear of the House, years since given over to their carefree Assaults. Here have come to rest a long scarr'd sawbuck table, with two mismatch'd side-benches, from the Lancaster County branch of the family, – some Second-Street Chippendale, including an interpretation of the fam'd Chinese Sofa, with a high canopy of yards of purple Stuff that might be drawn all 'round to make a snug, dim tent, – a few odd Chairs sent from England before the war, – mostly Pine and Cherry about, nor much Mahogany, excepting a sinister and wonderful Card Table which exhibits the cheaper Wave-like Grain known in the Trade as Wand'ring Heart, causing an illusion of Depth. (Pynchon 1998: 5)

While Pynchon's novel is a historical epic, it is narrated neither from the point of view of a character from the past, nor from a present recollecting narrator. If we ask 'Who speaks?' of this novel we are not only given a number of voices (including a talking dog) we are also given a language beyond speech. (And this would make sense of Fredric Jameson's (1991) claim that the postmodern does not *quote*; it does not incorporate *voices* so much as sound, noise and simulation.) But whereas Joyce's *Ulysses* had already incorporated newspaper headlines into the stream of consciousness of Leopold Bloom or the voices of Dublin, Pynchon's language resists even this insecure location. The disembodied voices of high modernism are still *voices*: local dialects, quotations, stream of consciousness and recorded lyrics. The language of *Mason & Dixon* is not the language of a genre, a character of a locale. As the novel proceeds the language pulverises into a chaotic overlay of impersonal, unfamiliar and near-surreal ways of writing (rather than ways of speaking or ways of seeing). We are taken from the readable to the unreadable; it's not just this or that concept, this or that style, that is disrupted but the very conditions of style and meaning.

It is possible, then, to see postmodernity as a consequence of the failure of modernism. The panoramic impersonality that culminates in

Finnegan's Wake or *The Cantos* is articulated as the voice of the west in general (Joyce 1977). After these epic projects to locate the very emergence, limit or origin of sense in consciousness or culture, postmodernity 'returns' to those local, limited, particular projects of character or sensibility. This has been described by Fredric Jameson as a retreat from the sublime to the beautiful, from the limits of the concept to the 'aesthetic' or the 'sensible' (Jameson 1998: 123). But Jameson also offers a dialectical way of reading this historical 'transition' and he does this through the notion of 'epochality' (90). This demands seeing the postmodern as more than an empty repetition or pastiche of past styles (99). Indeed, we might see the *sensibility* of postmodern art and literature as a confrontation with the very force that gives history, style and meaning. To use Deleuze's terminology: rather than thinking the sensibility *of being* – as though the sensible were a mere sign or indicator of some ultimate real – we might think the *being of the sensible* (Deleuze 1994: 140). This would be a sensibility experienced in all its difference and immanence: not a sensibility that was given through concepts but a sensibility from which concepts and sense emerged. We normally think of the sensibility of being as though the sensible were always the sign of some underlying presence; to think the being of the sensible reverses this series. It is the sensible itself, and not some (limit) meaning or intention, that is the very medium of the postmodern.

Rather than see the postmodern, then, as one more literary period, we might regard it as a challenge to the very sense of periodicity. Modernity is often defined as a project of coming to oneself, of reducing alienation, of recognition, transparency and universalisability (Habermas 1985). Postmodernity, on the other hand, is *both* an inscription of the very limits of 'our' epoch (through quotation, pastiche and repetition) *and* the impossibility of a sense of ownness (taking us to the impersonal or eternal force that gives repetition in the very sound and materiality of art and literature).

Superior Irony

While Deleuze has described his project as a reversal of Platonism – turning the series of 'being plus representation' into a series of 'image plus image plus image . . .' – his work on irony can also be read as a reversal of Hegelianism. Hegel regarded irony as a precursor to recognition and modernity. It is when we overcome the ironic distance between our concepts and the world that subject and substance will coincide; the world will be the medium of subjective recognition, and the subject will be the medium through which world history recognises itself. For Deleuze, by contrast, it is only when we no longer treat our concepts as mirrors or reflections of things, but as positive creations or events that we will really be doing philosophy and really affirming style.

In *The Logic of Sense* Deleuze describes philosophy as traditionally occupying one of two forms: either metaphysics or transcendental philosophy; either a gesture to some transcendental field outside the 'I' (a formless ground, absolute, abyss) or the location of all sense within the subject (1990: 106). Interestingly, Deleuze defines this 'fundamental problem' of philosophy as the question of 'who speaks?' (107), and it is this question that Deleuze's own philosophy seeks to surpass, and through a more profound transcendentalism. For, according to Deleuze, the supposed shift in point of view or perspective (from God to the subject) which occurs with Kant is no shift at all precisely because we still remain within a *problem of point of view*.[2] This problem, coupled with the question of 'who speaks?', is only overcome, Deleuze argues, with Nietzsche's discovery of 'a world of impersonal and pre-individual singularities' (Deleuze 1990: 107). What this suggests is that a sense of the philosophical epoch is intimately connected to style. If philosophy has always been generated by the attribution of what is said to a voice who speaks, then new thought might demand a style or grammar that dislocates point of view and enunciative position. Point of view locates speech or language as the speech *of* some speaker (or as the literature *of* some epoch). Deleuze and Guattari, on the other hand, will argue that speech is in the first instance a collective assemblage, not located within a subject but a movement from which subject positions are derived (Deleuze and Guattari 1986: 17).

Indeed, it is the very possibility of point of view that has traditionally enabled the idea that beyond the 'saying' of an utterance there is an expressed 'said' or meaning. Irony, traditionally theorised as *saying something other than what is understood* (Quintillian, quoted in Vlastos 1991: 21), is perhaps the clearest instance of a disjunction between speaker meaning and sentence meaning, or a 'said' that exceeds the 'saying'. When Socrates demonstrates, in the first book of the *Republic*, that the Sophist's concept does not meet with its supposed definition, he is able to posit a realm of ideas above worldly definitions. If, for example, we were to say that justice is paying back what one owes then, Socrates argues, we would also have to mean that justice would require returning a weapon that we borrowed from a deranged man. But, as Socrates gets his interlocutors to admit, justice *can't mean* that (Plato 1961: 580). When Thrasymachus then claims that justice is 'the advantage of the stronger'

(588) he tries to reduce the concept of justice to an act of force or will. The Socratic irony lies in soliciting further remarks from Thrasymachus to show that he *can't mean what he says*. There is a disjunction between saying and meaning (which means that there is a meaning of concepts that governs what we say). Thrasymachus is forced to acknowledge that if justice were 'the advantage of the stronger' then this would *mean* that justice would also be obedience to the 'stronger', even if the stronger were tyrannical or in error. But if the stronger were in error, then they might be deluded about their advantage, and so obedience (justice) would also be to the *dis*advantage of the stronger. And so Thrasymachus has to follow Socrates and admit that justice *can't have this contradictory meaning* (590). Thrasymachus responds, finally, by arguing that if a ruler were to make such a mistake he could not *really* be a ruler, just as a physician who acted counter to the health of a body could not *really* be a physician. And so it is the truly just ruler who acts to maintain his advantage, the advantage of the ruling strength. However, by extending Thrasymachus's *own* analogy of the practice of justice and medicine, Socrates is able to lead Thrasymachus to what he did not mean, for if justice is a practice like medicine, then it has an end other than itself. Medicine furthers the advantage of the body, and justice must do more than further the advantage of those who practise justice:

Then medicine, said I, does not consider the advantage of medicine but of the body?

Yes.

Nor horsemanship of horsemanship but of horses, nor does any art look out for itself – for it has no need – but for that of which it is the art.

So it seems, he replied.

But surely Thrasymachus, the arts do hold rule and are stronger than that of which they are the arts.

He conceded this but it went very hard.

Then no art considers or enjoins the advantage of the stronger but every art that of the weaker which is ruled by it.

This too he was finally brought to admit though he tried to contest it. (Plato 1961: 592)

The dialogue continues with Socrates leading Thrasymachus through a series of 'reversals of form' (593). This movement of the dialogue is effected through a certain commitment to the concept. When Thrasymachus uses the word 'art' then he *must mean*, Socrates declares, that there is an end other than the practice of that art. When Thrasymachus uses the word 'stronger' then he *must mean* those who are tyrannical as well as democratic, those who are in error as well as those who know their advantage. By accepting that concepts have a meaning that lies beyond their use, Socrates and his interlocutors are able to follow where that concept will take them. Thrasymachus is compelled to change his definitions, not by any positive content offered by Socrates, but by Socrates unfolding the meaning of what Thrasymachus has said. This means that the concept has a movement and force of its own. The ironic movement of a Socratic dialogue takes a concept that we use, only to demonstrate how that concept takes us beyond ourselves to the height of an Idea beyond our representation.

Socrates, Hegel and Dialectic

It is just this disjunction – between the meaning of a concept and what we think we say – that provided Hegel with his motor of historical development and recognition. Hegel's overcoming of irony is, according to Deleuze, a passage to 'infinite representation' and the 'infinitely large' (Deleuze 1994: 42). For Hegel what lies beyond the concept is not an empty negativity or absolute but itself a movement of the concept. Any idea beyond representation or concepts is effected through the labour of the concept. It's not that there's an infinite or Absolute that our concepts can't reach. The absolute or pre-conceptual is posited from the concept, and if our concepts appear inadequate this is what will lead us to extend their domain. We should not think of some pre-conceptual undifferentiated abyss that concepts then negate or order, or some infinite Idea of which our concepts are finite representations. There is nothing other than the negating activity or movement of the concept and it is from this movement that both the pre-conceptual and the conceptual are formed. In the case of justice, for example, if our concept of justice can meet with no worldly definition this is because of an inadequate development of the concept. The response to this conceptual limit or negation ought not to be the positing of some Absolute beyond the concept. Rather, this negativity needs to be taken up by the concept. First, our concept of justice will have to move beyond its pure form and not just be an empty idea – and so the definition of the concept will also have to include its worldly instantiation.

Second, our world will have to meet our concept. If the Greek concept of justice seemed elevated above this world, this was because they had not yet concretised the universal concept. This concretisation will occur, Hegel insists, with his own philosophy, which is an actual realisation of the history of philosophy's concepts. Philosophy is not the conceptual interpretation of the world; it is the formation of the world through concepts.

If Socratic dialogue allows the concept its own movement it does so through a certain style, where the various voices follow and respond to a question, a question that is formed in relation to some pre-given sense: what is x? Hegelian dialectic takes a different form, arguing that the 'x' is itself effected-through the question. Philosophy is not the discovery of concepts that exist prior to some act of knowing; philosophy is the formation of concepts. And in this regard Deleuze and Guattari will agree. Philosophy *is* the creation of concepts. But for Deleuze and Guattari such creations are *events*: they are neither determined, nor grounded, nor timely. Concepts are *eternal*; they express the ever-repeating power of renewal, difference and disruption. For Hegel, however, the concept has a *proper* and *historical* itinerary. Only the concept of Absolute spirit can conclude the teleology of the west. Only with Spirit will philosophy realise that it does not *apply* concepts to the world or *discover* concepts. Philosophy reaches maturity when it recognises itself as nothing other than conceptual activity. For Hegel, when philosophy defines a concept it does not merely attach definitional predicates to some already existing substance, as though the concept unfolded some pre-conceptual real. The 'is' of a 'speculative proposition' does not passively link a subject to a predicate but *recognises* itself as an act of conceptual unfolding. By contrast, the 'is' of a standard subject/predicate proposition merely accepts the distinction between a ground and its attributes (Hegel 1977: 25). In the *speculative* (rather than 'mathematical') proposition the 'is' is not just a link between two pre-existing terms; rather the 'is' effects the relation of difference and identity that constitutes the two terms in their difference and relation (1977: 37):

> The philosophical proposition, since it *is* a proposition, leads one to believe that the usual subject-predicate relation obtains, as well as the usual attitude toward knowing. But the philosophical content destroys this attitude and this opinion. We learn by experience that we meant something other than we meant to mean; and this correction of our meaning compels our knowing to go back to the proposition, and understand it in some other way. (Hegel 1977: 39)

Hegel therefore identifies his own dialectic with a certain style of proposition. To say that the real *is* rational is not just to describe a certain feature of the real. The proposition performs or effects the unity it describes. In the case of defining what justice *is*, we need to see this 'is', not just as the adding of predicates to a subject; the passage from subject to predication is the very movement of justice itself. A just state would be one in which the very act of defining justice was essential. A just state does not accept the concept of justice as some already given and external law (that we then define); a just state is one that determines for itself what justice is. Only then, Hegel insists, does the concept come to maturity.

This is why the exemplary style of the Hegelian dialectic is the chiasmus: 'the real is rational and the rational is real'.[3] The subject and predicate of the speculative proposition are not just attached by the 'is': the 'is' is actively recognised as the driving power of propositions. For Hegel, then, the voice of the proposition is more than a vehicle for the articulation of concepts. It is through the voice of philosophy that reason speaks itself, and recognises itself (and all that 'is') as effected through this saying: 'The *proposition* should express *what* the True is; but essentially the True is Subject. As such it is merely the dialectical movement, this course that generates itself, going forth from, and returning to, itself' (Hegel 1977: 40). Deleuze, of course, takes voice in the opposite direction. Voice is not an elevation to a self-present concept, such that the tone, style or materiality of voice would be nothing more than a passage to recognition. For Deleuze, voice is at first noise and nonsense. It is the 'depressive' position that recognises voice as a superego coming from 'on high' – imposing a meaning or law. For the schizo, by contrast, 'speaking will be fashioned out of eating and shitting' (Deleuze 1990: 193). And there are forms of literature that affirm this event of sense: where concepts are not elevated forms expressed through voice, but vocalisations that take on an incorporeal dimension. Lewis Carroll's nonsense words, for example, imbricate noise and sense. But all language has passed through this event, from the corporeal to the metaphysical surface, from eating to speaking. *The Logic of Sense* draws on Carroll to reaffirm the event of sense as it emerges from the mouth; in so doing we retrace the very opening of style:

> We have seen this struggle for the independence of sounds go on, ever since the excremental and alimentary noises which occupied the mouth-anus in depth; we followed it to the disengagement of a voice high above; and finally we traced it to the primary formation of surfaces and words. Speaking, in the complete sense of the word, presupposes the

verb and passes through the verb, which projects the mouth onto the metaphysical surface, filling it with the ideal events of this surface. (Deleuze 1990: 240–1)

The pre-Socratic philosophers, according to Deleuze, also possessed this 'schizophrenic' art of the surface; and it is from this surface of sound that a distinction between depth and height is subsequently inaugurated in Platonism (Deleuze 1990: 191). This Platonic distinction between depth and height takes noise and the mouth as both the expression of some underlying subject and as the articulation of a universal meaning (182). Socratic dialogue, for example, allows the voices to gather around the meaning of the concept and this creates a clear hierarchy: between the Sophists who feel their worldly definitions capture the concept and the Socratic questions that allow the concept to exceed the given definition (256). This creates a clear distinction between the saying and the said, between the use of the word 'justice' and its higher meaning, a meaning that transcends any worldly use (259).

Hegel's style, by contrast, extends infinitely – beyond an opposition between the 'saying' of the concept and the concept's sense (or said). The 'end' of philosophy will be that moment of full recognition when the saying and the said are united, when the voice who speaks is at one with the content spoken. This drive for unity of voice accounts for the extraordinary difficulty of reading Hegel. For his writings, like Socratic dialogue, seek to follow the movement of the concept. But the concept is no longer fixed in some idea above and beyond the world. And the voice or point of view of dialectic is no longer divided between the fixed definition and the Socratic question. Rather, Hegel's sentences move from a certain limited understanding of the concept to a higher or speculative meaning. Once a concept is voiced at a certain level it is forced to move beyond itself.

Deleuze, by contrast, does not include all finite points within the general self-regard of the concept; rather, any specific point of view is not a point of view overlooking some object world, but a proliferation of points, a pre-personal field of singularities. There is not some higher speculative point that could encompass the look in general; looking is not located within point of view. For Deleuze, from a series of impersonal looks, imagines, reflections and repetitions something like a personal point of view can be effected (Deleuze 1993). This means that we have to take seriously Deleuze's emphasis on viewing apparatuses along with his emphasis on style. We can't subordinate looking, receptivity or the givenness of the world to the site of the subject, as though the world were located *within* point of view. Before the representing power of the subject there is an infinite series of looks or 'contemplations'. Genetic codings, reflective surfaces, the passive responses of bodies, cells, life and animality are all, to use Bergson's terminology, forms of perception (Deleuze 1988). What makes this (non-human) perception *pure* is its immediate relay. When one point of life responds to another it does so immediately, and is thus a pure instance of perception. When there is a delay in response – when the human mind considers how to act in relation to a perception – then the subjective or representational point of view is formed. This means, strictly, that there is not a subject *who then comes to perceive the world*. There is pure perception. From a 'contraction' of this perception a subject is formed (Deleuze 1993). The subject does not reach the world by looking. From a field of looks something like subject and object are contracted: 'Perhaps it is irony to say that everything is contemplation, even rocks and woods, animals and men, even Actaeon and the stag, Narcissus and the flower, even our actions and our needs. But irony in turn is still a contemplation, nothing but a contemplation' (Deleuze 1994: 75).

It would be an extreme reactivism, on this Deleuzian model, to see point of view as the origin of images. This is the error of representation, an error that has dogged philosophy. If we accept the affirmation of eternal return then we accept a single and univocal field of images, not the image *of* some real, not the giving *of* some given, but a giving, imaging or perpetual difference *from which* identity and the given are effected. Imaging and giving cannot be contained within or subordinated to some privileged image, for the subject is itself an image among other images. Despite this original multiplicity of points, both philosophy and its concomitant style have produced the subject, not as an image among others, but as the ground or origin of all images. This is where the question of style intervenes. Like Hegel, Deleuze will insist that it's not as though there is a subject who is then expressed through propositions. It is the style of the proposition that unfolds the subject. For Hegel the proper grammar that would extend the subject beyond its finite location would be the speculative proposition. Here the 'is' would not assume a ground (or subject) that then has certain attributes (or predicates). For Hegel, the difference between subject and predicate is achieved through the 'is' of the proposition. It is through the proposition that the subject unfolds itself as being what it is.

Both Deleuze and Hegel work against a tradition of irony that had subordinated thought to the 'elevation' of the concept. For Hegel the subject is nothing other than the concept, and it requires a certain style of philosophy to realise the subject's identity. For Deleuze both subject and concept are effects of style. But style for Deleuze is not just the expression of what is, as though style were a way of capturing a certain perspective or point of view. On the contrary, perspective and point of view are enabled by style. Style is not the expression of the human point of view; the human is an effect of a certain style. If style were extended faithfully *as style* then it would take us beyond point of view:

> the conditions under which a book is a cosmos or the cosmos is a book appear, and through a variety of very different techniques the ultimate Joycean identity emerges, the one we find in Borges and in Gombrowicz: chaos = cosmos. Each series tells a story: not different points of view on the same story, like the different points of view on the town we find in Leibniz, but completely distinct stories which unfold simultaneously. The basic series are divergent: not relatively, in the sense that one could retrace one's path and find a point of convergence, but absolutely divergent in the sense that the point or horizon of convergence lies in a chaos or is constantly displaced within that chaos. (Deleuze 1994: 123)

Kierkegaard and the Ironic Point of View

Consider this question of point of view and its dissolution in relation to the question of irony. Irony takes the meaning of a concept beyond its immanent use. When a concept is elevated ironically, a higher point of view is generated, *even if this point of view is not our own*. Kierkegaard makes this clear in his reading of Socrates. When Socrates detaches a concept from its everyday utterance he leads us to the possibility of the *idea*, a meaning which, according to Kierkegaard, is 'absolute infinite negativity'. And it is this negativity of the idea that delimits the specific personality of our existence. The idea is given negatively, as what lies beyond the finitude of our existence. Because we live the difference between the worldly concept and the idea that lies beyond the concept, irony elevates us above our finite point of view (Kierkegaard 1989: 154). It is in this manner of elevation that Kierkegaard describes Aristophanes' Socrates:

> Whether he is in a basket suspended from the ceiling or staring omphalopsychically into himself and thereby in a way freeing himself from earthly gravity, in both cases he is hovering. But it is precisely this hovering that is so very significant; it is the attempted ascension that is accomplished only when this staring into oneself allows the self to expand into the universal self, pure thought with its contents. The ironist, to be sure, is

lighter than the world, but on the other hand he still belongs to the world; like Mohommaed's coffin, he is suspended between two magnets. (Kierkegaard 1989: 152)

From this elevation of the idea, we are brought back to the specific finitude of our point of view. It is as though our point of view, or our world, was suddenly being examined from above. To use a concept is to invoke an impersonal force or meaning; irony is the intensification of this impersonality. Irony, from Socrates to Kierkegaard, has worked by delimiting the world we thought we knew and the words we thought were ours. And this delimitation is achieved through the thought, or idea, of a higher point of view.

Kierkegaard is insistent that this point of view within which concepts are thought ought not to collapse into a positive, determined or reified *self* that could be delimited as a thing within the world. The power of the Socratic position, according to Kierkegaard, is its capacity to sustain a certain 'height' or 'hovering'. Whatever the world *is*, it can never fulfil the demand of the Idea. But this Idea does not indicate, as it did for Plato, an existing realm of Ideas towards which the worldly soul can successfully ascend (Kierkegaard 1989: 153). Kierkegaard makes a clear distinction between Plato's assertion of a realm of Ideas and the Socratic irony that sustains itself in a relation of absolute infinite negativity towards the Idea. The ironic position is at once directed towards the Idea, but the ironist also acknowledge his own worldly position or *existence*. (This is what differentiates Socrates from the complacency of the Sophists, for the Sophists are all to ready to define their concepts whereas Socrates sustains the gap of the question.) Socratic existence is at once aware of its worldly location alongside its capacity to adopt a point of view above that location. This bifurcation is effected through the concept. On the one hand, the concept is used in everyday dialogue. On the other hand, it is possible to *exist* in such a way that one's concepts are open to question. It is this predicament of existence that places one in an infinitely negative relation to the idea, and which admits of no sublation in the Hegelian sense. Not only does the Idea 'hover' over dialogue, never capable of being grasped from within the exchange of voices. The Idea's negativity is also effected from the very limits of voice. Indeed, there is much in Kierkegaard's work that suggests that there is not an idea that is subsequently grasped inadequately in dialogue. Rather, from the very movement of dialogue a negativity is generated. The Idea does not lie in some pure position beyond the limits of voice, but is effected from the limit. Let's say there are two positions regarding the limits of the concept.

The first is Platonic/Socratic: there *are* ideas that our concepts can only grasp in limited form. The second is Hegelian: it is only because of the delimiting movement of concepts that we are able to think of some pre-(or supra-)conceptual idea. *Where* is Kierkegaard and his theory of irony in all this? Neither affirming that presence which is elevated above our concepts (Plato), nor including all that is within the movement of representation (Hegel), Kierkegaard places himself within the personality of Socrates. *The Concept of Irony* traces the emergence of a certain type of personality: a personality that recognises itself not as a thing within the world, but as a way of relating between one's worldly existence and the (non-worldly) concepts of that existence:

> [S]ituation was immensely important to Socrates' personality, which must have given an intimation of itself precisely by a secretive presence in and a mystical floating over the multicolored variety of exuberant Athenian life and which must have been explained by a duplexity of existence, much as the flying fish in relation to fish and birds. This emphasis on situation was especially significant in order to indicate that the true center for Socrates was not a fixed point but an *ubique et nusquam* [everywhere and nowhere], in order to accentuate the Socratic sensibility, which upon the most subtle and fragile contact immediately detected the presence of idea, promptly felt the corresponding electricity present in everything, in order to make graphic the genuine Socratic method, which found no phenomenon too humble a point of departure from which to work oneself up into the sphere of thought. (Kierkegaard 1989: 17)

What needs to be understood in all this is not just Kierkegaard's difference from Hegel, but the ways in which this difference is effected from different styles of dialectic and point of view. Much has been made of Kierkegaard's use of personae in his other works. While *The Concept of Irony* is not written in an explicit persona, Kierkegaard establishes the movement of his argument from the position of Socrates. What Kierkegaard traces is not any Socratic position – propositions or statements – so much as the style with which the Socratic point of view is achieved. *The Concept of Irony* is a book *about* the Socratic viewpoint; but the work is written in such a manner that it also resists a stable viewpoint, always speaking through Socrates. The 'position' of *The Concept of Irony* is not that of a philosopher making statements about the world. Kierkegaard negotiates the very possibility of the philosophical statement. Like the Socrates he describes, Kierkegaard hovers above this text: listing readings of Socrates, quoting philological studies at length, comparing Plato's and Xenophon's portraits of Socrates. The irony of this book lies not only in its topic, but also in its excessive volubility. The history of philosophy, for

Kierkegaard, is not just a series of statements. What Socrates presents us with is the very *existence* of the philosopher as one who recognises the difference between the idea of philosophy and the worldly grasp of that idea. From that gap one can see oneself as more than a point of view within the world, but as a possibility for viewing the world in general. Grasping Socrates as a historical possibility means that we must not reduce the force of his existence to being a mere vehicle for the explication of concepts. Socrates must be more than an *object* of philosophical activity. He offers Kierkegaard the challenge of a certain style: not to be present within the text as some expressed self, but to remain everywhere absent. Irony is just this ruthless resistance to allowing oneself to appear as a recognisable being. If one allows one's concepts, or what one says, to exceed one's point of view, then one can always remain other than, different from, or 'above' the merely said. This is why Kierkegaard's *The Concept of Irony* is both 'about' ways of saying and viewing, as well as being the enactment of a disjunction between voice and point of view. When Kierkegaard 'speaks' in *The Concept of Irony*, he repeats the Socratic position; he quotes various interpretations and descriptions of Socrates, and allows the authorial point of view of the text to remain above and beyond the totality of its utterances.

Hegel's history, by contrast, examines each philosophical position as an example of the manifestation of the concept, such that it is not *Plato* who is speaking so much as a certain level of understanding. For Kierkegaard, however, the style of philosophy that *seems* to articulate concepts is really the unfolding of personality or existence. Indeed, the very concept of irony only opens, or becomes possible, through the originally historical existence of Socrates (an existence that then inaugurates a possibility of exceeding history) (Kierkegaard 1989: 9). *Ironically*, however, this existence is best expressed in its absence. When one becomes identified with some authorial point of view, one has been reduced to a character, as though one's existence were nothing more than a certain position. If what I say in a philosophical text is fully owned by me, then I present myself as adequately re-presented in the external work. If, however, one adopts a 'voice' – as does Kierkegaard – one sustains the impersonality of *existence*, not reducible to a position within the world. When one displaces oneself through a persona one's existence is sustained as different from, or other than, point of view. Irony, for Kierkegaard, is both the very heightening of one's existence and a hyperbolic impersonality. Indeed, this is what enables Kierkegaard to distinguish between two forms of irony. Like Deleuze, Kierkegaard insists that there is the irony that allows an argument to move forward and then there's a higher irony.

The first form of irony shows the limits of this or that definition. The higher irony is demonstrated in the life or personality of Socrates. The ironist who speaks in a dialogue is always at an infinite distance from what is said, and this because the ironist – unlike the Sophists – keeps the *Idea* or the *meaning of what is said* in view (147). I may use the word justice, but I also see that this concept exceeds the force of any use I may make of it. We cannot mean what we say. The ironist's existence is poised in this negativity. And so when Kierkegaard 'speaks' in *The Concept of Irony* it is not *from* a position, but always in relation to a possible position. The idea of the ironist – as one who maintains a distance between what is said and what is meant – can never itself be fully presented, but only acted, voiced or performed.

Deleuze

Deleuze describes irony as ascent – a movement tied to the infinitely large (and aligned with the infinite representation of Hegelian dialectic). In contrast, humour is descent – a movement progressing to the infinitely small (and aligned both with finite representation and with the thought of Leibniz) (Deleuze 1994: 11). There are two broad responses that Deleuze makes to his distinction. The first is a preference for Leibniz over Hegel, for descent over ascent, for a voice from the depths as opposed to a voice from on high, humour over irony, the infinitely small over the infinitely large (Deleuze 1994: 51). (We can see the crude reification of this debate in the 'opposition' today between Deleuze and Derrida. Derrida will ask the question of a concept and demonstrate the concept's force or elevation above and beyond any context or voice – such that all speech is a 'becoming theological' (Derrida 1989). Deleuze by contrast describes the creation of concepts from the very depths of being, and the ways in which voices emerge from sounds and the pulsations of the body – such that philosophy to come would be a 'becoming animal' or 'becoming machine', an affirmation of the inhuman.) But Deleuze does not just opt for the movement of humour over irony. Deleuze's second response is the retrieval of dialectic and irony in a *superior form*: beyond Hegel and Leibniz, beyond representation, and beyond the good voice of reason (Deleuze 1994: 268–9). Such retrieval will demand a new style of philosophy – no longer a style that proceeds from the movement of concepts grounded in good sense.

Representation, Deleuze argues, is tied to two moral commitments: good sense and common sense. Good sense contains all thought within a grounding subject, while common sense directs all thought to an object of recognition. Both good sense and common sense establish a clear and unambiguous representational point of view. The subject is the ground of good sense: that point from which thinking proceeds. The object is that towards which all thought is directed. What is assumed is that there is a general point of view that characterises thinking in general, and that there is a world of recognition that corresponds to this viewpoint of good sense. This is, of course, most easily recognised in the style of high realism and omniscient narration. Here, the point of view comes from 'nowhere' and can pass from character to character, as though there were a general human thinking, given particular form in each of its psychological viewpoints. Good sense is given in the very possibility of this style, a style that captures each character's way of seeing by attributing attitudes, values and propositions and by locating all these different positions within a single style of description – as though style were the mere vehicle for a thought that preceded stylistic particularity. Consider the following passage from Anthony Trollope's *The Warden*:

> There is living at Barchester, a young man, a surgeon, named John Bold, and both Mr Harding and Dr Grantly are well aware that to him is owing the pestilent rebellious feeling which has shown itself in the hospital; yes, and the renewal, too, of that disagreeable talk about Hiram's estates which is now again prevalent in Barchester. Nevertheless, Mr Harding and Mr Bold are acquainted with each other; we may say, are friends, considering the great disparity in their years. Dr Grantly, however, has a holy horror of the impious demagogue, as on one occasion he called Bold, when speaking of him to the precentor; and being a more prudent far-seeing man than Mr Harding, and possessed of a stronger head, he already perceives that this John Bold will work great trouble in Barchester. He considers that he is to be regarded as an enemy, and thinks that he should not be admitted into the camp on anything like friendly terms. As John Bold will occupy much of our attention, we must endeavour to explain who he is, and why he takes the part of John Hiram's bedesmen. (Trollope 1928: 13)

On the one hand the voice passes from character to character, as though psychological states were open for viewing: 'Mr Harding and Dr Grantly are well aware that to him is owing the pestilent rebellious feeling which has shown itself in the hospital.' At the same time the voice is also that of everyday opinion or town gossip, referring to 'that disagreeable talk' and using the frequent point of view of 'we' and our obviously unanimous concerns. It has long been noted that omniscient narration harbours an implicit politics: as though there were a subject in general that preceded any stylistic variants or voices (MacCabe 1979). Irony can be considered both an extension and a disruption of this grounding voice of common sense. In the forms already discussed, irony shares with omniscient narration the postulation of a view from nowhere or a God's-eye view. In omniscient narration this higher point of view is the very subject of the narrating voice. The style speaks from the ground of good sense. In irony, most frequently, this higher viewpoint does not itself speak but is generated from the limited viewpoint of the speaking voice.

In Jonathan Swift's *A Modest Proposal*, for example, the speaking voice is using all the discourse of a strict and calculating rationalism. The proposal – to solve the problems of poverty and hunger by consuming the poor – is *ostensibly* the very height of reason, but the discourse, by extending reason as mere calculation to its extreme version, generates a critique of that reason. Reason *can't mean* simple calculation and interest. The proposal begins with an invocation of shared voice or common sense: 'It is a melancholy object . . .'; 'I think it is agreed that . . .' (1984: 492). However the 'we' that is invoked is disrupted in the extension of our common concepts. 'Our' language of reason, calculation and utilitarian charity is spoken so faithfully that it yields the most absurd outcomes. 'We' can no longer share this voice, and yet no other voice is articulated:

> I have already computed the charge of nursing a beggar's child (in which list I reckon all *cottagers*, *labourers*, and four fifths of the *farmers*) to be about two shillings *per annum*, rags included, and I believe no gentleman would repine to give ten shillings for the *carcass of a good fat child*, which, as I have said, will make four dishes of excellent nutritive meat, when he hath only some particular friend, or his own family to dine with him. Thus the Squire will learn to be a good landlord, and grow popular among his tenants, the mother will have eight shillings net profit, and be fit for work until she produces another child. (1984: 494)

Swift also presents a classic example of Deleuze's distinction between irony as elevation and humour as descent. In irony the speaking voice continually limits itself, and thus generates a higher point beyond that limit. *A Modest Proposal* speaks through a reason that is mechanical and arithmetical, and entirely devoid of any more subtle considerations. The reader is thereby able to see above the point of view of the speaker: reason *can't mean* that it's rational to consume one's children. But there's a point at which the *Proposal* also 'descends' into humour and this is when a duplicity of voice enters:

> I have reckoned upon a medium, that a child just born will weigh 12 pounds, and in a solar year if tolerably nursed increaseth to 28 pounds.

I grant this food will be somewhat dear, and therefore very *proper for landlords*, who as they have already devoured most of the parents, seem to have the best title to the children. (1984: 494)

There's a joke, here, in the Freudian sense. The word 'devoured' is being used 'literally', for the proposal is suggesting the consumption of flesh; but it also deploys the figural meaning of the devouring landlord. In this slip into humour the irony descends. We are given more than the single point of view of the rationalist and his limited computational way of seeing. The play on words allows the everyday voice of humour to erupt. Irony generates a higher point of view by delimiting a way of seeing; but humour returns any supposedly elevated viewpoint to the depths: in the case of Swift the proposal is reduced to a position, not of social concern, but of literal consumption. What makes this a 'descent' of humour is that the 'other' voice is actually articulated. Humour, here, criticises the devouring landlord, whereas irony generates a higher point that sustains itself above and beyond any articulation.

Irony, as deployed by Swift, extends the demands of representation. In the case of irony what is delimited is a way of viewing the world, such that irony then demands ascent to a higher viewpoint. In humour, by contrast, a putative elevation into concepts and high reason is dragged back down into its worldly interests. (Think of how Beckett's humour draws the questions and concepts of existence and meaning down to the level of machines, bodies and stray objects. Or how Henry Fielding shows the concepts of 'virtue', 'honour' and 'character' to be rhetorical ploys for characters' interests.) Both irony and humour play off the gap between concepts and world. In irony our world is inadequate to the lofty strivings of our concepts. In humour these elevated concepts are shown to be masks or veils for the uses and desires of our world.

Against this separation of representational logic Deleuze will put forward the possibility of a logic of *immanence*: where the event of the given is nothing other than itself, and not the givenness *of* some grounding presence. This means that rather than finding propositions that unify subjects with predicates (Hegel), or concepts that transcend their articulation (irony), Deleuze will demonstrate the emergence of concepts *from life* or modes of style. If style is not the expression *of* 'what is', if style is not the becoming *of* some subject, it is because for Deleuze style is not an overlay. It is not that there is a being that differentiates itself through style. There is just stylistic differentiation. Certain styles – such as the proposition – lead us to think that style is the style *of some voice*. Other styles show voice to be the effect of style itself. This means that there are not points of view that then mark themselves with a certain style. Rather point of view is effected from style.

Free-indirect style, to take one example favoured by Deleuze and Guattari, is not a way of speaking that describes something external; it is a way of being in itself (Deleuze and Guattari 1987: 84). Deleuze's appeal to style, then, is not 'aesthetic'. It refuses to think of writing as the effective laid over the actual. If actuality is nothing other than its effects then *style will itself be a mode of being* (Deleuze 1997: 113).

Consider the following instance of free-indirect style that opens D. H. Lawrence's 'The Ladybird':

> How many swords had Lady Beveridge in her pierced heart! Yet there always seemed room for another. Since she had determined that her heart of pity and kindness should never die. If it had not been for this determination she herself might have died of sheer agony, in the years 1916 and 1917, when her boys were killed, and her brother, and death seemed to be mowing with wide swaths through her family. But let us forget.
>
> Lady Beveridge loved humanity, and come what might, she would continue to love it. Nay, in the human sense, she would love her enemies. (Lawrence 1960: 9)

If we ask the question of 'Who speaks?' with regard to the above quotation we are presented with an equivocation or dislocation of voice. The passage is not in quotation marks, but it is spoken in the discourse of humanism – a humanism that the narrative movement of Lawrence's story contradicts. Lady Beveridge's humanism is depicted as otiose, and her negation of life is inscribed in her physiognomy: she is 'a little, frail, bird-like woman' with a 'long, pale, rather worn face, and . . . nervous gestures' who speaks 'with a thin, English intonation' (Lawrence 1960: 10). Lawrence's use of free-indirect style creates a distance from humanism without establishing another point or voice. It is not *Lawrence* who is speaking in the opening of the story, for the style of the speech is that of Lady Beveridge herself. The hyperbole, mawkish sentimentality and *psychological* inwardness of the language is in direct opposition to the novella's subsequent technique that describes characters through their physiognomy. (Count Dionys is dark and 'aboriginal' while Daphne is described through a 'splendid frame, and . . . lovely, long, strong, legs' (13).) Lawrence's story acts as a diagnosis or symptomatology of the very style of humanist pity. Rather than being 'owned' by the voice of a character or located in an authorial point of view, the language of humanism – of charity, pity, self-abnegation and feeling – is seen for what it *does*. In free-indirect style, characters or points of view are produced through ways of speaking. Lawrence's despised humanists repeat a voice that comes from elsewhere, a voice that is not created by any subject, but is already spoken. Voice is not a becoming grounded in an autonomous subject; the subject is the effect of voice (Deleuze 1990: 248). In Lawrence's story it is the clichés and banalities of humanism that effect certain subject positions. Further, we are also given the thoroughly *inhuman* character of human voice in all those places in the story where there is 'speaking' without a located voice. In the above quotation the phrase, 'But let us forget' might be attributed to Lady Beveridge's slavish effacement before her clichéd ideals. But the following paragraph opens with an instance of what Deleuze describes as the 'collective assemblage' nature of all speech: 'Somebody had called her the soul of England.' Lawrence is freeing language from voice, showing the ways in which phrases repeat themselves, produce moral positions and operate apart from any inner intent or human decision.

We might distinguish free-indirect style's distance of voice *from within* by defining it against irony. Irony estranges or alienates voice in order to play off the particularity of voice against a transcendent idea that resists all articulation or determination. While irony shows the limits of voice it does so by showing the ways in which speakers *mean more than they say*. (When Plato's Thrasymachus says that justice is the advantage of the powerful, the *concept* of justice already undercuts Thrasymachus's attempt at moral relativism (Plato 1961: 588).) What makes free-indirect style different from irony is the peculiar ontological commitment of irony. In irony a way of speaking is identified as limited from within. And irony is not only, as Deleuze argued, the style that has always tied philosophy to the question of 'Who speaks?' It is also a style tied to establishing height and recognition (Deleuze 1990: 248; 1994: 5). When John Milton's Satan says 'Evil be thou my good' *we* can see Satan ironically undercutting himself. Satan has to use the very concept of good in his embrace of evil, and in so doing refutes his own project of embracing evil (Milton 1971: 196). Irony is a style that relies on the *sustained force of concepts*, so that a speaker can say one thing and be understood to mean another. Satan *wants to say* that he embraces evil, but we who hear him understand him differently; for to take evil as one's good is to recognise it as a good and therefore to remain within some unavoidable law of the good. Irony is inherently tied to this work of the concept and recognition. A concept has a form or force beyond its individual utterance, and it was this transindividual or grounding force of concepts that drove Plato's ironic dialogues and the moral projects of German idealism: irony is that collective form of a concept that 'comes from above' and situates speaking subjects *within* some more general logic (Deleuze 1990: 230). Free-indirect style on the other hand is beyond good and evil. In free-indirect style it is not as though there are concepts that can be recognised as the voice of law. In free-indirect style we are given highly particular, located, idiosyncratic ways of speaking that are, as Deleuze and Guattari describe them, 'collective assemblages' (Deleuze and Guattari 1986: 17). Whereas irony plays on the difference between the universal force of a concept and its individual utterance, free-indirect style traces the very becoming of concepts as highly particular events. In free-indirect style it is not as though there is a general concept that is then situated in a point of view – as in irony. Free-indirect style effects a located logic and concepts, demonstrating that concepts are always forms of speaking, that styles are ways of being and – most importantly – that styles are the expressions of places and not subjects.

Deleuze's attention to style is an affirmation rather than a critique. Rather than arguing that any point of view will raise the question of the ground from which it emerges, Deleuze aims to think a style that troubles the attributive and critical force of point of view. What is so difficult in free-indirect style is not just the answer to the question of 'Who is speaking?', but also the very possibility of this question. Free-indirect speech doesn't, like irony, 'come from on high'. It is the very wandering or nomadisms of style, dislocated from a speaking subject, producing a multiplicity of positions, a collage of voices or an assemblage. It is not as though there is a law or logic that is then belied by the particular utterance of the speech act (as in irony). In free-indirect style law or logic is the reaction or interpretation that comes after the event of voice, speech, tracing or wandering. And if *meaning* is just the reactive effect of certain ways of speaking, then we will only overcome our reactive submission to meaning and the law, if we regard speaking not as the vehicle of sense but as a movement or event alongside other events. From events of speech certain regularities, such as located speakers, are effected. And it is this event that is affirmed in free-indirect style.

But what do other styles do? How can Deleuze account for the overwhelming western corpus of literature and philosophy that deploys a representational grammar? If 'what is' is *not* a presence there to be represented, how did we come to think and speak in this way? Deleuze and Guattari's reading of Kafka offers some answer to this problem. Even those great texts of the Law and the father can be *activated*; the Law that seems to recede behind the text can be shown to be one of the text's

effects. What their reading of Kafka's text does is not ask what it *means* –
for this is the work of irony, showing how utterances have a meaning
beyond the speaker's intention. Rather they ask how texts *work*: how
laws are effected, subject positions carved out, desires instituted, and
ideas of presence and ground produced through textual events and
questions. There is, then, a two-fold tactic. First, we need to affirm a
style that is adequate to life. Free-indirect style is not the style *of* some
being; it is existence or language *speaking itself*, a way of being effected
through style. Second, we need to read in such a way that all those texts of
Law are not taken as *representations* of law, but as ways of speaking,
moving and writing that then effect a law they supposedly represent:

> A Kafka-machine is thus constituted by contents and expressions that
> have been formalised to diverse degrees by unformed materials that enter
> into it, and leave by passing through all possible states. To enter or leave
> the machine, to be in the machine, to walk around it, to approach it – these
> are all still components of the machine itself: these are the states of desire,
> free of all interpretation. (Deleuze and Guattari 1986: 7)

Postmodernism/PostDeleuzism

Since its earliest definitions irony has worked upon, and generated, a
distinction between the saying and the said. This is what ties irony to the
concept, and what ties western thought to the 'concept of the concept': the
idea that what we say is the sign of some higher meaning or 'said'. The
saying is the material word, the actual utterance, the corporeal movement
of sound, while the said is the meaning generated from that singular
articulation. When Thrasymachus utters the word 'justice' there is a
certain meaning that surpasses his 'saying'; and this is what allows
Socrates to insist that Thrasymachus *means* or *says* more than he is
saying. It is this notion of the said that, according to Michel Foucault,
opens the western 'will to truth' and coincides with the routing of the
Sophists. It is with Plato that attention was henceforward directed not to
what discourse *did* or *was* but to what it *said* (Foucault 1972: 218). And it
is this production of a *said* that inaugurates an 'ethics of knowledge'
(1972: 227). For with the idea of a 'said' or meaning that lies above and
beyond the force of an utterance we are able to subordinate discourse to
some general meaning. The 'said' that supposedly exceeds our singular
statements provides thought with a foundation and thereby disavows the
event of thinking or the production of the incorporeal meaning from
corporeal force (1972: 231). In Deleuze's terms, we reactively subordinate

the activity of thinking to some pre-given and recognisable ground, rather than affirming thought as the very event of difference.

Against this 'ethics of knowledge' we might consider Deleuze's ethics of *amor fati*, an ethics that resides in the transcendental movement of freeing the saying from the said and undoing the conceptual subjection of irony (Deleuze 1990: 149). What Deleuze will insist upon is not the ironic difference between saying and said, the corporeal and the incorporeal, but the passage or movement from one to the other. And it is literature that gives us this passage of sense, this event of the incorporeal. By not reducing sound (or the saying) to its meaning (or said) literature replays the emergence of concepts from style. Literature is most forceful, then, when it adopts a style beyond the human: not a voice that subordinates itself to the concept but a voice that moves pre-conceptually, nomadically or at the level of nonsense. Such voices are given in the nonsense words of Lewis Carroll, the shifting viewpoints of Woolf's stream of consciousness (as in *The Waves*) or the sound and vocality of poetry (such as that of e.e. cummings).

If free-indirect style shows the human to be an effect of a certain style, another possibility is to free voice from the human. It's not just that voice generates the human; voice extends beyond the human: not located in the higher point of the concept or idea but in the depths of noise, machines and the 'buzz' or anonymous murmur of discourse. The high modernism that is so often invoked by Deleuze can be characterised as a movement of speech that created, rather than expressed, human positions. Modernism is littered with speech that emanates from machines and objects, looks that extend from cameras and viewing apparatuses, and quotations that are repeated like so many found objects. T. S. Eliot's *The Waste Land* and Joyce's *Ulysses* repeat phrases of popular tunes, voices from radios, advertising slogans, and newspaper headlines – all in voices no longer located within a point of view. Thomas Mann's *Death in Venice* concludes with the 'look' of a camera left idle on the beach as the high romantic artist, Aschenbach, wanders to his death in the ocean. F. Scott Fitzgerald's *The Great Gatsby* is dominated by the image of an advertising billboard for an ocularist – the two giant and manufactured eyes staring out at the landscape of moving vehicles. Irony demonstrates the limits of the concept by generating a higher point of view – a point of view of the idea or the infinite. Modernism shifts the inhuman point of view, not to a point of higher meaning but to an inhuman machine, where the look is reduced to a lens or camera and the 'voice' is reduced to a recording or slogan. The extension of this modernist gesture is the postmodern disembodied voice: not the voice of a subject, but a voice from which subjects and concepts are interpreted. We can make sense of this through Jameson's (1991) distinction between parody and pastiche. The parodic voice of modernism gathers quotation and disembodied voices *behind which* the high point of authorship remains – like Flaubert's God – above and beyond his handiwork. Postmodern pastiche, by contrast, is a fragmentation without grounding unity: not a voice that has alienated itself *from* the human, but a voice from which the human might be derived. As an instance of this we can think of Deleuze's (and Deleuze and Guattari's) readings of high modernism: rather than a voice that has fallen away from its ground, Deleuze reads Lawrence, Woolf, Joyce and Kafka as the movement of a voice in its pure becoming. Alongside these invocations of modernism are all those inhuman forms of semiosis described in *A Thousand Plateaus* (the striations of space, the codings of genetics, the geological movements and animal burrowings that form the 'mechanosphere'). What is at stake in this superior irony is the very limit of the human. Could we have a dialectic that allowed the concept to move beyond the said? Is it possible to articulate a style of the inhuman – a style *of style* and not a style that would be the style *of some subject*? If a machine could speak, could we avoid humanising him or her?

Both Foucault and Deleuze were insistent that power or desire could not be reduced to the human. And both insisted that certain literary styles could take us back to the inhuman buzzing of discourse, to a white noise that plunges us from the heights of meaning to the depths of materiality. Foucault celebrated the 'silence' of Blanchot – a style that managed to speak without saying – and the sounds of Roussel and Mallarmé. Deleuze also proffered Roussel and a plethora of voices from Melville, Beckett, Lawrence and Woolf: authors who could revive voice in its event of becoming, rather than its grounding in a speaking subject. It is this movement in literature which takes us from the inhuman voices of high modernism – the voices of gramophones, quotations, newspaper headlines and received phrases – to those postmodern moments when objects themselves adopt a point of view. Two of the most famous works of postmodern literature open with the image of a television screen. Thomas Pynchon's *The Crying of Lot 49* opens with a voice which moves from its central character to the viewing screen that is within her hotel room. William Gibson's *Neuromancer* opens with a sky likened to a tuned-out television screen. Both of these examples are indicative of a strong *thematic* strain in postmodern literature that depicts points of view that exceed the human. Deleuze and Guattari had already drawn attention to Beckett's alignment of Molloy with his bicycle and Kafka's description of animal burrowings. Here, the subject or content is the inhuman, but this is achieved by having the inhuman 'speak' or 'look'. Is it possible that there might be a new *style* of the inhuman, and not just the description of the inhuman from the viewpoint of a speaking subject? Is it possible that beyond first person, third person and free-indirect narration machines might transform our grammar, or give us what Deleuze refers to as the 'fourth person'? The problem is this: if we extend voice beyond the human, this can have two effects. The first would be to dehumanise voice. The second would be to humanise the inhuman. And this might explain why postmodern literature can seem to be something like a 'retreat' after the radical anonymity of high modernism. After *Finnegan's Wake* most literature has been written within point of view, not in a sustained free-indirect style or stream of consciousness, but in what seems to be a return to the human.

Once modernist free-indirect style demonstrated that the human was the effect of a certain style, and once postmodernism then extended this style beyond the human, it was always possible that this very dehumanisation or posthuman would become one more site of recognition. Consider the controversial style of Brett Easton Ellis. *Glamorama* is composed from a series of brand-names, popular song lyrics, celebrity names and ephemeral and fashionable references. But far from this dissolving point of view, all these references become the very hallmark of the narrating character – a character who is not even the effect of a singular style so much as the simulation of received style. What is open to question here is the status of this form of postmodernism in relation to Deleuze's ethics of *amor fati*. According to Deleuze style is inextricably intertwined with affirmation and ethics. If we think of style as the style *of* some subject, ground or concept then we subordinate the event of style to one of its effects. We proceed as though our actions (of speech, thought or movement) were reactions to some determining ground. If we affirm style *as style*, however, we have no foundation upon which our events are grounded. We would be confronted with the groundlessness of events. And if no event could be given privilege over, or ground, any other event then there could never be a *proper* style (a style that was adequate or accurate). Rather, the challenge would be to affirm the difference of style eternally. If style were taken to be the style *of* some point of view it would lose its force as style. How, then, might we think of a postmodernism that has fallen-back into point of view?

The Glamour of the Postmodern

What Ellis' novel illustrates is one of the movements long ago identified in the theory of irony. As Kierkegaard argued, once voice has been freed

from the security of the self, it is always possible that this very impersonality might be taken as one more form of positive selfhood
(Kierkegaard 1989: 166). Isn't this just what happens in the tradition
of freeing voice from point of view that culminates in *Glamorama*?
Machinic repetition, quotation, simulation – all those devices once used
to disrupt the human – become one more recognisable style, one more
banal form of humanity. There's an irony here. We could regard
Glamorama as the ironic extension of Deleuze. Those theories of the
inhuman and the machinic voice that seemed so radical in *A Thousand
Plateaus* become, when cashed out, yet one more consumable, assimil-
able mode of the human. But to argue in this way would be to accept
Deleuze as the prescription of a certain style – a style that could have its
day and its moment of shock. But as Deleuze himself pointed out, the
truly new is eternally new (Deleuze 1994: 136). What Deleuze affirmed
was not a certain style – the free-indirect style of modernism – but the
event of style. We need to confront style as that which produces, rather
than expresses, thought. This means that instead of repeating Deleuze's
celebrations of modernism we need to face the event of the postmodern.
In the case of Ellis we have to ask, not what this style means or says, but
how it works and what it does. And this brings us back to irony, and the
eternal challenge of Deleuze's superior irony. What happens when the
inhuman, the machinic, the disembodied and the cybernetic become our
ground of recognition? What *Glamorama* demonstrates is not the awful
moral consequence of postmodern anti-humanism. Indeed it's the resistance to irony, the failure to generate a higher viewpoint above all the
vignettes of the novel, that makes this work truly postmodern. Rather
than this being a novel that delimits or thematises the horrors of
consumer culture, and rather than being a celebration of the posthuman,
Glamorama creates a style of misrecognition. On the one hand, all the
simulacra of postmodernity are reduced to utter banality – spoken from
the point of view of a character who is nothing more than the labels he
wears and the styles he identifies. On the other hand, while the radical
anti-foundationalism of postmodernism is reduced to a human point of
view, we are not given some higher critical viewpoint of judgement. If
there is an ethics of *amor fati* this cannot be reduced to a position: an
argument that, say, the indeterminacy of postmodern style is necessarily
a resistance to conservatism, dogma or quiescence. If there is a link
between style and ethics it is perhaps this: because style is difference
itself, and not the style *of* some ground, then we have to ask of each
stylistic event what its force is, and what positions it produces. Whereas
free-indirect style had repeated the human to disclose all those points

where the concepts of the human *mean nothing*, postmodern anti-humanism demonstrates that the repetition of the meaningless can suffice to produce one more form of the human. Ellis' sentences are frequently not propositions, and are often more like lists of brand-names and celebrities, or noun-phrases without any subject or predicate. Unlike high modernist stream of consciousness, where the string of words is generated from the system of language, *Glamorama*'s language is devoid of semantic, etymological, or even punning, modes of connection. We can contrast a passage from Joyce's *Ulysses* with *Glamorama* precisely in the extent to which, for Joyce, there is some inhuman system or assemblage that speaks through characters. In the following section from the 'Hades' section of *Ulysses* there is an equivocation of voice, but all the phrases are linked through a connection with death and burial. It is as though the stream of phrases is indeed a stream of *consciousness*, even if that consciousness is already invaded by voices from elsewhere, and passing through collections of objects:

> Mr Bloom walked unheeded along his grove by saddened angels, crosses, broken pillars, family vaults, stone hopes praying with upcast eyes, old Ireland's hearts and hands. More sensible to spend the money on some charity for the living. Pray for the repose of the soul of. Does anybody really? Plant him and have done with him. Like down a coal-shoot. Then lump them together and save time. All souls' day. Twenty-seventh I'll be at his grave. Ten shillings for the gardener. He keeps it free of weeds. Old man himself. Bent down double with his shears clipping. Near death's door. Who passed away. Who departed this life. As if they did it of their own accord. (Joyce 1977: 484)

The narrative voice opens in third person, describing Bloom, and then moves to phrases from Bloom's point of view ('More sensible to spend the money on some charity for the living'). But the voice shifts again to phrases that come from nowhere, phrases that wander through Bloom's stream of consciousness ('Pray for the repose of the soul of'). The voice then seems to become more like an errand list ('Ten shillings for the gardener' ... 'Twenty-seventh I'll be at his grave') or an advertisement ('He keeps it free of weeds'). And then the voice turns back to idly repeated phrases ('Who passed away') set alongside Bloom's reflection on those clichés ('As if they did it of their own accord').

Glamorama, by contrast, has an entirely different mode of construction. Phrases are linked, not by their meaning, their sound or their etymological connection, nor do they flow through a consciousness that provides a unifying character. *Glamorama*'s central character is nothing more than the names he repeats, the objects he finds and the songs that he quotes. And these phrases are merely found, often repeated in empty lists without a verb or subject, or with a subject occurring late in the sentence, well after a list of objects. The following 'sentence' opens section 28:

> Stills from Chloe's loft in a space that looks like it was designed by Dan Flavin: two Toshiyuki Kita hop sofas, an expanse of white maple floor, six Baccarat Tastevin wineglasses – a gift from Bruce and Nan Weber – dozens of white French tulips, a StairMaster and a free-weight set, photography books – Matthew Rolston, Annie Leibovitz, Herb Ritts – all signed, a Fabergé Imperial egg – a gift from Bruce Willis (pre-Demi) – a large plain portrait of Chloe walking seminude thorugh the lobby of the Malperisa in Milan while nobody notices, a large William Wegman and giant posters for the movies *Butterfield 8*, *The Bachelor Party* with Carolyn Jones, Audrey Hepburn in *Breakfast at Tiffany's*. (1999: 39)

There is a complete absence of psychology; there is no report of mental states or interior depth – just the repetition of surface effects. Often, the passive voice is used, as though there are just actions and objects with no grounding subject:

> Speedos after Bermudas, baseball caps are positioned backwards, lollipops are handed out, Urge Overkill is played, Didier hides the Polaroid, then sells it to the highest bidder lurking in the shadows, who writes a check for it with a quill pen. One of the boys has an anxiety attack and another drinks too much Taittinger and admits he's from Appalacjia, which causes someone to call for a Klonopin. (62)

We might believe that there *is* a style or grammar of becoming, and that whatever managed to free itself from the labour of irony would take us beyond ourselves and recognition to the 'chaosmos' or the 'mechanosphere'. But wouldn't this be to belie the very style of style? Style is style, not so much in its expressive dimension (as the style *of* a certain position) but in its production of positions. Confronting style's effective dimension is the challenge of Deleuze's thought. If we don't know what thinking is, if there's no good subject who might determine in advance what it is to speak, then we need to engage with literature in terms of the connections it makes and the problems it carves out. The upshot of this is that we are now presented with an ironic challenge *beyond irony*. Postmodernism has been celebrated as the playful repetition of phrases with no ground – and therefore as essentially libratory (Hutcheon 1995). And postmodernism has also been denounced as a naive loss of critique, reason and political force (Norris 1990). An ironic position would play between the two: any attempt to pulverise identity can fall back into one more identity, but any assertion of identity also relies on those pre-identical forces which it must negate. Deleuze suggests moving beyond this oscillation between identity and non-identity, and beyond the accompanying moral rhetoric of liberation and transgression.

And this is why I have chosen Ellis as an 'example'; for if we are truly to assert the style of postmodernity there can be no example. Rather, style would be the continual affirmation of singularity in the face of the threat of exemplarity. Whereas irony points beyond itself to a moral height, the banality of *Glamorama* takes all the moral rhetoric of postmodernism to its amoral extension. For some time now we have been celebrating (or berating) postmodernism as a moral conclusion, as though the dissolution of voice, the collapse of truth and the death of the subject might free us from the burden of the question or the problem. *Glamorama* presents us with the glamorous truth about non-truth: it's no answer at all. It's not even a question we can fully call our own. It is, perhaps, an instance (but not a type) of superior irony:

> Instead of the enormous opposition between the one and the many, there is only the variety of multiplicity – in other words, difference. It is, perhaps, ironic to say that everything is multiplicity, even the one, even the many. However, irony itself is a multiplicity – or rather, the art of multiplicities: the art of grasping the Ideas and the problems they incarnate in things, and of grasping things as incarnations, as cases of solution for the problems of Ideas. (Deleuze 1994: 182)

We have arrived in a new millennium where Deleuze might seem to herald an ethics that would take us beyond recognition to affirmation. And so we might rest easily, celebrate the voices of high modernism and recognise ourselves as having achieved the posthuman. Alternatively, we might remind ourselves – through the postmodern – that it is just when we think we have freed ourselves from subjectivism and recognition that we have fallen back into banality. Deleuze's superior irony is not a style to be found, a position to be lived, but a challenge to our relation to style. Once a style is 'ours' it is no longer *style*. Perhaps all those texts of post-modernity – texts that wander through machines, simulacra, phrases and voices – are best read not as the voice of the inhuman but as instances of the eternal challenge of style. The inhuman, then, is not a style we can discover, so much as the perpetual (and eternal) challenge of writing anew.

The risk of irony, as Kierkegaard insisted, is that the ironic existence, which hovers above the world, might fall back into being yet one more posited self. In this regard Deleuze's superior irony needs to be articulated through eternal return (Deleuze 1994: 7). The descent of voice away from meaning is not a position that can be achieved once and for all but needs to be affirmed again and again with each new movement of style. Postmodern literature is at one and the same time a movement beyond recognition to voice, sound and the inhuman *and* a diagnosis of the continual recuperation of the human.

Notes

1. Of course, one of the most provocative accounts of postmodernity defines the postmodern through its impossibility of quotation. According to Fredric Jameson, high modernism quotes past styles, precisely because it has a strong sense of periodicity and also of its own unique voice. By contrast, the postmodern can evoke the past, with a vague sense of nostalgia; but because there is no sense of history or definitive epoch there can be no 'quotation' or differentiation of the past (Jameson 1991: 9).
2. 'It is frequently said that philosophy throughout its history has changed its center of perspective, substituting the point of view of the finite self for that of the infinite divine substance. Kant would stand at the turning point. Is this change, however, as important as it is claimed to be? As long as we maintain the formal identity of the self, doesn't the self remain subject to a divine order and to a unique God who is its foundation?' (Deleuze 1990: 294).
3. In addition to the general structure of the work which follows each terms as it passes over into its other, other examples of the chiasmus in Hegel's Phenomenology include 'Notion corresponds to object and object to Notion' and ' "I" that is "We" and "We" that is "I" ' (Hegel 1977: 51, 110).

Bibliography

Deleuze, Gilles (1988), *Bergsonism*, trans. Hugh Tomlinson and Barbara Habberjam, New York: Zone.

Deleuze, Gilles (1990), *The Logic of Sense*, trans. Mark Lester and Charles Stivale, Constantin V. Boundas (ed.), New York: Columbia University Press.

Deleuze, Gilles (1993), *The Fold: Leibniz and the Baroque*, trans. Tom Conley, London: Athlone Press.

Deleuze, Gilles (1994), *Difference and Repetition*, trans. Paul Patton, New York: Columbia University Press.

Deleuze, Gilles (1997), *Essays Critical and Clinical*, trans. Daniel W. Smith and Michael A. Greco, London: Verso.

Deleuze, Gilles and Guattari Félix, (1984), *Anti-Oedipus: Capitalism and Schizophrenia*, trans., Robert Hurley, Mark Seem and Helen R. Lane, London: Athlone Press.

Deleuze, Gilles and Guattari, Félix (1986), *Kafka: Toward a Minor Literature*, trans. Dana Polan, Minneapolis: University of Minnesota Press.

Deleuze, Gilles (1987), *A Thousand Plateaus: Capitalism and Schizophrenia*, trans. Brian Massumi, Minneapolis: University of Minnesota Press.

Deleuze, Gilles and Guattari, Félix (1994 [1991]), *What is Philosophy?*, trans. Hugh Tomlinson and Graham Burchell, New York: Columbia University Press.

Derrida, Jacques (1989), 'How to Avoid Speaking: Denials', trans. Ken Frieden, *Languages of the Unsayable: The Play of Negativity in Literature and Literary Theory*, ed. Sanford Budick and Wolfgang Iser, New York: Columbia University Press, pp. 3–61.

Ellis, Bret Easton (1999), *Glamorama*, New York: Alfred A. Knopf.

Flaubert, Gustave (1980–2), *The Letters of Gustave Flaubert*, ed. and trans. Francis Steegmuller, Cambridge, MA: Harvard University Press.

Foucault, Michel (1972), *The Archaeology of Knowledge and the Discourse on Language*, trans. A. M. Sheridan Smith, New York: Pantheon.

Habermas, Jürgen (1985), 'Modernity – An Incomplete Project', trans. Seyla Benhabib, in *Postmodern Culture*, Hal Foster (ed.), London: Pluto, pp. 3–15.

Hegel, Georg Wilhelm Friedrich (1977), *Phenomenology of Spirit*, trans. A. V. Miller, Oxford: Oxford University Press.

Hegel, Georg Wilhelm Friedrich (1979), *Hegel's Introduction to Aesthetics: Being the Introduction to the Berlin Aesthetics lectures of the 1820s*, trans. T. M. Knox, Oxford: Clarendon Press.

Husserl, Edmund (1975), *The Paris Lectures*, trans. Peter Koestenbaum, The Hague: Martinus Nijhoff.

Hutcheon, Linda (1995), *Irony's Edge: The Theory and Politics of Irony*, London: Routledge.

Hutcheon, Linda (1996), 'The Power of Postmodern Irony', in *Genre, Trope, Gender: Critical Essays by Northrop Frye, Linda Hutcheon and Shirley Neuman*, ed. Barry Rutland, Ottawa: Carleton University Press, pp. 35–49.

Jameson, Fredric (1991), *Postmodernism, or, The Cultural Logic of Late Capitalism*, London: Verso.

Jameson, Fredric (1998), *The Cultural Turn: Selected Writings on the Postmodern, 1983–1998*, London: Verso.

Joyce, James (1977), *The Essential James Joyce*, intro. and notes Harry Levin, St Albans: Triad/Panther.

Kierkegaard, Sören (1989), *The Concept of Irony with Continual Reference to Socrates and Notes of Schelling's Berlin Lectures*, ed. and trans. Howard V. Hong and Edna H. Hong, Princeton: Princeton University Press.

Lawrence, D. H. (1960), *Three Novellas*, Harmondsworth: Penguin.

MacCabe, Colin (1979), *James Joyce and the Revolution of the Word*, London: Macmillan.

Milton, John (1971), *Paradise Lost*, ed. Alastair Fowler, London: Longman.

Nehamas, Alexander (1985), *Nietzsche, Life as Literature*, Cambridge, MA: Harvard University Press.

Nietzsche, Friedrich (1967), *The Birth of Tragedy and the Case of Wagner*, trans. with commentary by Walter Kaufmann, New York: Vintage Books.

Nietzsche, Friedrich (1996), *On the Genealogy of Morals: A Polemic by Way of Clarification and Supplement to my Last Book Beyond Good and Evil*, trans. intro. and notes Douglas Smith, Oxford: Oxford University Press.

Norris, Christopher (1990), *What's Wrong with Postmodernism: Critical Theory and the Ends of Philosophy*, Baltimore: Johns Hopkins University Press.

Plato (1961), *The Collected Dialogues of Plato*, ed. Edith Hamilton and Huntington Cairns, Princeton: Princeton University Press.

Pynchon, Thomas (1979), *The Crying of Lot 49*, London: Pan Books.

Pynchon, Thomas (1998), *Mason & Dixon*, London: Vintage.

Rorty, Richard (1989), *Contingency, Irony and Solidarity*, New York: Cambridge University Press.

Swift, Jonathan (1984), *Jonathan Swift: A Critical Edition of the Major Works*, ed. Angus Ross and David Woolley, Oxford: Oxford University Press.

Trollope, Anthony (1928 [1855]), *The Warden*, Oxford: Oxford University Press.

Vlastos, Gregory (1991), *Socrates, Ironist and Moral Philosopher*, Ithaca, NY: Cornell University Press.

Chapter 6

On the Uses and Abuses of Literature for Life

Gregg Lambert

> One day, perhaps, there will no longer be any such thing as Art, only Medicine.
>
> Le Clézio, *Haï*

Introduction to the Literary Clinic

The above title is an allusion to Nietzsche's famous treatise 'On the Uses and Abuses of History for Life', a question which I would like to take up in a parallel manner by asking what are the uses and abuses of literature for life; that is, what kind of health it may promote for 'an individual, a people, a culture' (1997: 63). In his final published work, *Essays Critical and Clinical* (1997), Gilles Deleuze responds to this question by outlining some of the aspects of a clinical as well as a critical use of literature. We might summarise this use along the following lines. First, certain writers have invented concrete semiotic practices that may prove more effective than psychoanalytic discourse in diagnosing the constellation of mute forces that both accompany life and threaten it from within. Second, as a result of this diagnostic and critical function, certain literary works can be understood to produce a kind of 'symptomatology' that may prove to be more effective than political or ideological critique in discerning the signs that correspond to the new arrangements of 'language, labour, and life' to employ Foucault's abbreviated formula for the grand institutions of instinct and habit. Some of the examples Deleuze gives of these new arrangements are 'the foldings proper to the chains of a genetic sequence, a new form of life based on the potential of silicon in third generation machines', or the political and economic stratification of the earth under the final stages of capitalism (1988b: 131). Finally, third, certain modern writers can offer us a manner of diagramming the potential forms of resistance, or 'lines of flight', which may be virtual to these new arrangements.[1]

Taken together, these tasks should be understood as creative and perhaps even 'vitalist' in the sense that Bergson had early on employed this notion. In other words, as Deleuze writes, 'there is a "use" of representation, without which representation would remain lifeless and senseless' (1990: 146). The realisation of this 'use', however, may require that we approach the question of writing 'from a point outside' the critical representation this question often receives in the institutions of literary study today; therefore, I would like to suggest that a clinical usage may radically alter the conditions of the practice of literature and emerge as a kind of 'war machine' against how the uses of literature have been determined by the dominance of institutional criticism in the modern period. Is it simply a question of 'style', in other words, that Deleuze's own commentaries on writers seem to pay no attention or even tribute to the field of criticism, but rather approach always from a point external to the historical representation of an author or body of work? Moreover, could we imagine something like a 'Deleuzian school of literary theory', understood as one approach among others in a pluralism of critical styles and methodologies, preserving the relative stability of the field of literary objects and the integrity of 'a set of individuals who are recognised and identify themselves as practitioners of the discipline' of literature (Godzich 1994: 275)?

For any student of Deleuze's writings, and especially those works written in collaboration with Guattari, the response to the above questions might seem all too obvious; however, in the academy today where the principle of 'marketing' is becoming an efficient cause which determines the uses of theory, we must always hold out the possibility that anything can be perverted against its own nature. Consequently, rather than speculating on the fortunate and unfortunate actualities that might flow from the proclamation, 'one day this century will be known as Deleuzian' (Foucault), in what follows I will offer a more preliminary discussion of some of the principles we might draw from Deleuze's own manner of treating literary expression and, in particular, the questions and problems of writing that have been associated with the works by those modern writers (Artaud, Beckett, Kafka and Proust in particular) who occupy a central role in all his writings on the question of literature. This discussion in some way represents my own attempt to define the characteristic marks of what Deleuze had early on proposed as a generalised 'literary clinic'; at the same time, it is an attempt to provoke creative dialogue around the very conditions that would make a Deleuzian pragmatics distinct from other hermeneutic models in the belief that such a dialogue should occur at this critical juncture when Deleuze's writings are being adopted by students of literature and culture today.[2]

The Critical and the Clinical

The discourse of psychoanalysis in the modern period constitutes the dominant representation of the conditions whereby the critical function of knowledge is given a clinical or diagnostic usage. The critique that Deleuze and Guattari launch against this representation in *Anti-Oedipus* (1983) and in *A Thousand Plateaus* (1987) is crucial and may help to clarify why the relationship between critical and clinical is somewhat complex and not always clear, since the clinical can always assume the form of a dominant 'method' and obscure the critical function of literary works, which is why Deleuze and Guattari write that 'today, psychoanalysis lays claim to the role of *Cogitatio Universalis* as the thought of the Law, in a magical return' (1987: 376). In the case of literary criticism, I will argue that the opposite could be seen to be true as well: that is, the dominance of the critical criteria of representation might have caused an original clinical impulse found in many literary works to fall into obscurity as well. In order to illustrate this, we might refer to an earlier example Deleuze himself employs to interrogate this relationship between critical and clinical: Sacher-Masoch. First addressing the question of the clinical determination of literary work in his introductory essay 'Coldness and Cruelty' to *Masochism* (1989b), Deleuze argues that, like the physician, the works of Sade and Masoch constitute a profoundly original clinical tableau by disassociating symptoms that were previously confused, and by grouping together symptoms that were previously disassociated and unperceived. Sade links the order of reason with the sadistic arrangement of the drives from the position of Law, or absolute right; Masoch links together the status of minorities and women and the position of Law arranged through the privileged instrument of the contract – in other words, as Deleuze writes, 'the masochist draws up contracts while the sadist abominates and destroys them' (1989b: 13). In the psychoanalytic treatment of both writers, however, Deleuze discerns that the extraction of the 'clinical entities' of sadism and masochism from the work of Sade and Sacher-Masoch results in an evacuation of the descriptions offered by these works themselves. There is a reduction of the language that was specific to Sade and Masoch in which symptoms later associated with the psychoanalytic terms that bear their names were first arranged together and displayed upon a critical tableau indistinguishable from the art of Sade and of Sacher-Masoch. As Deleuze writes,

'symptomatology is always an affair of art' and, moreover, 'the specifi-
cities of sadism and masochism are not separable from the literary values
proper to the works of Sade and Masoch' (1989b: 10).

In other words, it was the 'critical' creation of Sade and Masoch which
first raised these obscure affections, passions and perceptions to the status
of what Deleuze and Guattari will later call *affects* and *percepts*.[3]
Through this process of creation, their literary works caused what was
formerly unperceived, imperceptible and 'outside of language' to pass
into language where these *percepts* and *affects* become 'signs' that will
henceforth bear a certain visibility, and, as Deleuze writes, 'a tendency
toward greater specificity [which] indicates a refinement of symptomatology' (1989b: 13). If we are to regard Sade and Masoch as 'true artists
and symptomatologists', something curious happens when psychoanalysis appropriates their clinical discoveries: their own proper names are
employed to designate the 'syndromes' they themselves first brought to
light. In other words, the critical is obscured by the clinical at the same
time that Sade and Masoch are separated from their own language, and
the exceptional cases of Sade and Masoch are reduced to 'a clinical state'
of illness, rather than becoming a critical diagnosis of health. Following
Krafft-Ebing's earlier objections, Deleuze's criticism of the psychoanalytic
construction of sado-masochism is clear. First, Deleuze argues, because
psychoanalysis was not specifically attentive enough to the works of Sade
and Masoch, it botched the accuracy of its own clinical conception of
sadism and masochism by misinterpreting the symptomatology they had
originally created. Second, because the symptoms were abstracted from
their original contexts, they lost much of the critical force that was
specific to their literary production; in turn, this led to the subsequent
confusion of sado-masochism as a complementary and reversible structure, which Deleuze goes on to argue as, in fact, distinct and irreversible.
Deleuze's early work therefore functions as both an introduction and a
critical recovery of Masoch's own language accompanying the re-edition
of *Venus in Furs*. The title under which this work appears in French,
Présentation de Sacher-Masoch (1967), the term *'présentation'* assumes
the juridico-technical meaning of a legal process of discovery, the stage in
which evidence is gathered from an opposing party in the initial phase of a
juridical proceeding. Deleuze's critique of the clinical appropriation of
Masoch can be understood as pleading for the defence in the legal
proceeding against psychoanalysis, a proceeding that would finally come
to trial five years later in *Anti-Oedipus*.

This is why Deleuze writes concerning the case of the psychoanalytic
appropriation of Masoch and Sade that because the clinical judgement

may be too prejudiced, perhaps 'it is now necessary to begin again with an approach situated outside the clinic, a literary approach, from which these perversions originally received their names' (1967: 10; my translation). In an interview that took place about the same time he wrote the preface to Masoch's novel, Deleuze described this point outside as the place where 'the problem of symptomatology' must also be situated: 'at a neutral point, almost zero-degree, where artists and philosophers and doctors and patients can encounter one another' (1997: 177, n. 25). Both these remarks correspond to a strategy one can find throughout Deleuze's writings, from *Difference and Repetition* (1994), where this point is 'difference' – that is, as the repetition of the variable, or the 'new' – which must be located outside the western philosophical tradition; to *Foucault* (1988b), where Deleuze even formulates this strategy in the chapter of 'Strategies and the Non-Stratified' (1988b: 70–93); and finally, to the writings with Guattari where this point of 'the outside' (*le dehors*) is expressed in several different ways and itself becomes multiple points each inserted or discovered to be emerging within their own assemblage or plateau (for example, 'the war machine', 'the nomad', 'smooth space', 'the line of flight', 'deterritorialisation' and so on).

The above strategy of course receives its most forceful articulation in the following passage from *Anti-Oedipus*, where it is applied to the reconfiguration of the relationship of critical and clinical, and which necessarily entails the destruction of the previous relationship operated by psychoanalysis as one of the primary tasks of what Deleuze and Guattari call 'schizoanalysis':

> [T]he problem [of Oedipus] is not resolved until we do away with both the problem and the solution. It is not the purpose of schizoanalysis to resolve Oedipus, it does not intend to resolve it better than Oedipal psychoanalysis does. Its aim is to de-oedipalise the unconscious in order to reach [*from a point almost outside*] the real problems. Schizoanalysis proposes to reach those regions of the orphan unconscious – indeed 'beyond all law' – where the problem of Oedipus can no longer be raised. (1983: 81–2)

As Deleuze and Guattari explain in the next statement, this point outside is not necessarily outside psychoanalysis itself (for example, another discourse or branch of knowledge such as anthropology, philosophy, or science) as it is *the outside of psychoanalysis itself* which can only be revealed through an internal reversal of its analytical categories – namely, 'the schizo', a figure which must be sharply distinguished from the clinical entity of the schizophrenic, since many of the exemplary representatives of the figure of the schizo are drawn from literature (Artaud, Beckett,

Kafka, Lenz, Rimbaud and so on). This strategy is one of reversing the institutional priority of the two functions, critical and clinical, either by investing the clinical object with a critical function, or the critical with a clinical determination, and thereby folding one operation on to the other.

Applying the above example as an analogy to the critical institution of literature in the university today, we might perceive that certain literary works also bear a critical activity that is proper to their own creation, which occurs before (or even without) the representation of the *significance* of these works by 'criticism' or 'theory'. For example, the entry of structuralist categories into the study of language and literature after the 1950s marks the beginning of a scientific function which has dominated the major movements of literary criticism from that period onward; however, the need to guarantee a constancy of the object of knowledge (which is a major trait of structuralist and narratological theories of Gérard Genette, in particular, but also Gerald Prince, Michel Riffaterre, and Robert Scholes) shares many of the same attributes of what Deleuze-Guattari describe as 'Royal Science'.[4] Thus, literary criticism of this type may indirectly serve to inscribe the normative value of literary expression within an apparatus of specialisation, one that also bears a political function consonant with the institutional determination of its subject. In distinct contrast to this 'subject of literature', the writer often begins from 'a point outside' the critical representation of literary constants, with a certain series of concrete problematics. In each case, the solutions are always temporary and take the form of a story or narrative, a certain tale or novella, this or that character. (The fiction of Borges is perhaps the best example of this problem-solving approach.) This practice corresponds to a fundamental axiom in Deleuze's philosophy, often described as his 'radical empiricism' or even 'pragmatism'; that is, the condition of a statement on literature is at the same time a condition of literary enunciation itself, and the criteria by which literature appears as an object of real experience are at the same time the conditions of each particular expression or enunciation. It is for this reason that a critical image of literature cannot take on a major form without invoking a transcendental function, or without appealing to certain categories that would each time function as constants whether that of the 'author', 'narrator', the 'text', 'genre', or 'narrative mode'.

Here, we might begin to ask how this activity has often become obscured by the institutional consolidation of criticism in the university so that, today, we find a situation in which the problems of literature are often separated from their own expressions (solutions). That is, we might view this situation as being analogous to the situation of the schizophrenic within psychoanalytic interpretation who becomes subject to an analytic and clinical form of interpretation that makes him or her the 'object' of another system of classification and knowledge. Like the clinical subject, literature today is often stripped of any enunciatory power of its own, and, lately, often appears so helpless that its very representation predisposes it to the critic's ideological rectification or discourse of truth. As in the case of Sade and Masoch above, perhaps, like psychoanalysis and its regime of 'interpretation', the critical representation of literature may also be too full of prejudices to be of use any longer, and it is now necessary to begin all over again '*as if* from a point outside'. Therefore, we must ask in response to this situation, how do we discover a critical form of expression immanent to the clinical or diagnostic expression invented by writers themselves?

The Four Criteria

In the introductory essay to *Essays Critical and Clinical*, the plane of immanence upon which the question of literature is unfolded is defined as 'Life'. More specifically, Deleuze defines literature as 'the passage of life within language that constitutes Ideas' (1997: 5). In *The Fold* (1993), this 'passage' is described almost in the same manner that Whitehead had earlier spoken of Ideas themselves as the 'passage of Nature' into the location of a place (1993: 73). Recalling the strategy outlined from the preface of *Coldness and Cruelty*, since we can only hope to discover a point outside the critical representation of literature on a plane that is occupied by 'Life', then it is only from this point (or vista) that we might begin again to pose the question of literature itself. However, this last statement must be understood concretely, and without leaving the notion of 'Life' itself as a pure abstraction or metaphysical expression of vitalism. Keeping this in mind, that is, the strategic necessity of situating the question of the critical from a point 'outside' its historical representation (or representative discourse), I will turn to this introductory essay in order to interrogate the above passage, since it is from this point that Deleuze describes what happens when the questions of living are bound up with 'the problems of writing'. In this essay Deleuze outlines what could be called the four criteria for defining the relationship between literature and life. Because they may provide us with a good approximation of the reconfiguration of the critical and the clinical – that is, with the 'uses of literature for life' – in the sections that follow I will illustrate each of these criteria.

> First Criterion: 'Literature is a passage of life that traverses outside the
> lived and the liveable'. (1997: 1)

This is what Deleuze means by the first sentence that begins the leading
essay of *Essays Critical and Clinical*, 'Literature and Life': 'To write is
certainly not to impose a form of expression on the matter of lived
experience' (1997: 1). This statement recalls a question first proposed by
Proust: 'If art was indeed but a prolongation of life, was it worth while to
sacrifice anything to it? Was it not as unreal as life itself?' (*The Captive*
1993a: 339). Before Deleuze, Proust is probably the greatest apologist for
the 'duty' of literature. 'How many have turned aside from its task', he
asked, 'lacking the instinct for it, which is nothing less than the instinct for
life itself' (*Time Regained* 1993b: 298). On the other hand, '[r]eal life,
that is, life at last laid bare and illuminated – the only life in consequence
to which can be said to be really lived – is literature, and life thus defined
is in a sense all the time immanent in ordinary men no less than in the
artist' (*Time Regained* 1993b: 298). For Proust, as for Deleuze, literature
is perhaps the most 'real' of all things, since ideas that are formed by pure
intelligence may be logical, but are not necessary; moreover, perception
or knowledge which is either common or general is also not 'necessary',
because it has not been deciphered, developed, worked over – in other
words, created. (Thus, in a famous description, Proust writes that for
most people memory is a darkroom containing too many negatives that
have not been 'developed'.) Therefore, literature *is* life

> remote from our daily pre-occupations, [the life] we separate from
> ourselves by an ever greater gulf as the conventional knowledge we
> substitute for it grows thicker and more impermeable, that reality which
> it is very easy for us to die without ever having known and which is, quite
> simply, our life. (*Time Regained* 1993b: 298–9)

According to this principle, certain literary works often take the opposite
path: to discern beneath the merely personal the power of the impersonal.
Thus, literature sometimes concerns the question of living in the sense that
the writer struggles with the problem of life in order to extract movements
and becomings that are inseparable from the question of 'style'. 'Style',
however, does not reflect the individuated expression or personality of the
artist or writer. As Proust argues:

> [A]rt, if it means awareness of our own life, means also the awareness of
> the lives of other people – style for the writer, no less than colour for the
> painter, is not a question of technique but of vision: it is the revelation,
> which by direct and conscious methods would be impossible, of the

qualitative difference, the uniqueness in which the world appears to each one of us, a difference which, were it not for art, would remain the secret of every individual. (*Time Regained* 1993b: 299)

In the passage that traverses both the lived and the liveable, the identities of the terms do not remain the same, but enter into a process of mutual becoming. In *Dialogues* (1987), Deleuze defines this process as a 'double-capture', that is, a repetition that causes both to become unequal to their former definitions, and enter into a relation of becoming (1987: 2–7). Such a becoming, however, concerns the immanence of 'a life', and only in rare or exceptional cases does it emerge to touch upon the immanence of a life that is lived and liveable by others. We might ask then, what makes the life posed by literature exemplary; in other words, what causes its critical expression to pass over to the side of the clinical? It is with this question that the value of the literary enterprise is posed, whether it receives justification and a 'use' or falls into a miserable state of univocity. This is where the nature of this 'passage' receives a definite qualification: literature concerns the passage of a life into language. It is only through this passage that Life itself can achieve the repetition of a higher power, and the personal can be raised to the condition of 'a language'.

Deleuze often remarks that the plane of life surpasses both the lived and the liveable; the writer's encounter often proceeds from an encounter when life, defined in terms of the lived and the liveable, becomes impossible, 'too powerful, or too painful, too beautiful' (Deleuze 1989a: 51). Accordingly, the writer often returns from the land of the dead and is himself or herself 'a stranger to life' (Deleuze and Guattari 1987: 208). In other words, the writer does not simply write from experience or memory, but also from something too painful for memory or too light for experience – even 'an unbearable lightness' although perhaps in a different sense than in the novel by Milan Kundera. It is for this reason, second, that the act of writing and the figure of the writer always entertain a relationship with a fundamental stupidity (*bêtise*), which is not simply a lack of experience as the fictionalising factor, as well as with a fundamental amnesia or 'forgetting', which is not simply a weak memory as the factor of an overly active imagination. (The *récits* of Marguerite Duras are exemplary in this regard.) Both stupidity and forgetting are the forces that define the writer's strangeness and estrangement from the 'lived and the liveable'. For example, is there not a stupidity proper to Kafka's relationship with women that initiated the desire of the bachelor (hence, his famous statement, 'Prometheus was a bachelor'), or a forgetting that one finds in Artaud, Beckett and Joyce? As in the famous case of the '*jeune homme schizophrène*' (an earlier essay of which is included in *Essays Critical and Clinical*), the relationship to a maternal language has undergone a fundamental trauma and dispossession and must either be invented anew (as in the case of Joyce and Proust) or pushed to its extreme limit to the point where Language itself confronts its impossibility (*impouvoir*, using Blanchot's term) and comes into contact with its own outside. The latter can find its various strategies in Artaud (where the outside is the cry beyond words), or in Beckett, who pushed the language of the novel to an extreme repetition that unravels into tortured fragments at the same time that his characters devolve into partial objects (for example, a mouth, a head, an eye, a torso, a stomach, an anus). Perhaps we can illustrate the immanence of a life with the following statement which Deleuze takes from Primo Levi, although in a manner that implicitly points to the example of Kafka: 'The shame of being a man – is there any better reason to write?' (Deleuze 1997: 1). Here, 'shame' defines the fundamental trait of 'a life' that cannot simply be identified with the life of Kafka, but rather with a 'situation' that is particular to his case. For Kafka, therefore, the problem of writing is posed within an immanent relation to the escape from a 'situation' of shame. Benjamin had earlier perceived this shame as an 'elemental purity of feeling' that is fundamental to Kafka's writings and, consequently, 'Kafka's strongest gesture [*gestus*]' (1968: 25). What is the 'shame of being human?' For Benjamin, therefore, shame is primarily a social feeling: it is something one feels in the presence of others, something one feels for others. Because of this origin, the individual is innocent and cannot be found to be its cause; on the contrary, the situation of shame always returns to find its causality in the character of the Law and its officers (the judge, the father, the mother, even the son and the daughter, or sister); the character of Law is that of an incredible filth that covers everything and everyone – a defilement of being. The father in 'The Judgement' wears a dirty nightshirt; in 'The Metamorphosis', the father's uniform is covered in filth; in *The Trial*, the Examining Magistrate pages through a dusty volume of the Law, which turns out to be filled with dirty pictures. One might think this is a characteristic particular to the fathers and the officials only; however, nothing could be further from the truth. In fact, the son has become the embodiment of filth; he is vermin. Woman doesn't escape either since she is touched with the filth of the Law that defiles her own sex, and appears as a slut, a court prostitute, or a hunchback among the assembly of harpies who assemble on the stairs outside the painter Titorelli's studio. Shame – that is, the shame of being human – is nothing 'personal', but rather 'the Universal' or 'the general', an unknown 'family' which includes both humans and domesticated animals alike. Kafka writes concerning his indefinite relationship to this 'family of Man': 'He feels as though he were living and thinking under the constraint of a family . . . Because of this family . . . he cannot be released' (Benjamin 1968: 25).

> Second Criterion: 'To write is not to recount one's memories and travels, one's loves and grief, one's dreams and fantasies; neither do we write with our neuroses, which do not constitute 'passages', but rather those states into which we fall when our desire is blocked or plugged-up' – consequently, 'literature then appears as an enterprise of health'.
> (Deleuze 1997: 2–3)

Why does Deleuze seem to love children and writers so much? Or rather, why are writers so often described in the process of 'becoming-child'? Kafka's letters often demonstrate this process directly, particularly those to Felice, where he takes a child's point of view in talking about her 'teeth' or in day-dreaming over the idea of curling up in her dresser drawer next to her 'private articles', or, finally, in the passages where he describes a thousand agitated hands fluttering and out of reach, which can be understood as prefiguring Gregor Samsa's thousand tiny legs waving helplessly in front of him. In addition to Kafka, we might think of Beckett as well, particularly the trilogy, where the characters (Molloy, Malone, Jacques, Mahood, the Unnameable) are all shown undergoing incredible and hilarious journeys and transmigrations, or are haunted by endoscopic perceptions. The answer, it seems, would be simple enough: because the child knows how to play (that is, to experiment), and the writer in the process of 'becoming-child' does not imitate children but repeats a block of childhood and allows it to pass through language. However, we must avoid allowing the notion of 'play' to remain too simplistic (since most adults will claim they know what 'playing' is); therefore, we might turn back to Freud's original intuition of the child-at-play in his 'Creative Writers and Day-Dreaming'.

Freud noticed that the child, contrary to the adult, plays in the full light of day, plays openly, and even causes his or her creations to transform the external world of perception. In contrast, adults can only play in secret and often actively hide their creative activities – even from themselves! The 'unconscious' is a kind of hidden or secret form of play, a game that goes on in the darkness and randomly chooses its own players. Adults are, first and foremost, guilty; they have lost the innocence of play, have repressed it, meaning also that they aggressively prohibit all 'public displays' of such an activity by transforming the nature of play itself into an unconscious source of pleasure. Freud used this distinction primarily to distinguish the play of child from the fantasy life of the adult in order to show that the origin of the phantasm itself has this sense of 'hiding', a guilty source of satisfaction for the adult who can only play in secret (and alone). At the same time, even Freud noticed that the artist constitutes the exceptional case to this internalisation and continues to play out in the open. What's more, Freud exclaims with a certain amount of surprise – society allows it! However, the artist (or the 'creative one') must usually pay the price in terms of a suffering that compensates for the artist's enjoyment and seems to satisfy the cruelty of society itself towards the artist for enjoying too much and in a manner that civilisation first of all demands to be sacrificed, cut off. This economic arrangement of cruelty and pleasure, according to Freud, is the only guarantee that the creative writer and artist have to exist. This is why the old adage is an accurate description – that the price of art (enjoyment, creativity) is suffering.

Returning now to the writer, who like the child plays openly and in the full light of day, this implies that the nature of the creative activity of writing cannot find its source in the secret, internalised and guilty affects of the adult. As Deleuze argues, 'we do not write with our neuroses' (1997: 3). Wouldn't this imply that we should look for the sense of the process on the surface of the writer's activity, for a process that seeks to hide nothing? It seems odd, therefore, that the tendency of 'interpretation' is to reveal or to expose a 'secret' behind the appearance of the literary effect, underneath the more overt and all-too-evident transformations: to locate the 'figure in the carpet' or the 'figure of ideology'. Is there any difference? Moreover, couldn't this activity be seen as an extension of the earlier repression: to transform what is out in the open, on the surface, to what is hidden and secret? Wouldn't this transform the very intentionality of the writer in such a way that the figure itself would appear to have been ferreted away, and desire would in turn become a desire of the phantasm? This is why interpretations of ideology begin with a false premise: that the writer was hiding anything to begin with. And perhaps this is also why Deleuze-Guattari choose the most problematic of writers from the perspective of normal adult morality (for example, Carroll and his love for little girls, Faulkner's and Melville's racism, or that of Céline, the misogyny of Miller and Burroughs, Proust's 'closeted' homosexuality, Artaud's mania and crypto-fascism, Kafka's bachelor-desire, Woolf's frigidity and so on), as if to say, 'Well now, there's nothing hidden here!' 'All perverts – everyone of them!' Or, 'If we are to judge, if we must arrive at a judgement, then we must find better evidence; but at least, we must find something more interesting to say.' But then, finally, 'perversion' may not be the right word. Again, this evokes the sense of symptomatology of literary expression, since the writer 'plays' – that is, openly and without shame, or guilt – with what the adult would otherwise choose to keep 'secret', even though this secrecy which defines the unconscious source of morality makes these symptoms no less determining of a life and perhaps even more so. How many times have we had to suffer the moralism of perverts, racists, misogynists and pederasts who choose to persecute others for their own most secretive desires? Thus, the publicity with which the writer plays with his or her desires is not perverse in the least; rather, the function of 'perversion' describes the position of a normative morality under the condition that enjoyment either remains 'a dirty little secret' of the individual, or undergoes a strange reversal into sadism and cruelty.

> Third Criterion: 'Health as literature', as writing, consists in fabulation, which Deleuze defines as 'the invention of a people who are missing'; thus, 'the ultimate aim of literature is to set free, in the delirium, in this creation of a health, in this invention of a people, the possibility of a life'. (Deleuze 1997: 5)

Under this criterion, we should recall the three characteristics that belong to the concept of 'minor literature': first, a certain situation occurs when a major language is affected with a high coefficient of deterritorialisation; second, everything is political and the 'individual concern' or 'private interest' disappears or serves as a mere environment or background; third, everything takes on a collective value. From these three criteria, we can locate the specific conditions that give rise to what Deleuze calls 'fabulation'. The concept of 'fabulation' first appears in *Bergsonism* (1988a [1966]) and then disappears almost entirely until it is highlighted in the later writings, particularly in *Cinema 2: The Time-Image* (1989a [1985]) and again in the interviews conducted between 1972 and 1990 that appear in the English edition under the title of *Negotiations* (1995), where Deleuze makes the following pronouncement: 'Utopia is not a good concept, but rather a "fabulation" common to people and to art. We should return to the Bergsonian notion of fabulation to provide it with a political sense' (1995: 174). In light of our effort to understand this concept from the perspective of a generalised literary clinic, we might define the concept of fabulation as having two sides: creation and prognosis. Fabulation is the art of invention as well as a conceptual avatar of a 'problem-solving' instinct that remedies an unbearable situation, particularly as Deleuze often says with regard to the situation of the 'people who are missing' (1997: 4). In *Cinema* 2 (1989a), the goal of fabulation is a process by which the writer and the people 'go toward one another' (1989a: 153); in this sense they share a common function. Deleuze writes, 'To write for this people who are missing . . . ("for" means less "in place of" than "for the benefit of")' (Deleuze 1997: 4). That is, they share a process, a vision beyond words, and a language beyond sounds. Consequently, fabulation could be said to resemble the function of dreamwork and, by extension, the moments of selective rearrangement that marks historical discontinuities. What is power unleashed in revolution but the ideal game deployed within what is essentially a fiction; that is, the power to select and re-order the objects, artefacts and meanings that belong to a previous world? Utopia, then, rather than designating a static representation of the ideal place, or *topos*, is rather the power of the 'ideal' itself, which can bifurcate time and create possible worlds. This is why Deleuze calls 'fabulation' a better concept than 'utopia', since it designates a power or a vital process rather than representing a static genre: an ideal form of repetition, rather than the repetition of an ideal form.

Let us examine this process a little more closely. Fabulation entails a 'becoming' that happens from both directions: it is both the becoming-popular of the creator or intellectual, and the becoming-creative of a people. In many ways, this movement echoes the description of the cultural process of nationalist or postcolonialist art which was first examined by Frantz Fanon in *The Wretched of the Earth* (1963), which can be used to illustrate the concept of fabulation. First, in Fanon's own analysis of this process of creation – which must be understood differently than it has been by his critics[5] – the process of fabulation is what determines the people's 'presence' or 'absence' in colonial culture, as well the forms of 'socialisation' and 'identification' that underlie the perspective of the modern 'creator'. Fanon writes:

> At the very moment when the native intellectual is anxiously trying to create a cultural work he [sic] fails to realise that he is utilising techniques and language which are borrowed from the stranger in his country. He contents himself with stamping these instruments with a hallmark he wishes to be national, but which is strangely reminiscent of exoticism. The native intellectual who comes back to his people [as Fanon previously qualifies, 'whatever they were or whatever they are' (1963: 222)] by way of culture behaves in fact like the foreigner. Sometimes he shows no hesitation in using a dialect in order to show his will to be as near as possible to the people; but the ideas he expresses and the preoccupations he is taken up with have no common

yardstick to measure the real situation which the men and women of his country know. (1963: 223)

This non-commensurability which underscores the initial appearance of the colonised intellectual also belongs to a preliminary phase in the creation of national conscience of culture in Fanon's reading. It must be followed by other phases which reconfigure the attributes (or 'property') of culture between its contingent and exterior genres and its interior collective expression of 'inner truth' (1963: 225). (Fanon articulates the latter as culture's muscularity, in relation to political action, and rhythm, in relation to ethnic and regional identities.) In a postcolonial culture's incipient phase, however, these attributes are uncoordinated and this non-coordination can be seen to inform the very appearance of hybridity in the image of the cultural producer and his or her creative work. From the perspective of the postcolonial 'people' – which, at this stage, 'is still missing' – the initial schizoid image of culture, which is also manifested in the appearance of the colonised intellectual, is the result of the mutilating psychological effects and dehumanisation of the colonising situation. This addresses the problem of becoming from the perspective of the native intellectual and writer, where 'going back to your own people means to become "a dirty wog", to go native as much as possible, to become unrecognisable, and to cut off those wings that before you had allowed to grow' (1963: 221). Part native and part stranger, near and distant at the same time, the creator only 'appears' to manifest a characteristic of proximity by imitating native dialects and speech patterns; however, this creator's 'ideas' are at first both unfamiliar and strangely distant from a people's perception of their own image.

Fanon himself accounts for this hybridity by assigning it two causes. First, hybridity results from an appearance of 'culture' itself that is uncoordinated with political and national conscience (that is, a direct consequence of a colonial process which 'alienated' and even 'negated' any relationship between these two sites of mentality). Second, this appearance of the indigenous cultural producer and national conscience of culture precedes the actualisation of political revolt. This peremptory and premature appearance gives the creator and the cultural work the characteristics of 'a-temporality' and 'affective remoteness' in the minds of the people themselves:

The artist who has decided to illustrate the truths of the nation turns paradoxically toward the past and away from actual events. What he [sic] ultimately intends to embrace are in fact the cast-offs of thought, its shells and corpses, a knowledge which has been stabilised once and for all. But the native intellectual who wishes to create the authentic work of art must realise that the truths of a nation are in the first place its realities. He must go on until he has found the seething pot out of which the learning of the future will emerge. (1963: 225)

This diagnostic and therapeutic narrative structures the dialectical stages that the creator (and the 'people') must pass through in order to arrive at the synthesis of collective political and cultural expression. Fanon traces these stages from the alienation of an internalised cultural identification with the coloniser; to the spark of an original memory (which Fanon compares to the return of infantile and maternal associations); to a period of malaise, nausea and convulsion (expressions of 'vomiting out' the poison of the earlier cultural identification); and at last to the final stage of combat in the martyrological expression of a true popular culture, where the writer becomes 'the mouth-piece of a new reality in action' (1963: 223). Thus in Fanon there is a deep analogy between the becoming of a 'people' and the story of the coming-to-conscience of the creator's voice, the manifestation of a culture's essential 'property' and authentic expression of its innermost nature. At the end of the dialectic of culture outlined by Fanon, the 'mental space of a people' that had been distorted by the instruments of colonisation gradually draws close to itself in the image of the creator and remembers in the voice of the poet the sound of its own voice. The final image of proximity occurs when the creator and the people become one mentality in which culture thinks itself in – and as – the substance of its own ideational life. The 'organic co-ordination' between the poet's plastic expression and the people's inner thought achieves such a synthesis of muscularity and natural rhythm that those who before would never have thought to compose a literary work 'find themselves in exceptional circumstances . . . [and] . . . feel the need to speak to their nation, to compose a sentence which expresses the heart of the people, and to become the mouth-piece of a new reality in action' (1963: 223).

We could see here in Fanon's description of the process shared by the marginalised writer and 'a people who are missing', an echo of a lesson from Kafka that Deleuze and Guattari often emphasise in the context of their discussion of fabulation:

The author can be marginalised or separate from his more or less illiterate community as much as you like; this condition puts him all the more in a position to express potential forces and, in his very solitude, to be a true collective agent, a collective leaven, a catalyst. (1986: 221–2)

This is the solitude Kafka addressed in terms of impossibility, where the 'problem of writing' is fundamentally related to a collective impossibility:

the situation of a people who either live in a language not their own, or who no longer even know their own and know poorly the major language they are forced to serve (1986: 19). To use an expression invoked throughout Deleuze's work, and is principally inspired by Blanchot's writings, the writer's solitude cannot be reduced to a normal situation of solitude in the world, to an experience of being-alone and apart from others. Writers do not experience their aloneness from the perspective of this world, from this or that society, or from the presence of others who exist, but rather from the perspective of another possible world or another community that these figures anticipate, even though the conditions for this community are still lacking. Often this desire or longing, which brings about the condition of an exceptional solitude, is expressed in the discourse of love as in the example of Kierkegaard with Regina, or Marcel with Albertine. As Deleuze and Guattari write, 'the highest desire desires both to be alone and to be connected to all the machines of desire' (1986: 71). Thus, in the novels of Proust, Marcel is *haunted* by the fact that no matter how close he comes to Albertine, or no matter how he draws her near him (even to the point of holding her hostage), behind the face of Albertine, there always lies another Albertine, a thousand other Albertines, each breaking upon one another like waves of an infinite ocean. This is the experience of solitude which burns into his mind the image of desire: the impossible and delirious plan of capturing each one, of 'knowing' all the possible Albertines, as the highest goal of Love.

Returning to the case of Kafka, according to Deleuze, the solitude of the writer is related most profoundly to the situation of the people who are missing. This is why the solitude of certain writers is in no way a private affair for Deleuze, and why the concept of 'solitude' must be qualified to evoke the uncanny experience of inhabiting a strange language, a language that is not and may never be one's own, where the very act of speaking brings with it the feeling of self-betrayal, or of 'falsifying oneself', and where the alternative of remaining silent bears the threat of extinction. It is in this sense that the position of the writer is virtual to that of the collective, and, therefore, the so-called 'private' is immediately collective as well, that is, 'less a concern of literary history than of a people' (Kafka 1948: 149). Deleuze writes concerning this situation which was specific to Kafka's predicament, but which can describe the situation of other writers as well (such as Melville or Woolf), that 'the most individual enunciation is a particular case of the collective enunciation' (Deleuze and Guattari 1986: 84). Moreover, 'this is even a definition: a statement is literary when it is "taken up" by a bachelor who precedes the collective conditions of enunciation' (Deleuze and

Guattari 1986: 84). This last definition appears to reclassify the entire sense of the literary as emerging from 'a bachelor-machine', a concept that Deleuze and Guattari derive from Michel Carrouges and apply to Kafka, but also to other writers as well. The condition of the 'bachelor-desire', however, must be redefined, outside its gender determination, to describe or refer to a situation in which one prefers the state of being alone (exceptional, singular, anonymous) than to 'take on' the identity of a subject one is assigned by the majority. The situation of preferring to remain a bachelor therefore finds affinities in the situation of the Jew in eighteenth-century Europe, of a woman in nineteenth- and twentieth-century societies, or in the situation faced by minorities in the United States and other first-world countries today. This is why they write that a literary 'machine is all the more social and collective insofar as it is solitary, a bachelor, and that, tracing the line of escape [from one of these situations, for example] is equivalent itself to a community whose conditions haven't yet been established' (1986: 71).

> Fourth Criterion: 'Finally, literature opens up a kind of foreign language within language' (Deleuze 1997: 5).

This final criterion has three aspects: first, through syntax, the destruction of the maternal language; second, through delirium, the invention of a new language that carries the first outside its usual furrows (*habitus*), which, in turn, entails a secondary destruction: the shattering of the clichés of visibilities and statements that although not completely reducible to language, are nevertheless inseparable from it, being the 'ideas' and 'habits' that determine the forms of seeing and saying. In the third aspect, as a result of the destruction of the maternal language and of the clichéd statements and stock visibilities (which are like its ghosts), the literary process bears language to its limit, turning it towards its own 'outside', which Deleuze describes as its inverse or reverse side made up of visions and auditions, which 'are not outside language, but the outside of language' (1997: 5). As I introduced above, the final aim of these three aspects, according to Deleuze, is the concept of literature defined as 'the passage of life within language that constitutes ideas' (1997: 5).

Taking up the first aspect, through the destruction of the maternal language, literature functions as what Deleuze and Guattari call 'a war machine'. 'The only way to defend language is to attack it' (Deleuze 1997: 4). This is the principle behind many works of modern literature and its axiomatic articulates the exact sense of a process that aims beyond the limit of language. As noted above, however, this limit beyond which the outside of language appears is not outside language per se, but rather appears in its points of rupture, in the gaps, or tears, in the interstices between words, or between one word and the next. The examples of writers who define their relationship to language under the heading of this principle are too numerous to recount, although I will provide a few significant examples for the purposes of illustration. First, we might point to the post-holocaust, German-language poet Paul Celan, whose poetry is precisely the systematic destruction of the language of 'the Masters' (that is, the language of Goethe and Rilke). The objective of the poem itself is to express a word that no German mouth can speak (the deterritorialisation of language from the teeth and the lips), the end being nothing less than a materialisation of the mother's corpse which is gradually interred within the German language and given a specific place of mourning. (Thus, the image of the mother is a shadow of the lost object by which Celan draws the entire German language into a process of mourning.) This is Celan's process: the 'passage' of the mother's death into the German language; in other words, the passage of the living German language into an encounter with his mother's death and, by extension, with the murder of his maternal race. Moreover, the use of colour in Celan's poetry gives us a vivid illustration of the Deleuzian and Proustian notion of vision. The poet is a true colourist who causes colours to appear as nearly hallucinatory visions in language; however, in Celan's poems, the descriptive and neutral function of colour is poetically transformed into the attributes of his mother's body – her hair, her skin, her eyes, the green of her decaying corpse. It is as if the enunciation of each colour will henceforth bear a reference to his mother's body, and in this manner the German language is modified to incorporate this cryptic reference into its poetic and descriptive functions. Thus, the green is the colour of summer grass, but it is also the colour of my mother's decaying shadow; blue is the colour of the sky, but it is also the colour of the sky the day it wore my mother's hair; red is the colour of the tulip, but it is also the colour of the 'silent one' who comes that day 'to behead the tulips' (Celan 1972: 53). Finally, gold is the lovely hair of Marguerite (in the vision of Goethe), but it is also the colour of 'my mother's star', the star that marked her for extinction.

Kafka also approaches the German language with the statement of his swimming champion, 'I speak the same language as you, but don't understand a single word you're saying' (Deleuze 1997: 5), and at the same time draws on the resources of the all too vernacular and deterritorialised Czech-German and the all too symbolic and allegorical Yiddish ('a language of the heart' (Kafka 1948: 151)) in order to purify the German language and the syntax of Goethe from its own cultural signification. In other words, as Deleuze often recounts, Kafka 'creates a kind of foreign language within language' (1997: 5). Although it may bear an uncanny and perfect resemblance to the major language, this new language no longer bears the significance for German culture and emerges as a kind of war machine within its majoritarian sense. As Deleuze and Guattari write, by a kind of schizo-politeness hidden beneath an almost too-perfect German syntax, 'he will make the German take flight on a line of escape . . . he will tear out from the Prague German all the qualities of underdevelopment it has tried to hide; he will make it cry with an extremely sober and rigorous cry . . . to bring language slowly and progressively to the desert . . . to give syntax to the cry' (1986: 26). This marks the importance of animals in Kafka's shorter works – the musical dogs that appear in 'Investigations of a Dog', the singing mouse-folk in 'Josephine, the Mouse-Singer', the song of the Ape in 'Report to the Academy', the low cry of the Jackals in 'The Jackals and Arabs' – but also the musical auditions of the other fabulous creatures that Kafka creates, such as Odradek in 'Cares of a Family Man', whose laughter bears the airy sound of dried leaves, or the silence of the Sirens in the tale of the same name. In all these cases, we have examples of pure sonorous auditions that are introduced into the German language. It is through the deterritorialisation of the human that the German language passes through a becoming-animal, that animals introduce the notes of a strange music that has never been heard before in German literature, that Kafka introduces new possibilities into the German tongue, 'a music made up of deterritorialised sounds' (Deleuze and Guattari 1986: 26). In themselves, as pure sonorous material, these sounds may have already been possible: the melody of a dog's howl, the shrill silence of a mouse, the low moan of the jackal. However, in the form they take in Kafka's language – for example, the first song that the Ape learns from a drunken sailor, which becomes his primitive language lesson – an animal's song becomes an 'idea' in its passage through language, an 'audition' of a cry of humiliation and oppression that Kafka first introduces as such into the German ear. It is in this manner that he both escapes the oppressive, classical harmonies of the German language and, at the same time, institutes a pedagogy of syntax in which he teaches the German language to cry.

Taking up the second aspect, the invention of 'a delirium, which forces it out of its usual furrows' (Deleuze 1997: 5), we should recall that one of the principle axioms of *Anti-Oedipus* is that desire always directly invests or is immanent to the social field of production, in order to apply this axiom to 'the desire to write'. The desire to write, at one level, is a delirium that is immediately social. How could we otherwise explain the institution of criticism that has built up around the work in societies based upon writing if not as an effort to submit this delirium to the identifiable categories of a 'proper delirium' that functions their ground. At the same time, if we were to attempt to grasp 'the desire to write' from its immanent perspective within society, we would need to conceive of the function of writing in all its occasions: from the legal or juridical and the legislative, to the hermeneutic and confessional modes of writing. Perhaps, then, the figure of the writer emerges to 'represent' this delirium and, thereby, to isolate the 'problem of writing' to rare and exceptional cases we call 'writers', almost in the same manner that Derrida had illustrated around the function of the *pharmakon*. It is as if society, which itself is constructed by and from writing, must also produce a being who embodies writing in order to protect itself from the madness that belongs to its own order of possibility. Is there any wonder then that the writer has so often been defined by the attributes of illness or bad health? Again, this may explain Deleuze and Guattari's selection of the series of problematic writers to combat this definition. To close the work off by applying these symptoms to the ethical or psychological character of an author, and thereby to 'psychologise' or to 'impeach' the writer, is to alienate the critical function of these writers: that is, the 'lens' they offer to perceive what otherwise remains obscure and misapprehended by its individuated or psychological forms. Recalling again the second criterion, the principle distinction is that the incredible 'openness' these symptoms receive in the writing must be set against the usual secret forms that determine the expression of unconscious fantasies, or individual symptoms.

Here, the Borgesian formula of 'Fang has a secret', often recounted by Deleuze from *Difference and Repetition* on, can be used paradigmatically of this moment of turning, or decision, in which nothing is guaranteed (1994: 116). That is, 'Fang has a secret' and 'there is a stranger at the door'. In order to illustrate the paradigmatic value of this formula, we could substitute for the nameless identity of the stranger the forces signalled by the emergence of a life based on silicon, the formation of the capitalist in the final stages of planetary deployment, the deterritorialisation and crisis of disciplinary regimes and their reterritorialisation by mechanisms of the 'control society', the emergence of racialised identities and new fascisms of the flesh. In turn, each of these 'strangers' marks turning points for the human form, as well as a fullness of time, a time pregnant with possibility, the moment of a 'dice-throw'. (These are the 'sombre precursors' spoken of in *Difference and Repetition* (1994: 145).) That is, each arrangement presents us with diverse possibilities, with possible futures that bifurcate, tracing the curve of the present that goes towards the future announced by the new assemblage of Life that appears on the horizon. Borges, for example, discovered a possible means of escaping a colonising relationship with the past through a comic procedure of overturning the European library and parodying the God of European history in its colonial situation. Kafka discovered through the fictional personage of 'K' a manner to research the diabolical assemblage of law and the institution of the state-form. Burroughs diagnosed the secret filiation of the alien, the homosexual, and the junkie as victims of the paranoia unleashed by the 'bio-power' of the modern state that defines its internal enemies in terms of a virus. And there are countless more examples of these 'sombre precursors' in Deleuze's work (Buchner's Lenz, Nietzsche's Zarathustra, Melville's Ahab or Benito Cereno, Duras and Resnais's Hiroshima).[6]

In *Anti-Oedipus*, it is with the discovery of the production proper to the schizophrenic that Deleuze and Guattari find a degree-zero of the delirium that the schizophrenic shares with society: 'he hallucinates and raves universal history, and proliferates the races' (1983: 85). Thus, the schizo refers to the function of a delirium as the principle of 'desiring-production' that society itself uses to 'distribute races, cultures, and gods' – in short, to 'make itself obeyed' – on the body without organs, that is, the full body of the earth (1983: 84). In Deleuze and Guattari's use of the concept of delirium we might detect a certain cosmological theory of madness (a thesis of 'madness as work' or a style of *'grand politique'* which they share in some ways with Blanchot and Foucault), which was first presented by Freud in his famous commentary on Daniel Schreber, who created a universe with his delirium and then proceeded to populate it with gods, demi-gods (or demons), as well as with new races and sexes. These were the personages of Schreber's fabulous delirium; however, the structure of this delirium also describes the origin of the prohibitive mechanisms that society itself produces. In other words, the language of madness simply locates in the 'story-telling function' of figures like Schreber the very same mechanisms that society itself uses to engender a world populated with gods, cultures, races and peoples. Given the conservative function of this 'myth-making' faculty, we might ask how, according to the major thesis of *Anti-Oedipus*, the delirium proper to schizophrenic production and social production can lead to the potential of fabulation as a relay to revolutionary force. This is the point around which many protests against Deleuze-Guattari's use of the schizo fall into error by taking the clinical entity of the schizophrenic as a kind of model creator, a turn to romanticism. However, the equation of the fabulation of the clinical schizophrenic with social fabulation has the subtle effect of rendering social production as the truth of the clinical equation, since the clinical personage of the schizophrenic constitutes that point where desiring-production is blocked, falls into an impasse, becomes reactive or sick. If the clinical entity of the schizophrenic is identical with society, then we find the true subject of schizoanalysis, which is social production. Therefore, within the literary process delirium undergoes a positive 'transvaluation' (Nietzsche) which differentiates it from its repressive or conservative functions in madness and society. That is, if the world itself 'is the set of symptoms whose illness merges with man [sic]', it is by means of this process that 'literature is a health' (Deleuze 1997: iv).

Finally, concerning the third aspect of these criteria, Deleuze writes, 'the final aim of literature . . . is the passage of life within language that constitutes ideas' (1997: 5; my emphasis). In *Foucault*, Deleuze situates this aspect that belongs to modern literature in what is essentially a psychology of the fold, whereby language is disarticulated from the 'grand unities of discourse' which structure the possibilities of enunciation (1988b: 14–15). In *Essays Critical and Clinical*, Deleuze recalls the above formulation when he describes the event of literature as, 'in effect, when another language is created within language, it is a language in its entirety that tends toward an "a-syntactic", "a-grammatical" limit, or that communicates with its own outside' (1997: iv). Deleuze locates this aspect of modern literary practices in an analysis that owes much to Foucault's stubborn privileging of the question of literature in a time when it was being subordinated to the forces of the negative (work, communication, information, identity), particularly its possibilities of resistance which are potential in the recent and overt tendency of modern writers to uncover a strange language within language. Accordingly, modern literature creates within language a non-linguistic stammering that inclines towards "a-typical expression" and "a-grammatical effects" (for example, Berryman, Celan, Queneau, cummings, Mallarmé).

As a result of this process, ideas emerge from the process that Deleuze calls visions and auditions; these are the forms of seeing and hearing that are specific to the literary process in its passage within Language. As Deleuze further describes, however, these ideas appear only when the literary process achieves its aim and breaks through the limit of language, a limit that is not outside language, but rather the outside of language which language alone makes possible. 'These visions are not fantasies, but veritable Ideas that the writer sees or hears in the interstices of language, in its intervals' (Deleuze 1997: 5). Although they bear a certain hallucinatory quality specific to the literary effect (for example, Proust's *'madeleine'*, Gombrowizc's 'hanged-sparrow', Melville's 'white whale',

Silko's 'spider-web'), they cannot be reduced to the psychological fantasies of the author nor to 'ideologemes' of a collective unconscious, since they take place, as Kafka said, 'in the full light of day' and not 'down below in the cellar of structure' (1948: 197). Consequently, it is to break through words or between words that the implicit aim of the literary process can be located; this desire on the part of the writer is accompanied by a certain destruction of the stock forms of visibilities and statements, of linguistic and syntactical habits, clichés of the quotidian and common utterances, stock and made-to-order descriptions and categorical prescriptions that all too often imprison what is seen and heard in a fog of nothingness.

> This labour of the artist, this struggle to discern beneath matter, beneath experience, beneath words, something that is different from them, is a process exactly the reverse of that which, in our everyday lives in which we live avoiding our own gaze, is at every moment satisfied by vanity and passion, intellect and habit, extinguishing our true impressions that are entirely concealed from us, buried underneath a junk heap of verbal concepts and practical goals that we falsely call 'life'. (Proust, *Time Regained* 1993b: 299–300)

In a certain sense, then, we might say that modern literature creates the conditions for 'good habits' of language use. 'What are we but habits of saying "I"?' Deleuze first proposes this question in his early study of Hume (1991: x). The question of language that both philosophy and literature expound upon in different manners, therefore, is one of developing and promoting 'good habits' of language usage and diagnosing 'bad or destructive' habits. Philosophy has always concerned itself with the 'uses and abuses' of language for the purpose of living (and dying) well; however, this image of good sense is not an object of logic, but of ethics or even etiquette. Nietzsche understood this as the essence of logic, as well as an image of philosophy as 'the transvaluation of values', which, first of all, include linguistic values, or 'signs', whose proper sense can only be the object of a genealogical study, such as Foucault later described in his essay 'Nietzsche, Genealogy, History' (1977). Consequently, we find in Foucault's work an original relationship of language to the 'body' (the materiality of the self), a relationship which is given a historical and diagnostic expression. Habits (*habitus*), understood as the modern form of repetition, stand for those institutions of the statements that interpellate us and which define us by determining the possible attributes that can belong to the 'I'.[7] As a certain species of repetition, moreover, habits achieve a degree zero of memory (where the particular equals the universal), producing the condition in which 'what we do not remember, we repeat' (Deleuze 1994: 19). Thus, certain uses of language can be defined as the cause of our illness, since they lead to a botched form of life, self, individuality, power and so on. Deleuze writes:

> These thousands of habits of which we are composed – these contractions, contemplations, pretensions, presumptions, satisfactions, fatigues; these variable presents – thus form the basis of the domain of the passive syntheses. (1994: 78)

We must recognise the effects of these 'habits' upon the process of thinking as well, particularly in the sense that the 'interiority of thought' (the grand circuit of associations, signs, concepts, memory and feeling) is 'limited' (contracted or disciplined) by the external forms of discourse and language. It is not a question of thought without language, but rather of thinking, which in its most extended circuit enters into combinations with the elements of seeing and speaking that are 'exterior' to a language defined by formed statements and the visibility of objects. Consequently, this problematic is a part of the Deleuzian critique of repetition since our repetitions, or habits of language, use, determine the unconscious of our representations.

On the other hand, certain modern literary practices, rather than being founded by their representational function, can be understood as a profound experimentation that reveals the positivity and the limits of our language-habits (our addiction to saying 'I'). What Deleuze refers to as 'the curve of the sentence' is a profound experimentation that reveals the limits of certain expressions, negates their abstractness for a 'new' positivity of language. Deleuze writes as early as *Difference and Repetition* that the event of positivity occurs necessarily in the advent of the 'new' that introduces variables into a previous repetition. Statements such as Kafka's 'I am a bug' or Fitzgerald's 'I am a giraffe' lead to the discovery of the non-sense that belongs to the statement 'I am a man' (Deleuze and Guattari 1987: 377). Consequently, the first two statements repeat the last one and at the same time introduce a new predicate, causing the statement 'I am a man' to be lacking definition and, in a certain sense, in need of rectification. In other words, the statement 'I am a man' leads to nothing and can be criticised as a bad use of definition. It defines no-one and, thus, makes the 'abstract' predicate of man possible as a real relationship. Rather than representing, Kafka's proposition 'selects' and corrects the imperfections of the former definition. It reveals the limits of the statement as well as the visibility of the predicate. It introduces new variables into old habits of being, new possibilities, clearer and more definite articulations, new possibilities for the passage of a life into language.

The Question: 'What is Minor Literature Today'?

In conclusion, we should situate the question of literature as one of the principle themes of the two volumes of *Capitalism and Schizophrenia*. In order to do so, it would be necessary to pay more specific attention to the status of the literary in the work of Deleuze and Guattari. When and in what manner is it evoked? For example, what is being addressed in the cries of poor A.A., the stroll of Lenz, the sucking-stones of Molloy, Kleist's Marionettes or Michael-Kolhaus on his horse. In each case, literary expression is allied to a 'war machine', which means it draws its force directly from 'the outside'. Deleuze and Guattari constantly pit this condition of literary enunciation against any representation that subjugates it to a form of inferiority (whether that of the subject-author, the private individual, a culture, or even of a race). It is not by accident that the lines of Rimbaud are always recited like the lyrics of a favourite song: 'I have always been of an inferior race . . . I am of an inferior race for all eternity . . . I am a beast, a nigger' (Deleuze and Guattari 1987: 379). The relationship of the concept of literature to a war machine is essential, and we should note that many of the examples of the war machine are drawn from writers (Artaud, Büchner, Kafka, and Kleist), as well as philosopher-artists such as Nietzsche and Kierkegaard. In *A Thousand Plateaus*, the conflict between the literary war machine and the critic as 'man of the state' is first attested to by the confrontation between Artaud and Jacques Rivière. Although not a man of the state, Rivière according to Deleuze was not the first or last critic to mistake himself for 'a prince in the republic of letters'. He found Artaud incomprehensible and poorly organised and he had no hesitation in giving his advice to '*pauvre A.A.*': 'Work! Work! If you revise, then soon you will arrive at a method (*Cogitatio Universalis*) to express your thoughts more directly!' (1987: 377). Next, the literary war machine is attested to by Kleist's conflict with Goethe, 'of all literary figures a veritable man of the state' (1987: 378). In the case of the figures like Nietzsche and Kierkegaard, however, there is the conflict between the 'public professor' and the 'private thinker', although Deleuze qualifies the latter notion in order to argue that, in fact, the 'private thinker' may not be a good term, since it too closely follows the reductive notion of the 'private individual', and too simple a form of inferiority where the so-called spontaneity of thought is said to occur. Instead, Deleuze and Guattari argue that the 'solitude' one approaches in the writings of Nietzsche, or in Kafka, is a solitude that is extremely 'populated' (1987: 467).

The concept of literature we have been discussing all along fundamentally invokes a situation of language where the collective subject of enunciation (different from the official enunciation a 'people', or of a 'national consciousness') exists only in a latent or virtual state that cannot be located in the civil and juridical language of statutes and laws, the 'paper language' of bureaucracy, or the technocratic and vehicular language of administrators, entrepreneurs and capitalists. It would not be an exaggeration to assert that most technical and administrative language, even in the first world, bears a historical relationship to the early techniques invented by colonial administrations. It is a language composed purely of 'order-words' (*les mots d'ordre*), a language of command in which the law finds its purest expression, just as Sade discovered the essence of Enlightenment reason, not by accident, in the categorical imperatives of pornographic speech: 'Do this!' 'Submit!' 'Obey!' Concerning the status of this language, as Fanon asserts, we have every reason to believe the coloniser when he says, 'the colonised, I know them!' since he (the coloniser) has created the categories that were installed at the deepest point of their interiority by the colonising process, categories which continue to legislate their own knowledge of themselves as 'a subjected people'. Moreover, Fanon writes, 'colonialism is not satisfied merely with holding a people in its grip and emptying the native's brain of all form and content. By a kind of perverted logic, it turns out to be the past of the oppressed people, and distorts, disfigures, and destroys it' (1963: 210). Deleuze and Guattari refer to this as the condition by which a 'people as Subject' falls to the condition of a 'people-subjected' (1987: 164). As we have witnessed many times, the question of 'identity' is always a dizzying and even treacherous problem from the position of the colonised, leading often to the very 'impasse' from which this category was created, underscoring an 'intolerable situation', since the identity they assume in speaking, in saying 'I (the colonised)', has been essentially fabulated and only serves to subject them further. This intolerable condition of enunciation is a condition that is specific to the concept of 'minor literature'. At the same time, we must take inventory of the fact that the history of literature in the west is full of examples of this impossible situation: Hippolytus and Phaedra, Antigone; Kafka's 'metamorphosis', there is Gregor who cannot speak, but rather emits a shrill note that can barely be discerned; but also in Melville, we have the character of Babo in 'Benito Cereno' who refuses to speak 'as the accused' and chooses to remain silent (therefore, in full possession of his speech), but also in the figure of Bartleby with his '*I would prefer not to*'.

Why does this situation appear as a fundamental problematic, if not to signal something genetic to the literary enunciation: the problem and the power of 'falsehood', of the fictional status of the enunciation that essentially haunts the situation of writing? Taking up the notion of the 'public sphere', such a concept already refers to the particularly 'striated openness' (*Offendlichkeit*) which is established when the dominant institutions of language and culture reflect the pre-conscious interests of the nation-state or class. In such conditions, the literary machine itself has already been 'reterritorialised' so that it now functions to reflect the genius of the national character or the spirit of Culture. Thus, we might refer to this moment as one that has prepared the way for the strictly ideological representation of literature in the academy today, which is reduced to a sub-compartment of the 'political unconscious' or to a poetics of the State-form. This representation of literature is necessarily one-dimensional. It must sacrifice the variable relationships that originally belonged to the production of the art-work, and above all, it must repress the whole question of art (often by reducing it to the category of aesthetics, which can, in turn, be prosecuted for its falsifying production). When a literary machine is captured by the State-form and provided an end, what is that end except a war directed against 'the people' in the form of national memory and an official story-telling function? Recalling the problems of criticism raised in the beginning of this discussion, the very taxonomy and organisation of literature soon repeats the rank-and-file order of major and minor tastes, as well as the striated organisation of the story-telling function into a form of Canon. On the contrary, the writer does not often seek to represent the truth since 'truth' is often the category invented by the coloniser and the oppressor. Rather, citing another anecdotal phrase that Deleuze often employs, the writer seeks to raise the false to a higher power, that is, beyond the moral-juridical opposition of true-false that is maintained by the model of truth (1989b: 133–5). To raise the false to a higher power is to discover the principle of fabulation that governs even truthful representation, to turn this principle into a critical force which addresses the intolerable situation of 'a people who are missing'. Accordingly, literature bears within its fragmented body – scattered, torn to pieces, or 'dispersed on the four winds' – the seeds of a people to come. These seeds are the germs of a 'collective assemblage of enunciation', which, as Deleuze often declares, are real without necessarily being actual, and ideal without necessarily being abstract.

Today, Deleuze and Guattari situate the conditions for the emergence of minor literature in a world where the forms of collective enunciation and national consciousness are breaking down on several fronts, as a result of the immigration patterns and displacement of national labour forces, and the decline of the 'State-form' itself.

> How many people today live in a language that is not their own? Or no longer, not yet, even know their own and know poorly the major language that they are forced to serve? This is a problem of immigrants, and especially of their children, the problem of minorities, the problem of minor literature, but also a problem for all of us: how to tear a minor literature away from its own language, allowing it to challenge the language and making it follow a sober revolutionary path? How to become a nomad and an immigrant and a gypsy in relation to one's own language? (1986: 19)

In order to determine the status of the 'literary', the primary emphasis must fall upon the absence of a particular collective enunciation from official and public institutions of language and national culture. In the absence of a distinct majoritarian formation of the 'public sphere', which gives enunciation weight and reference – which 'orders reality', in so many words – a body of literature assumes the shadowy and non-essential region of a collective enunciation, a 'minor public' whose existence is always haunted by the 'imaginary' (or fabulous) nature of its *agora* (its open space). But, as Deleuze and Guattari write,

> The literary machine thus becomes the relay for a revolutionary machine-to-come, not at all for ideological reasons but because the literary machine alone is determined to fill the conditions of collective enunciation that is lacking elsewhere in the milieu: literature is the people's concern. (1986: 17–18)

Finally, in order to strip this last statement of any romanticism in association with the nationalist or ethnic entity of a people invented during the nineteenth century, I should stress that without specific attention to the position of enunciation that is evoked here, we lose both the status of what Deleuze and Guattari call the 'literary machine' and the specific relationship that is being drawn up between a collective enunciation and the concept of minor literature. Here, the status of a minor literature is the problem of its multiple forms and locations, since it does not have an institution that organises and disciplines its forms. This does not mean it is formless, but rather is an organisation of collective enunciation which is dispersed across several registers of the major language it inhabits (legends, private letters, songs, heated conversations, stories, fables and so on) and has the character of dream-language in the various operations it performs upon the form of visibilities and on the organisation of statements. Finally, only when these criteria of minor literature are fulfilled can we begin to understand the statement that 'literature is a concern of the people', perhaps even a vital concern of public health – a concern that may demand both a clinical and a critical approach to the uses (and the abuses) of the question of literature for life.

Notes

1. The function of this vitalist logic (or 'radical empiricism') echoes the fabulous 'problem-solving' instinct of Life that is first presented in Bergsonism. See 'Élan Vital as a Movement of Differentiation', *Bergsonism* (1988a: 91–113).
2. At times the reader may notice a certain Nietzschean tone – or as Deleuze himself describes it, 'becoming a bit of a guerrilla' (1993: 158) – in my representation of the current critical approach to the question of literature. This is not accidental. In my view, there is a weakness inherent in those commentaries today which appropriate Deleuze's writings without also admitting what is potentially dangerous in it as well. It is to raise the possibility of something dangerous or inherently risky that I have alluded to Nietzsche's essay 'The Uses and Abuses of History for Life', which itself concerns a similar set of problems and issues that surrounded the dominant epistemological orientation of his age. Although my implicit aim is to cause the current critical image of literature to 'explode', this objective is justified by the belief that only what is worthy of being valued can be submitted to destruction with the faith that this 'will promote rather than injure the general propriety' of its uses for life (Nietzsche 1997: 86).
3. See 'Percept, Affect, Concept' (Deleuze and Guattari 1994: 163–200).
4. See 'Treatise on Nomadology – The War Machine' (1987: 351–423). For example, in *Structuralism in Literature: An Introduction* (1974), Scholes writes: 'By moving from the study of language to the study of literature, and seeking to define the principles of structuration that operate not only through individual works but the relationships between works over the whole field of literature, structuralism has tried – and is trying – to establish for literary studies a basis that is as scientific as possible' (Scholes 1974: 10).
5. I am thinking, in particular, of the criticism by Henry Louis Gates, Jr. See his essay 'Critical Fanonism' (1991), *Critical Inquiry*, vol. 17, pp. 457–70.
6. For a fuller discussion of this aspect, see my 'Deleuzian Critique of Pure Fiction' (1997), *Sub-Stance* 84, vol. 26, no. 3, pp. 128–52.
7. In *Difference and Repetition* Deleuze revises his earlier notion of 'habit' from Hume following, on the one hand, the 'molecular sociology' of Gabriel Tarde and, on the other, the phenomenological understanding of habits as the 'passive syntheses' which are the 'larval subjects that comprise the system of the self' (1994: 78–9). Deleuze's use of this term, therefore, has no relation to the sense it receives in Bourdieu's work. See also Ian Buchanan (1997), 'Deleuze and Cultural Studies', *South Atlantic Quarterly*, vol. 96, no. 3, p. 487.

Bibliography

Benjamin, Walter (1968), *Illuminations*, New York: Schocken Books.
Buchanan, Ian (1997), 'Deleuze and Cultural Studies', *The South Atlantic Quarterly*, vol. 96, no. 3, pp. 483–97.

Celan, Paul (1972), *Poems of Paul Celan*, trans. Michael Hamburger, New York: Persea Books.

Deleuze, Gilles (1988a [1966]), *Bergsonism*, trans. Hugh Tomlinson and Barbara Habberjam, New York: Zone Books.

Deleuze, Gilles (1988b [1986]), *Foucault*, trans. Sean Hand, Minneapolis: University of Minnesota Press.

Deleuze, Gilles (1989a [1985]), *Cinema 2: The Time-Image*, trans. Hugh Tomlinson and Robert Galeta, Minneapolis: University of Minnesota Press.

Deleuze, Gilles (1989b [1967]), *Masochism: An Introduction to Coldness and Cruelty*, trans. Jean McNeil, New York: Zone Books.

Deleuze, Gilles (1990 [1969]), *The Logic of Sense*, trans. Constantin Boundas, Charles Stivale and Mark Lester, New York: Columbia University Press.

Deleuze, Gilles (1991 [1953]), *Empiricism and Subjectivity: An Essay on Hume's Theory of Human Nature*, trans. Constantin V. Boundas, New York: Columbia University Press.

Deleuze, Gilles (1993 [1987]), *The Fold: Leibniz and the Baroque*, trans. Tom Conley, Minneapolis: University of Minnesota Press.

Deleuze, Gilles (1994 [1968]), *Difference and Repetition*, trans. Paul Patton, New York: Columbia University Press.

Deleuze, Gilles (1995 [1992]), *Negotiations*, trans. Martin Joughin, New York: Columbia University Press.

Deleuze, Gilles (1997 [1994]), *Essays Critical and Clinical*, trans. Daniel W. Smith and Michael Greco, Minneapolis: University of Minnesota Press.

Deleuze, Gilles and Guattari, Félix (1983 [1972]), *Anti-Oedipus: Capitalism and Schizophrenia*, trans. Robert Hurley, Mark Seem, and Helen R. Lane, Minneapolis: University of Minnesota Press.

Deleuze, Gilles and Guattari, Félix (1986 [1975]), *Kafka: Toward a Minor Literature*, trans. Dana Polan, Minneapolis: University of Minnesota Press.

Deleuze, Gilles and Guattari, Félix (1987 [1980]), *A Thousand Plateaus: Capitalism and Schizophrenia*, trans. Brian Massumi, Minneapolis: University of Minnesota Press.

Deleuze, Gilles and Guattari, Félix (1994 [1992]), *What is Philosophy?*, trans. Hugh Tomlinson and Graham Burchell, New York: Columbia University Press.

Deleuze, Gilles and Parnet, Claire (1987 [1977]), *Dialogues*, trans. Hugh Tomlison and Barbara Habberjam, New York: Columbia University Press.

Fanon, Frantz (1963), *The Wretched of the Earth*, trans. Constance Farrington, New York: Grove Press.

Foucault, Michel (1977), *Language, Counter-Memory, Practice: Selected Essays and Interviews*, trans. Donald Bouchard and Sherry Simon, Ithaca: Cornell University Press.

Freud, Sigmund (1963), 'Creative Writers and Day-Dreaming', *The Standard Edition*, vol. 9, (ed. Ernst Jones), New York: Grove Press, pp. 143–53.

Godzich, Wlad (1994), *The Culture of Literacy*, Cambridge: Harvard University Press.

Kafka, Franz (1948), *Diaries*, ed. Max Brod, New York: Shocken Books.

Lambert, Gregg (1997), 'The Deleuzian Critique of Pure Fiction', *Sub-Stance*, vol. 26, no. 3, pp. 128–52.

Le Clezio, J.-M. G. (1971), *Haï*, Paris: Flammarion.

Gates, Henry Louis Jr (1991), 'Critical Fanonism', *Critical Inquiry*, vol. 17, pp. 457–70.

Nietzsche, Fredrick (1997), 'On the Advantages and Disadvantages of History for Life', *Untimely Meditations*, trans. R. J. Hollingdale, Cambridge: Cambridge University Press, pp. 57–124.

Proust, Marcel (1993a), *In Search of Lost Time, Volume V: The Captive and the Fugitive*, trans. C. K. Scott Moncrieff and Terrance Kilmartin, revised by D. J. Enright, New York: The Modern Library.

Proust, Marcel (1993b), *In Search of Lost Time, Volume VI: Time Regained*, trans. Andreas Mayor and Terrance Kilmartin, New York: The Modern Library.

Scholes Robert (1974), *Structuralism in Literature: An Introduction*, New Haven: Yale University Press.

Chapter 7

'A Question of an Axiomatic of Desires': The Deleuzian Imagination of Geoliterature

Kenneth Surin

It is a question of a more luminous life which, on the edge of independence and with aid of its appeal, will be made imminent, dazzling us by the rapidity of its comprehension of things and of beings. It is a question of an axiomatic of desires, of being luxuriously swathed in the drizzle of their satisfactions.

Tristan Tzara, Noontimes Gained

She was off like a bird, bullet, or arrow, impelled by what desire, shot by whom, at what directed, who could say? What? What?

Virginia Woolf, To the Lighthouse

Gilles Deleuze, in his interview-essay translated as 'On the Superiority of Anglo-American Literature' (Deleuze 1987), advances a number of interesting and perhaps remarkable propositions contrasting French and 'Anglo-American' literature, perhaps none more intriguing than the claim that in the end the superiority of the latter over the former arises from Anglo-American literature's elective affinity with three philosophical movements: British empiricism, Spinozism and Stoicism.[1] In this essay I shall outline the main features of this interview-essay, and then focus on the constitutive affinity that Deleuze takes to exist between Anglo-American literature and the three philosophical movements, an affinity that (for Deleuze) exists because the exemplary representatives of Anglo-American literature are possessed by the insight, which is all the more effective for not being explicitly entertained or promulgated, that the book is an assemblage, and that one is a writer precisely because one invents assemblages (of a particular and quite specific kind).[2]

The Deleuzian Anglo-American 'canon' includes such seemingly diverse figures as Charlotte and Emily Brontë, Hardy, Melville, Stevenson, Whitman, Lewis Carroll, Henry James, Joyce, Virginia Woolf, Faulkner,

Thomas Wolfe, D. H. Lawrence, T. E. Lawrence, Malcolm Lowry, Lovecraft, Fitzgerald, Henry Miller, Beckett, Wilfred Thesiger, Edmund Carpenter, Arthur Miller, Burroughs and Kerouac. At the same time, Deleuze makes it clear that the propensity to use the book in order to invent assemblages is not confined to those who happen to write in English (albeit in certain ways and in certain registers). A cursory look at his texts will reveal: (1) that the Bible, 'the first novel', is regarded by Deleuze as something of a prototypical 'Anglo-American' work; and (2) that other non-anglophone writers, including several who happen to be French, also partake of this defining propensity, so that Lautréamont, Hölderlin, Ghérasim Luca, Artaud, Genet, François Villon, Gombrowicz and Tournier all feature in what can be described as an 'honorary' Anglo-American canon.[3] So how is the distinction between these two kinds of literatures to be marked?

The aim, never declared as such, is obviously to overturn the tradition associated with Saint-Beuve, Taine and Lanson, with its gridded systems of literary classification (a kind of *anatomie comparée* in Saint-Beuve's parlance, or 'tree-system' in Deleuze and Guattari's) intended to identify the 'spirit' of a pedagogically-useful national literary tradition. Deleuze's efforts to motivate an Anglo-American literature can thus be seen as something of a *Contre Saint-Beuve Mark II*; that is, as an attempt to bypass a monumentalised 'French literature' confected by Saint-Beuve and his successors, by adverting to an assortment of American and English novelists and poets (as well as a few German and renegade French writers) who are taken by Deleuze to constitute a counter-tradition whose emblematic form is 'the rhizome' and not 'the tree-image' or 'tree-system'. We don't need to negotiate this 'French literature', Deleuze seems to be saying, because we can have Hardy, Lawrence, Virginia Woolf and so on, in the same way in which, philosophically, he has constructed an assemblage consisting of the Stoics, Scotus, Spinoza, Hume, Nietzsche and Bergson to show that there is an alternative to the French tradition ruled by the impression that everything philosophically worthwhile somehow has to involve the *cogito* and that 'philosophically' everything has to go through Hegel and thus to involve dialectics.[4] The differences between Anglo-American and French literature as these are characterised by Deleuze can be presented schematically in the terms set out in Table 7.1.[5]

Obviously, and this reiterates the point made in the previous paragraph, the differences between 'French' and 'Anglo-American' literature are somewhat stylised on this rendering, since, given Deleuze's criteria, Trollope or Walter Scott clearly have more in common with Zola or

Table 7.1 Differences between Anglo-American and French literature, as perceived by Deleuze

'French Literature'	'Anglo-American Literature'
'poverty of the imaginary and the symbolic, the real always being put off until tomorrow'	line of flight
kings: land, inheritance, marriages, lawsuits, ruses, cheating	kings: movements of deterritorialisation, wanderings, renunciations, betrayals, passing by at breakneck speed
invents the bourgeois apparatus of power capable of blocking the English, calling them to account	unleashes the flood of capitalism
voyage	flight
interiority	relationship with the outside
seeks beginning or end as point of origin, point of anchor	the English zero is always in the middle
trees	crabgrass
too human: person, subject	collection, packet, bloc of sensations
gods: fixed attributes, properties, functions, territories, codes, rails, boundaries	daemons: jump across intervals
trickery, trickster (plagiarisms)	betrayal, traitor (creative theft)
secrecy	clandestiny
Oedipus	Cain, Jonah
. . .	Old Testament
Old World, East coast of America	New World, West coast of America, Indians
priest, soothsayer, statesman, courtier, characters in French novels	experimenter, man of war (not marshal or general)
domesticity	the Anomalous, the outsider, terror
'Madam Bovary, *c'est moi*'	becoming-woman
interpretation	experimentation
phantasms, the survey	programmes
life is reduced to the personal: personal conflicts, perfecting of perfectings, neurotic toadying, narcissistic tribunals	strict impersonality, the personal is an empty category
history, the chronicle	geography, the map
too concerned with past and future, therefore does not know how to become	knows how to become
filiation	alliance
'future of the revolution'	'revolutionary becoming'
'salvation through art'	'salvation in life'

Anatole France, and would therefore presumably qualify as 'French', just as, conversely, the 'deviant' Frenchmen Artaud and Genet are regarded by Deleuze as being in principle more 'Anglo-American' than 'French'.[6] The terms 'Anglo-American' and 'French' are thus *façons de parler*, and derive their sense and their saliency from the ability of the former, and the complementary inability of the latter, to invent the appropriate assemblages. If it is their inexhaustible capacity to invent assemblages – assemblages that are, among other things, 'philosophical', but also inextricably ethical and political where Deleuze is concerned – that marks the 'Anglo-Americans' and sets them apart from the 'French', then Deleuze's grouping of these two dozen or so figures as exemplars of an Anglo-American writing has itself to be viewed as an assemblage, that is, as a constellation which allows 'populations, multiplicities, territories, becomings, affects, events' to be brought into conjunctive relationships with each other (Deleuze 1987: 51/65).[7] 'Anglo-American literature' is in effect the assemblage constructed by Deleuze on behalf of Virginia Woolf, Hardy, Faulkner and others, or more precisely, it is the assemblage that is generated when a 'Woolf-assemblage', a 'Hardy-assemblage', a 'Faulkner-assemblage' and so on is 'plugged into' (*être branché*, one of Deleuze's favourite images) a specifically philosophical assemblage, in this case an irreducibly ethical and political assemblage whose lineaments have been traced in now well-known ways by Deleuze (and Guattari). But what is this assemblage whose name is 'Anglo-American literature'? What kind of assemblage is a literature whose books constellate 'populations, multiplicities, territories, becomings, affects, events' into an ensemble plugged into the three primary components of this philosophical assemblage (British empiricism, Spinozism and Stoicism)? What kind of event is the event of 'writing' such a constellation, of moving along such a line? Is this the veritable reinvention of the concept of a literary tradition?

An assemblage, according to Deleuze, is,

> a multiplicity which is made up of many heterogeneous terms and which establishes liaisons, relations between them, across ages, sexes and reigns – different natures. Thus, the assemblage's only unity is that of co-functioning: it is a symbiosis, a 'sympathy'. It is never filiations which are important, but alliances, alloys; these are not successions, lines of descent, but contagions, epidemics, the wind. (1987: 69/84)

Where the book, *qua* machinic assemblage is concerned, one side of the assemblage faces what Deleuze and Guattari call 'the strata', that is, a plethora of codes and milieux characterised above all by a ceaseless mobility (Deleuze and Guattari 1987: 502/627). The other side of the assemblage faces 'the body without organs', that is, what is fundamentally an agglomeration of part-objects that interrupts the functioning of the three great strata (the organism (*l'organisme*), signifiability (*la signifiance*) and subjectification (*la subjectivation*) as organising principles). In *A Thousand Plateaus* Deleuze and Guattari say that the book possesses several bodies without organs, 'depending on the nature of the lines considered, their particular grade or density, and the possibility of their converging on a "plane of consistency" assuring their selection' (4/10). The upshot of the functioning of the bodies without organs is the injunction that writing thus be quantified (*quantifier l'écriture*). This injunction carries with it the following implications which are explicitly drawn by Deleuze and Guattari:

> There is no difference between what a book talks about and how it is made. Therefore a book also has no object. As an assemblage, a book has only itself, in connection with other assemblages and in relation to other bodies without organs. We will never ask what a book means, as a signified or signifier; we will not look for anything to understand in it. We will ask what it functions with, in connection with what other things it does or does not transmit intensities, in what other multiplicities its own are inserted and metamorphosed, and with what bodies without organs it makes its own converge. A book exists only through the outside and on the outside. A book itself is a little machine; what is the relation (also measurable) of this literary machine to a war machine, love machine, revolutionary machine, etc. – and an *abstract machine* that sweeps them along?[8]

Several examples are provided in *A Thousand Plateaus* of the other 'machines' literary works are plugged into: Kleist and Kafka insert themselves into 'a mad war machine' and 'bureaucratic machine' respectively (4/10); Woolf (in *The Waves*) a 'wave machine' (252/308); Ken Kesey a 'fog machine' (520 n. 18/29 n. 17); Charlotte Brontë a 'wind machine' (261/319);[9] Melville a 'delirious machine'; and T. E. Lawrence a 'machine for manufacturing giants'.[10] Writing has perforce to do with something other than itself, it measures this exteriority by surveying and mapping it, including domains that are yet to come.[11] Writing, in other words, has to do with the creation of worlds that are specified by the assemblages the writer enters into, even as he or she is invented by still other assemblages. The insertion into an assemblage thus constitutes a kind of therapy, a proposition that is integral to several of the essays in Deleuze's late work *Essays Clinical and Critical*.

An assemblage has two components. One is a state of things and bodies, which commingle and transmit affects to each other, in the way that, for instance, the prison is an assemblage because cells and dungeons and the bodies of those made prisoners constitute each other affectively. The other component consists of utterances and regimes of utterances. Regimes of utterances in turn comprise 'two non-parallel formalizations', namely, *Sentences* or forms of content (*formalisation de contenu*) and *Figures* or forms of expression (*formalisation d'expression*), the former being attributes of bodies, the latter constituting the 'expressed' of the utterance.[12] The distinction between *Sentence* and *Figure* is adapted from the linguist Louis Hjelmslev, and it and its accompanying notions are used by Deleuze (and Guattari) to abolish the traditional three-decker division between object ('the world'), representation ('the book') and subjectivity ('the author'), this triadic schema viewing the book as the indispensable mediating link between the external world and the internal world of the author. In place of this triptych, the authors of *A Thousand Plateaus* propose the assemblage as an organising device which links sets of multiplicities extracted from each of these three orders. The upshot is that a book is always written from and through its outside; it is defined by this 'outside' and not by the figure of the author (its putative 'subject') or that of the world (its equally specious 'object'). This outside is a multiplicity, and into it is plugged a collective assemblage of enunciation and a machinic assemblage of desire, each permeating the other. The function of the book is thus to assemble with this heterogeneous outside, to move 'rhizomatically', and not to represent 'the' world. Deleuze believes that Anglo-American literature exemplifies this 'rhizomatic' principle, it knows 'how to move between things, establish a logic of the AND, overthrow ontology, do away with foundations, nullify endings and beginnings. They know how to practice pragmatics' (Deleuze 1987: 23–5/34–7).

Although he is not mentioned by Deleuze and Guattari, the target of the barely suppressed polemics of this passage, with its insistence on the centrality of the 'outside' of the text, has to be Derrida, whose famous (some would say 'notorious') claim in *De la grammatologie* that 'there is nothing outside of the text' (*il n'y a pas de hors-texte*) crisply encapsulates the notions of intertextuality Deleuze (and Guattari) are keen to repudiate.[13] While the proponents of intertextuality (an admittedly rather amorphous term encompassing such diverse but sometimes overlapping items as the displacement of 'meaning', the 'infinite play of semiosis', the heterogeneity of the text and its contexts of 'origin', the determination of a discourse by other discourses, a text's 'influences', the text's constitutive 'undecidability' as it confronts its readers, the circulation of ideology, and so forth) make some claims in the course of formulating their positions that would be acceptable in principle to Deleuze, such as the Tel Quel's group's emphasis on the 'death' of the subject; their dependence in the end on an 'ontology' of the signifier and signified, with the correlative assertion of a fundamental disruption of the relation between signifier and signified, *is* ultimately incompatible with the 'pragmatics' of writing that Deleuze is advocating. Deleuze is certainly not against the notion of a text having its organising principles controverted or dismantled, but the qualified objection he has to structuralism – that it is necessarily 'a system of points and positions' – is one that is also applicable to Derrida and other poststructuralists, who want to insist on the irremediable 'instability' and 'decentredness' of this system, but who have to retain it precisely in order: (1) to affirm that it is marked by these characteristics; and (2) to demonstrate the system's 'aporetic' qualities by working rigorously within it, by tracking down the points and the ways in which the 'structurality' of its structure becomes so attenuated or fraught that it can be seen to be less than that.[14] For Deleuze, the text's instability comes not so much from the absence of a semiotic Archimedean point intended to guarantee or establish a determinate and monocentric meaning (the fantasy promulgated by the 'logocentrism' undermined by Derrida and his followers), but from the 'power of the false', a Nietzschean conception that Deleuze uses as the basis for the account of simulation he developed in *Logique du sens*. According to Deleuze, the purported 'essence' of 'the same' and 'the similar' can only be *simulated*, and so there is no essential congruence between the copy and its 'original', with the 'anarchic' and 'nomadic' consequence that the book or work is a non-hierarchised 'condensation of coexistences and a simultaneity of events'. The simulacrum preempts the participation of the ostensible replica in its 'origin', it dissolves all foundations, and it 'assures a universal breakdown (*effondrement*), but as a joyful and positive event, as an un-founding (*effondement*) . . .' (Deleuze 1990: 262–3/303).[15] Deleuze then goes on to say: 'That the Same and the Similar may be simulated does not mean that they are appearances or illusions. Simulation designates the power of producing an *effect*' (263/304); emphasis as in original.) The Deleuzian book, in short, is always and unavoidably a series of effects generated by the 'power of the false', a power that functions as the book's 'outside' in order to overwhelm the text's aspirations to fixity and hierarchy.

Derrida does of course acknowledge the force of the Nietzschean *Pseudos* when he makes his well-known distinction, in 'Structure, Sign, and Play in the Discourse of the Human Sciences', between two fundamental 'interpretations of interpretation'; one 'dreaming' of 'deciphering a truth or an origin that escapes play and the order of the sign', and another, 'the Nietzschean', in his words, which 'is no longer turned toward the origin', and 'affirms play and tries to pass beyond man and humanism' (Derrida 1978: 292–3). But Derrida prefers not to choose between these two approaches, on the grounds that to 'choose' today is 'trivial' in any case, and also because any such 'choice' would be nugatory as long as we do not determine what precisely the 'differenceness' *is* in the 'irreducible difference' between these two approaches. Deleuze is not detained by such reticences. His espousal of the power of *Pseudos* is positive rather than optative, and he gives an account of it that differs significantly from Derrida's. Where Derrida views this power as a decomposing principle or propensity lodged inextricably in the text's structure, Deleuze, as several key passages from *Logique du sens* make clear, regards the power of *Pseudos* primarily as the power to create effects. In other words, Deleuze's espousal of the Nietzschean *Pseudos* takes the form of the positing of a *vitality* or *vitalism* of the text or book, and it is this vitality or vitalism, drawn from the text's 'outside' – because for Deleuze the power of simulation is the *sine qua non* of the text's emergence, its enabling anteriority/exteriority, so to speak, and thus one it cannot create for itself even as it transmits its force – that undermines the text's 'foundations'. Where the book is concerned, there can for Deleuze only be inventing and assembling, never interpretation. If Deleuze is a 'poststructuralist' (a term whose provenance is American, not French!), then it has to be acknowledged that his 'poststructuralism' is as much Bergsonian as it is Nietzschean, and that it is this unquenchable vitalism of the text that sets him fundamentally apart from Derrida, whose approach does not require him to say anything about the power which possesses the book and its writer so that they can affect or be affected by other assemblages.[16] But what is this power, derived as it is from *Pseudos*, of invention and assembling?

According to Deleuze (and Guattari), the writer is responsible to this power, which also happens to be the source of his or her becoming-other.

> If the writer is a sorcerer, it is because writing is a becoming, writing is traversed by strange becomings that are not becomings-writer, but becomings-rat, becomings-insect, becomings-wolf, etc . . . Writers are sorcerers because they experience the animal as the only population before which they are responsible in principle. The German preromantic Karl Philipp Moritz feels responsible not only for the calves that die but before the calves that die and give him the incredible feeling of an unknown Nature – *affect*. For the affect is not a personal feeling, nor is it a characteristic, it is the effectuation of a power of the pack that throws the self into upheaval and makes it reel. Who has not known the violence

of these animal sequences, which uproot one from humanity, if only for an instant, making one scrape at one's bread like a rodent or giving one the yellow eyes of a feline? A fearsome involution calling us towards unheard-of becomings.[17]

The book belongs to an order in which utterances and bodies commingle to bring about unanticipated 'becomings-other'. The vitalism which subtends Deleuze's account of how this traffic between bodies and utterances occurs is also the basis for his treatment of the so-called problematic of dualisms. Deleuze maintains that it is a question not simply of undermining the hold of dualisms, but of getting language per se to flow between the terms of dualisms (he calls this the invention of 'stammering'), and that it is this flow or stammering, 'the AND', which constitutes the multiplicity that transposes the terms of a dualism into a completely new infrastructure of relationships, not just semiotic and syntactic, but also assemblages that, in the manner identified by Spinoza, transmit affects and other 'powers of the body'. The 'AND' between the two terms of the dualism 'is neither the one nor the other, nor the one which becomes the other', but a line of flight 'which passes between the two terms . . . the narrow stream which belongs to neither one nor to the other, but draws both into a non-parallel evolution, into a heterochronous becoming'.[18] The objective is to avoid retaining the structure of the dialectic, a structure that, ostensibly, is kept in place even by those who try to undermine it by bringing out the suppressed 'undifferentiatedness' that is lodged in the 'difference' between the two terms that are (dialectically) counterposed – this being the Heideggerian heart of Derrida's strategy for dealing 'deconstructively' with the dialectic of identity-and-difference.[19]

It has already been noted that the concept of a 'simulation-effect' is one of the decisive features of the conceptual armature developed in *Logique du sens*. The simulacrum sets things in motion, because if each 'copy' is the 'original' of itself (the theme of the famous first appendix in *Logique du sens* that seeks a 'reversal' of Platonism), then repetition of this or that 'copy' can only be repetition of difference (the primary theme in *Différence et répétition*), each and every time necessarily (hence the convergence of the respective thematics of *Différence et répétition* and *Logique du sens*). Since variation is the defining feature of repetition, every repetition carries with it possibilities for the emergence of new lines of flight and becomings-other, and thus for the creation of new assemblages. Every repetition, therefore, is an event or 'incorporeal transformation' that contains within it the 'components of passage' that will set up a new line of flight and the possible emergence of a new assemblage: repetition provides the conceptual ground or axiomatics for the emission of singularities or *haecceities* ('thisnesses'), and assemblages are the systems which transmit and receive intensities and *haecceities*.[20] If the book is an assemblage and the writer an inventer of assemblages, then the question of what it is that the book receives and transmits, and what it is that the writer does in the course of inventing assemblages becomes important for Deleuze.

Deleuze insists that there is no significant difference between painting, music and writing, and says in an important passage in the 'Anglo-American Literature' interview-essay that 'these activities are differentiated from one another by their respective substances, codes, and territorialities, but not by the abstract line they trace, which shoots between them and carries them towards a common fate' (74/89). Deleuze maintains that painters, musicians and writers can produce philosophy when they find an 'outside' to painting, music and writing, when 'the melodic line draws along the sound, or the pure traced line colour, or the written line the articulated voice'. There is thus no real need for philosophy: for Deleuze 'it is necessarily produced where each activity gives rise to its line of deterritorialization', and philosophers themselves necessarily produce their work from the outside. Deleuze goes on to say: 'Writing is very simple . . . [I]t is becoming, becoming something other than a writer, since what one is becoming at the same time becomes other than writing. Not every becoming passes through writing, but everything which becomes is an object of writing, painting or music. Everything which becomes is a pure line which ceases to represent whatever it may be' (1987: 40) In other words, since writing (both 'philosophical' and 'novelistic'), painting and music involve the creation of lines of flight first and foremost, and cease to traffic in representations by virtue of this creation of a becoming-other, what is crucial for them all is this becoming-other, the 'delirium' that constitutes an 'outside' for philosophy, literature, painting and music.[21]

There is of course for Deleuze a crucially important difference between the characters or aesthetic figures that the novelist creates and the conceptual personae who are the subject of the philosopher's thinking and writing, namely, that conceptual personae 'are the powers of concepts' while aesthetic figures are 'the powers of affects and percepts'.[22] That is to say, concepts are effective by virtue of being images of 'Thought-Being', while aesthetic figures do so by being images of 'a Universe', so that philosophy is 'the [constitution] of immanence or concepts' while literature is the 'constellation of a universe of affects and percepts'.[23] At the same time, Deleuze (and Guattari) allow the possibility of a crossing-over of these two forms into each other 'in a becoming that sweeps them both up in an intensity which co-determines them' (66/64). As examples Deleuze and Guattari point out that Kierkegaard uses the operatic character Don Juan as a conceptual persona, and that Nietzsche's conceptual persona Zarathustra has become an exemplary figure in music and theatre, so that 'it is as if between them, not only alliances but also branchings and substitutions take place' (66/64). They also refer to Michel Guérin's *La terreur et la pitié* and credit him with being the foremost discoverer of the role of conceptual personae in philosophy by using them within a 'logodrama' or 'figurology' that imbues thought with affect, so that 'the concept as such can be concept of the affect, just as the affect can be affect of the concept' (66/64–5). The 'planes' from which art is composed and from which philosophy is written can permeate each other, and entities from the one 'plane' can move on to the other. Philosophical innovation occurs when a thinker creates a new image of thought, and produces a new 'plane' (the 'plane of immanence') for the writing of philosophy. But this philosophical 'plane' can also be occupied by poetic, novelistic, pictorial or musical figures. For Deleuze (and Guattari) the opposite is also true: philosophical figures can also be transported on to the artist's 'plane of composition'. To quote them:

> These thinkers are also 'half' philosophers but also much more than philosophers. But they are not sages. There is such force in those unhinged works of Hölderlin, Kleist, Rimbaud, Mallarmé, Kafka, Michaux, Pessoa, Artaud, and many English and American novelists, from Melville to Lawrence or Miller, in which the reader discovers admiringly that they have written the novel of Spinozism. To the sure, they do not produce a synthesis of art and philosophy. They branch out and do not stop branching out. They are hybrid geniuses who neither erase nor cover over differences in kind but, on the contrary, use all the resources of their 'athleticism' to install themselves with this very difference, like acrobats torn apart in a perpetual show of strength. (Deleuze and Guattari 1994: 66–7/65)

And if Melville, Lawrence, Miller and others (for example, such exponents of 'Anglo-American literature' in the expanded sense as Artaud) can invent assemblages that are plugged into the assemblage that is Spinozism to form a 'co-determining intensity', they can also invent functionally similar 'branching-out' assemblages that plug into the assemblages that are British empiricism and Stoicism.[24] Why write about British empiricism?, why write about Spinozism?, why write about Stoicism?, ask Claire Parnet/Deleuze each time in the 'Anglo-American Literature' essay before providing the lineaments of an answer.

Deleuze's answer to the first of these questions is succinct: 'Because empiricism is like the English novel. It is a case of philosophizing as a novelist, of being a novelist in philosophy' (1987: 54/68). The primary philosopheme taken by Deleuze to mark British empiricism is the procedure or 'function' – never 'principle', for Deleuze insists that empiricism does violence to *all* principles – that all relations are external, and that terms and relations constitute all that there is. This extraordinary 'function' carries with it the implication that a relation can change without affecting its terms (something that Hegel and his followers would regard as incongruous), so that relations always exist 'in the middle': a change in the relation, say, moving a glass off the table, does not alter the terms in this relation, the glass or the table. 'If one takes this exteriority of relations as a conducting wire or as a line,' Deleuze goes on to say, 'one sees a very strange world unfold, fragment by fragment: a Harlequin's jacket or patchwork, made up of solid parts and voids, blocs and ruptures, attractions and divisions, nuances and bluntnesses, conjunctions and separations, alternations and interweavings, additions which never reach a total and subtractions whose remainder is never fixed' (55/69). Empiricism, in short, is able to substitute the AND for IS, the AND being the path which underlies all relations, and in this way empiricism creates yet another remarkable function: 'a multiplicity which constantly inhabits each thing' (57/71). Hence to write like Lawrence or Woolf or Miller is already to write as an empiricist, and in his early *Empiricism and Subjectivity*, Deleuze identifies several features of Hume's empiricism that will later appear, whether explicitly or implicitly, in his account of the assemblage that is 'Anglo-American literature' (Deleuze 1991).

These include: relations are external and irreducible to their terms (123/139); 'we should not ask what principles are, but rather what they do' (132–3/151),[25] 'the subject is constituted by means of principles and . . . is grounded in the fancy (*fantasie*)' (127/143); the mind is a collection of impressions (132/150); the understanding is grounded in the imagination (127/143); 'the exception is a natural thing' (56/48); the passions transcend the mind (63/57); the given is the product of the powers of nature (109/122); and 'subjectivity' is a process (113/127). These formulations embody 'territorialities' that furnish the ground for concepts, and their agglomeration ensues in a 'Hume-assemblage' with its constituting emphasis on the anomalous and the exceptional, as well as on multiplicities – multiplicities generated by the substitution of AND for IS necessitated by the externality of relations – that inhabit all beings. Empiricism corrupts and undermines Being, and puts experimentation and blocs of becoming in its place. It renders these in the form of concepts, but their functions can also be expressed through affects and percepts, which in Deleuze's eyes is how the great American and English novelists come to 'write' their versions of this empiricism.

From Spinoza the Deleuze of the 'Anglo-American Literature' essay derives a similar emphasis on the AND, and in doing this characterises the 'Spinoza-assemblage' in terms of the injunction 'to make the body a power which is not reducible to the organism, to make thought a power which is not reducible to consciousness' (62/76). The components of this kinetic assemblage include 'soul and body, relationships and encounters, powers to be affected, affects which realize this power, sadness and joy which qualify these affects', so that Deleuze's Spinoza, unexpectedly but not implausibly, is somehow a bastard ancestor of the bastard Kerouac, someone for whom 'the soul is neither above nor inside, it is "with", it is on the road, exposed to all contacts, encounters, in the company of those who follow the same way, "feel with them, seize the vibration of their soul and their body as they pass", the opposite of a morality of salvation, teaching the soul to live its life, not to save it' (62/76–7). So like the 'Hume-assemblage', the 'Spinoza-assemblage' is one whose *raison d'être* is an unceasing experimentation.[26]

Like Spinoza and Hume, the Stoics found ways of getting rid of the indicative IS by substituting for it any verb of the infinitive form that emerges from a state of things ('to flee', 'to arrive', 'to stop' and so on), these verbs in turn designating events ('Caesar arriving', 'Deleuze writing' and so on). This in turn is tied to an ethics/politics, because

> making an event – however small – is the most delicate thing in the world: the opposite of making a drama or making a story. Loving those who are like this: when they enter a room they are not persons, characters or subjects, but an atmospheric variation, a change of hue, an imperceptible molecule, a discrete population, a fog or cloud of droplets. Everything has really changed. Great events, too, are made in this way: battle, revolution, life and death . . . True Entities are events, not concepts. It is not easy to think in terms of the event. All the harder since thought itself then becomes an event. Scarcely any other than the Stoics and the English have thought in this way. (Deleuze 1987: 66/81)

The Deleuzian philosophical counter-tradition is formed from a concatenation of the Stoic, Spinozan and Humean, as well as the Scotist, Nietzschean and Bergsonian assemblages (Leibniz becomes important for

Deleuze later on), each with its history of the clandestinies of becoming, all coming together to constitute an alternative to the history of Being that extends in a meandering trajectory from Plato and Hegel to the present, a tradition in which Heidegger and Derrida have to be included as dissident members.[27] Anglo-American literature for Deleuze is distinctive precisely because its exemplary writings can be 'mapped' on to these assemblages and not any other (such as the Platonic-Hegelian). The determining criterion or set of criteria for what constitutes 'Anglo-American literature' is thus an ensemble of philosophemes, albeit with the significant proviso that for Deleuze (and Guattari) this philosophy is always one based on the proposition that philosophy is necessarily constituted from its 'outside', from the event, *this* event, which it then has to construct from affects and percepts, though never as a drama or story. And not just any philosophy, and therefore necessarily by implication not just any literature: where Deleuze is concerned, only the Stoic-Scotist-Spinozan-Leibnizean-Hu-mean-Nietzschean-Bergsonian 'super-assemblage' qualifies as this thinking of the 'outside', this thinking with affects and percepts. Thus Hermann Broch, whose *Der Tod des Virgil* is surely one of the great novels of the Hegelian assemblage – 'Nothing unreal will survive', declares Broch's protagonist Virgil, using 'real' very much in the sense of 'actual' in Hegel's famous aphorism 'What is rational is actual and what is actual is rational' – is not likely to have a place in Deleuze's Anglo-American literary canon. This is not because it is 'German' (for as we have seen Kleist and Kafka are grouped by Deleuze with the great Anglo-Americans), but precisely because it is not a book that can be plugged into the Stoic-Scotist-Spinozan-Leibnizean-Humean-Nietzschean-Bergsonian 'super-assemblage'. In fact, given Deleuze's literary and philosophical criteriology, *Der Tod des Virgil* is perhaps more appropriately to be categorised as a novel whose basic affinity is with the assemblage that is 'French literature'.

But why, in this case, is there no Anglo-American philosophical tradition that parallels its extraordinary literary counterpart? Deleuze and Guattari have noted that American philosophy departments are dominated by the study of logic, with phenomenology as a small adjunct, and those of us who have studied in philosophy departments in either Britain or the United States will know that Hume, for instance, is never studied in a way that accords with Deleuze's understanding of him, namely, as one of the great exponents of constructivism in philosophy.[28] Instead, in the version of the history of philosophy typically promulgated in British and American philosophy departments, Hume is depicted as someone with an abiding interest in something called 'sense-data' and is lumped by virtue of this interest with Locke and Berkeley as 'British empiricists', who in turn are pitted against a 'Rationalist' tradition whose primary exemplars are Descartes, Spinoza and Leibniz, so that in the end a Strawsonian or Bennettian Kant can be viewed as the towering figure who brings about a *rapprochement* between these two contending traditions. The nineteenth century is omitted, or rather is given over to 'Continental Philosophy' because *that* is where Fichte, Hegel, Schelling, Kierkegaard, Schopenhauer and Nietzsche are deemed to belong, while the history of ('real') philosophy resumes early in the twentieth century with Frege and Russell, before going through Wittgenstein and Austin in order to end up with Quine and Davidson (and with this terminus the student has been brought 'up to date'). It would never occur to anyone schooled in this tradition to regard Hume and Spinoza as two philosophical allies in the way proposed by Deleuze, and to have them aligned with Nietzsche against 'the rest' (with Leibniz as a possible exception for the later Deleuze). Given this syllabus, and all the 'arborescent' assessments normatively built into it, it is hardly likely that anyone thinking along its lines will be able to conceive of an Anglo-American philosophical tradition capable of serving as an appropriate complement to the Anglo-American literary tradition identified by Deleuze (and Guattari). If anything, the literary complement of this overwhelmingly 'arborescent' Anglo-American philosophical tradition in Deleuze's scheme of things is quite likely to be 'French literature'! If the Anglo-Americans write in affects and percepts in order to form multiplicities, then only a philosophy whose basic tenor is 'constructivist' will accord with the decidedly modernist writers assigned by Deleuze to this countertradition.

In the 'Geophilosophy' chapter of *What is Philosophy?* Deleuze and Guattari maintain that philosophy has known three major 'reterritorialisations', each with their associated modalities: on the Greeks in the past (Hegel and Heidegger being the preeminent figures of this 'reterritorialisation');[29] on the democratic State in the present, so that philosophy comes to be marked by national characteristics ('German philosophy', 'French philosophy', 'English philosophy' and so on, with the *cogito* being used as the primary instrument for accomplishing this 'national' conquest of the plane of immanence (102–11/98–106)); and 'on the new people and earth in the future' (110/106). This future constitutes the 'moment' for the geophilosophy proposed by Deleuze and Guattari.

The reterritorialisation of philosophy is also the occasion for conceptual renovation. The first of the two reterritorialisations mentioned above – the Greeks and democratic State – do not provide adequate conditions for the creation of concepts. The first because for this reterritorialisation to be more than just a vapidly nostalgic longing for the Greeks, the Greeks will have to be reterritorialised on us even as philosophy is reterritorialised on them (Deleuze and Guattari, with Heidegger's egregious identification of the Greek *polis* with the Nazi *Gleichschaltung* in mind, his rejoining of the Greeks through the Germans, quote Nietzsche who asked if there was 'anything worse . . . than to find oneself facing a German when one was expecting a Greek?' (108/104). The reterritorialisation of philosophy on the modern state will not work either. The modern State is a seamlessly incorporated element in the history of capitalism, and thus prevents both the liberation of subjugated peoples and the emergence of concepts: it, and that means 'we', cannot create and it/we 'lack resistance to the present' (108/104). So the generation of new concepts has to await a philosophical reterritorialisation of the future, for a new earth and a people who are yet to come, who will provide philosophy and politics with the 'correlate of creation', the wherewithal for a becoming-other, that is presently lacking.

If philosophy and art converge in the project of beckoning this new earth and new people, then

> the race summoned forth by art or philosophy is not the one that claims to be pure but rather an oppressed, bastard, lower, anarchical, nomadic, and irremediably minor race – the very ones that Kant excluded from the paths of the new Critique. Artaud said: to write *for* the illiterate – to speak for the aphasic, to think for the acephalous. But what does 'for' mean? It is not 'for their benefit', or yet 'in their place'. It is 'before'. It is a question of becoming. (109/104–5)

For Deleuze and Guattari it is not a matter of the thinker 'doing something for' the illiterate and so on but rather it is that the thinker becomes illiterate, becomes Indian, becomes rat, so that the illiterate, the Indian, the rat, can become something else: 'The agony of a rat or the slaughter of a calf remain present in thought not through pity but as the zone of exchange between man and animal in which something of one passes into the other. This is the constitutive relationship of philosophy with nonphilosophy' (109/104–5). Becoming is two-way, which is not to say that it is reciprocal or involves the exchange of attributes. It is this double becoming which brings forth the new earth and the people who are to come: 'The philosopher must become nonphilosopher so that nonphilosophy becomes the earth and people of philosophy', so that the people constitute the thinker's becoming-other by virtue of their becoming-people, even as the thinker is internal to the people as part of their becoming (109/105).

In this deterritorialisation-reterritorialisation of the double becoming between people and art/philosophy, neither the artist nor the philosopher are capable as such of creating the new people. Art and philosophy can only 'summon' the new people in their becoming-other, and share in the same resistance 'to death, to servitude, to the intolerable, to shame, and to the present' (110/105). Deleuze and Guattari link the creation embodied in 'pure becomings' and 'pure events' on the plane of immanence to this fundamental resistance, and then pose the question of this resistance at the level of thought: thinking is experimentation above all, and experimentation is always a 'becoming-other' that makes greater demands on us than the appearance of truth itself. This is the line on which a thinking based on the anomalous, experimentation, manifests itself, and it is from this experimentation that the new earth and the new people emerge from under the shadow of the Greeks and States.[30] Philosophy, geophilosophy in this case, takes experimentation into the domain of concepts, and literature into that of affects and percepts. It follows from this that geophilosophy ('concepts') will have its complement in a geoliterature ('percepts' and 'affects'). But is Anglo-American literature this geoliterature? If geophilosophy emerges from a new reterritorialisation on the future, then does it not follow that Anglo-American literature will itself have to undergo a similar reterritorialisation on the future in order to become geoliterature? Or is Anglo-American literature already reterritorialised on the future in such a way that it is capable of functioning as the equivalent of a geoliterature. Is it the latter in all but name?

This is the age of national philosophies which perforce also partake of 'the modern' and its appurtenances. Deleuze and Guattari believe that it is the mark of the philosophical 'modern' to possess the concept but to have lost cogniscance of the plane of immanence. (It's possible therefore to understand the two volumes of *Capitalism and Schizophrenia* as an immense orchestration or collocation of concepts intended to reclaim the plane of immanence for philosophy, their 'postmodernity', so to speak.) There is a French philosophy that creates its personae who manage concepts by submitting them to the exigencies of 'epistemology', whose basic function is the reterritorialisation of consciousness; a German philosophy whose personae have retained the absolute but who, unlike the French, deterritorialise consciousness in order to find absolute foundations for philosophy, which in turn is viewed as the science of consciousness. Deleuze and Guattari's description of English philosophy shows their profound affinity for it and needs to be quoted in full because it defies summary:

[T]he English are precisely those nomads who treat the plane of immanence as a movable and moving ground, a field of radical experience, an
archipelagian world where they are happy to pitch their tents from island
to island and over the sea. The English nomadize over the old Greek earth,
broken up, fractalized, and extended to the entire universe. We cannot
even say that they have concepts like the French and Germans; but they
acquire them, they only believe in what is acquired – not because everything comes from the senses but because a concept is acquired by
inhabiting, by pitching one's tent, by contracting a habit. In the trinity
Founding-Building-Inhabiting, the French build and the Germans lay
foundations, but the English inhabit. For them a tent is all that is needed.
(105/101)

Clearly inspired by the account of *habit* given by C. S. Peirce, Deleuze and
Guattari transpose the lineaments of the Peircean account into an
ethnology of 'the English':

They develop an extraordinary conception of habit: habits are taken on by
contemplating and by contracting that which is contemplated. Habit is
creative. The plant contemplates water, earth, nitrogen, carbon, chlorides,
and sulphates, and it contracts them in order to acquire its own concept
and fill itself with it ('enjoyment') [Deleuze and Guattari use the English
word in the original]. The concept is a habit acquired by contemplating the
elements from which we come (hence the very special Greekness of English
philosophy, its empirical neo-Platonism). We are all contemplations, and
therefore habits. *I* is a habit. Wherever there are habits there are concepts,
and habits are developed and given up on the plane of immanence of
radical experience: they are 'conventions'. That is why English philosophy
is a free and wild (*sauvage*) creation of concepts. (105/101)

The reader of this passage quickly realises that the authors of *Capitalism
and Schizophrenia* are thus to be reckoned 'English philosophers' (they
are hardly French and not remotely German!), and that the perspective of
geophilosophy is attained largely through the generalisation, their generalisation, of the *modus operandi* of English philosophy.[31] Of all the
national philosophies of the 'imagined community' type, English philosophy alone has not abandoned the plane of immanence that geophilosophy seeks to restore in the name of a new earth and a people yet to
come, an ethical and political 'project' it will moreover undertake through
'a free and wild creation of concepts'.

This provides a clue as to how one can extract 'geoliterature' from the
lineaments of Anglo-American literature. We simply try to generalise the
latter's way of creating and organising percepts and affects, since, as we
have seen, Anglo-American literature derives its primary features from its

capacity to be plugged into the conceptual reticile of Hume-Spinoza-Stoic philosophical assemblage: what this assemblage renders in terms of concepts, Anglo-American literature transposes into percepts and affects. Both summon, in their respective modes, the new earth and the new people in ways not possible for the national philosophies (though English philosophy expresses this summons inchoately) and their precursor transcendental philosophies, and of course French literature (though Anglo-American literature anticipates geoliterature).

But how can the assemblage that is Anglo-American literature undergo this generalisation into geoliterature when, with a few exceptions (Kleist, Hölderlin, Charlotte and Emily Brontë, Robert Louis Stevenson and mystery – and travel – writers like Lovecraft and Thesiger), the novelists in Deleuze's 'canon' are so emphatically modernist? Will a certain parochialism – geoliterature as hinted at here seems suspiciously like a repristinated modernism – stand in the way of this generalisability? I do not see why it should. If the primary desideratum determining what geophilosophy is is the reclaiming of the plane of immanence for the creation of new concepts (what Deleuze elsewhere calls 'experimentation') in the name of a new earth and a new people, then, the risk of some simplification notwithstanding, it could be argued that any literature will in principle qualify as 'geoliterature' so long as it can be plugged into the adjacent geophilosophical assemblage, that is, provided it creates affects and percepts capable of functioning as the necessary correlate to geophilosophy's concepts. So why not Garcia Márquez or Julio Cortázar or Salman Rushdie or anyone similar bypassed in the initial Deleuzian specification of the Anglo-American literary *Nachlass*, such as the overlooked Victorian poet-physician Thomas Lovell Beddoes (who significantly influenced Beckett)? Does a writer 'write with a view to an unborn people that doesn't yet have a language?' asks Deleuze, and he certainly should not object to the inclusion in geoliterature's wayward 'canon' of anyone who wrote in this vein, and in the name of the ethical and political project that for Deleuze is the writer's (as opposed to the author's) reason for becoming.[32] To ask what such an ambition might mean is to have begun to imagine what the possible contours of a geoliterature might be. But are Garcia Márquez, Cortázar, Rushdie, Vargas Llosa, and others like them, sufficiently 'exhausted' or 'sparse' (in the way that Beckett and Kafka obviously are for Deleuze) to belong plausibly to a geoliterature constructed according to broadly Deleuzian specifications?

Deleuze, albeit with some exceptions (Melville and Henry James are hardly 'sparse' and 'exhausted'), is palpably wedded to authors firmly lodged in the experimentally minimalist wing of modernism, and it will be hard for many of his commentators to see how the exponents of a literary 'magical realism' (say), whose works are typically marked (some would say 'trademarked') by a well-known narrative exuberance and prolixity, can be accommodated within the purview of a literary movement or tradition established on the basis of recognizably Deleuzian 'axioms'. Nevertheless, I think a case of sorts can be made for the inclusion of Garcia Márquez and others in the 'canon' of such a geoliterature.

Making a case for including authors such as Garcia Márquez and Rushdie in a 'Deleuzian' 'geoliterature' will require the bringing together of two different but related and overlapping Deleuzian theoretical accomplishments. One is the axiomatics for organising the sensuous created by Deleuze (and Guattari) in *Capitalism and Schizophrenia*: the sensuous being of course the domain that Deleuze and Guattari take to be embodied in percepts and affects and constituted by desire. This axiomatics – whose architectonic heart is adumbrated in the two volumes of *Capitalism and Schizophrenia*, though it is 'complicated' in later works, primarily *Le Pli* – has the scope of an immense *conceptual* orchestration of the domain of the sensuous.[33] This axiomatics of desire, or appropriate segments of it, underlies Deleuze (and Guattari's) work on literary figures such as Kafka, on cinema, on artists like Francis Bacon, on semiosis (in the Peircean as opposed to the Saussurian register), on music, on the history of philosophy, and so forth. The second area of accomplishment is the extraordinary theory of images developed by Deleuze in the two *Cinema* books. It is striking that in both these areas Deleuze evinces a powerful interest in the capacity of the text and the image to proliferate and multiply, to fold, unfold, and fold again, even to infinity.[34] It is as if Deleuze, his fondness for Beckett notwithstanding, is compelled to eschew a Beckettian ascesis of the text in his own textual production, and that, moreover, he explicitly acknowledges the force of this irresistible semiotic and graphic mobility in his treatment of cinematic conceptual production, even if his own preference in literature happens in the main to be for this or that version of a modernist minimalism.

One thinks here immediately of the brilliantly suggestive discussion of the oeuvre of Werner Herzog in the first *Cinema* book (Deleuze 1986: 184–6). In this remarkable disquisition on Herzog, Deleuze declares that Herzog is a 'metaphysician' who deals in forms and conceptions ('the Large' and 'the Small') that 'designate Visions which deserve even more to be called Ideas'.[35] Herzog's films are populated by visionaries and dreamers who are larger than life, who inhabit an environment that is itself larger than life, and who are fated or doomed to find an action or mode of being commensurate with this largeness. This metaphysical structure conduces to the hypnotic and hallucinatory qualities which mark Herzog's films: the latter are displayed when the hopelessly vision-ary protagonist soars over a necessarily bounded nature, and the former when this protagonist comes up against the limits of an unrelenting nature. The 'action' of the Herzogian film involves a modulation of the landscapes and the actions, in the process 'realising' the Large as a pure Idea. Herzog treats the Small in a similarly metaphysical way: the dwarves and weaklings who populate his films unavoidably bring nature down to their scale and thereby enfeeble it. But they transcend this diminished nature through 'vast hallucinatory visions of flight, ascent, or passage, like the red skier in mid-jump in *Land of silence and Darkness* or the three great dreams of landscapes in *The Enigma of Kaspar Hauser*' (186). The Large and the Small therefore modulate each other as well, since the counterpart of the red skier (who transmutes the Small into the Large) is Fitzcarraldo, whose gigantic vision of a shrine to Verdi in the Amazon jungle culminates in a tawdry performance by a bedraggled troupe of singers in front of a small audience (the transmutation of the Large into the Small).

A similar hallucinatory quality pervades literary magical realism, with its well-known propensities for disjointed temporalities, the 'exchange of qualities' between the dead and the living, the haphazard merging of personas, as well as the by now hackneyed piquancy of musicians who can play their instruments simply by placing the mouthpieces against their necks and moving their throat-muscles, animals who can count and talk, and so on. But more significantly, the metaphysically–prescient modulation between the Large and the Small which Deleuze finds in Herzog is, for instance, also to be found in a novel like Rushdie's *Midnight's Children*. Rushdie's main protagonist, Saleem Sinai, through sheer inadvertence, has a biography that is virtually coextensive with the history of post-independence India (the instantiation of the Idea of the Large, in Deleuzian terms). At the same time Saleem has a preternatural sense of smell, one so acute that he achieves preeminence in his career – pickle-making – because he can identify with his nose, in a kind of miraculating interchangeability of the senses, flavours that are indis-cernible to others (the manifestation of the Idea of the Small). Moreover, Saleem's unique and distinctive nasal passages also allow his sense of smell to serve as a conduit for memories and ideas; he smells out the past and his thinking is a veritable sniffing out. He does metaphysics through the nose. And Saleem is possessed by an extraordinary desire: to be something like an Indian Everyman by savouring, and not banishing as intrinsically alien, the experiences of everyone he comes across. The desire in this case is not the aggrandising desire to be 'all', but the very Deleuzian quest to have as many facets of the multiple refracted into interstices of one's being.

This convergence, if that is the way to describe it from my admittedly brief sketch, between the film-maker Herzog and the novelist Rushdie should not be surprising, given Deleuze's several statements to the effect that both the great film-makers and the primary novelists of the 'Anglo-American' tradition have always been philosophers. In which case, the power of Hume, Spinoza and Bergson as creators of concepts, as inaugurators of the philosophical 'super-assemblage' delineated by Deleuze, is a power that can be manifested in film and novel alike. This power is the basis of a geoliterature that will, at any rate where its axioms are concerned, be an amplification of the 'Anglo-American' literature that Deleuze uses as the primary instrument for the reinvention of the concept of a literary tradition.

Notes

1. Wherever possible page references will be given first to the English translation, and then to the original after a slash (e.g. 51/65).
2. Deleuze and Guattari 1987: 4/10. After their collaboration in *Anti-Oedipus* it becomes virtually impossible to separate the positions of Deleuze and Guattari. But since the pivot of my discussion is Deleuze's 'Anglo-American Literature' piece, I shall refer throughout to 'Deleuze' rather than resort to the neologism 'deleuzoguattarian', while bearing in mind at the same time Guattari's function as an indispensable 'intercessor' for Deleuze's thinking.
3. In the interview published as 'On *Anti-Oedipus*'. (Deleuze 1995: 23/37), Deleuze says that in comparison to the 'great English and American novelists . . . [a]ll we've got in France is Artaud and half of Beckett'. It is clear however from other texts and interviews that Deleuze's list of French writers who approximate to the Anglo-Americans is considerably less abbreviated than this passage indicates; elsewhere Deleuze has characterised Lautréamont (as interpreted by Bachelard), Genet, Villon, and Tournier as having significant affinities with the Anglo-American novelists. The omission of Proust from this list is perhaps surprising, but Proust is indicted in *A Thousand Plateaus* for seeking a salvation through art, 'a still Catholic salvation', as opposed to finding a salvation 'in real life', which is where the Anglo-American novel locates it (186–7/228–9). The question of the criteria used by Deleuze (and Guattari) to determine the composition of the Anglo-American 'canon' will be taken up in note 24 below.

   The absence of any engagement with 'magical realism' in Deleuze's oeuvre is striking and may need to be accounted for. Would there be room in an expanded 'Anglo-American canon' for such writers as Garcia Márquez and Wilson Harris? It is hard to see why these writers should not in principle have a place in this heteronomous 'canon', and Deleuze's apparent failure to take them into account will be taken up later.
4. As Deleuze and Guattari say humorously: 'The French are like landowners whose source of income is the cogito.' See Deleuze and Guattari 1994: 104/100.

5. As Paul Patton points out (Patton 1981), Deleuze and Guattari often proceed by enumerating a list of contents, perhaps the best known being the filigree of notions that begins the plateau titled 'Rhizome' in *Mille plateaux*:
   All we talk about are multiplicities, lines, strata and segmentarities, lines of flight and intensities, machinic assemblages and their various types, bodies without organs and their construction and selection, the plane of consistency, and in each case the units of measure. Stratometers, BwO units of density, BwO units of convergence. (Deleuze and Guattari 1987: 4/10–11)
   My delineation of the differences between 'French' and 'Anglo-American Literature' follows this modus operandi, and simply enumerates their respective characteristics as identified by Deleuze (and Guattari).

6. Where literary criticism or the philosophy of criticism are concerned, the clear implication of Deleuze's position is that someone like Lukács must generally be reckoned 'French' on account of the canonical primacy he accords such 'classical realists' as Balzac, Scott, Tolstoy, Thomas Mann and Gorky. The writers preferred by Deleuze tend invariably to belong to the experimental wing of a broadly defined modernism, and this would certainly set him apart from Lukács, who, for instance, contrasted the 'mixture of decadence and reaction' displayed by Deleuze's favourite Kleist with Goethe, whom Lukács esteemed for 'wrestling to create glorious islands of human culture against the pressing flood of bourgeois barbarism', and this despite being a 'representative' of his class. See Lukács 1981. I am grateful to Ian Buchanan for urging me to try to contrast Lukács and Deleuze, and for making several suggestions that helped to improve this chapter.

7. Elsewhere in this essay Deleuze says:
   To fly is to trace a line, lines, a whole cartography. One only discovers worlds through a long, broken flight. Anglo-American literature constantly shows these ruptures these characters who create their line of flight, who create through a line of flight . . . In [Hardy, Melville, Stevenson, Woolf, Wolfe, Lawrence, Fitzgerald, Miller, Kerouac] everything is departure, becoming, passage, leap, daemon, relationship with the outside. (37/47–8)

8. Deleuze and Guattari 1987: 4/10. Emphasis as in original.

9. See also the interview-essay 'Dead Psychoanalysis: Analyse', in Deleuze and Parnet 1987: 120/143, where it is asserted that 'Brontë designates a state of winds more than a person'.

10. For Melville and Lawrence, see Deleuze 1997: 68ff and 118 respectively/89ff and 147 respectively.

11. Deleuze and Guattari 1987: 5/11. Deleuze says that 'an assemblage may have been in existence for a long time before it receives its proper name which gives it a special consistence as if it were thus separated from a more general regime to assume a kind of autonomy: as in "sadism", "masochism".' See 'Dead Psychoanalysis', in Deleuze 1987: 120/143. Fredric Jameson's suggestion that the Hegel of *The Phenomenology of Spirit* be regarded as the prescient 'inventor' of the category of reification, albeit before it got its name, while not concerned with this aspect of Deleuze's work, provides another interesting example that provides grist for a Deleuzian characterisation of the assemblage. See Jameson 1997: 393–4.

12. Deleuze 1987: 70–1/85–6. Deleuze says of the regime of utterances that in them 'signs are organized in a new way, new formulations appear, a new style for new gestures (the emblems which individualize the knight, the formulas of oaths, the system of "declarations", even of love, etc.)' (70–1/85–6).

13. Derrida 1976: 158. It has to be said however that the claim that 'there is no outside-text' is sometimes wilfully misrepresented by Derrida's more intemperate

critics, who seem more eager to make him sound ridiculous than to find ways of understanding what this assertion may be about. (It could after all be the quite benign insight that an irreducible element of 'constructiveness' or 'contingency' goes into the constitution of the text. The problem for Deleuze (and Guattari) would then not be with this claim in itself, since they would, in all likelihood, be disposed to regard this version of it as salutary and anodyne, but with the ontological edifice used by Derrida and others to buttress it.) Another target of this polemics could be Jean Starobinski, well known for his proposal, which is something like an axiom for the Geneva School, that 'data' lodged in the interior of the text can be suitably transcoded to reveal marks of the author's consciousness or imagination. See Starobinski 1961: 158–9. As 'founding' proponents of the doctrine of intertextuality, Julia Kristeva and Roland Barthes would also be susceptible to criticism on the grounds adduced by Deleuze (and Guattari).

14. François Dosse is right therefore to depict Derrida as a 'superstructuralist', i.e. someone intent – when he reads texts by philosophers, ethnologists and representative structuralists – on working within the terms of the structure of the text in order to expose its impasses and undecidabilities. See Dosse 1997: 17ff.

15. I am grateful to Janell Watson for drawing my attention to the relevance of this passage from *Logique du sens* for an understanding of the claims made by Deleuze (and Guattari) about the text's 'outside' in *Mille plateaux* and in the 'Anglo-American Literature' essay.

16. Of Deleuze's many commentators, Keith Ansell Pearson is perhaps the one who has most explicitly brought out the part played by his Bergsonism in his elaboration of the notion of multiplicity. Ansell Pearson has also stressed (perhaps overstressed for some) the importance of Deleuze's Bergsonism for his critique of dialectics. See Ansell Pearson 1999: especially 156.

17. Deleuze and Guattari 1987: 240/293–4. This therefore is an ethics of writing, but also a politics (more about which later).

18. Deleuze 'A Conversation: What is it? What is it for?', in *Dialogues*, pp. 34–5/43. Though Deleuze does say that some lines of flight can be motionless. See 'Anglo-American Literature', p. 37/48–9.

19. Brian Massumi uses the term 'hyperdifferentiation' to describe the position of Deleuze and Guattari, and contrasts it with the 'identity-undifferentiation' that is more typical of the viewpoints of Lacan, Barthes, Althusser, Derrida, Kristeva and Baudrillard. I am inclined therefore to agree with Massumi when he says that these thinkers 'can still be said to repose in the shadow of Saussure's tree, even if they claim to have closed the door on it'. See Massumi, *A User's Guide to Capitalism and Schizophrenia: Deviations from Deleuze and Guattari* (Cambridge, MA: MIT Press, 1992), pp. 77–8 n. 73. See also p. 78 n. 74.

20. An 'intensity' communicates a difference, and the haecceity is either an 'assemblage haecceity', i.e. an individuated multiplicity that receives and projects intensities, or an 'interassemblage haecceity', i.e. the expression of the potential becoming-other that resides in an assemblage when it enters into combinations and conjunctions with another assemblage or group of assemblages. See Deleuze and Guattari 1987: 262–3/320. Deleuze and Guattari say that the two kinds of haecceity cannot really be separated from each other.

21. 'A flight is a sort of delirium'. See Deleuze 1987: 40/51. In his 'Literature and Life' (Deleuze 1997: 1/11), Deleuze says:

> Writing is a question of becoming, always incomplete, always in the midst of being formed, and goes beyond the matter of any livable or lived experience . . . These becomings may be linked to each other by a particular line, as in Le Clezio's novels, or they may coexist at every level, following the doorways, thresholds, and zones that make up the entire universe, as in Lovecraft's

powerful oeuvre. Becoming does not move in the other direction, and one does not become Man, insofar as man presents himself as a dominant form of expression that claims to impose itself on all matter, whereas woman, animal, molecule always has a component of flight that escapes its own formalization. The shame of being a man – is there any better reason to write?

22. See Deleuze and Guattari 1994: 65/64.

23. Deleuze and Guattari 1994: 66/64. Deleuze and Guattari remind us that 'affects' and 'percepts' are not to be confused with 'affections' and 'perceptions' respectively. An affects is not a state of being in the way that an affection is, rather it is the becoming that ensues when two sensations are coupled without resembling each other; and a percept is a bloc of sensations and relations that has an actuality that is independent of the perceiving subject (which is not the case with perceptions). For a succinct statement of this distinction see the interview 'On Philosophy', in Deleuze 1995: 137/187. The next few pages references in the main body of the text will be to *What is Philosophy?*

24. In the interview 'On Philosophy' Deleuze says that 'the great English and American novelists often write in percepts, and Kleist and Kafka in affects' (Deleuze 1995: 137/187). A similar demarcation seems to be at work in Deleuze and Guattari 1994: 168–9/159–60. The conclusion that the English and Americans write essentially in 'percepts' while the Continental Europeans who have affinities with them write in 'affects' should however be resisted. Though Deleuze and Guattari do not say this in so many words, affects ('nonhuman becomings of man') and percepts ('nonhuman landscapes of nature') are not distributed in this neatly compartmentalised way. Indeed, it is clear from their accounts that Melville wrote in affects and percepts and D. H. Lawrence wrote almost exclusively in affects. Just as interesting, and this is a point that needs to be explored elsewhere, is Deleuze's suggestion that Spinoza's *Ethics* is written not just in concepts, but also percepts and affects. See 'Letter to Réda Bensmaïa, on Spinoza', Deleuze 1995: 164–6/223–5.

25. Deleuze goes on to say of principles that they 'are not entities; they are functions. They are defined by their effects. These effects amount to this: the principles constitute, within the given, a subject that invents and believes . . . [T]he principles are principles of human nature. To believe is to anticipate. To communicate to an idea the vividness of an impression to which it is attached is to anticipate; it is to transcend memory and the senses' (133/151).

26. In his essay 'Spinoza and Us' Deleuze says: '[Spinoza's] approach is no less valid for us . . . because no one knows ahead of time the affects one is capable of; it is a long affair of experimentation, requiring a lasting prudence, a Spinozan wisdom that implies the construction of a plane of immanence or consistency. Spinoza's ethics has nothing to do with a morality; he conceives it as an ethology, that is, as a composition of fast and slow speeds, of capacities for affecting and being affected on this plane of immanence.' See Deleuze 1988: 125.

27. Deleuze and Guattari regard Hegel and Heidegger alike as 'historicists' because they view history as the interior site in which the concept unfolds or reaches its point of completion. See Deleuze and Guattari 1994: 95/91.

28. For Deleuze and Guattari on philosophy in the American university, see their 1994: 143/136.

29. We can still undertake a 'reterritorialisation' of ourselves among the Greeks, say Deleuze and Guattari, but, and this is something that Heidegger failed to understand, it will be 'according to what they did not possess and had not yet become', i.e. it will be more like a 'reterritorialisation' of the Greeks on us. See their 1994: 102/98.

30. Deleuze and Guattari provide a fascinating account of the temporality that

subtends the Now of our becoming in this experimentation, which they distinguish from the present of history. This infinite Now runs counter to the past and the present, because (and here they follow Foucault) this Now is the actuality of our becoming which is incommensurate with the present of what we are. See 112/107.

31. Of course Deleuze and Guattari's estimation of what it is that constitutes English philosophy is highly selective and, as I pointed out earlier, hardly approximates to the kind of thing that is purveyed in British philosophy departments. 'English philosophy' for them encompasses all of Hume, Russell's doctrine of the externality of relations, and Whitehead's account of 'the event' (which as Deleuze makes clear in *Le Pli* is heavily influenced by Leibniz in any case). The rest of English philosophy is done in hybrid fashion by its novelists.

32. For Deleuze's remark on writers, see 'On Philosophy', Deleuze 1995: 143/196.

33. In arguing for this claim one must of course enter the caveat that problems unavoidably arise when we try to encompass so rich and diverse a body of work as that of Deleuze and Guattari within a single interpretive armature like that of an 'axiomatics of desire'.

34. Tom Conley has persuasively argued that this dynamism of the text and the image is characteristic of all of Deleuze's writings, with the possible exception of the more explicitly philosophical studies. See Conley 1997.

35. Deleuze therefore overturns Kant's separation of Vision from Ideas (Kant had assigned the former to the Sensibility and the latter to the Understanding), or rather he imputes this overturning to the cinematic conceptualising of a Herzog.

Bibliography

Conley, Tom (1997), 'From Multiplicities to Folds: On Style and Form in Deleuze', *The South Atlantic Quarterly*, 96, no. 3, pp. 629–46.

Deleuze, Gilles (1986), *Cinema 1: The Movement-Image*, trans. Hugh Tomlinson and Barbara Habberjam, Minneapolis: University of Minnesota Press. Originally published as *Cinéma 1: L'image-mouvement*, Paris: Minuit, 1983.

Deleuze, Gilles (1987), 'On the Superiority of Anglo-American Literature', in Gilles Deleuze and Claire Parnet, *Dialogues*, trans. Hugh Tomlinson and Barbara Habberjam, New York: Columbia University Press, pp. 36–76. Originally published as *Dialogues*, Paris: Flammarion, 1996; original edition in 1977.

Deleuze, Gilles (1988), *Spinoza: Practical Philosophy*, trans. Robert Hurley, San Francisco: City Lights. Originally published as *Spinoza: philosophie pratique*, Paris: Presses Universitaires de France, 1970.

Deleuze, Gilles (1990), *The Logic of Sense*, ed. Constantin V. Boundas, trans. Mark Lester with Charles Stivale, New York: Columbia University Press. Originally published as *Logique du sens*, Paris: Minuit, 1969.

Deleuze, Gilles (1991), *Empiricism and Subjectivity: An Essay on Hume's Theory of Human Nature*, trans. Constantin V. Boundas, New York: Columbia University Press. Originally published as *Empirisme et subjectivité: essai sur la Nature Humaine selon Hume*, Paris: Presses Universitaires de France, 1953.

Deleuze, Gilles (1995), *Negotiations, 1972–1990*, trans. Martin Joughin, New York: Columbia University Press. Originally published as *Pourparlers*, Paris: Minuit, 1990.

Deleuze, Gilles (1997), *Essays Critical and Clinical*, trans. Daniel W. Smith and Michael A. Greco, Minneapolis: University of Minnesota Press. Originally published as *Critique et clinique*, Paris: Minuit, 1993.

Deleuze, Gilles and Guattari, Félix (1987), *A Thousand Plateaus: Capitalism and*

Schizophrenia, trans. Brian Massumi, Minneapolis: University of Minnesota Press. Originally published as *Mille plateaux: capitalisme et schizophrénie*, Paris: Minuit, 1980.

Deleuze, Gilles (1994), *What is Philosophy?*, trans. Hugh Tomlinson and Graham Burchell, New York: Columbia University Press. Originally published as *Qu'est-ce que la philosophie?*, Paris: Minuit, 1991.

Derrida, Jacques (1976), *Of Grammatology*, trans. Gayatri Chakravorty Spivak, Baltimore: Johns Hopkins University Press. Originally published as *De la grammatologie*, Paris: Minuit, 1967.

Deleuze, Gilles (1978), 'Structure, Sign, and Play in the Discourse of the Human Sciences', in his *Writing and Difference*, trans. Alan Bass. London: Routledge and Kegan Paul. Originally published as *L'écriture et la différence*, Paris: Seuil, 1967.

Dosse, François (1997), *History of Structuralism (vol. 2): The Sign Sets, 1967-Present*, trans. Deborah Glassman, Minneapolis: University of Minnesota Press. Originally published as *Histoire du structuralisme, II. Le chant du cygne, de 1967 à nos jours*, Paris: La Découverte, 1992.

Jameson, Fredric (1997), 'Marxism and Dualism in Deleuze', *The South Atlantic Quarterly*, 96, no. 3, pp. 393–416.

Lukács, Georg (1981), *Essays on Realism*, ed. and intro. Rodney Livingstone, trans. David Fernbach, Cambridge, MA: MIT Press. Originally published in Georg Lukács, *Werke, vol. 4: Essays über Realismus*, West Germany: Luchterhand, 1971.

Patton, Paul (1981). 'Notes for a glossary', *I & C* 8, pp. 41–8.

Pearson, Keith Ansell (1999), *Germinal Life: The Difference and Repetition of Deleuze*, London: Routledge.

Starobinski, Jean (1961), *L'Oeil vivant*, vol. 2, Paris: Gallimard.

Chapter 8

Transvestism, Drag and Becomings: A Deleuzian Analysis of the Fictions of Timothy Findley

Marlene Goldman

Gilles Deleuze outlined his 'problematological' method in a letter, claiming that any worthwhile book on philosophy must fulfil three criteria:

> Firstly, it must address itself to a sort of general 'error' which other books on the subject commit. Secondly, it must attempt to reinstate something essential which has been forgotten on the given subject. Thirdly, it should create a new concept: error, neglect, concept.[1]

Although not a book on philosophy, my study adopts Deleuze's method both to reflect a debt to Deleuze and to redress an oversight in Deleuze and Guattari's writing on the subject of the relationship between transvestism and becomings. In *A Thousand Plateaus*, Deleuze and Guattari make two brief, yet ambiguous, pronouncements on the supposed distinction between authentic instances of deterritorialisation and the practices of 'imitation, or moments of imitation, among certain homosexual males' and transvestites (Deleuze and Guattari 1987: 275). Although they insist that they do not want to overlook the importance of imitation among homosexuals, 'much less the prodigious attempt at real transformation on the part of certain transvestites' (Deleuze and Guattari 1987: 275), their comments nevertheless suggest that the path to deterritorialisation lies elsewhere and that transvestism may be too closely aligned with imitation to unleash true becomings.

While it is tempting to accept their view, their subsequent and final comment on the subject contradicts their initial assertion. Describing the rites of transvestism in primitive societies, they acknowledge that these rites *can* instigate a deconstruction of gender stereotypes that highlights the inherent instability and synthetic quality of what was taken to be natural. As they explain, transvestism poses a challenge to the social structure – a challenge that very often eludes sociological and psychological explanations (Deleuze and Guattari 1987: 278).

By adopting the framework of Deleuze's 'problematological' method, I hope to demonstrate that something essential has, indeed, been forgotten. For one, in speaking of transvestism, Deleuze and Guattari fail to distinguish between transvestism and drag; second, although they discuss transvestism, they never once speak of drag's potential to instigate becomings. To reinstate the 'forgotten' element, namely, drag, and to offer a more precise map of the complex relationships among deterritorialisation, transvestism, camp, drag and literature, this chapter examines the portrayals of transvestism, camp and drag in the works of the celebrated gay Canadian writer Timothy Findley. A Deleuzian analysis of Findley will, I hope, clarify the remarkable extent to which Findley's obsession with challenging fascism, promoting becomings and exploring the deterritorialising potential of literature mirrors many of the fundamental goals of Deleuze and Guattari's philosophical project.

Owing to their obsession with what Findley terms the 'seeds of fascism',[2] his fictions engage with the central concern outlined in the writings of Deleuze and Guattari. Their analysis of fascism shares with Findley's narratives the same impulse to counter the desire to be led. As one critic puts it, Deleuze and Guattari's writing interrogates the desire 'to have someone else legislate life. The very desire that was brought so glaringly into focus in Europe with Hitler, Mussolini, and fascism; the desire that is still at work, making us all sick, today' (Seem 1983: xvi). In his preface to *Anti-Oedipus*, Michel Foucault likewise refers to Deleuze and Guattari's attempt to highlight the dangerous aspect of fascism, not simply 'historical fascism', but 'also the fascism in us all, in our heads, and in our everyday behaviour, the fascism that causes us to love power, to desire the very thing that dominates and exploits us' (Foucault 1983: xiii).

To counter fascism, Deleuze and Guattari argue that rather than defend 'the rights of the individual, who is the product of power, the aim of politics and philosophy should be to "de-individualise", to find a connection with the collectivity at a level which is underneath that of the individual' (see Marks 1998: 94–5). According to Deleuze and Guattari, subverting fascism's Oedipalisation of the individual, which concretises flows into identities doomed either to lead or to follow, involves experimentation with ego-loss and processes of transformation which they term 'becomings'. All becomings, they argue, 'begin with and pass through becoming-woman. It is the key to all the other becomings' (Deleuze and Guattari 1987: 277).[3] Although the process begins at this point, it constitutes a journey that takes one beyond 'becoming-woman' into the becoming of animals, vegetables and even minerals.[4] As Deleuze and Guattari explain, 'on the near side, we encounter becomings-woman, becomings-child . . . On the far side, we find becomings-elementary, -cellular, -molecular, and even becomings-imperceptible' (Deleuze and Guattari 1987: 248).

By analysing Findley's fictions – specifically, the relationships among fascism, camp, transvestism and drag – in the light of Deleuze and Guattari's notion of 'becomings', this chapter aims to illuminate a Deleuzian method and to address the 'error' of Deleuze and Guattari's dismissal of transvestism as well as their absolute silence on the topic of drag. Whereas Deleuze and Guattari align transvestism with imitation, dismissing both in what is, in part, a rhetorical move to make the concept of becoming more distinctive, I argue that specific performances of drag in Findley's writing, particularly those found in *Not Wanted on the Voyage*, must not be conflated with imitation, and, in fact, set the stage for what might be considered true becomings. At the same time, this study will broaden the critical discussion of Findley's anti-fascist sentiments by offering an alternative account of the prevalent images of transformation in his texts-images that range from the figure of the transvestite to the drag queen to individuals who forge alliances with non-human entities.

In Findley's first novel, *The Last of the Crazy People*, the eleven-year-old protagonist announces, 'It isn't fair that I have to marry a woman' (1967: 54). Pondering his mother's psychological illness, which results in her retreat from the family, the boy concludes, 'Mama shouldn't have been married at all' (1967: 54). Later, holed up in a barn, after gazing into the 'pale bronze eyes' of his beloved cat – eyes that uncannily mirror his own – he responds to the repressive social order by gunning down his entire family. The violence directed at the social order and the family, in particular, is not simply an idiosyncratic feature of this novel. Subsequent works by Findley continue to call into question the private and public discourses that structure reified notions of gender identity, and many of his texts forge links between gender hierarchies and fascist politics.[5] Findley's novels, like Deleuze's writings, emphasise that 'just as we pay a price for disorder, we also pay a price for order' (Marks 1998: 2–3).

Recently, critics have begun to discuss Findley's critique of gender politics and his representations of the transvestite and drag queen, interpreting his challenge to hierarchical constructions of identity and gender relations within the context of camp aesthetics.[6] While recognising that Findley's texts utilise camp performance and solicit camp recognition, this chapter argues further that the figures of the transvestite and, to an even greater extent, the drag queen, reflect what Deleuze would describe as the desire to invent new possibilities of life; relying on style and gesture, the rites of the transvestite and the drag queen undermine ego-based notions of identity and interiority. Ultimately, I argue that the graphic, sometimes humorous, but more often sombre, representations of the disruption and fragmentation of human identity throughout his corpus signal a process of deterritorialisation that exceeds the goal of troubling contemporary constructions of gender identity. As we will see, in novels such as *Not Wanted on the Voyage* and *Headhunter*, and in short stories such as 'Foxes', processes of transformation, typically initiated by 'becomings-woman', inscribe lines of flight that also include 'becomings-animal'. To challenge Deleuze and Guattari's dismissal of cross-dressing and to explore the limits of becoming articulated in Findley's writing, I will forge links among slightly different elements including becomings, transvestism, camp, drag and the Japanese theatrical traditions of Kabuki and Noh.

While virtually all of Findley's works throw fixed gender roles into question, his fifth novel, *Not Wanted on the Voyage* (1984), the focus of this study, offers a fanciful retelling of the biblical story of Noah that launches the most explicit attack on western culture's fixation with fascist notions of perfection, predicated on a masculine norm. In his parody of the story, the author portrays Noah as the sadistic tyrant, Dr Noyes ('no/yes'); Yaweh ('he-way') as a decrepit old man who opts for his own death; and Lucifer as Lucy, a fantastically tall woman in Japanese attire, with a 'great, moon-white face and jet black hair' (Findley 1984: 59). As Lucy herself boasts, she is '[s]even-foot-five; and every inch a queen' (Findley 1984: 249). In this version, the cross-dressing, androgynous, rogue angel with a penchant for kimonos marries Dr Noyes' son, Ham, and, after swishing aboard the ark, combats divine and human fascist notions of identity and stages a revolution that paralyses the apocalyptic plot.

Findley's novel opens with the standard account of the flood as depicted in Genesis 7: 7. However, the narrator immediately counters the official version of the story. In accordance with Deleuze's insistence that thought begins with something that 'does violence to the expectations and self-possession of consciousness' (see Hughes 1998: 18), the prologue paints a disturbing and ultimately confounding image of violence – a flaming pyre that Noah's wife struggles to comprehend:

> Nothing she saw that moved had feet or legs – but only arms and necks and heads – and everything was floating – heaving up through the waves of smoke, like beasts who broke the surface of a drowning-pool, then sank and broke again. And again – and then were gone. (Findley 1984: 4)

Catherine Hunter, a critic of Findley's work, notes that for Findley the 'beginning of writing is a form of violence' (Hunter 1998: 14). In this case,

the unrecognisable image that instigates new thoughts turns out to be a funeral pyre; before embarking on the ark, Noah offers a final, earthly sacrifice to Yaweh and burns alive all of the animals not wanted on the voyage. The image of the pyre, a synecdoche for the destructive nature of fascism that runs rampant in the text, and a not-too-subtle allusion to the smoke-stacks of the Nazi concentration camps, raises questions that, according to Deleuze, were posed initially by Spinoza:

> Why are the people so deeply irrational? Why are they proud of their own enslavement? Why do they fight 'for' their bondage as if it were their freedom? Why is it so difficult not to win but to bear freedom? Why does a religion that invokes love and joy inspire war, intolerance, hatred, malevolence, and remorse? (Deleuze 1988: 10)

In Findley's text, Noah adores and obeys a god who confounds the idea of love with slavery. During his final visit to earth, just before willing his own death, God thanks Noah for his love and proposes a toast:

> '*Love*,' Yaweh's eyes were now ablaze with passionate emotion – '*love*' is the one true bond . . ."
> 'Hear, hear . . .'
> 'Between God and His angels . . .'
> 'Hear, hear . . .'
> 'God and man . . .'
> 'Hear, hear . . .'
> 'King and subject . . .'
> 'Hear, hear . . .'
> 'Lord and vassal . . .'
> 'Hear, hear . . .'
> 'Master and slave . . .'
> 'Hear, hear . . .' (Findley 1984: 87)

As noted earlier, according to Foucault, for Deleuze, the goal lies in 'freeing ourselves from our own love of the very things that dominate us' (Foucault 1983: xiii). The goal of liberation constitutes the driving force behind Findley's novel, as well. Moreover, in keeping with Deleuze and Guattari's ethics of 'schizoanalysis', whose slogan is 'You haven't seen anything yet . . . More perversion! More artifice!' (Deleuze and Guattari 1987: 321), Findley's narrative responds to the cruelty and perversion of fascism, not by calling for a different order, but by instigating a deterritorialisation of order and identity through 'artifice' – the over-the-top, perverse aesthetics of camp.

In her study of the text, Cecilia Martell observes that one of the 'most intriguing (and, by now, obvious) manifestations of Camp' is the character of Lucy. Martell goes on to recall Susan Sontag's claim that 'the androgyne is certainly one of the great [camp] images' and that 'the hallmark of Camp is the spirit of extravagance' (Martell 1996: 103). In her 'Notes on Camp', Sontag defines camp as 'a woman walking around in a dress made of three million feathers' (Sontag 1966: 283). Lucy, who sports kimonos and, beneath them, her own natural, angelic gown of 'long bronze feathers', offers a magnificent illustration of Sontag's definition.

In addition to adopting virtually every aspect of camp's visual iconography, Lucy's behaviour also adheres to the unwritten rules of traditional camp performance. Following the routines of established female impersonators, Lucy's drag act involves offering a credible female personae and, at strategic moments, drawing attention to the fact that the illusion is fabricated by a male actor.[7] On several occasions, Lucy utilises this tactic to undercut humourless characters who uphold God's repressive, heterosexist edict of two-by-two.

For instance, when confronted by Ham's brother, Japeth, who demands that the rest of the family appear before Dr Noyes, Lucy proceeds to mock her brother-in-law. Owing to the difficulty of paraphrasing humour, I have cited the passage below:

'Are we to come up?' said Mrs Noyes.
'Yes. The lot of you.'
Mrs Noyes had her foot on the lower step when Japeth added; 'and be quick about it.'
'I beg your pardon?'
Mrs Noyes stepped all the way back into the corridor.
Lucy said; 'I think he said' (and here she lowered her voice at least an octave below the tentative tenor of Japeth) '. . . "*be quick about it!*"'
'Don't you make fun of me!' said Japeth, swinging the lamp instead of brandishing the sword, but realizing his mistake too late to correct it. 'I'm not in any mood to be tampered with.'
He scowled.
Lucy said; 'I hadn't really thought of "tampering" with you, ducks. Is it something you want me to consider?' (Findley 1984: 201–2)

Taken together, the lowering of the voice, which effects a momentary dropping of the feminine 'mask', the irreverent epithet 'ducks', and the barely veiled sexual innuendo conveyed by the word 'tamper' illustrate how faithfully Findley's narrative adheres to the conventions of the traditional drag show. While camp elements abound in Findley's text, the role they play in promoting and/or inhibiting the transformation of traditional gender roles is not self-evident.

According to Sontag, camp's transformative power stems from what Deleuze and Guattari label 'artifice', a connection to an anti-essentialist, theatrical view of identity. As Sontag explains, theatricality is the fundamental aspect of camp: 'To perceive Camp in objects and persons is to understand Being-as-Playing-a-Role. It is the farthest extension, in sensibility, of the metaphor of life as theatre' (Sontag 1966: 280). In Findley's novel, Lucy's rebellious power likewise draws its strength from a vision of 'life as theatre'.

In an early episode, Lucy's brother, Michael Archangelis, chastises her for 'dressing as a woman. *And* a foreigner' (Findley 1984: 107). He goes on to remind her that, as an angel, she is, if not a man, then certainly 'male'. To counter his criticism, Lucy insists on her love of acting: 'I like dressing up,' she says. 'I always have. You know that. Me as the Pope – me as the King. Why not? It's harmless enough' (Findley 1984: 107). Whereas her love of theatricality enrages those obsessed with maintaining order, individuals who are marginalised by the system appreciate her subversive, theatrical bent.[8]

Findley, who pursued a successful career as an actor before embarking on his career as a writer, repeatedly links transgressive behaviour with this type of playful, non-essentialist attitude towards one's role. Rather than portray Satan as an angry child, getting back at Daddy/God, Findley eschews the model of a static, Oedipalised identity in favour of a model that identifies Lucy with a series of flows. Satan emerges as a shape-shifter who enters into relations with other forces in an effort to combat a deathly, fascist hierarchy.

Deleuze asserts that becomings are predicated on two forms of combat: one involving an external opposition and the other involving an internal struggle between one's own parts. In the episode cited above, Lucy engages in two distinct forms of combat. On the one hand, she enters into an external combat against God's external, repressive order, enforced, in this case, by Japeth. But she also engages in an internal combat between angelic/human and masculine/feminine forces. This type of internal combat, which Deleuze terms 'combat-between', tries to take hold of a force 'in order to make it one's own' (Deleuze and Guattari 1997: 132). By adopting the gestures and affects of a human and, more specifically, a woman, Satan instigates this type of 'combat-between' – a process through which 'a force enriches itself by seizing hold of other forces and joining itself to them in a new ensemble: a becoming' (Deleuze and Guattari 1997: 132).

As Deleuze points out, however, it is not enough to enter into relations with other equal forces; there must be differentials among the forces that facilitate transformation: 'A power is an idiosyncrasy of forces, such that the dominant force is transformed by passing into the dominated forces, and the dominated by passing into the dominant – a centre of metamorphosis' (Deleuze and Guattari 1997: 133). Findley's text constructs this centre of metamorphosis when Lucy, an angel and dominant force, enters into an ensemble with a series of dominated forces, including human, woman, homosexual, animal and, finally, the small force of insects.

To gain a greater understanding of the first stage of Lucy's becoming, it is useful to consider Findley's long-standing interest in the figure of the transvestite and his implicit insistence on the strengths and limits of the challenge posed by cross-dressing and drag. For example, the author's more recent novel *Headhunter* (1993) similarly underscores the connection between drag and 'Being-as-Playing-a-Role'. In a key episode, a power-hungry psychiatrist asks his patient to write an essay outlining why she wants help, who she thinks she is, and how she sees herself. Although the patient dutifully completes the assignment, she upholds a camp vision of the world and refuses to conform to the model of a fixed, essential identity. 'We're all in drag . . .' she writes. 'Me in black. You in grey. It's a drag act – men pretending to be men – women pretending to be women – but only the artists will tell us that. The rest of us cannot bear the revelation' (Findley 1993: 341). Despite the power of the 'revelation' that identity and, more specifically, gender is an act, *Headhunter* clarifies that drag alone cannot necessarily effect a radical transformation of the social order. Although 'we're all in drag', an earlier episode emphasises that becoming-woman does not necessarily liberate individuals from traditional gender roles and other repressive, hierarchical social mechanisms.

In his insightful study of camp, Kim Michasiw categorises camp and camp-recognition as forms of irony. Yet, as a number of critics have observed, irony 'can be a weapon equally of hegemonic groups and of the oppressed' (Michasiw 1994: 153).[9] Warnings about the complexity of camp's ironic codes are especially pertinent to a key episode in *Headhunter's* third section, which portrays the struggle between a young boy, Warren Ellis, a budding transvestite, and his mother, Freda Manly, who uses feminine wiles to climb the corporate ladder. As the narrator explains:

> Warren Ellis first wore women's clothes when he was five years old. Caught in his mother's closet one afternoon while she entertained her lover, Tony Bloor, Warren believed he could escape their notice by pretending to be someone else. Emerging from his hiding place, he wore a large black hat with a veil . . .

'Is that you, Warren?' his mother asked, looking out from beneath Tony Bloor. Warren had his answer ready.
'No,' he said. And left the room. (Findley 1993: 121)

As a child, Warren believes that he can transform himself into someone else by cross-dressing, but he revises this view after subsequent transvestic experiments.

He appears in women's clothes for the second time when he plays the role of Katerina in *The Taming of the Shrew* at a school performance. His rendition is so convincing that several parents complained that a girl had been brought in to play the role, and the boy who played Petruchio 'was beside himself with desire. He became so disturbed by Warren's charms that he failed an English exam' (Findley 1993: 122). On this occasion, Warren, who is both loved from afar by one youth and raped by another, experiences the power and the danger that attend becoming-woman.[10]

The third time Warren cross-dresses, he consciously uses this power to foil his mother's attempt at a takeover of the family business, following the death of her second husband. When Warren learns that the final and key shareholder in the company (and, consequently, his mother's next sexual target), Gordon Perry, longs to 'dress athletic youths in women's clothing', Warren once again puts his transvestic talents to use. At her husband's funeral, Freda Manly wonders at the mysterious, fashionable woman who arrives with Perry:

> All at once, Freda turned. Her mouth fell open. The profile beside her had come at last into focus. It produced a low and masculine cough.
> Freda leaned away and stared in horror. 'Is that you, Warren?' she said.
> Warren knew it was best to have his answer ready.
> 'Yes,' he said.
> And he gave his mother a dazzling smile. (Findley 1993: 147–8)

Warren's response to his mother seemingly attests to his delight in taking up a position as a multiple, rather than unified Oedipalised subject. However, the outcome of his cross-dressing intimates that he does not so much subvert gender roles as identify with his mother, assume her place, and cement his alliance with another powerful male. In this case, it remains difficult to conceive of his transvestism as truly subversive. The symbolic order hardly grinds to a halt when Warren dons a Balenciaga and pearls to outdo his mother in the male-dominated corporate game. Masculine and feminine stereotypes remain firmly entrenched when Warren takes his place beside Perry and, as the 'truly' phallic woman (in comparison to the 'fake' pretender, Freda Manly), lays claim to his admirer's heart and corporate shares. As the text demonstrates, the rites of transvestism alone cannot destabilise entrenched binary constructions. For Deleuze and Guattari and, it would seem, for Findley, as well, becoming-woman does not represent the end point of deterritorialisation; *Headhunter* demonstrates how this strategy can get bogged down and fall back into Oedipal patterns.

In *Not Wanted on the Voyage*, the transvestic situation is ostensibly far less conservative because Lucy, although male, is not a *man*, but an angel.[11] Second, she cross-dresses, not to pass as a woman and gain financial clout, but to flaunt convention and escape from the repressive, homosocial order of heaven. In Findley's version of Lucifer's fall, Satan was not defeated by the heavenly hosts: he chose to leave. Although the war with Lucifer is 'proclaimed a victory in Heaven', Michael Archangelis knows that Lucifer 'had not been vanquished; he had escaped' (Findley 1984: 101). In this case, the unrelenting masculine sameness of heaven, orchestrated by a moribund God and his all-male contingent (a parody of the male-dominated corporate structure) instigates Lucifer's flight.[12] In her challenge to God's private homosocial perversity and public support for heterosexism, Lucy does not so much reverse God's order as fight for a more inclusive and tolerant perspective.[13]

Towards the end of the novel, Lucy discloses her angelic status and admits to her sympathetic friends aboard the ark that she travelled to earth in search of a world that would accept difference. Although lengthy, her monologue is worth quoting in full:

> Where I was born – the trees were always in the sun . . . The merciless light. It never rained – though we never lacked for water. *Always fair weather*! Dull. I wanted storms. I wanted difference. And I heard this rumour . . . about another world. And I wondered – does it rain there . . . I wanted, too, someone I could argue with. Someone – just once – with whom I could disagree. And I had heard this rumour: about another world. And I wondered . . . might there be people there, in this other world, who would tell me the sky was green? Who would say that dry is wet – and black is white? And if I were to say; '*I am not I – but whoever I wish to be*,' would I be believed – in this other world? (Findley 1984: 282)

With its insistence on the need to accept difference and to embrace a non-essentialist view of identity, Lucy's statements seem unequivocally and compellingly progressive. Yet a closer reading of the particulars of her oriental-inspired drag act expose the less overt strengths and limitations of Satan's line of flight.

Surprisingly, critics have remained silent on the topic of the Kabuki or 'oriental' style of Lucy's glamour drag, despite the fact that it remains a central aspect of her performance.[14] As noted earlier, Lucy's brother Michael criticises her specifically because she imitates, not simply a woman, but 'a foreigner', someone 'not of these parts' (Findley 1984: 107). She responds by interrogating his terms: 'And what, may one ask, do you mean by "a foreigner"? . . . The slanted eyes, et cetera? The black, black hair – the white, white face? You don't like it? I *love*' (Findley 1984: 107). While Satan may well be delighted, readers may be less certain about what to make of Findley's gleeful, kimono-clad devil, mincing across the ark.

Lucy's passion for things foreign raises important questions about the politics of becomings outlined in Findley's novel. Depending on the reader, Satan's attraction may be understood as a pernicious symptom of orientalism or it may be taken as an ironic gesture that paradoxically offers itself as a remedy for this type of gender and racial stereotyping. If, as Linda Hutcheon argues, the recognition or attribution of irony depends on a range of clues that signal that irony is being used (Hutcheon 1994: 151), then readers must carefully interrogate the visual references associated with Satan's becoming-woman.

For my part, I found it intriguing that Lucifer's costume – which includes, among other things, a variety of silk kimonos and a wig of 'jet-black hair' – is drawn from Kabuki, the Japanese theatrical tradition. The 'strange white powder' that covers her face and the 'finely drawn eyebrows' are likewise adopted from the highly stylised *kumadori*, the elaborate makeup used in Kabuki.[15] Not only does Lucy adopt the Kabuki costume and makeup, but, throughout the novel, she also makes use of the two favourite stage properties of the Kabuki actor, the fan and the paper umbrella (Ernst 1956: 184; Yoshida 1977: 116). Even the physical aspects of her performance, which include speaking in a falsetto voice, adopting a mincing walk, and changing costumes on stage, allude to the standard practices of the Kabuki actors who impersonate women (Komparu 1983: 51).

On one level, by aligning Satan's line of flight and the process of becoming with both the performances of drag queens and Asian theatrical traditions, Findley's narrative doubly reinforces a non-essentialist and non-mimetic approach to identity. Although some readers might be tempted to interpret Satan's drag act as reinscribing an orientalist perspective, the text prevents anyone from naturalising the stereotypical image of the exotic, submissive, hyper-feminine oriental woman. The ironic repetition of this image in a diabolical context substantially changes its meaning; right from the start, readers know that Lucifer lies underneath the kimonos. While the costume and makeup recall the racial stereotype, the text undermines its legitimacy by clarifying that the Other, in this case, the 'foreigner', is fabricated from the archive of the self. After all, it is a male angel, and God's favourite at that, who constructs the most believable representation of the 'foreigner'. Thus, rather than simply reinscribe the cliché, the novel traces the orientalist production to its source to reveal how gender stereotypes are woven together with racist, colonial fantasies. The fact that Lucy, decked out in her oriental costume, manages to fool God and his earthly servants attests to the power of racist stereotypes and divine and human ignorance concerning non-western cultures.[16]

Findley's treatment of the stereotype cannot be considered imitation and should not be confused with mimesis because Satan does not simply copy a woman. As suggested earlier, his drag act forcibly demonstrates the simulated nature of a supposedly natural femininity. Mimesis, according to Deleuze and Guattari, is bound up in a practice that seeks to distinguish the 'thing' from its images, the original from the copy (Deleuze 1990: 253). This practice aims to assure 'the triumph of the copies over simulacra, of repressing simulacra . . .' (Deleuze 1990: 257). This key element, the simulacra, possesses the ability to disrupt the supposedly natural relationship between original and copy. Although the simulacra is often defined as 'a copy of a copy, an infinitely degraded icon', Deleuze insists that it should be understood 'not simply [as] a false copy', but as an image that 'places in question the very notations of copy and model' (Deleuze 1990: 256).

I would suggest that Lucifer's drag act functions as a simulacrum. When Satan dresses as Lucy, in full Japanese Kabuki regalia, readers are faced with an angel self-consciously producing an image of a male fantasy of a woman. This is not mimesis because Satan is not simply imitating a woman and trying to pass as one. Instead, the flamboyant gestures and costume force readers to interrogate the very structure that posits original and copy. Critics of transvestism and drag likewise warn that drag should not be confused with imitation and mimesis, practices more properly associated with transvestism. According to Daniel Harris, in contrast to the transvestite, who imitates women and tries to 'blend seamlessly into the general public' (Harris 1997: 203), the drag queen experiments with style and calls attention to the very constructed nature of woman, the supposedly 'natural' original.

Findley's Asian intertext not only draws the reader's attention to the power of the simulacrum, it also affords additional information about the politics implicit in his rewriting of the story of the Flood. In their writings on becomings, Deleuze and Guattari highlight the relationship between this series of transformations and the resistance of minoritarian groups – groups that have been 'oppressed, prohibited, in revolt, or always on the fringe of recognized institutions' (Deleuze and Guattari 1987: 247). Before we go on to analyse the links between Lucy's drag and minoritarian politics, a brief review of the history of Kabuki might be helpful.

According to tradition, Kabuki was first performed in Kyoto in 1596, but reached its peak in the Tokugawa, or Edo, period (1603–1868). Although Kabuki was said to have been invented by a woman in Kyoto in 1596 and was initially open to women actors, Women's Kabuki was quickly banned early on by the government. The decree, issued on 23 October 1929, was based on the supposed immorality of the performers, many of whom were prostitutes (Ernst 1956: 10–11).

After women were prohibited from appearing on stage, their roles were taken over by long-haired handsome boys. Young Men's Kabuki enjoyed tremendous popularity until it, too, met the fate of Women's Kabuki in 1652, when certain of the samurai found themselves 'unduly attracted to the boys' (Ernst 1956: 11).[17] Henceforth, Kabuki was performed by adult males, who lessened their attractiveness by cutting off their hair. The actors who portrayed women, known as *onnagata*, were expected to play them 'offstage as well, living the self-effacing roles expected of Japanese women'. For generations a small number of men 'spent their lives playing and acting as women' (Bullough and Bullough 1993: 242).

Owing to its association with transgressive desire, the contemporary term 'Kabuki' is derived from the word *kabuku*, a now obsolete verb from the Momoyama period (1573–1603), which originally meant 'to incline'. By the beginning of the seventeenth century, 'Kabuki' had come to mean 'to be unusual or out of the ordinary', but it still 'carried the connotation of sexual debauchery' (Ernst 1956: 10). Homosexuality has always been associated with the Kabuki theatre (Bullough and Bullough 1993: 242).

Furnished with only this cursory knowledge of Kabuki – one of the best known of the Asian transvestite theatres – readers can begin to appreciate how Findley's narrative simultaneously invokes the process of becoming-woman, camp aesthetics and Kabuki to form specific alliances with historically oppressed groups,[18] in addition to signalling the unstable and constructed basis of gender and racial identities. By covertly drawing parallels between Lucy, the exiled drag queen, who is clearly 'not straight', and the Kabuki *onnagata*, who were likewise deemed 'aslant', the text situates the devil's plea for the acceptance of difference within the historical context of the prohibition and oppression of homosexuals.

Despite its efficacy in making a bid for the acceptance of difference, the novel intimates that challenges to God's oppressive, hierarchical order cannot solely rely on becoming-woman. As we will see, sustained dependence on Kabuki and drag ultimately limits the impact of the revolutionary protest and the radical challenge posed by becomings – of which becomings-woman is only the first step.[19]

The impact of Satan's revolt is compromised largely because both Kabuki and drag work within (and therefore tend to reinscribe and re-essentialise) the gender stereotypes that they seek to overturn. Their complicity with the system they seek to overturn becomes apparent when one recognises that in both drag and Kabuki the standard means of signalling that an actor is constructing the illusion of femininity involves removing an article of clothing or changing costume on stage. In Japanese theatre, this gesture obeys the Kabuki principles of 'displaying frankly the means by which its effects are produced' (Ernst 1956: 186). Traditional performances of drag queens likewise typically conclude with the removal of a key article of clothing.

Findley's text makes use of these conventions in the scene cited earlier, in which Lucy sheds most of her feminine garb and describes her quest for a world tolerant of difference. When Lucy removes her costume, she likewise abandons the use of falsetto. We are told that her voice 'was not a voice that any of those who were present had ever heard before. It was a darkened voice – with a harshness to it that was foreign to the woman they had known' (Findley 1984: 282). Even the blind cat Mottyl 'could sense that something was happening to Lucy. She could feel the other Lucy being erased: departing' (Findley 1984: 283). Without her makeup, Lucy's face is completely transformed:

> The face beneath the face that had been was sallow in colour – almost grey. Its mouth was wider and its lips fuller than the mouth and the lips that had been. Its nose was longer – sharper – stronger – more divisive. The face it halved was angular and harsh: a face without room for laughter, or even smiles. Above it, there was a short-cropped crown of copper hair – and right down the centre of this hair – a strand of white. (Findley 1984: 284)

In this instance, the text may once again be drawing both on drag and established Asian theatrical practices, in which a change of costume, particularly on female characters, is one of the standard methods of 'renewing audience interest' (Ernst 1956: 186). But what exactly are the implications of this transformation?

According to critics who study drag, even when the wig is doffed, ceremonially, at the end of a transvestic stage performance, this does not mean that rigid gender identities are re-established. As Marjorie Garber states:

> What is the 'answer' that is disclosed? Only another question: is *this* the real one? In what sense real? What is the 'truth' of gender and sexuality that we try, in vain to see, to see through, when what we are gazing at is a hall of mirrors? (Garber 1992: 389)

Although the removal of Lucy's costume does not necessarily reinscribe fixed sex-gender roles, it is nevertheless significant that Satan chooses, in a moment of crisis, to reveal what are traditionally considered more masculine traits.[20] The repeated emphasis on Lucy's underlying 'harshness' also lends support to the suspicion that Satan's success in portraying a strong woman – a woman capable of fighting for the rights of minorities – is due to these underlying, masculine traits.

It is also useful to view Lucy's change of costume in terms of the evolving aesthetic of drag. As it turns out, Findley's portrait of Lucy shifts from an exotic hyper-feminine creature to a more masculine, butch warrior and recalls two distinct early phases of the aesthetic, both of which are heavily invested in traditional gender roles.[21]

In addition to drawing on the history of drag, Satan's exposure of a more masculine harshness also recalls the tenets of traditional Kabuki, which holds that only a man can portray ideal feminine beauty.[22] Whether or not Lucy's underlying 'harshness' is informed by the 'strong line' that can supposedly only be provided by a man and is deemed essential in Kabuki, the adoption of a more masculine personae highlights the limitations of any challenge to traditional gender roles that does not venture beyond becomings-woman. As Deleuze and Guattari warn, it is as 'deplorable to miniaturize, internalize the binary machine as it is to exacerbate it; it does not extricate us from it' (Deleuze and Guattari 1987: 276). By oscillating between stereotypical feminine and masculine gender roles, even Satan himself cannot completely destabilise the entrenched binary system.

Although I recognise the limitations of drag, I do not accept Deleuze and Guattari's dismissal of transvestism and conflation of the practice with imitation. Instead, I argue that transvestism must be distinguished from drag, and that while a distinction needs to be drawn between the self-conscious performance of drag and true becomings, the former can pave the way for more radical forms of deterritorialisation.

To its credit, Findley's novel makes no attempt to conceal the limitations of working within the system that one opposes. Throughout the text, readers are reminded that Lucy remains attracted to and repulsed by the homosocial order that she attempts to overthrow. This defiant yet complicit position *within* the fascist system is underscored both by the enduring bond shared with her militant Michael Archangelis – a bond that partly accounts for her nostalgia for heaven – and by her love of camp performance.

The text forcibly exposes Lucy's nostalgia for God's male-dominated order and her connection to Michael in the scene cited earlier, in which Michael criticises Lucy's experiment with drag. When Michael strides away, Lucy watches him with 'a mixture of relief and regret', and the text offers us insight into her deep feelings for her brother:

> Human company was not the same as angel company. Only an angel knew that. Lucy would miss Michael above all her brothers. Like enemies everywhere and always, in their hatred there was devotion. Even love. 'Goodbye!' she called.
> Michael went on marching. He did not turn.
> 'Goodbye!' Lucy called again. 'Remember – alway remember – only Michael Archangelis can kill me! No one else! No one! Ever!' (Findley 1984: 109)

This emotionally and erotically charged episode exposes Lucy's devotion to the heavenly order and those whom she ostensibly hates.[23] More importantly, this scene also clarifies that her camp performance of the hyper-feminine oriental woman remains tied to the hyper-masculine performance of western male identity (what Kim Michasiw calls 'masquerade') offered by Michael Archangelis and his earthly protégé, Japeth.[24] The text hints at the interdependent relationship between camp and masquerade by repeatedly juxtaposing camp and masquerade in scenes featuring Lucy and Michael. After Michael disappears from the text when Lucy boards the ark, Japeth takes the militant angel's place. It seems far from coincidental that Lucy's campiest moments occur when Japeth, emulating his angelic hero, straps on his leather breastplate, grasps his sword, and performs the macho masquerade.[25]

Through this type of juxtaposition, the text subtly confirms Michasiw's insight that camp and masquerade represent the two 'interdependent modalities of the masculine' (Michasiw 1994: 147). Thus, rather than propel the individual towards authentic transformation, which would involve ego-loss, both camp and masquerade maintain and discipline the contradictory forces of repulsion and attraction that surface in the face of the potential 'deliquescence of gendering' (Michasiw 1994: 167).[26] In accordance with Michasiw's analysis of camp's elaborate and ambivalent strategies of defence, the deployment of both camp and its cognate, masquerade, in *Not Wanted on the Voyage* is likewise neither wholly capable, nor completely desirous of dismantling the prevailing phallocentric order. Lucy's nostalgia for angelic, masculine company together with the 'harshness' that surfaces in her demeanour mark the limits of Findley's representation of drag and becomings-woman.[27]

To conclude the analysis of images of transformation at this point, however, would be to overlook what may well be the strongest challenge in Findley's text to the fascist desire to order humanity on the basis of a misguided notion of masculine perfection. Within the novel, becomings-woman represent only one phase in a series of even more radical images of the fragmentation of human identity. The connections among various forms of deterritorialisation become apparent when one traces the hostile responses directed at those who experiment with different modes of ego-loss. Not surprisingly, the contempt directed at those who cross-dress is minimal compared to the hatred reserved for those who explore the more transgressive possibility of forging alliances with animals.

The increasingly severe penalties meted out to those who transgress the social codes clarify that assuming a gendered position is merely one means by which the subject perpetuates itself: individuals must also take up a position as 'human' as opposed to 'animal'. In the novel, the opportunity to transgress this boundary, to form hybrids and demonic alliances is everywhere apparent and everywhere brutally controlled.

Right from the start, the text alerts readers to the instability of the socially construed human/animal opposition. For example, in the opening section, the narrator subtly aligns Noah's beloved sons with animals: Shem, the eldest, is dubbed 'Shem The Ox', and the macho Japeth is repeatedly associated with his beloved wolves.[28] Readers must also come to grips with the fact that one of the central focalisers is Mrs Noyes' cat, Mottyl. She regularly makes forays into the forest to converse with her animal friends. At bottom, in a fiction such as this, where animals speak and reason like humans and humans behave like animals, the boundary between the categories of human and non-human repeatedly blurs.

Virtually all of the human characters negotiate the possibility of becoming-animal. For instance, before the ark is swept off the hill, Mrs Noyes flees the vessel in search of her beloved cat. Released from Noah's surveillance, Mrs Noyes gorges on forbidden apples:[29] '*I am like a cow*', she thinks. '*Standing in the rain and staring into space. At any minute, I will begin to chew my cud!*' (Findley 1984: 143). For the first time, she escapes from the constraints of the patriarchal order and the necessity of maintaining her Oedipalised identity as wife and mother. As the narrator explains:

It was such a curious time for Mrs Noyes – what with her being so utterly alone, losing track of the days, feeding entirely on apples and sleeping in the trees. But she did have moments – wandering through the fields or walking along some trackless path – when she felt that civilization was falling away from her shoulders, and she was gratified. What a burden it had been! . . . One morning, Mrs Noyes lifted her skirts and – squatting in full view of the windows of an abandoned carriage – she peed. (Findley 1984: 146)[30]

Mrs Noyes becomes increasingly animal-like in foraging for food (Findley 1984: 132), in moving through the river 'crablike-sideways' (Findley 1984: 153) and in giving herself what Donna Pennee describes as 'paws of sorts' and a new hide or coat made of bits of torn cloth (Pennee 1993: 181–2). When Mrs Noyes almost completely succumbs to the process of becoming animal, she recognises that she is not even 'afraid of rats any more. Now, she was one of them' (Findley 1984: 183).[31] Her relief at the waning forces of civilisation and her comment about the rats recall Deleuze and Guattari's discussion of the film *Willard* and their insight that, of all animals, the 'proliferation of rats, the pack, brings a becoming-molecular that undermines the great molar powers of family . . . and conjugality' (Deleuze and Guattari 1987: 233). As she herself observes, by becoming-rat, Mrs Noyes escapes the 'oppression of time – the daily ritual of violence – all that prayer and blood and wine – and the dreariness of protocol: having to ask permission to speak and touch and move' (Findley 1984: 146).

As mentioned earlier, in their discussion of becomings, Deleuze and Guattari map a series of transformations that culminate in becoming-invisible, becoming-imperceptible. But these constitute end-points that neither Findley nor any of his characters attain. Although more will be said about Findley's own negotiations with becomings in his role as writer, at this point, it is important to clarify that Mrs Noyes never completely relinquishes her civilised identity. In the episode cited above, just after she urinates, she catches sight of another person. Like a soldier off duty who suddenly hears a command and instinctively salutes, she immediately 'scurrie[s] to her feet and thr[ows] down the hems of her skirts. She even felt her hand – unbidden – rising to touch her hair and adjust the closing at her neck' (Findley 1984: 147).[32] Thus, only within the limits demarcated by the Other, does Mrs Noyes willingly engage in the process of becoming-animal.[33]

By contrast, her husband Noah dedicates his life to cutting off this line of flight. Both Noah and his wife, however, possess tangible proof of their potential for deterritorialisation and difference – proof that the latter takes great pains to conceal. Initially, only they know that Japeth's twin, whom they drowned at birth, was what they term an 'ape-child'. To prevent anyone from tracing this so-called defect to him, Noah married Japeth to Emma – a girl whose sister Lotte was also an 'ape-child'. Noah reasoned that if Japeth and Emma bore a deformed child, Emma could be held responsible. Despite his devious plotting, there is no way to escape the evidence of difference; towards the end of the novel, the stillborn child that Noah adulterously fathers with Shem's wife, Hannah, also turns out to be an 'ape-child'.

Because he cannot accept the non-human strain within himself, Noah lives in fear that everyone is on the verge of slipping off his or her appointed rung on the evolutionary ladder. To borrow the words of Deleuze and Guattari, Noah has internalised the 'threat of Oedipus', which states that, 'if you don't follow the lines of differentiation daddy-mommy-me, and the exclusive alternatives that delineate them, you will fall into the black night of the undifferentiated' (Deleuze and Guattari 1983: 78). Dr Noyes remains tormented and torments others owing to his binaristic conviction that '*you cannot be an ape and be of God*' (Findley 1984: 239). His conviction that everyone should conform to their appointed role prompts him to rape Japeth's twelve-year-old wife with the unicorn's horn, so that she will finally submit to so-called normal conjugal relations.

In contrast to Noah's brutal and hysterical efforts to maintain order, Satan serenely engages in a process of becomings that dissolve the human/non-human opposition on which the social order rests. Viewed in the context of the tension between human and animal, the name 'Lucy' specifically recalls the famous discovery in East Africa of the fossil of an unusual hominid, which led to major revisions in the understanding of human biological evolution. The discovery of 'Lucy' furnished evidence that, in the period from one to three million years ago, the genus Homo ('true human') coexisted with other advanced man-ape forms. Both of these hominids appear to be descendants of an Ethiopian fossil, the 3–13.7 million-year-old Australopithecus afarensis – the famous 'Lucy' skeleton found in 1974. The retrieval of Lucy and related fossils in the 1970s and 1980s proved that different types of early humans coexisted: a revelation that put serious kinks in the theory of a single evolutionary chain ('Lucy').

By casting Satan as a drag queen who chooses the name 'Lucy', the text creates a convergence between two semiotic regimes and reminds readers of the importance of these pre-historic findings. The narrative also paints a moving portrait of the coexistence of various hominids in biblical times.

As noted earlier, in Noah's and Emma's family 'ape-children' and more recognisably 'human' children spring from the same source.

As in the case of Satan's Kabuki-inspired drag, which calls into question the essential nature of the feminine stereotype, the use of the name 'Lucy' also highlights the inability to distinguish a single, pure, origin. In both instances, readers experience what Deleuze and Guattari describe as the simulacrum's 'positive power which denies *the original and the copy, the model and the reproduction*' (Deleuze 1990: 262). This same denial of a pure origin surfaces in Deleuze and Guattari's *A Thousand Plateaus*, a work that articulates the primordial interdependence of the State and the nomad. Likewise, *Not Wanted on the Voyage* disrupts the project of selecting lineages – a project that aims 'to distinguish pretenders; to distinguish the pure from the impure, the authentic from the inauthentic' (Deleuze 1990: 254). The world portrayed by Findley – a world in which God opts for suicide and his disciple Noah, in the absence of divine authority, invents the Truth – is neither secured by a divine origin nor an original image of perfection.

In his fascist quest to secure a singular origin and instantiate perfection, Dr Noyes takes it upon himself to select lineages, separate the pure from the impure: a process that involves inscribing an artificial boundary between human and animal. He sees to it that Japeth's twin is drowned at birth, and when Mrs Noyes brings Lotte aboard the ark, Noah arranges for Japeth to slit her throat; finally, he ensures that Hannah throws her stillborn 'ape-child' into the sea. Grieving at the injustice of it all, Lucy prophesies holocausts to come and tells Ham that people like Dr Noyes 'will go on throwing all the apes and all the demons and all the Unicorns overboard for as long as this voyage lasts' (Findley 1984: 349).

In a final bid to resist these brutal dictates, Lucy engages in a series of becomings that forcibly illustrate proliferation and multiplicity. Towards the end of the novel, Satan, appearing in yet another incarnation, rises from the stairwell surrounded by a strange sound:

> The humming sound that accompanied this woman's entrance grew very loud – and soon it was clear exactly what it was, when the woman lifted two large, woven beehives onto the deck and set them in the sun.
> [. . .]
> At first it had not been clear this woman was Lucy. Only her great height was reminiscent of her other incarnations. Now her hair was neither black nor red – but honey-coloured – and neither rolled and set in piles on top of her head, nor close-cropped and wavy. This hair was long and straight and it hung down her back as far as her shoulder blades. The face – this time – was neither round nor angular, but wide and flat, with extra-

ordinary eyes of an almost golden colour: animal eyes, fierce and tender. The eyes of a prophet whose words, like an animal's warning cries, would be ignored. (Findley 1984: 343, 344)

In this scene, Satan's face is neither 'round nor angular', that is to say, neither symbolically feminine nor masculine. Instead, as Lord of the flies (in this case, Lord of the bees), Satan traces a line of flight that forges an alliance with the insect-world and moves beyond the angel and human orders altogether.[34] The description of Satan's eyes as the 'eyes of a prophet' who 'would be ignored' suggests, further, that Satan (and, by extension, Findley) recognises that he is not addressing his contemporaries. Instead, he communicates in order to 'summon forth' what Deleuze calls 'a people yet to come' (Deleuze and Guattari 1994: 176). According to John Hughes the people yet to come are a collective entity located on 'the far side of a deconstituted subjectivity, narrative, and knowledge'; moreover, their coming is 'announced through making the standard or major language [to borrow Deleuze and Guattari's words], "stammer, tremble, cry or even sing"' (Hughes 1998: 68–9; see Deleuze and Guattari 1994: 176).

By following the sequence of transformations that constitute Satan's line of flight, readers can appreciate 'the linkage, unleashing, and communication of the becomings triggered by the transvestite; the power of the resultant becoming-animal; and above all the participation of these becomings in a specific war machine' (Deleuze and Guattari 1987: 278).

In its representation of becomings, *Not Wanted on the Voyage* is not unique in Findley's corpus. His fictions repeatedly feature transformations that undermine oppositions between male and female, sane and insane, and human and animal. On occasion, his narratives draw explicit connections between acting (particularly, Japanese theatre traditions) and the process of becoming. Perhaps the most explicit representation to date of the relationship between performance and becomings can be found in his short story 'Foxes'.

Commissioned by the Royal Ontario Museum (ROM) and published in its publication *Rotunda* in 1987, 'Foxes' is set in the Museum's Far Eastern Department. The story traces the mysterious transformation of a famous communication's expert, Morris Glendenning. When the story opens, Glendenning, equally renown for his expert opinions and for his reclusiveness, has journeyed to the ROM to analyse its collection of Japanese theatre masks. Glendenning's interest in the masks was sparked when he glimpsed a photograph on the cover of *Rotunda* featuring a mask recently purchased and brought from the Orient. Although the caption read 'Fox', he recognised that the mask was not quite a fox: it was 'a *human fox*' (Findley 1988: 64). Through reading about the masks, he learns that they were of a series created for a seventeenth-century Japanese drama, in which a fox becomes a man; each of the masks illustrates a separate stage in the transformation.[35]

While contemplating the photograph and peering into the lacquered face of the mask, Glendenning imagines 'stripping off the layers of the human face. Not to the bone, but to the being' (Findley 1988: 65). In this case, the impulse to view the actual masks exceeds mere curiosity. As the narrator explains, 'a trigger was pulled in the deeps of his consciousness. Something had been recognized' (Findley 1988: 65). Glendenning realises that, under 'the weight of all his personal masks, there was a being he had never seen. Not a creature hidden by design – but something buried alive that wanted to live and that had a right to life' (Findley 1988: 65–6). Later that same day, standing in front of a mirror, he catches sight of his unmasked self. What had been unmasked had not been human: 'What he had seen – and all he had seen – was a pair of pale gold eyes that stared from a surround of darkness he could not identify' (Findley 1988: 66). The image of golden 'animal eyes' recalls Lucy's final incarnation in *Not Wanted on the Voyage*.[36] Here, too, transformations in the eye/I signal the formation of alliances between human and animal, 'creative involutions bearing witness to an "*inhumanity immediately experienced in the body . . .*"' (Deleuze and Guattari 1987: 273).

In keeping with *Not Wanted on the Voyage*, 'Foxes' juxtaposes transformations of this sort against the dangerous sterility and oppressiveness of the individualistic, Oedipal social order. As he makes his way to the museum, walking along Toronto's busy Bloor Street, Glendenning contemplates the crowd rushing past: 'Not one person was looking at any other . . . Why were they so unconcerned with one another? When had they all become collectively impassive?' (Findley 1988: 67–8).[37] As if to defy this repressive social code, which rests on the opposition between self and other, Glendenning enters into a relationship with the vulpine pack. Slipping into the Museum, he makes his way to the storage area unnoticed and places the mask against his face.

Here a mask, rather than cross-dressing, triggers the process of becoming-animal.[38] When Glendenning places the mask on his face, he initiates a transformation and enacts an age-old ritual familiar to the main actor of the Noh play, known as the 'shite'. Using only his willpower, the 'shite' calls forth multiple identities:

Just before going on stage the *shite* sits before a mirror . . . facing his own reflected image and puts on the mask. As he gazes intently through the tiny pupil eyeholes at the figure in the mirror, a kind of willpower is born, and the image – another self, that is, an *other* – begins to approach the actor's everyday internal self. (Komparu 1983: 7–8)

There is, according to a critic of Noh theatre, a tremendous difference 'between taking on the appearance of another while retaining the self, which is accomplished with makeup [what happens in Kabuki], and becoming a completely different being through transformation [what happens in Noh]' (Komparu 1983: 226). In accordance with this latter transformation, when Glendenning dons the mask, he encounters a self that is neither unified nor domesticated.

The first time he tries on the mask, Glendenning discovers that the self is only 'a threshold, a door, a becoming between two multiplicities' and he finds himself transported (Deleuze and Guattari 1987: 249). Earth replaces the tile floor beneath his feet and seated around him are non-human creatures, which turn out to be foxes.[39] As the narrator explains, 'never in all of Morris's life had he been so close to anything wild' (Findley 1988: 72). When one of the animals gazes at him, seemingly desirous of communication, he finds himself overcome with the desire to speak. But the force of the 'sound of something rising through his bowel' is 'so alarming' that he pulls the mask from his face (Findley 1988: 72). The next time he puts the mask on, he finds his voice; it is not 'his human voice but another voice from another time' (Findley 1988: 73). To reinforce the reader's awareness of the fracturing of Glendenning's ego, the narrator adds that '[n]ow – at last – he was not alone' (Findley 1988: 73).

In their discussion of becomings, Deleuze and Guattari insist that it involves a creative symbiosis which creates a deterritorialisation of both bodies involved (see Hughes 1998: 44–5). Likewise, in 'Foxes' both the foxes and Glendenning undergo a metamorphosis. In forming an assemblage, both the foxes cease to be recognisable as foxes (they become something else) as does Glendenning. As the latter recognises, the fox is 'on its way to becoming a man' (Findley 1988: 70). Those familiar with Deleuze and Guattari's discussion of becomings-animal in *A Thousand Plateaus* will recognise the fox that 'came and sat at his feet and stared up into [Glendenning's] . . . face' as the 'anomalous' – 'a specific animal that draws and occupies the borderline, as leader of the pack' (Deleuze and Guattari 1987: 245). Anyone tempted to dismiss these transformations as a hallucination must contend with the fact that, when Glendenning flees the Museum, the secretaries in the office remark on the presence of strange odour. They both smell dog.

While it is interesting to trace Findley's obsession with becomings, it is perhaps equally important to learn what would prompt an author to champion multiplicity, connectedness and collective alliances so relentlessly in his fiction. According to Findley, the desire to oppose fascism crystallised when he stumbled on the pictures of Dachau taken by Ivan Moffat, the first official photographer allowed through the gates of the Nazi concentration camp. Learning what the Nazis and the fascist programme had accomplished was, for him, an epiphanic moment. As he explains, 'I was never to see myself again as a being apart. How, after all, can you be *apart* when everyone else is standing *apart* beside you?' (qtd Roberts 1994: 39). In interviews, he admits that he wrote *Not Wanted on the Voyage* fired by the conviction that civilisation started to fall apart when humans put their faith in unity and identity rather than in multiplicity – when they chose 'one God over a belief in the holiness of all living things' (qtd in Roberts 1994: 89).

As a writer, Findley remains deeply concerned about the author's relationship to his community – a a relationship that is informed by the author's connection to his art. These are also issues of tremendous concern to Deleuze and Guattari, who view art as an ensemble that can instigate becomings. What is perhaps most intriguing about their respective visions is that neither Findley nor Deleuze and Guattari articulate a singular model of this relationship. For example, in their text *What is Philosophy?* (first published in French in 1991), Deleuze and Guattari offer a description of the relationship between creator and created that draws on familiar modernist conceptions of art which stress the independence of the art from the artist. At one point, they directly address this topic:

> What about the creator? [The work] . . . is independent of the creator through the self-positing of the created, which is preserved in itself. What is preserved – the thing or the work of art – is *a block of sensation, that is to say a compound of percepts and affects.* (Deleuze and Guattari 1994: 164)

Later, in this same text, Deleuze and Guattari refer to the artist as 'a seer' (Deleuze and Guattari 1994: 171), and they reiterate that the aim of art is to 'extract a bloc of sensations, a pure being of sensation' (Deleuze and Guattari 1994: 167). Taken together, their insistence on the work's independence from the creator and their choice of terms, including words such as 'seer' and 'pure', echo modernist conceptions of the author as a genius or master, a seer or prophet who extracts epiphanic blocks of pure form, sensations divorced from the sordid material world. Perhaps the literary critic Frank Kermode puts it best when, in his discussion of modernist writers who espoused this type of perspective, he says, 'What we feel about these men at times is that they retreated into some paradigm, into a timeless and unreal vacuum from which all reality had been pumped' (Kermode 1967: 113).[40]

By contrast, in their earlier study entitled *Kafka: Toward a Minor Literature* (first published in 1975), Deleuze and Guattari outline an entirely different conception of the relationship between writer and text. In Chapter 3, 'What is a Minor Literature', they describe a collective and materially grounded view of art. This view, seemingly informed by postmodern and poststructuralist reactions to modernism's elitism, stresses art's embeddedness in social and historical structures. In listing the central characteristics of minor literature, they suggest that it 'takes on a collective value' and that 'there are no possibilities for an individual enunciation that would belong to this or that "master"' (Deleuze and Guattari 1986: 17). In an important passage, they elaborate on their sense of the work's communal nature:

> When a statement is produced by . . . an artistic singularity, it occurs necessarily as a function of a national, political, and social community, even if the objective conditions of this community are not yet given to the moment except in literary enunciation. (Deleuze and Guattari 1986: 84)

It is difficult to reconcile this earlier refusal of singularity and mastery in favour of a communal conception of art, found in their study of Kafka, with the later view, articulated in *What is Philosophy?*, of the artist as 'seer' whose art constitutes an autonomous 'bloc of sensations'. My sense is that these two contradictory views of the relation of the author to the work mirror the relation of the nomad to the State. In their book on Kafka, the model proposed more closely resembles the type of ensemble composed of a series of forces that Deleuze and Guattari associate with becomings. However, in the later model, which seemingly springs from a desire to sever the ties among the work, author and the community, and thereby rescue art from potentially reductive Oedipal narratives, Deleuze and Guattari posit a relationship between artist and work that guarantees the autonomy and impersonality of the art at the cost of reifying and concretising the artist as 'seer'. This is a line of flight that has already been absorbed by the State.

As a contemporary writer, Findley can not escape western culture's debate about the relationship between artists and their work; he, too, oscillates between the antithetical models that I align with Deleuze and Guattari's conception of the nomad versus the State. In his autobiographical work *Inside Memory*, for example, Findley implicitly invokes the modernist, State narrative of the artist as master when he describes his response to Conrad's *Heart of Darkness* and claims emphatically that, in the face of this 'masterpiece', he 'put away even the thought' that he might write a story on the same subject because whatever he 'wanted to say had been so *perfectly* said'.[41] Ironically, Findley could not resist the temptation to disobey his own internalised sense of the law of the State. In *Headhunter* he rewrites Conrad's *Heart of Darkness*; the latter serves as the novel's primary intertext. Within *Headhunter*, allusions to canonical texts as well as the presence of the author in his own novel do not simply install the modernist narrative of author as master/seer. Instead, they serve as reflexive gestures that highlight not so much the mastery and genius of Conrad as the importance of the poststructuralist mode of enlarging the aesthetic framework and viewing the once-isolated work of art as a communal narrative located within a world conceived as a vast web of texts. As noted, Findley climbs down into his own text – inviting the reader to read him – and succumbs to the label of 'ranter' bestowed on him by Marlow, his psychiatrist. In doing so, he mocks the cult of genius and challenges perceptions of identity based on notions of essentialism and interiority.

Rather than posit a singular answer to the riddle of the relationship between art and artist, both Findley and Deleuze and Guattari articulate the polyphonic debate between nomad and State. The contradictions and different models for this relationship that these authors generate keep the debate alive and open, which is likely the aim of anyone interested in instigating becomings. Not surprisingly, despite their differences, all parties stress that writing must aim beyond identity politics to address for a 'people yet to come', and that the artist is also one who becomes.

In *Essays Critical and Clinical* and in *A Thousand Plateaus*, Deleuze and Guattari repeatedly insist on the relationship between writing and becomings. Likewise, for Findley, writing constitutes a process that reinforces his own multiplicity, a becoming that is 'transversed by strange becomings that are not becoming-writer, but becomings-rat, becomings-insect, becomings-wolf' (Deleuze and Guattari 1987: 240). In fact, while penning his version of the Flood, Findley modified his human perspective to gain insight into his animal characters (see Roberts 1994: 87). In his memoirs, he records his attempt to journey into the being of a cat:

Just came into the cabin from being on the beach at low tide. As usual, I was crawling around in my shorts on my hands and knees – with my bum in the air and my nose in the sand. All this to garner what I can of a cat's-eye-view of the world – so I will get some part of it right when I put the cats on paper. Besides which, I have come to enjoy this new perspective because it reveals so much that I've never seen before. Not even as a child. (Findley 1990: 224)

It is worth noting that Findley recognises that becomings-animal provide him with new knowledge, but he refuses to associate this knowledge with thought; nor does he believe that humans are denied access to this information. Speaking of his own cat, Mottyl (the prototype for Mrs Noyes' cat in the novel), he explains:

She has a wisdom of her own that has nothing to do with thought as we know it. Nor with 'instinct' as we describe it for ourselves. Whatever it is, it lies on that same plane where we are creatures together in this one place where we share our existence. As human beings, we have forgotten how to play our role in that dimension. Why? (Findley 1990: 224)

As a trained actor, who has clearly not forgotten how to play a role in that dimension, Findley regularly experiments with becomings.[42] I would argue further that his commitment to deterritorialisation involves the impersonal experience of 'drifting'. In using this term, I am referring to the way in which Deleuze has been characterised as a philosopher who accepted Nietzsche's invitation 'to embark on a period of "drifting" or "deterritorialisation", to experiment with an escape from the framework of contract, law and institution' (see Marks 1998: 58).

Although one might associate drifting with ease and forgetfulness, Findley's narrative of the voyage underscores the courage it takes to let go of the known order and recalls Deleuze's questions about fascism cited earlier:

Whey are people so deeply irrational? Why are they proud of their own enslavement? Why do they fight 'for' their bondage as if it were their freedom? Why is it so difficult not to win but to bear freedom. Why does a religion that invokes love and joy inspire war, intolerance, hatred, malevolence, and remorse?

In *Not Wanted on the Voyage*, experiments with deterritorialisation – instigated by a Satanic cross-dresser who loses herself in the small force of insects and addresses a people yet to come – crystallise in a singular image at the novel's conclusion. With Mottyl on her lap, Mrs Noyes sits aboard the drifting ark. In a final gesture that has puzzled and angered readers (but would no doubt have pleased Deleuze), she looks up at the empty sky. Perversely rejecting the promise of an end to the voyage and a return to order, she acquiesces to the motion of drifting and she prays – 'not to the absent God . . . but to the absent clouds' – for more rain (Findley 1984: 352).

Notes

1. John Marks lists these criteria in his study of Deleuze (1998: 24–5) and refers to the letter written by Deleuze, which is discussed in Arnaud Villani's essay 'Méthode et théorie dans l'oeuvre de Gilles Deleuze', *Les tempes modernes*, no. 586 (janvier-février 1996), pp. 142–53.
2. According to Findley, the 'seeds of fascism', which he defines as a neurotic refusal to face reality, lie dormant within us all, and the realisation of this fact is 'our best defence against it' (qtd in Roberts 1994: 73). By this he means that rather than accept a complicated and chaotic reality, people prefer to cling to impossible ideals, including those propagated by the Nazis. Only by becoming aware of this impulse to flee reality and to install the ideals of order and perfection, can we counter fascism.
3. Note that the phrase 'becoming-woman' comes from Deleuze and Guattari's discussion in *Anti-Oedipus* of Freud's patient, Schreber, and, in fact, is their means of rejecting Freud's reading of Schreber's donning of women's clothes as transvestism (1983: 19). For an analysis of feminist responses to the writings of Deleuze and Guattari, see pp. 143–4 of my book *Paths of Desire*.
4. For a detailed discussion of the implications of Deleuze and Guattari's theory of becomings, see Elizabeth Grosz's study 'A Thousand Tiny Sexes: Feminism and Rhizomatics', pp. 18–24. As she explains:
   > There is . . . a kind of direction in the quantum leap required by becomings, an order in which becoming-woman is, for all subjects, a first trajectory or direction: becoming-woman desediments the masculinity of identity; becoming-animal, the anthropocentrism of philosophical thought, and becoming-imperceptible replaces, problematizes the notion of thing, entity. Indiscernibility, imperceptibility and impersonality remain the end-points of becoming. (Grosz 1992: 23)
5. In *The Wars* (1977), Robert Ross, a Canadian soldier in the World War I, likewise resists the brutal dictates of familial and military orders. Similar concerns regarding gender, power and dominance surface in *Famous Last Words* (1981), which documents the fatal attraction of fascism for a group of elites (including the Duke and Duchess of Windsor), who become embroiled in a cabal instigated by high-ranking Germans during the Second World War. For a more information about Findley's treatment of fascism, see Barbara Gabriel's essay, ' "The Repose of an Icon" in Timothy Findley's Theatre of Fascism: From "Alligator Shoes" to *Famous Last Words*', and Anne Geddes Bailey's *Timothy Findley and the Aesthetics of Fascism: Intertextual Collaboration and Resistance* (Burnaby, British Colombia: Talon, 1998).
6. For instance, Cecilia Martell, relying on Andrew Ross's essay 'The Uses of Camp', claims that Findley's reliance on camp 'transforms, destabilizes and subverts the existing balance of acceptance of sexual identity and sexual roles' (Ross qtd in Martell 1996: 99). Peter Dickinson (1998) likewise reads Findley's fiction in the light of camp aesthetics in his essay ' "Running Wilde": National Ambivalence and Sexual Dissidence in *Not Wanted on the Voyage*'.
7. In her study of camp and female impersonation, Esther Newton discusses this convention:

The art of these impressions [performed by drag queens] depends on a sharply defined tension between maintaining the impersonation as exactly as possible and breaking it completely so as to force the audience to realise that the copy is being done by a man. A common method of doing this is to interject some aside in the deepest possible bass voice. A skilled performer can create the illusion, break it, and pick it up again several times . . . and the effect can be extremely dramatic and often comic. (Newton 1972: 48)

    More recent studies of traditional drag likewise confirm that the drag queen does not 'fear disclosure as the transvestite does; he invites it. A gesture of electrifying revelation is often central to the comedy' (Harris 1997: 204).

8. Trapped aboard the ark and banished to the lower deck by her despotic husband, Mrs Noyes takes comfort in Lucy's talents and muses, 'What a strange, enchanting creature Lucy was . . . a woman of such taste and wealth and fortitude. And such a great actress, too; "with all them funny voices!" ' (Findley 1984: 249).

9. In her study of irony, Linda Hutcheon likewise stresses that irony 'has often been used to reinforce rather than to question established attitudes' (Hutcheon 1994: 10).

10. There is danger because one can enter into an ensemble that allows one a measure of freedom from the repressive social order but, at the same time, leaves one vulnerable to attack.

11. In Norman Cohn's *Cosmos, Chaos, and the World to Come*, he points out that in two works, *Jubilees* and *I Enoch*, the sex of the angels is discussed. *Jubilees* states that all angels were male and that God had created the two highest ranks of angels already circumcised (Cohn 1993: 180).

    I Enoch, however, tells the story of miscegenation between angels and humankind. The first part of *I Enoch*, known as the *Book of Watchers*, explains that as mankind multiplied, some of the angels were so overcome by the beauty of the daughters of men that they came down to earth, took on human form, and acquired a wife each. By doing so, they polluted themselves and forfeited the spiritual qualities with which God had endowed them. [These angels] also taught people what they were never to have known: how to make weapons, how to dress seductively and how to practise magic. (Cohn 1993: 183)

    Perhaps Findley's portrait of Lucy was inspired by these ancient writings.

12. As Mrs Noyes points out, there is 'not a single female angel – not a single female presence' among His acolytes:

Yaweh, of course – as anyone knew – had never taken wives in the formal sense – and, indeed, it had never been rumoured there was even a single mistress. He seemed content and supremely comfortable with all his male acolytes and angels about him. And why not? They had been so impeccably trained to minister to His every need . . . Mrs Noyes was in a quandary as to whether they were the gentlest creatures she had ever seen – or the most severe. And still, no women and no female angels. It was troubling to Mrs Noyes – and she had to admit it. (Findley 1984: 71–2)

Here, Findley once again intimates that 'sameness' constitutes a perversion, reflecting Deleuze's alternative approach to the issues of identity and sameness, which reduces identity and sameness to a secondary function: '[t]hey are the masks of a drama of becoming whose essence is that the nature of things is only transformation and dissimilation' (Hughes 1998: 67).

13. In her 'Notes on Camp', Sontag claims that camp 'doesn't reverse things. It doesn't argue that the good is bad, or the bad is good. What it does is to offer for art (and life) a different – a supplementary – set of standards' (Sontag 1966: 86).

14. Peter Dickinson proves the exception; he argues that Findley's deliberate orientalising of the transvestite figures in his text 'adds another elements of national

ambivalence to Lucy's already evident sexual dissidence' (Dickinson 1998: 138–9).

15. In Kabuki, the standard makeup consists of a 'dead white face' on which the eyebrows 'are painted in black, higher on the forehead than the actual eyebrows'; in the case of women, 'rouge is used to produce a small mouth in which the thickness of the lips is minimized.' (Ernst 1956: 196). When Lucy removes her makeup and discusses her quest for difference, readers can see how faithfully she adopts the conventions of Kabuki:

> Lucy withdrew a piece of cotton from her pocket and began to remove her make-up. All her white powder – all her dark rouge – her finely drawn eyebrows and the kohl that coloured her lids . . . Lucy removed her rich, sable wig and set it aside. The face beneath the face that had been was sallow in colour – almost grey. Its mouth was wider and its lips fuller than the mouth and the lips that had been. (Findley 1984: 283)

16. In her discussion of David Henry Hwang's play *M. Butterfly*, based on the famous scandal involving a French diplomat and transvestite Chinese opera singer, who were sentenced to six years in jail for spying for China, Marjorie Garber argues that, in the play, the transvestite functions as a figure not only for 'the conundrum of gender and erotic style, but also for other kinds of border-crossing, like *acting* and *spying*, as well' (Garber 1992: 239). In Findley's novel, which also foregrounds acting and spying, the transvestite likewise marks the tensions that surround a series of boundary violations including those between west and east, man and woman, homosexual and straight, human and animal.

17. Although it might be tempting to read becoming-Kabuki as a becoming-irreal, as a refusal of the limits of reality, and as a virtualisation of identity, the history of Kabuki suggests otherwise. As we have seen, the boys' becomings were viewed as a threat, not owing to their refusal of reality, but because they were deemed too sexual and all too real.

18. Newton's ground-breaking study of female impersonators directly addresses this issue:

> [T]he role of the female impersonator as a public homosexual accounts for all the popularity, with room to spare. The impersonator . . . is flaunting his homosexuality on a stage without any apology. Not all gay people want to wear drag, but drag symbolizes gayness . . . The drag queen symbolizes an open declaration, even celebration, of homosexuality. The drag queen says for his gay audience, who cannot say it, 'I'm gay. I don't care who knows it; the straight world be damned.' (Newton 1972: 64)

19. Both Deleuze and Findley appreciate that, as John Marks explains, identity 'marginal or not, can easily become a ghetto; and arguments which are based upon privileged experience of marginal activity are, Deleuze says, "reactionary". Rather than claiming an identity, it is a question of becoming and experimenting' (Marks 1998: 9).

20. In his production of *Not Wanted on the Voyage* at the National Theatre School of Canada in 1991, the director, Richard Rose, outfitted Lucy as a warrior, after she removes her geisha costume. Her more masculine apparel consisted of a moulded breastplate with silken ruffles extruding from the top; a military 'skirt' with feathers protruding from behind; and knee-high buccaneer-style leather boots; in her hand, she carried a spear.

21. As Daniel Harris states:

> Embedded within the aesthetic of drag is the sensibility of the heterosexual tourists who constituted the first dumbstruck audiences for which drag queens camped it up, succumbing to the self-dramatizing impulse of turning them-selves into theatre for voyeuristic onlookers. To borrow from feminist theory

the metaphor of the so-called male gaze, the 'gaze' of drag is a heterosexual gaze. (Harris 1997: 206)

After the Stonewall riots, however, the aesthetic altered, becoming politicised and more masculine:

[G]oing out in public in women's clothing was transformed into an act of solidarity, a form of civil disobedience that celebrated the gutsiness of a new gay rights heroine, the warrior drag queen.

The flaming assertiveness of this quasi-militaristic figure ironically began to masculinize a hyperfeminine aesthetic, exaggerating its already extravagant mannerisms. The politicizing of drag had a concrete visual impact on the nature of the costumes men began to wear as they came to see themselves as saber-rattling cross-dressers. (Harris 1997: 210)

Understood in this context, Lucy's transformation from oriental 'femme' to masculine warrior maps important historical shifts in the aesthetic of drag. Moreover, an awareness of this context helps readers to appreciate the relationship of this aesthetic to the overdetermined binary opposition of masculine and feminine.

22. In the words of the eighteenth-century *onnagata* Yoshizawa Ayame:

If an actress were to appear on the stage she could not express ideal feminine beauty, for she would rely only on the exploitation of her physical characteristics, and therefore not express the synthetic idea. The ideal woman can be expressed only by an actor. From the point of view of the design of the production, the *onnagata* is necessary because, according to the Japanese, although the surface of the woman portrayed should be soft, tender, and beautiful, beneath this surface there should be a strong line which can be created only by a man. (Qtd in Ernst 1956: 195)

Once again, readers are reminded that, in Findley's novel, Satan is not simply engaged in mimesis. He is not offering a copy of an original – a woman. He is copying a copy of femininity generated by a man.

23. Lucy's relationship to God's order recalls the fundamental question Foucault argues Deleuze and Guattari's writing poses concerning fascism, namely, 'why do we love the very things that dominate us?'

24. Peter Dickinson likewise observes that Japeth and Lucy – 'in their respective self-stylings as hypermasculine and hyperfeminine – occupy opposite poles on the camp continuum' (Dickinson 1998: 135).

25. See pp. 201 and 233, for example.

26. According to Michasiw camp constitutes a defence against the truly unknown nature of the Other:

The elements of the masculine construction of the feminine which the camp-performer identifies are exactly those where masculinity shades over into terror, where an increasing panicked defence against what the female might signify produces monsters of semiosis. Hence, the camp-performer identifies with exactly that weak point in the male heterosexist symbolic order, that point at which groping to symbolize, thus to contain, has encountered intimations that can be kept at bay only through hyperbole, and only then if the hyperbole is understood as parodically abjectable. (Michasiw 1994: 162)

27. Daniel Harris puts it quite bluntly, when he states:

Contrary to the notion that drag fosters experimentation with sex roles and blurs oppressive distinctions between masculinity and femininity, it is in fact sexually reactionary and all but allergic to androgyny . . . [D]rag is not a liberating event in which one breaks out of the sartorial prison of one's gender. The sartorial prison has already been unlocked. We have escaped it. Drag knocks to be let back in. (Harris 1997: 209)

28. Japeth's devotion to the lupine pack is so strong that when, owing to a

premonition of the incipient flood, the wolves refuse to drink, Japeth urges them to quench their thirst by drinking 'as an animal drinks, with his mouth wide open, drawing the water in with his tongue' (Findley 1984: 34).

29. As Mrs Noyes explains, women 'were absolutely forbidden to eat them, as were children and domestic animals. Only the elders like Noah – men who had been inducted into the mysteries – could feed from the orchard' (Findley 1984: 133).

30. Mrs Noyes' experience recalls the comments made by Robert Ross' friend Harris, in *The Wars*. On his deathbed, Harris tells Robert about the joys of swimming in the ocean:

    'Where I swam, there was a shelf . . . Sitting on the shelf at low tide, my head was just above the water. Then I'd slide. Like a seal. Out of the air and into the water. Out of my world into theirs. And I'd stay there hours. Or so it seemed. I'd think: I never have to breathe again. I've changed. It changes you. But the thing was – I could do it. Change – and be one of them. (Findley 1977: 95)

31. See Donna Pennee's study pp. 53–58.

32. In his essay 'Michael Tournier and the World without Others' in *The Logic of Sense*, Deleuze suggests that the Other is not simply a particular object or another subject, but is fundamentally 'a structure of the perceptual field, without which the entire field could not function as it does' (Deleuze 1990: 307). In a world without Others, Deleuze argues that 'things end up being organized in a manner quite different than their organization in the presence of the Others' (Deleuze 1990: 319). The episode in which Mrs Noyes is confronted by another person and returns to her Oedipalised self confirms Deleuze's hypothesis about the primary function of the Other.

33. For a thorough explanation of Deleuze and Guattari's view of the function of the Other, see his essay 'Michael Tournier and the World Without Others', pp. 301–21, in *The Logic of Sense* (Deleuze 1990).

34. Earlier we are told that, fascinated by the 'deep, urgent sound of their awakening', Lucy often presses her ear against the hive and begins to hum. Gradually, Lucy's connection to the insects causes her to fall into a trance and, at these times, she no longer responds to other people. When Mrs Noyes finds Lucy in this state, she consults her son, Ham, who confesses that this isn't the first time that Lucy has lost consciousness. He explains that Lucy's trances began when she started feeding the other insects (Findley 1984: 319). Mrs Noyes tells her son that Lucy's behaviour reminds her of a 'cat-trance'. As she says, 'I've never seen a person do it. Not before Lucy, anyway' (Findley 1984: 320). While Lucy remains in this insect-trance, she hears 'the voices' – voices that offer knowledge about the best way to wage war against Dr Noyes (Findley 1984: 320). In its depiction of the voices of the fairies 'like bits of glass blown in the wind' (Findley 1984: 192), as well as the voices of the insects, Findley's text betrays the urge to express what Deleuze and Guattari describe as the forces that cannot be seen, heard, or thought (see Marks 1998: 27, 49).

35. Many thanks to Hugh Wylie of the ROM's Far Eastern Department for helping me track down the masks. The fox masks described in the story actually exist (the ROM has two such masks), and were used for kyogen plays: the comic-relief performances staged between Noh plays. The transforming masks described in the story were specifically used for the kyogen role Hakuzosu, a fox that changes into a monk; as Wylie notes, in the story, Findley mistakenly refers to him as a priest. One play in which these masks were used was Tsurikitsune (or Tsurigitsune), which translates as 'To Catch a Fox' or 'Fox Trapping'. For a summary of the plot in English, see Don Kenny's *A Guide to Kyogen* (1968: 276–7).

36. Note that they recall the eyes of Hooker Winslow's cat in *Last of the Crazy People*. As he sits in the barn, waiting to murder his entire family to release them

from their pain, Hooker ponders the 'pale bronze eyes' of his cat. It strikes him that they are 'deadly, vibrant, yet clouded, gathered. They were explosions – like his. Just like his own eyes' (Findley 1967: 9).

37. This episode echoes Engels' contempt for this type of monadisation, which, as he notes, is particularly apparent in cities:

> [People] . . . crowd by one another as though they had nothing in common, nothing to do with one another, and their only agreement is the tacit one, that each keeps to his own side of the pavement, so as not to delay the opposing streams of the crowd, while it occurs to no man to honour another with so much as a glance. The brutal indifference, the unfeeling isolation of each in his private interest becomes the more repellent and offensive, the more these individuals are crowded together, within a limited space. And, however much one may be aware that this isolation of the individual, this narrow, self-seeking is the fundamental principle of our society everywhere, it is nowhere so shamelessly barefaced, so self-conscious as just here in the crowding of the great city. The dissolution of mankind into monads, of which each one has a separate principle, the world of atoms, is here carried out to its utmost extremes. (Engels 1934: 24)

38. As the narrator explains, the mask possesses this power because the Curator of the Far Eastern Department, who returned with these treasures from another time, brought them 'with all their magic intact': 'Not with ancient spells, of course, since all such things are nonsense – but the magic they released in others: but those who behold them without the impediment of superstition' (Findley 1988: 66–7). In referring to magic in this way, the story specifically alludes to the Japanese understanding of magic, which is seen 'not as the power of other beings but as a supernatural power that all human beings possess when they believe without doubt – that is, in the power of the will' (Komparu 1983: 7).

39. Are we dealing with a pun or is it merely a coincidence that the protagonist's name is 'Glendenning', and the dens of these foxes are located in a glen?

40. As John Marks notes, Peter Hallward criticises Deleuze for underestimating the elevated status that his philosophy accords to the 'agent of redemption', which is usually the thinker, artist or philosopher. The writer/artist's privileged position enables him or her to function in a space akin to Kermode's vacuum, 'alone, outside history' (Hallward 1997: 13).

41. As he explains:

> There was nothing left to add – except my appreciation of what Joseph Conrad had done. And I thought that what I should do is publish a one-page book, between neat blue covers. And on that single page it would say: 'In lieu of writing his own book, the would-be author respectfully draws your attention to *Heart of Darkness* by Joseph Conrad. In it, all that the would-be author would say – is said. The End.' (Findley 1990: 157)

42. In his account of becomings-cat cited above, Findley goes on to confess that while he was scrambling about on the beach, he was interrupted by a happy family out for a stroll. Needless to say, they were appalled to find a man on all fours with his face in the sand. Assuming that he was mad or on drugs, they fled in horror. To my mind, this anecdote, which pits the supposedly sane family against the seemingly insane individual, provides a graphic summary of the anti-fascist politics that inform Findley's writing. As if in response to this family's horror at the sight of a grown man abandoning his humanity, his texts relentlessly expose the horrors committed in the name of maintaining humanity and the nuclear family. He and his protagonists counter these horrors by strategically submitting to the violence of becomings, those 'animal sequences which uproot

one from humanity, if only for an instant . . . giving one the yellow eyes of a feline' (Deleuze and Guattari 1987: 240).

Bibliography

Bailey, Geddes Anne (1998), *Timothy Findley and the Aesthetics of Fascism: Intertextual Collaborations and Resistance*, Burnaby, British Columbia: Talon.

Bullough, Vern and Bullough Bonnie, (1993), *Cross Dressing, Sex and Gender*, Philadelphia: University of Pennsylvania Press.

Cohn, Norman (1993), *Cosmos, Chaos and the World to Come: The Ancient Roots of Apocalyptic Faith*, New Haren, CT: Yale University Press.

Deleuze, Gilles (1988), *Spinoza: Practical Philosophy*, trans. Robert Hurley, San Francisco: City Lights.

Deleuze, Gilles (1990), *The Logic of Sense*, trans. Mark Lester with Charles Stivale, ed. Constatin V. Boundas, New York: Columbia.

Deleuze, Gilles (1997), *Essays Critical and Clinical*, trans. Daniel W. Smith and Michael A. Greco, Minneapolis: University of Minnesota Press.

Deleuze, Gilles and Guattari, Félix (1983), *Anti-Oedipus: Capitalism and Schizophrenia*, Minneapolis: University of Minnesota Press.

Deleuze, Gilles and Guattari, Félix (1986), *Kafka: Toward a Minor Literature*, trans. D. Polan, Minneapolis: University of Minneapolis Press.

Deleuze, Gilles and Guattari, Félix (1987), *A Thousand Plateaus: Capitalism and Schizophrenia*, Minneapolis: University of Minnesota Press.

Deleuze, Gilles and Guattari, Félix (1994), *What is Philosophy?*, trans. H. Tomlinson and G. Burchell, New York: Columbia University Press.

Dickinson, Peter (1988), ' "Running Wilde": National Ambivalence and Sexual Dissidence in *Not Wanted on the Voyage*', *Paying Attention: Critical Essays on Timothy Findley*, ed. Anne Geddes Bailey and Karen Grandy, Toronto: Essays on Canadian Writing. 125–46. Also published in the *Timothy Findley Issue*, ed. Anne Geddes Bailey and Karen Grandy. Spec. issue of *Essays on Canadian Writing*, 64 (1998), pp. 125–46.

Engels, Friedrich (1934), *The Condition of the Working Class in England in 1844*, trans. F. K. Wischnewetzky, London.

Ernst, Earle (1956), *Kabuki Theatre*, London: Secker and Warburg.

Findley, Timothy (1967), *The Last of the Crazy People*, Toronto: Penguin.

Findley, Timothy (1977), *The Wars*, Toronto: Penguin.

Findley, Timothy (1981), *Famous Last Words*, Toronto: Penguin.

Findley, Timothy (1984), *Not Wanted on the Voyage*, Toronto: Penguin.

Findley, Timothy (1988), 'Foxes', *Stones*, Toronto: Penguin.

Findley, Timothy (1990), *Inside Memory: Pages From a Writer's Workbook*, Toronto: HarperCollins.

Findley, Timothy (1993), *Headhunter*, Toronto: HarperCollins.

Foucault, Michel (1983), Preface, in Gilles Deleuze and Félix Guattari, *Anti-Oedipus: Capitalism and Schizophrenia*, Minneapolis: University of Minnesota Press.

Gabriel, Barbara (1998), ' "The Repose of an Icon" in Timothy Findley's Theatre of Fascism: From "Alligator Shoes" to *Famous Last Words*', *Paying Attention: Critical Essays on Timothy Findley*, ed. Anne Geddes Bailey and Karen Grandy, Toronto: Essays on Canadian Writing, pp. 149–80. Also published in the *Timothy Findley Issue*, ed. Anne Geddes Bailey and Karen Grandy. Spec. Issue of *Essays on Canadian Writing*, 64 (1998), pp. 149–80.

Garber, Marjorie (1992), *Vested Interests: Cross Dressing and Cultural Anxiety*, New York: HarperCollins and Routledge

Goldman, Marlene (1997), *Paths of Desire: Images of Explanation and Mapping in Canadian Women's Writing*, Toronto: University of Toronto Press.

Grosz, Elizabeth (1992), 'A Thousand Tiny Sexes: Feminism and Rhizomatics', Deleuze and Guattari Conference, Trent University, Ontario, 15–17 May 1992.

Hallward, Peter (1997), 'Gilles Deleuze and the Redemption from Interest', *Radical Philosophy*, 81 (Jan–Feb), pp. 6–21.

Harris, Daniel (1997), *The Rise and Fall of Gay Culture*, New York: Hyperion.

Hughes, John (1998), *Lines of Flight: Reading Deleuze with Hardy, Gissing, Conrad, Woolf*, Sheffield: Sheffield Academic Press.

Hunter, Catherine (1998), ' "I Don't Know How to Begin": Findley's Work in the Sixties', *Paying Attention: Critical Essays on Timothy Findley*, ed. Anne Geddes Bailey and Karen Grandy, Toronto: Essays on Canadian Writing, 13–31. Also published in the *Timothy Findley Issue*, ed. Anne Geddes Bailey and Karen Grandy. Spec. issue of *Essays on Canadian Writing*, 64 (1998), pp. 13–31.

Hutcheon, Linda (1994), *Irony's Edge: The Theory and Politics of Irony*, London and New York: Routledge.

Kenny, Don (1968), *A Guide to Kyogen*, Tokyo: Hinoko Shoten.

Kermode, Frank (1967), *The Sense of an Ending*, New York: Oxford University Press.

Komparu, Kumio (1983), *The Noh Theatre: Principles and Perspectives*, New York and Tokyo: Weatherhill/Tankosha.

'Lucy' (1992–4) *Encarta '95*. Diskette. Microsoft.

Marks, John (1998), *Gilles Deleuze: Vitalism and Multiplicity*, London: Pluto.

Martell, Cecilia (1996), 'Unpacking the Baggage: "Camp" Humour in Timothy Findley's *Not Wanted on the Voyage*', *Canadian Literature*, 148, pp. 96–111.

Michasiw, Kim (1994), 'Camp, Masculinity, Masquerade', *Differences* 6.2+3, pp. 146–73.

Newton, Esther (1972), *Mother Camp: Female Impersonators in America*, Chicago and London: University of Chicago Press.

Pennee, Donna (1993), *Praying for Rain: Timothy Findley's Not Wanted on the Voyage*, Toronto: ECW.

Pronko, Leonard (1973), *Guide to Japanese Drama*, Boston, MA: G. K. Hall.

Roberts, Carol (1994), *Timothy Findley: Stories From a Life*, Toronto: Essays on Canadian Writing.

Rose, Richard (director) (1991), *Not Wanted on the Voyage*, National Theatre School of Canada. Video.

Seem, Mark (1983), Introduction to *Anti-Oedipus*, xv-xxiv.

Sontag, Susan (1966), 'Notes on Camp', *Against Interpretation*, New York: Farrar, Strauss and Giroux.

Yoshida, Chiaki (1977), *Kabuki: The Resplendent Japanese Theatre*, Tokyo: The Japan Times.

Chapter 9

Only Intensities Subsist:
Samuel Beckett's *Nohow On*

Timothy S. Murphy

The prose writings of Samuel Beckett are consistently privileged points of reference for Gilles Deleuze's philosophy, in both his solo works and his collaborations, yet Deleuze never produced an extensive reading or exegesis of Beckett's prose. His two essays on Beckett, 'The Greatest Irish Film (Beckett's *Film*)' and 'The Exhausted',[1] are focused on the smallest subset of Beckett's dramatic work, his film and television projects. Instead, Deleuze offers a significant number of what I would call 'intensive' readings of Beckett's prose: brief, allusive references to scenes (which assume the reader's familiarity) that are supposed to explicate key aspects of Deleuze's own philosophical creation. These intensive readings demonstrate that Beckett's prose works perform a crucial function within the context of Deleuze's philosophy: they exemplify the role and power of the pure intensity. After I have established this by examining the tactical deployment of Beckett's prose in Deleuze's writings, I will argue that Beckett's last prose works, the three novellas collected as *Nohow On*, can help Deleuze's readers to grasp the implications of the most radical and difficult aspect of his concept of intensity: the anti-Kantian differential theory of the faculties that forms the core of Deleuze's 'transcendental empiricism' in *Difference and Repetition*. In other words, I will first show how Deleuze's thought stages or dramatises (rather than reads or explicates) Beckett's prose, then how Beckett's prose stages Deleuze's thought. This profoundly philosophical conjunction of Beckett and Deleuze is all the more striking because Beckett appears never to have read Deleuze,[2] and Deleuze does not begin to refer to Beckett's prose until the early 1970s, long after he had completed *Difference and Repetition* in the mid 1960s.

I

Deleuze (with and without Guattari) often invokes Beckett when he is constructing a chain or series of exemplary aesthetic cases, as in this passage from *A Thousand Plateaus*:

> Because a style is not an individual psychological creation but an assemblage of enunciation, it unavoidably produces a language within a language. Take an arbitrary list of authors we are fond of: Kafka once again, Beckett, Ghérasim Luca, Jean-Luc Godard. It will be noted that they are all more or less in a bilingual situation: Kafka, the Czechoslovakian Jew writing in German; Beckett, the Irishman writing in English and French . . . But this is only circumstantial, an opportunity, and the opportunity can be found elsewhere. (Deleuze and Guattari 1987: 97–8)[3]

This list of authors is also a series of distinctive points that define the problem of style for Deleuze and Guattari. A problem is not a question having a single fixed answer (as in a catechism), nor one that places the answer on a fixed and continuous scale of identities (as in a graded or diagnostic test), but rather an equation containing variables that gives rise to a discontinuous range of solutions. In *Difference and Repetition*, Deleuze insisted that:

> It is never enough to solve a problem with the aid of a series of simple cases playing the role of analytic elements: the conditions under which the problem acquires a maximum of comprehension and extension must be determined, conditions capable of communicating to a given case of solution the ideal continuity appropriate to it . . . To solve a problem is always to give rise to discontinuities on the basis of a continuity which functions as Idea. (Deleuze 1994: 162)

The Idea of style as a 'language within a language' offers an Ideal or transcendental continuity to the series of authors, but it does so by providing a variable basis for their conjunction rather than a vague generality of which the authors would be specific cases. The apparently shared bilingualism of the authors is only 'circumstantial'; they are not all writers and thus their styles cannot be identified as minor 'dialects' within natural languages. For example, Beckett's theatre and especially television works constitute an 'elsewhere' in which he finds a non-linguistie 'opportunity' to create a style (Deleuze and Guattari 1987: 98).[4] That is, theatre and television can be understood as languages provided that they are considered pragmatically, as performatives rather than referential utterances, and thus that Beckett's dramatic style is seen as a contextual pragmatics of the voice and the visual image.

But just what does Beckett's style amount to? The contexts in which Deleuze cites Beckett offer a first clue. The pattern of intensive readings of Beckett appears for the first time in *Anti-Oedipus* in the opening exemplification of the 'schizo's stroll' via scenes from *Molloy* and *Malone Dies* (Deleuze and Guattari 1983: 2–3, 12–14), but more pertinently for my purposes in the description of the third or conjunctive synthesis of consumption-consummation, which produces effects of identity and subjectivity:

> It is a matter of relationships of intensities through which the subject passes on the body without organs, a process that engages him in becomings, rises and falls, migrations and displacements . . . When we speak here of a voyage, this is no more a metaphor than before when we spoke of an egg, and of what takes place in and on it – morphogenetic movements, displacements of cellular groupings, stretchings, folds, migrations, and local variations of potential. There is no reason to oppose an interior voyage to exterior ones: Lenz's stroll, Nijinsky's stroll, the promenades of Beckett's creatures are effective realities, but where the reality of matter has abandoned all extension, just as the interior voyage has abandoned all form and quality, henceforth causing pure intensities – coupled together, almost unbearable – to radiate within and without, intensities through which a nomadic subject passes. (Deleuze and Guattari 1983: 84)

The 'body without organs' is a limit, one that enables thought, feeling and action without being thought, feeling or action itself. In this way, the 'BwO' is Deleuze and Guattari's version of Kant's space-time co-ordinates that are the necessary preconditions of all possible experience (Kant 1929: 67–82). The BwO is the zero degree of intensity, a neutral and non-spatio-temporal stage on which various kinds of subject can be constructed and on which those subjects experiment with their polymorphously perverse identities, desires and affects (Deleuze and Guattari 1987: 149–54). These identities, desires and affects, these unstable states of the subject's extremely permeable interiority are one form of the pure intensity, which Brian Massumi has glossed as the 'virtual intensity [having] only *in*tension' but not physical extension in time and space' (Massumi 1992: 66).[5]

Intensities are not only the fundamental components of subjects and their states, but also the ultimate goal of Deleuze and Guattari's ethical imperative to 'deterritorialise' or destabilise and dismantle the ossified structures and constraints of the social world. This imperative resounds with particular force in their extensive discussion of Kafka's 'minor literature', by which they mean his choice to write in German against the dominant style of German literature rather than to adopt a minority language like Yiddish for his fiction. They further imply that Kafka's practice is akin to Beckett's. Deleuze and Guattari identify two ways of creating minor literature within a major language. The first is a method of linguistic inflation 'through all the resources of symbolism, of oneirism, of esoteric sense, of the hidden signifier'. This would be a kind of deterritorialisation through excessive allusion or reference, which they call 'reterritorialisation', a multiplication and overlapping of stabilising patterns of signification that would give the reader many possible ways to evade a unified reading but also many new ways to pin the writing down. The very abundance of patterns can lead, paradoxically, to a breakdown in which deterritorialisation grinds to a halt in a new stasis.

The second method, which Deleuze and Guattari see at work in Kafka's writings, is to:

> Go always farther in the direction of deterritorialization, to the point of sobriety. Since the language is arid, make it vibrate with a new intensity. Oppose a purely intensive usage of language to all symbolic or even significant or simply signifying usages of it. Arrive at a perfect and unformed expression, a materially intense expression. (For these two possible paths, couldn't we find the same alternatives, under other conditions, in Joyce and Beckett? As Irishmen, both of them live within the genial conditions of a minor literature. That is the glory of this sort of minor literature − to be the revolutionary force for all literature. The utilization of English and of every language in Joyce. The utilization of English and French in Beckett. But the former never stops operating by exhilaration and overdetermination and brings about all sorts of world-wide reterritorializations. The other proceeds by dryness and sobriety, a willed poverty, pushing deterritorialization to the point where only intensities subsist). (Deleuze and Guattari 1986: 19; translation modified)[6]

This 'materially intense' (rather than extensively referential or signifying) method can produce a breakthrough to minor literature in cases where the first method produces only breakdowns. In *Finnegans Wake* Joyce's writing, by means of its reliance on puns and polylinguistic accretion, deterritorialises or destabilises the referentiality of English in a radical way. The sheer number of possible parsings as well as significations of the text forestalls every attempts to bring it to the closure of unified meaning, but the very multiplicity of superimposed linguistic potentialities that it puts into play can serve as a second-order grid to contain the text.

> [T]he most resolutely fragmented work can also be presented as the Total Work or Magnum Opus . . . Joyce's words, accurately described as

having 'multiple roots,' shatter the linear unity of the word, even of language, only to posit a cyclic unity of the sentence, text or knowledge. (Deleuze and Guattari 1987: 6)

The circular structure of *Finnegans Wake* reflects this, as does the largely hagiographic body of scholarship that has sprung up around it.[7]

Beckett, on the other hand, foregoes Joycean linguistic lushness with its attendant dangers to embrace a style of 'willed poverty', what Deleuze later calls 'exhaustion': 'The tired person has merely exhausted the realization, whereas the exhausted person exhausts the whole of the possible' (Deleuze 1997: 152). This sense of the exhaustion of possibility is drawn from mathematics and cryptography, and refers to the systematic, almost mechanical process of determining a solution for every possible value of a variable within an equation or coded message. The method of exhaustion is not limited to Beckett's works; Deleuze and Guattari claim that both Antonin Artaud and Louis-Ferdinand Céline, in different ways, also exhaust the possible to produce writings of pure intensities (Deleuze and Guattari 1986: 26). I would add that Gertrude Stein's permutations and William S. Burroughs' cut-up experiments also produce uniquely exhaustive styles of writing. What is specific to Beckett's style is the fact that it exhausts the whole of the possible in four systematic ways:

1. By 'forming exhaustive series of things' as in Molloy's exhaustive permutation of his sucking stones (Beckett 1958: 69–74),[8] which concludes with his admission that 'deep down it was all the same to me whether I sucked a different stone each time or always the same stone, until the end of time. For they all tasted exactly the same' (Beckett 1958: 74).

2. By 'drying up the flow of voices' as in Mahood's admission that the characters from Beckett's earlier fiction, from Murphy and Watt to Malone and Worm, are merely arbitrary names for an ultimately unnamable 'me' (Beckett 1958: 390–1):[9] 'Is there a single word of mine in all I say? No, I have no voice, in this matter I have none. That's one of the reasons I confused myself with Worm. But I have no reasons either, no reason, I'm like Worm, without voice or reason . . .' (Beckett 1958: 347).

3. By 'extenuating the potentialities of space' as in the scrupulously measured and described space of *The Lost Ones* or *For To End Yet Again*, which despite its apparent specificity remains an indeterminate 'any-space-whatever', 'a space with neither here nor there where all the footsteps ever fell can never fare nearer to anywhere nor from anywhere further away' (Beckett 1996b: 246).[10]

4. By 'dissipating the power of the image', producing an indefinite image that escapes the dialectic of general and specific or real and imaginary, as in the confused musings of the speaker in the mud in *How It Is*: 'they are not memories no he has no memories no nothing to prove he was ever above no in the places he sees no but he may have been yes skulking somewhere yes hugging the walls yes by night yes he can't affirm anything no deny anything no so one can't speak of memories no but at the same time one can speak of them yes' (Beckett 1964: 97).[11] I will return to this issue of the image and its confusion or dissipation below.

The result of this process of exhaustion is a theatre, a cinema, a television and finally a prose writing of pure intensities, of subjectivity and its component parts focused down to a timeless, dimensionless point, a singularity.[12]

II

Nohow On is Beckett's own title for a 1989 collection of three novella-length prose pieces originally published separately: *Company* (1980), *Ill Seen Ill Said* (1981) and *Worstward Ho* (1983).[13] The situation explored in each text is different, as is the narrative technique. In *Company*, 'A voice comes to one in the dark' (Beckett 1996a: 3) and speaks of a past that may or may not belong to the one in the dark; the play of pronouns produces other subjects in the dark as illusory 'company' for the one spoken to, only to leave him as it found him, 'Alone' (Beckett 1996a: 46). In *Ill Seen Ill Said*, the narrator describes a solitary old woman and her bleak cabin as objects of uncertain and unstable perception and assertion. In *Worstward Ho*, a powerful repudiation of language's ability to describe and narrate is assembled bit by bit out of the abortive rudiments of a description and narration of fragmentary bodies. In each of these texts, the narrating/narrated mind finds it impossible to bring its faculties into harmony, to represent or recognise the external world revealed by its senses, or the self or selves correlative to that world, as stable and reliable objects of thought. All three of them, therefore, can be read as investigations of the paradoxical limits of the mind's abilities that are strikingly similar to Deleuze's differential theory of the faculties. Both Beckett and Deleuze 'dis-order' the faculties in order to expose the dogmatic assumptions of 'common sense' and to bring the unique and singular limits of each faculty to light.[14]

To understand how Beckett's novellas explore and embody the limit-objects of the faculties, I must begin with a detour that may seem strange at first. I must begin with the middle text, *Ill Seen Ill Said*, rather than the first, *Company*, because *Ill Seen Ill Said* poses the problem of an unrecognisable sensory encounter, what Deleuze calls a *sentiendum* that impels thought, the most directly. Then, following Deleuze's series delineating the 'chain of force and fuse along which each [faculty] confronts its limit' (Deleuze 1994: 141), I will double back to examine the resonance of the unrememberable, immemorial *memorandum* and its social counterpart (which Deleuze does not name but which I will provisionally call the '*sociendum*') which is named in the title of *Company*. Finally, *Worstward Ho* will provide a thorough staging of the *loquendum*, the act of language that, paradoxically, 'would be silence at the same time' (Deleuze 1994: 143). This re-sequencing of Beckett's text is necessary in order to clarify its relation to Deleuze's thought, and it might be justified first of all by the fact that Beckett's novellas themselves do not form a linear narrative in which sequence determines meaning according to causal links. Instead, they are constructed largely out of the permutation, that is the differential repetition, of a limited set of images and phrases. This dis-ordering might also be justified by reference to Deleuze's focus on the 'between' as the crucial set of relations defining every multiplicity; as Claire Parnet says, apparently with Deleuze's agreement:

> Beckett's characters are in perpetual involution, always in the middle of a path, already *en route* . . . the path has no beginning or end . . . because it cannot do otherwise. If not it would no longer be a path, it only exists as a path in the middle. (Deleuze and Parnet 1987: viii, 30)

Thus my path through *Nohow On* will parallel my path through *Difference and Repetition*, beginning in the middle and remaining there (like the nomad who moves in order to stay put), even as my argument doubles both backward and forward (Deleuze and Guattari 1987: 380–1).[15]

The differential theory of the faculties, the centerpiece of Deleuze's transcendental empiricism, itself first appears in the middle of the third chapter of *Difference and Repetition*, 'The Image of Thought'. In his preface to the English translation, Deleuze has identified this chapter as 'the most necessary and the most concrete' step in his effort to break free of the traditional image of thought as 'common sense or the employment of all the faculties on a supposed same object' (Deleuze 1994: xvi–xvii). Like Beckett's style, Deleuze's thought works to 'dissipate the power' of this 'image'. The third chapter outlines the pernicious consequences of seven dogmatic postulates of thought's representational image, consequences that reduce thinking to the sterile, exact repetition of unexamined clichés, but it is interrupted in the midst of its enumeration by the propositions of the differential theory, which describes thought's origin in interruption.[16] Thought for Deleuze is never the reflection or modelling of reality, but rather creation; for any thought to be actual thought it must be unforeseen and new.

Such new thought does not arise from any natural goodwill of the thinking subject, nor from any recognition of the objective world of extension, but rather from 'an original violence inflicted upon thought . . . a strangeness or an enmity which alone would awaken thought from its natural stupor or eternal possibility . . . Thought is primarily trespass and violence, the enemy, and nothing presupposes philosophy: everything begins with misosophy.' We break out of 'misosophy', the hatred of thinking that blocks thought, into philosophy, the love of thinking that makes thought flow, whenever '[s]omething in the world forces us to think' – not an object of recognition but an object of 'a fundamental *encounter* . . . [that] can only be sensed' (Deleuze 1994: 139). Beckett himself made a very similar argument in his study *Proust*:

> [T]he intelligence . . . abstracts from any given sensation, as being illogical and insignificant, a discordant and frivolous intruder, whatever word or gesture, sound or perfume, cannot be fitted into the puzzle of a concept. But the essence of any new experience is contained precisely in this mysterious element that the vigilant will rejects as an anachronism. It is the axis about which the sensation pivots, the centre of gravity of its coherence. (Beckett 1957: 53–4)[17]

This encounter cannot be recognised because recognition, the empirical exercise of a faculty, requires a coming to agreement of the sensible (sensory) faculty with the faculty of memory, imagination or reason in identifying the object. Empirical recognition presupposes that sensibility will form a clichéd 'common sense' with the other faculties, while the encounter provides only a paradoxical *aistheteon* or *sentiendum*, 'not a sensible being but the being *of* the sensible' that 'can only be sensed (and is at the same time imperceptible [*insensible*])'. Through this encounter sensibility 'finds itself before its own limit, the sign, and raises itself to the level of a transcendental exercise: to the "nth" power' (Deleuze 1994: 140).[18]

As its title suggests, *Ill Seen Ill Said* is largely concerned with the relation between sensibility, in this case faulty vision, and expression, or failing language. Everything begins, and constantly begins again on virtually every page, with misosophy, with a sensible encounter or unrecognisable event: 'Ope eye and at them to begin . . . Far behind the eye the quest begins. What time the event recedes. When suddenly to the rescue it comes again' (Beckett 1996a: 82–3). The old woman who is the object of the narration is first introduced as a seer: 'From where she lies she sees Venus rise' (Beckett 1996a: 49). But she is more often the seen, the baffling sign, described haltingly by a self-narrating 'imaginary stranger' (Beckett 1996a: 53) possessing an 'eye having no need of light to see' (Beckett 1996a: 50). This eye of the imagination shares the point of view with the physical eye: at times the woman can only be 'ill half seen' (Beckett 1996a: 54), at others she cannot be seen 'by the eye of the flesh nor by the other' (Beckett 1996a: 56). As vision strains to see, so language strains to say: she occupies a near-empty old cabin, '[a]nd from it as from an evil core . . . the what is the wrong word the evil spread' (Beckett 1996a: 50). Language cannot reliably name the object of unreliable vision, cannot recognise and categorise it accurately: 'what is the word? What the wrong word?' (Beckett 1996a: 56).[19] Language offers only vague abstractions, clichés like 'evil', to the seeking eye and mind. This linked unreliability of both seeing and saying reaches its most extreme point in the following passage:

> No matter now. Such the confusion now between real and – how say its contrary? No matter. That old tandem. Such now the confusion between them once so twain. And such the farrago from eye to mind. For it to make what sad sense of it may. No matter now. Such equal liars both. Real and – how ill say its contrary? The counter-poison. (Beckett 1996a: 72)

The traditional division between real and imaginary has become confused and blurred just as the narrator's visions of the cabin 'blurs' into indiscernibility (Beckett 1996a: 57), signifying a failure of recognition and agreement between the faculties of '[t]hat mock brain' (Beckett 1996a: 82).

The eye, whether of flesh or mind, cannot identify the old woman: 'What is it defends her?' the narrator asks. 'Even from her own. Averts the intent gaze. Incriminates the dearly won. Forbids divining her' (Beckett 1996a: 55). Nor can the eye follow her movements: like the 'lightning leap' of the second hand of a watch (Beckett 1996a: 76–7), 'she can be gone at any time. From one moment of the year to the next suddenly no longer there. No longer anywhere to be seen' (Beckett 1996a: 56). And later, she reappears in '[a] flash. The suddenness of all! She still without stopping. On her way without starting. Gone without going. Back without returning' (Beckett 1996a: 58). Her paradoxical mobility makes her unrecognisable, poses a profound problem for the eye:

What remains for the eye exposed to such conditions? To such vicissitude of hardly there and wholly gone. Why none but to open no more. Till all done. She done. Or left undone. Tenement and unreason. No more unless to rest. In the outward and so-called visible. (Beckett 1996a: 71)

She and her cabin become impossible objects, *sentienda* that are visible but neither intelligible to 'unreason', reason severed from its correlation to sensibility, nor retrievable from memory: 'Suddenly enough and way for remembrance. Closed again to that end the vile jelly or opened again or left as it was however that was. Till all recalled . . . Remembrance! When all worse there than when first ill seen' (Beckett 1996a: 81).[20]

The hearer who acts as the protagonist of *Company* also experiences a series of encounters that force him to think but do not allow him the simplicity and solace of recognition. His encounters are almost entirely auditory rather than visual. The voice that comes to him initially insists that '[y]our mind never active at any time is now even less than ever so' (Beckett 1996a: 5), and even near the end of the text the question arises, '[w]ould it be reasonable to imagine the hearer as mentally quite inert? Except when he hears. That is when the voice sounds.' These voice sounds are what trigger his mind to something like thought, making him 'wonder to himself what in the world such sounds might signify' (Beckett 1996a: 37). The voice's address forces him to think, as well as he can: 'with what reason remains he reasons and reasons ill' (Beckett 1996a: 7), producing only '[u]nformula gropings of the mind' (Beckett 1996a: 16) that do not confirm or confirm to the statements the voice makes. The sensory impact of the voice itself, not its referents or contents, serves as the *sentiendum*, and its unintelligible force propels the hearer to seek other encounters by crawling about in his darkened space, '[t]ill having encountered no obstacle discouraged he heads back the way he came' (Beckett 1996a: 36).

The limit-object of the encounter forces thought to take place, for both the hearer and his readers, by creating a differential resonance between the distinct faculties. 'Thus sensibility, forced by the encounter to sense the *sentiendum*, forces memory in its turn to remember the *memorandum*, that which can only be recalled' (Deleuze 1994: 141). Just as the *sentiendum* confronts sensibility with its own limit and raises it to a transcendental exercise, so the '*memorandum* here is both unremember-able and immemorial . . . [I]t exists within essential memory as though it were the "nth" power of memory with regard to its own limit or to that which can only be recalled' without ever having been present to sensibility or reason (Deleuze 1994: 140). Not a recognisable past being but rather the unrecognisable being of the pure past, the *memorandum* is also the transcendental forgetting that founds the faculty of memory.[21]

The first image in *Company* is that of a voice addressing the hearer, a voice that repeatedly 'tells of a past' (Beckett 1996a: 4), '[r]epeatedly with only minor variants the same bygone. As if willing him by this dint to make it his' (Beckett 1996a: 10), '[t]o have the hearer have a past and acknowledge it' (Beckett 1996a: 24). But the hearer refuses to accept the past because it cannot be verified by reference to some other faculty, for example sensibility:

> Only a small part of what is said can be verified. As for example when he hears, You are on your back in the dark. Then he must acknowledge the truth of what is said. But by far the greater part of what is said cannot be verified. As for example when he hears, You first saw the light on such and such a day. (Beckett 1996a: 3)

Episodes of such an unverifiable, unrecognisable past fill the text: a boy asking his mother about the nearness of the sky (Beckett 1996a: 6), 'an old man plodding along a narrow country road' (Beckett 1996a: 9), a young man meeting his lover, whom he discovers to be pregnant with his child, in a summerhouse (Beckett 1996a: 28–31), and others. None of these scenes of the past are acknowledged as his own by the hearer, however, and none of them allow him to identify himself now, for '[a]s then there was no then so there is none now' (Beckett 1996a: 15). The scenes constitute a past forgotten beyond the merely empirical forgetting of memories that could be recalled with subjective effort. They are pure *memoranda*, limit-objects that can only be 'remembered' transcendentally because they cannot be remembered empirically, that is, remembered as events that passed through the other faculties of the mind in a present, a 'now', that has passed and become a 'then'. In the normal sense of the term, these *memoranda* cannot be remembered at all.

Following in the expanding wake of the *memorandum* comes the next point of Deleuze's series, in which

> transcendental memory . . . forces thought to grasp that which can only be thought, the *cogitandum* or *noeteon* . . . [which is] not the intelligible, for this is still no more than the mode in which we think that which might be something other than thought, but the being of the intelligible as though this were both the final power of thought and the unthinkable. (Deleuze 1994: 141)

Thus the *cogitandum* is the only form of 'Pure reason' because its paradoxical violence pushes established thought out of the empirical realm, '[s]tirring now and then to wonder that mind so lost to wonder', into a transcendental exercise '[b]eyond experience', as Beckett writes (1996a: 38). No form or content of thought is transmitted from faculty to faculty, but only the shock wave of the original encounter, refracted into a unique limit-object at each point of transition.[22] Unlike recognition or common sense, which requires the faculties to converge and form a harmonious consensus on the object, the differential theory produces 'divergent projects in which, with regard to what concerns it essentially, each faculty is in the presence of that which is its "own." Discord of the faculties . . .' (Deleuze 1994: 141).

This forced resonance is not only the first or ultimate cause of thought in general, but also the efficient or local cause of every singular thought that escapes from doxa, dogma. What Beckett calls:

> The periods of transition that separate consecutive adaptations [to common sense or doxa] . . . represent the perilous zones in the life of the individual, dangerous, precarious, painful, mysterious and fertile, when for a moment the boredom of living is replaced by the suffering of being . . . The suffering of being: that is, the free play of every faculty. (Beckett 1957: 9)

Thus Deleuze makes these 'periods of transition' or forced resonance, like the Beckettian literary deterritorialisation they closely resemble, the object of a powerful imperative:

> Each faculty must be borne to the extreme point of its dissolution, at which it falls prey to triple violence: the violence of that which forces it to be exercised, of that which it is forced to grasp and which it alone is able to grasp, yet also that of the ungraspable (from the point of view of its empirical exercise). This is the threefold limit of the final power. Each faculty discovers at this point its own unique passion – in other words, its radical difference and its eternal repetition, its differential and repeating element along with the instantaneous engendering of its action and the eternal replay of its object, its manner of coming into the world already repeating. We ask, for example: What forces sensibility to sense? What is it that can only be sensed, yet is imperceptible at the same time? We must pose this question not only for memory and thought, but also for the imagination – is there an *imaginandum*, a *phantasteon*, which would also be the limit, that which is impossible to imagine?; for language – is there a *loquendum*, that which would be silence at the same time?; and for the other faculties which would find their place in a complete doctrine vitality, the transcendent object of which would include monstrosity; and sociability, the transcendent object of which would include anarchy – and even for faculties yet to be discovered, whose existence is not yet suspected. (Deleuze 1994: 143).[23]

In this eloquent, Promethean (and thus at least implicitly modernist) demand for a constant renewal of thought through an increased receptivity to the encounters out of which it is born, we can also hear a paean to the pure intensities that constitute the limit-objects of every encounter.

The text of *Company* not only stages the encounter with the *sentiendum* and resonates with the force of the *memorandum*, but also, as its title implies, finds the limit-object of subjective relations or sociability, which I will call the *sociendum*:

> What visions in the dark of light! Who exclaims thus? Who asks who exclaims, What visions in the shadeless dark of light and shade! Yet another still? Devising it all for company. What a further addition to company that would be! Yet another still devising it all for company. (Beckett 1996a: 44)

The repeated question 'who?' poses the problem of how sociability as a virtual or potential function of the mind is actualised. In *Company* there are apparently three stable positions whose interactions form the text's 'social' relations: the hearer 'on his back in the dark' (Beckett 1996a: 3), the voice that repeatedly 'tells of a past' (Beckett 1996a: 4), and finally the narrator who recounts this situation. These relationships, however orderly and objective they may initially appear, are entirely pronominal and are even defined metalinguistically by the narrator:

> Use of the second person marks the voice. That of the third that cankerous other [the narrator]. Could he [the hearer] speak to and of whom the voice speaks there would be a first. But he cannot. He shall not. You cannot. You shall not. (Beckett 1996a: 4)

The positions are defined not by their subject (speaker) pronouns but by their object (addressee) pronouns, and most significantly by their refusal of the continuously implied first person.

> Who asks, whose voice asking this? And answers, His soever who devises it all. In the same dark as his creature or in another. For company. Who asks in the end, Who asks? And in the end answers as above? And adds long after to himself, Unless another still. Nowhere to be found. Nowhere to be sought. The unthinkable last of all. Unnamable. Last person. I. (Beckett 1996a: 16–17)

Later comes the admission that 'the first personal and a fortiori plural pronoun had never any place in your vocabulary' (Beckett 1996a: 45). Thus despite the apparent conflicts between positions, there is actually only one continuously disavowed subject, who is ultimately the '[d]eviser of the voice and of its hearer and of himself. Deviser of himself for company. Leave it at that. He speaks of himself as of another. He says speaking of himself, He speaks of himself as of another. Himself he devises too for company. Leave it at that' (Beckett 1996a: 18).[24] The apparently distinct pronominal subjects are merely prefabricated grammatical states of intensity through which the single narrative subject passes, temporarily comforting but ultimately unstable roles the subject plays on the darkened plain or plane of his body without organs.

The situation is virtually a parody of Hegel's logic of the political state as the resolution of the class conflicts within civil society (Hegel 1952: 160–3), but instead of advancing the cause of Spirit and reason in an orderly, progressive, teleological fashion, Beckett's 'deviser' takes comfort in disorder: 'Confusion too is company up to a point' (Beckett 1996a: 18).[25] Confusion is the hearer's almost constant state of mind, one from which he cannot escape, think as he might. Sociability itself appears as a faculty of mind: 'In order to be company he must display a certain mental activity. But it need not be of a high order' (Beckett 1996a: 7). He imagines the many forms that such mental company could take, from the dim light of his featureless any-space-whatever (Beckett 1996a: 13) to the 'possible encounters. A dead rat. What an addition to company that would be! A rat long dead . . . [or] A live fly mistaking him for dead' (Beckett 1996a: 19–20). These hoped-for external manifestations of company never materialise. Since there is no company outside of his confused and 'unformulable gropings', ultimately the hearer must realise that he himself is a multiplicity, the first and only source of company to himself, not merely by his invention of pronominal company but 'by such addition to company as a movement of sustained sorrow or desire or remorse or curiosity or anger and so on. Or by some successful act of intellection as were he to think of himself referring to himself' (Beckett 1996a: 33), an action which he does manage to perform. His fluctuating emotional and intellectual states, like the proliferation of pronouns, are themselves 'additions to company', intensities or desiring machines on his body without organs. Their differentiation and instability constitute the *sociendum* or limit-object of his faculty of sociability: an intensive confusion or metastable anarchy, a disordered order or discordant harmony that would make an extensive, that is truly interpersonal, sociability possible, should actual things or people ever appear.[26] The hearer's fate at the end of *Company*, which as the voice says is to 'find yourself imagining you are not alone while knowing full well that nothing has occurred to make this possible' (Beckett 1996a: 45), does not alter the fundamentally open virtuality or potentiality of this faculty of sociability.

Worstward Ho, the final text of the set, restages in condensed form all the earlier transcendental exercises of the faculties: *sentiendum* ('No mind and pain? Say yes that the bones may pain till no choice but stand' (Beckett 1996a: 90)), *memorandum* ('No once in pastless now . . . Onceless till no more' (Beckett 1996a: 110)), *cogitandum* ('Know better now. Unknow better now' (Beckett 1996a: 92)), *sociendum* ('In the dim void bit by bit an old man and child. Any other would do as ill' (Beckett 1996a: 93)). Its primary task, however, is the staging of the *loquendum*, the limit-object of the faculty of language 'that would be silence at the same time'.[27] From its very first line (which provides the title of the set of novellas), the text engages reflexively with its own status as language: 'On. Say on. Be said on. Somehow on. Till nohow on' (Beckett 1996a: 89). Many of the statements that follow explicitly invoke the verb 'say', ironically implying the weak first-person plural imperative of invitation 'Let's say', as the precondition of its claim to any specific content or expression whatsoever: 'Say a body. Where none' (Beckett 1996a: 89). The implied 'Let's say' suggests hypothetical or fictional creation of the referent. This creative precondition is immediately qualified quite drastically: 'Say for be said. Missaid. From now say for be missaid' (Beckett 1996a: 89). The original term 'say' is grammatically restructured in impersonal or passive form as 'be said', and then redefined to mean its contrary or negation, 'missaid', just as vision is later redefined as its own passive negation: 'See for be seen. Misseen. From now see for be misseen' (Beckett 1996a: 93). The redefinition is reiterated later, apparently as a reminder: 'Whenever said said said missaid' (Beckett 1996a: 109). This places the narrator of *Worstward Ho* in a worse position than that of the narrators of the previous novellas, who only had to deal with 'ill seeing' (or hearing) and 'ill saying', not 'misseeing' and 'missaying'.

As in *Company*, the narrative voice of *Worstward Ho* refuses the first person, but it goes on to repudiate most of the other pronominal positions that were available to the previous narrators as well. 'Whose-words? Ask in vain. Or not in vain if say no knowing. No saying. No words for him whose words. Him? One. No words for one whose words. One? It. No words for it whose words. Better worse so' (Beckett 1996a: 98). Yet something continues to narrate, even as its words predictably begin to fail, only to fail fully to fail: 'The words too whosesoever. What room for worse! How almost true they sometimes almost ring! How wanting in inanity!' (Beckett 1996a: 99). The narrator goes on, as Beckett's narrators always have, trying to 'worsen' its words and hence its situation to the point at which it can finally rejoin the pure void. It sinks to a level at which there is '[n]o knowing what it is the words it secretes say. No saying. No saying what it all is they somehow say' (Beckett 1996a: 105).

With this equation of knowing and saying it reaches the point at which it can begin to think about the absence of thought and the absence of words, even though such thought still uses a minimum of words and there would have to be '[n]o words for what when words gone. For what when nohow on. Somehow nohow on' (Beckett 1996a: 104). Here 'nohow on', the title of the collection and opening line of *Worstward Ho* itself, is equated with the anticipated point 'when words gone', though the persistence of the indefinite but positive 'somehow' weakens the negative force of 'nohow on'.

The narrator tries two other gambits to reach that limit before falling silent. First, it proposes to use words to 'unsay' the unstable world it has 'missaid' into existence, but this does not work as it hoped: 'Unsay then all gone. All not gone. Only nohow on. All not gone and nohow on. All there as now when somehow on . . . Only words gone' (Beckett 1996a: 110). Clearly the words are not gone, because the 'somehow on' that occupies the place of the absent words remains and so the 'nohow on' cannot yet stand alone and paradoxically (un)said. As the narrator fatalistically expected, all remains '[a]s when first said. Ununsaid when worse said' (Beckett 1996a: 106). The double negation 'ununsaid' does not eliminate either the 'said' or the 'unsaid', but merely extends the 'missaid'. Finally, the narrator proposes to use '[b]anks for when words gone. When nohow on. Then all seen as only then. Undimmed. All undimmed that words dim. All so seen unsaid' (Beckett 1996a: 112). But this too does not appear to work, at least not immediately, leaving the narrator in its '[u]nmoreable unlessable unworseable evermost almost void' (Beckett 1996a: 113), at which point it finally cries, 'Enough. Sudden enough . . . Best worse no farther. Nohow less. Nohow worse. Nohow naught. Nohow on. [line break] Said nohow on' (Beckett 1996a: 116). Here, in the final differential reiterations of 'nohow' freed from 'somehow', Beckett's narrator finally reaches the threshold of the *loquendum*, offering a paradoxical language of the 'unword' that rigorously effaces itself in its own production via anti-grammatical grammar and subjectless, objectless and (almost) verbless predication. The empty continuation of 'nohow on', the threshold beyond which words will be gone, is spoken intensively, not extensively, in the convoluted silence of the reader's mind at the end of the narrative and written imperceptibly in the blank space that follows the final line of text.[28] This *loquendum* is the paradox towards which all of Beckett's work has aimed, the harshest possible extension of *The Unnamable*'s famous final statement:

[Y]ou must go on, perhaps it's done already, perhaps they have said me already, perhaps they have carried me to the threshold of my story, before the door that opens on my story, that would surprise me, if it opens, it will be I, it will be the silence, where I am, I don't know, I'll never know, in the silence you don't know, you must go on, I can't go on, I'll go on. (Beckett 1958: 414)

The *loquendum* is the story at the limit of stories, the silent story that Beckett approaches most perfectly in this late prose, a story that makes audible or legible not the content or referent of language, nor even the structure and materiality of the signifier, but rather the mute, illegible force of language itself.[29] Beckett himself puts it elegantly in his posthumously published first novel, *Dream of Fair to Middling Women*:

The experience of my reader shall be between the phrases, in the silence, communicated by the intervals, not the terms, of the statement, between the flowers that cannot coexist, the antithetical (nothing so simple as antithetical) seasons of words, his experience shall be the menace, the miracle, the memory, of an unspeakable trajectory'. (Beckett 1993: 138)

Silence is language in unextended, intensive, virtual form. In seeking to speak that silence that comes in the wake of words, Beckett's narrators embody the open, generative paradox of a language in which the difference between speaking and silence becomes imperceptible.[30]

If what I have argued is correct, then it may not be too much to claim that Beckett's work also offers itself as a limit-object for the most fundamental 'faculty' of all: vitality, life itself. Deleuze suggests that this limit of vitality, this *viviendum* would have to include monstrosity. This is the most general situation of Beckett's grotesque narrators, who often find themselves reduced to skulls, the archetypal image of death. As its last narrative act, *Worstward Ho*'s narrator does this death's head image one better (or rather worse), starting with '[t]wo black holes. Dim black. In through skull to soft. Out from soft through skull. Agape in unseen face' (Beckett 1996a: 114). These self-blinding eye sockets are still too human an image, too representational, too recognisable, too clichéd, so the narrator must '[t]ry better worse set in skull. Two black holes in foreskull. Or one. Try better still worse one. One dim black hole mid-foreskull. Into the hell of all. Out from the hell of all' (Beckett 1996a: 114). The human face turns monstrous and Cyclopean at its paradoxical limit, offering a single blind socket as unreliable conduit between the unrecognisable outer world and the inner 'hell of all'. This monstrous image is no longer simply one of death, however, for this skull will persist or subsist just as all of Beckett's narrators do: 'So skull not go. What left of skull not go. Into it still the hole. Into what left of soft. From out what little left' (Beckett 1996a: 116). The little that is left, the soft, receptive, living matter of the mind, awaits the encounters that will pass through the hole and set it resonating, turning its misosophy into feeling, thought, relation and even speech. As Deleuze says, '[i]t is not the gods which we encounter: even hidden, the gods are only the forms of recognition. What we encounter are the demons, the sign-bearers: powers of the leap, the interval, the intensive and the instant; powers which only cover difference with more difference' (Deleuze 1994: 145). Echoing Nietzsche, then, I would conclude by demanding that 'Whoever encounters monsters should see to it that in the process he or she *does* become a monster',[31] does become, that is, one whose thought is born and constantly reborn in the unrecognisable violence of the encounter with the outside.

Notes

1. Both essays are included in Deleuze 1997.
2. This despite the fact that Beckett and Deleuze shared a publisher, Les Éditions de Minuit, and even a personal editor, Jérôme Lindon, for over twenty years. But see Cronin (1997: 570), where he cites evidence provided by André Bernold, one of Deleuze's philosophy students, of conversations Bernold had with Beckett about Deleuze and Jacques Derrida in the 1980s.
3. Other versions of this series appear in, Deleuze and Parnet 1987: 4; Deleuze 1995: 23, 128; Deleuze 1997: 68, 109–10.
4. See also 'The Exhausted' in Deleuze 1997.
5. See also Deleuze and Guattari 1983: 20, where Beckett's *Unnamable* is cited as an example of the circulation of the decentred subject through various identity 'states'.
6. Polan translates the conclusion of this passage, which reads in French 'ce que ne subsistent plus que des intensités' (Deleuze and Guattari 1975, p. 35), as 'nothing remains but intensities'. However, in Deleuze 1994, Deleuze uses the verb 'subsister' in a technical sense that does not allow it to be equated with 'remain'. There, he describes the 'ideal event' as 'an objective entity, but one of which we cannot say that it exists in itself: it insists or subsists, possessing a quasi-being or an extra-being, that minimum of being common to real, possible and even impossible objects' (Deleuze 1994: 156). The intensities that 'subsist' in Kafka's and Beckett's works are not immediately given, brute objects but insistent or subsistent quasi-objects, variables that have a range of virtual or potential states which they can actualize or occupy. Hence the title of my essay.
7. But see my essay 'The Eternal Return of the "Seim anew": Joyce's Vico and Deleuze's Nietzsche' for a more affirmative assessment of Joycean punning and circularity.
8. See also Deleuze and Guattari 1983: 3; Deleuze 1997: 153.
9. See also Deleuze 1997: 157.
10. See also Deleuze 1997: 160.
11. See also Deleuze 1997: 159.
12. Obviously the preceding account of Beckett's style is an intensive and abstract interpretive machine rather than an extensive empirical explication, but I do not

believe that it misrepresents that style or contradicts the sensitive and detailed work of Beckett's critics. The most comprehensive and meticulous empirical analyses of style in Beckett's prose that I know of are Rabinovitz's two studies (1984 and 1992), and Brienza (1987).

13. The most comprehensive and sophisticated explication of *Nohow On* that I have found is Locatelli 1990: 157–270. Although I do not entirely agree with the complex 'phenomenological/hermeneutic/deconstructive' framework she constructs to situate Beckett's prose (12–15), I will cite her work throughout the remainder of my argument because her account of Beckett's methods in these texts parallels and, in some places at least, supports my own.

14. In his book *The Implied Reader: Patterns of Communication in Prose Fiction from Bunyan to Beckett* (1974), Wolfgang Iser reads Beckett as representative of the modern novel's patterns of formal and syntactical difficulty in that his innovative style 'concerns the functioning of our own faculties of perception. The reader is meant to become aware of the nature of these faculties, of his own tendency to link things together in consistent patterns, and indeed of the whole process that constitutes his relations with the world outside himself' (1974: xiv). Iser presents this demystification of the faculties as a learning process that the reader undergoes in order to become able to read Beckett's texts at all, while I am arguing, following Deleuze, that the disordering of the faculties is not merely a precondition of reading these texts but a precondition of their very writing and every other creative activity of the mind. As such Deleuze's 'dis-ordering' of the faculties extends Foucault's analysis of rationalist 'order' as thought's relation to its outside through the categories of identity and difference (see Foucault 1970: 50–8).

15. For another, very different example of this non-linear 'reading through the middle', see my analysis of William S. Burroughs' cut-up Nova trilogy in Murphy 1997: 136–9.

16. I have argued elsewhere (Murphy 1992) that this interruption rhetorically enacts the very theory of encounter that it describes.

17. In fact this conjunction of Beckett and Deleuze that I am outlining may ultimately be traced back to their common interest in Proust, whose work provided the occasion for both writers to propose theories of perception, memory and thought that break with the model of recognition. See Deleuze 1994: xviii; Deleuze 1972: 159–67, as well as note 21 below.

18. It might be objected here that Beckett's work is consistently, if idiosyncratically, committed to a radical empiricism (see for example the project for 'Film' in Beckett 1984a), which begins with an invocation of Berkeley's famous dictum 'Esse est percipi' (p. 163) and which Deleuze has analysed in 'The Greatest Irish Film' (Deleuze 1997: 23–6) and that thus the elaboration of a 'transcendental exercise' of the faculties is fundamentally alien to his perspective. However, such an objection would have little force because Deleuze's transcendental empiricism is not a traditional idealism or rationalism but rather an account of the genesis and enabling limits of the faculties, an investigation of the material forces that make empiricism possible.

19. Locatelli argues that '[t]he reproduction of visibility in Beckett's recent works is achieved by means of a suspension of designation, and shows the role of language in the structuring of reality. Suspension hampers an immediate grasp of reference, but can show the fact that saying is responsible for visibility. In fact, a suspended designation makes reference difficult to assess, but reproduces, at least in part, the process through which visibility is achieved' (1990: 211).

20. Even if her visibility is purely a function of the eye of the imagination, the 'eye [that] closes in the dark and sees her in the end' (Beckett 1996a: 69), she would

still act at best as an *imaginandum*, a *phantasteon* that can only be imagined but is at the same time impossible to imagine. See Deleuze 1994: 143.

21. Deleuze (1994: 141–3) attributes the foundational connection of memory to forgetting to Plato (see for example the *Phaedrus* in Plato 1961: 492–6), but does not note that Freud also establishes that connection (for example, in Freud 1965, Chapters I to IV). Beckett himself evokes this paradox of memory founded on forgetting in *Proust*: 'The man with a good memory does not remember anything because he does not forget anything. His memory is uniform, a creature of routine, at once a condition and function of his impeccable habit, an instrument of reference instead of an instrument of discovery' (1957: 17).

22. Deleuze's formulation clearly draws upon Nietzsche's critique of truth in 'On Truth and Lies in a Nonmoral Sense': 'To begin with, a nerve stimulus is transferred into an image: first metaphor. The image, in turn, is imitated in a sound: second metaphor. And each time there is a complete overleaping of one sphere, right into the middle of an entirely new and different one' (1979: 82). In Nietzsche's terms, then, Deleuze's differential theory of the faculties is metaphorical, but not in any purely linguistic sense that could be opposed to literality.

23. At this point in his argument (see 320 n. 10), Deleuze notes that Kant offers an example of a transcendental exercise of faculties in the disjunction between imagination and reason in the mathematical sublime: reason finds its limit in the suprasensible that can only be thought but not imagined (the infinite, for example) even as imagination discovers its limit in the formless image that inspires it to represent the unrepresentable. See Kant 1987, sections 26–27 and 29, pp 107–17, 124–6. Locatelli sees Beckett as 'exploit[ing] the power of the literary system in relation to the semiotics of the natural world, so as to reveal the primary role of the signifier . . . in the structuring of our cognitive systems', as opposed to Kant who discovers the unknowable 'infinite signified' of the suprasensible through his account of the sublime (1990: 199–200; my emphases).

24. As Locatelli observes, 'Company makes it clear that any formulation of self has to be relational, and so speaker and listener, as much as "you" and "he," provide the screen on which the "company of self" can be projected and seen' (1990: 167).

25. Recall also the 'confusion between real and – how say its contrary?' in *Ill Seen Ill Said*, Beckett 1996a: 72. See also Locatelli 1990: 195–6.

26. Locatelli describes this situation as one in which '[t]he correlation of subjects involved in the use of persons and subject(s) of the enunciation maps out the different positions of the self (selves) in relation to the "I." That is, it indicates the different ways in which the self is "other," without being "another" ' (1990: 175).

27. In a very early (1937) and often-cited letter, Beckett expresses a desire for a 'literature of the unword' that sounds very much like Deleuze's *loquendum*. See 'German Letter of 1937' and its English translation in Beckett 1984b: 53–4, 172–3. Locatelli glosses this phrase as follows: 'the prefix in the expression "unword" implies the dynamics of subtraction, the movement of a want which transforms the staticity and stability of words' (1990: 228).

28. Deleuze (1981) elaborates this paradoxical idea of the fullness or plenitude of the blank page in his discussion of painter Francis Bacon's 'fight against the cliché' of figurative or representational imagery.

29. Locatelli: 'the narrative movement deconstructs designation, and structural repetition corrodes semantic similarity. What remains, then, is the working of the texts, and what is made visible is the event of (its) communication' (1990: 226).

30. Locatelli: 'His work is intrinsically open: his communicative strategies question communication as they enact it; his subtractions transform words into echoes, and echoes into pure sound, still speaking; his endless combinations corrode the cultural marking of experience, and his impotence shows ineliminable creativity' (1990: 29).
31. See aphorism 146, in *Beyond Good and Evil*, in Nietzsche 1968: 279.

Bibliography

Beckett, Samuel (1957), *Proust*, New York: Grove Press.
Beckett, Samuel (1958), *Three Novels: Molloy, Malone Dies and The Unnamable*, trans. Samuel Beckett and Patrick Bowles, New York: Grove Press.
Beckett, Samuel (1964), *How It Is*, New York: Grove Press.
Beckett, Samuel (1984a), *Collected Shorter Plays*, New York: Grove Press.
Beckett, Samuel (1984b), *Disjecta: Miscellaneous Writings and a Dramatic Fragment*, ed. Ruby Cohn, New York: Grove Press.
Beckett, Samuel (1993), *Dream of Fair to Middling Women*, London: Calder Publications.
Beckett, Samuel (1996a), *Nohow On*, New York: Grove Press. Originally published in England in 1989.
Beckett, Samuel (1996b), *The Complete Short Prose 1929–1989*, ed. S. E. Gontarski, New York: Grove Press.
Brienza, Susan D. (1987), *Samuel Beckett's New Worlds: Style in Metafiction*, Norman: University of Oklahoma Press.
Cronin, Anthony (1997), *Samuel Beckett: The Last Modernist*, San Francisco: HarperCollins.
Deleuze, Gilles (1972), *Proust and Signs*, trans. Richard Howard, New York: George Braziller. Originally published in France in 1964.
Deleuze, Gilles (1981), *Francis Bacon: Logique de la sensation*, Paris: Editions de la Différence.
Deleuze, Gilles (1994), *Difference and Repetition*, trans. Paul Patton, New York: Columbia University Press. Originally published in France in 1968.
Deleuze, Gilles (1995), *Negotiations 1972–1990*, trans. Martin Joughin, New York: Columbia University Press. Originally published in France in 1990.
Deleuze, Gilles (1997), *Essays Critical and Clinical*, trans. Daniel W. Smith and Michael A. Greco, Minneapolis: University of Minnesota Press. Originally published in France in 1993.
Deleuze, Gilles and Guattari, Félix (1975), *Kafka: Pour une littérature mineure*, Paris: Editions de Minuit.
Deleuze, Gilles and Guattari, Félix (1983), *Anti-Oedipus*, trans. Mark Seem, Robert Hurley and Helen R. Lane, Minneapolis: University of Minnesota Press. Originally published in France in 1972.
Deleuze, Gilles and Guattari, Félix (1986), *Kafka: Toward a Minor Literature*, trans. Dana Polan, Minneapolis: University of Minnesota Press.
Deleuze, Gilles and Guattari, Félix (1987), *A Thousand Plateaus*, trans. Brian Massumi, Minneapolis: University of Minnesota Press. Originally published in France in 1980.
Deleuze, Gilles, and Parnet, Claire (1987), *Dialogues*, trans. Hugh Tomlinson and Barbara Habberjam, New York: Columbia University Press. Originally published in France in 1977.
Foucault, Michel (1970), *The Order of Things*, New York: Vintage. Originally published in France in 1966.

Freud, Sigmund (1965), *The Psychopathology of Everyday Life*, trans. James Strachey, New York: Norton.

Hegel, G. W. F. (1952), *The Philosophy of Right*, trans. T. M. Knox, Oxford: Oxford University Press.

Iser, Wolfgang (1974), *The Implied Reader: Patterns of Communication in Prose Fiction from Bunyan to Beckett*, Baltimore: Johns Hopkins University Press.

Kant, Immanuel (1929), *Critique of Pure Reason*, trans. Norman Kemp Smith, New York: St Martin's Press.

Kant, Immanuel (1987), *Critique of Judgment*, trans. Werner S. Pluhar, Indianapolis: Hackett.

Locatelli, Carla (1990), *Unwording the World: Samuel Beckett's Prose Works after the Nobel Prize*, Philadelphia: University of Pennsylvania Press.

Massumi, Brian (1992), *A User's Guide to Capitalism and Schizophrenia*, Cambridge, MA: MIT Press.

Murphy, Timothy S. (1992), 'The Theater of (the Philosophy of) Cruelty in *Difference and Repetition*', PLI: *Warwick Journal of Philosophy*, 4, pp. 105–35.

Murphy, Timothy S. (1997), *Wising Up the Marks: The Amodern William Burroughs*, Berkeley, CA: University of California Press.

Murphy, Timothy S. (1999), 'The Eternal Return of the "Seim anew": Joyce's Vico and Deleuze's Nietzsche', *James Joyce Quarterly*, 35, pp. 4.

Nietzsche, Friedrich (1968), *Basic Writings of Nietzsche*, ed. and trans. Walter Kaufmann, New York: Modern Library.

Nietzsche, Friedrich (1979), *Philosophy and Truth*, trans. Daniel Breazeale, Atlantic Highlands, NJ: Humanities Press.

Plato (1961), *Collected Dialogues*, ed. Edith Hamilton and Huntington Cairns, Princeton: Bollingen/Princeton University Press.

Rabinovitz, Rubin (1984), *The Development of Samuel Beckett's Fiction*, Urbana: University of Illinois Press.

Rabinovitz, Rubin (1992), *Innovation in Samuel Beckett's Fiction*, Urbana: University of Illinois Press.

Chapter 10

Nizan's Diagnosis of Existentialism and the Perversion of Death

Eugene W. Holland

My point of departure is Deleuze's idea that, rather than being expressive or reflective, works of literature are *diagnostic* (see Deleuze 1997 and 1989). Such a claim is akin to, but probably somewhat stronger than, the view advanced by Shoshana Felman (among others) that literature understands psychoanalysis, for example, at least as well as psychoanalysis understands literature (see Deleuze 1997: 3).[1] Freud, of course, frankly acknowledged how much he owed to literature and to poets, who he said had discovered the unconscious long before he did. And Karl Marx, in a similar vein, is reputed to have said that he learned more about class struggle from the novels of Balzac than from all the works of history and political economy he read. Literature makes discoveries about class and the unconscious, we might agree with Freud and Marx, and theoretical discourse then formalises them *ex post facto*. Deleuze's view – presented most strikingly, perhaps, in his study of the literary works of Sade and Masoch, but informing all his many literary analyses up to and including the posthumously translated collection of *Essays Critical and Clinical* – is this: literature often diagnoses syndromes for which psychiatry then develops an aetiology and a therapy, that is, ascertains the causes and proposes appropriate treatments. The authors whose proper names are often enough taken to designate the syndromes in question (as in 'sadism' and 'masochism') are thus not to be understood as passive vehicles through which perversion expresses itself, but as active and often self-conscious *analysts* of the psychic phenomena appearing in their literary works. As Deleuze puts it, 'the writer as such is not a patient but a physician, the physician of himself and of the world' – in much the same way that Nietzsche spoke of the philosopher as a physician of culture.[2] So Deleuzian literary reading suggests a two-fold transformation of conventional psychoanalytic approaches to literature: first of all, the literary work is to be considered diagnostic rather than expressive; and furthermore, it diagnoses social rather than individual ills. Along these lines, one aim of this chapter is to outline the diagnosis that Nizan's novels make of Heideggerian and Sartrean existentialism. The other aim will be to determine the extent to which Nizan's diagnosis is compatible with Deleuze's diagnosis of the perversion of the death instinct under capitalism – or more precisely: the perversion that *is* the death instinct qua 'instinct'. For according to Deleuze and Guattari in some rather enigmatic passages in *Anti-Oedipus*, death only *becomes* an instinct under specific historical conditions linked to the emergence of capitalism (Deleuze and Guattari 1983: 330–7 and passim).

More than Deleuze, Nizan will couch his diagnosis in terms of class – but not, I want to insist, of class in any narrow sense of the term. Nizan will indeed diagnoses existentialism as in some sense petty-bourgeois. But, as for Deleuze after him, what Nizan identifies as the petty-bourgeois mode of life has at least as much to do with Nietzsche as it does with Marx. The question Nizan raises is not so much whether existentialism can be considered a petty-bourgeois 'ideology', but rather, again in a Nietzschean vein, *who it is* that thinks and feels this way: what mode of existence or style of life does it imply?

There is little doubt that Nizan was in fact engaging Heideggerian and Sartrean existentialism in the two novels under consideration here, *Antoine Bloyé* and *The Trojan Horse* (Nizan 1973, 1975). It is widely known that Nizan and Sartre were classmates in philosophy at the Ecole Normale; that relation appears only thinly veiled in the largely autobiographical novel *The Trojan Horse*, as the relation between the hero, Bloyé, and his nemesis, Lange. Perhaps less well known is the fact that Nizan was the managing editor of the journal (*Bifur*) that published the first work of Heidegger in French ('What is Metaphysics?') – alongside essays by Sartre and Nizan himself. And any lingering questions about whether Nizan was responding to Heidegger in *Antoine Bloyé* (written just after Nizan had finished reading Heidegger's *Being and Time*) may be settled by noting the novel's epigraph – a passage from *The German Ideology* in which Marx and Engels insist that putting 'an end both to the "cares" of the bourgeois and the needs of the proletarian [requires] putting an end to the cause of both: "labour"'. Nizan appears intent on resituating the Heideggerian theme of care in a Marxist context.

And yet the central theme of both novels turns out to be not work, but death. As Youssef Ishaghpour has pointed out, *Antoine Bloyé* is probably the first French novel of directly Heideggerian inspiration (Sartre's *Nausea* will appear five years later), even though it is at the same time a pointed critique of Heidegger (Ishaghpour 1980: 97). Where *Being and*

Time does its best to ontologise and universalise the human condition as Heidegger sees it, Nizan will insist on historicising it, on diagnosing it as the condition of a *specific class* rather than of humanity as a whole and for all eternity. And nowhere does this diagnosis become clearer than in relation to death, a topic central to both the novelist and the philosopher – and indeed to so many others in the decades following the First World War.

The diagnostic force of *Antoine Bloyé* has not gone unfelt. In her study of what she calls 'the ideological novel as a literary genre', Susan Suleiman notes a discrepancy in the text between historical and universalist explanations of why Antoine Bloyé becomes so anxious about his impending death at the end of the novel (Suleiman 1983). She attributes the particularising explanation to the omniscient narrator, who sees Bloyé's life and anxiety in the face of death as rooted in class, and locates the universalising explanation in a passage in the text (Part III, Chapter 20), which seems to attribute a fear and avoidance of death to all men (sic):

> [E]verything forbids men from turning their attention to their eventual deaths. [. . .] They are surrounded by the barriers and ramparts which the species builds with coral-like obstinacy and patience to screen from living eyes the chasms and tremendous suction power of death. (Nizan 1973: 224)

In what appears as a classic 'strategy of containment', to recall Fredric Jameson's apt expression,[3] Suleiman tries to foreclose Nizan's diagnosis and what I'd like to call his 'classification' of death-anxiety by suggesting a deconstructive incongruity between the thesis of the *roman à thèse* and what the text appears to actually say, at least on one occasion, as quoted above. Suleiman nowhere acknowledges the relation between Nizan's novel and Heideggerian philosophy, nor the Heideggerian roots of the deconstructive reading she practises. But it is clear that her reading works against the diagnostic force of the historicising explanation in Nizan's text (even if what is ontologised in such a reading is the aporetic nature of all language use rather than the relation to death).

But Nizan's point in the novel is not to deny that all men may fear death, but rather to explain why death would become an *obsessive* theme for a *certain* class of men, such as Antoine Bloyé, in a particular historical conjuncture. The portrait Nizan presents of Antoine's working-class father provides a telling contrast with those like the son who have cause to obsess about death:

> A poor man, he realises that he is anchored to a certain lot in the world, a lot ordained for the rest of his life, a lot which he surveys as a tethered goat measures the circumference of its rope, a lot which, like every other lot in life, was willed by chance, by riches, by the rulers. [. . .] He knows neither ambition nor revolt. [. . .] He has reached a certain point, he is in a given place, and there he will remain. He sees how men of his station live, how their lives, their deaths, their meager heritage, follow one another. The end of the road can be seen from a long way off. At twenty, many men have reached a level above which they will never rise, a level below which they sometimes find it hard to sink. [. . .] Above them are other men [such as Antoine Bloyé] who know only that they will die, while the devious courses they will travel to reach their death are not so clear and pass many crossroads. In the [petty] bourgeoisie are men whose destiny may change, men who themselves do not always know what form it will take. (33)

Unlike his father's lot, as circumscribed and legible as that of a tethered goat,

> [Antoine's] existence [. . .] had the well-ordered pattern, the slowly-rising curve of the lives of functionaries marked for advancement. [. . .] Antoine Bloyé was following the trails blazed through western France by his company's [rail] lines. At each move he went up one step in the hierarchy. (142, 99)

Nizan is thereby able to show, in his account of the rise-and-fall trajectory of this ambitious yet unhappy life, that the meaning of petty-bourgeois existence depends crucially on where in the social hierarchy one ends up at the moment of death – rather like an earlier version of the late twentieth-century bumper-sticker that claims that 'in the end, whoever has the most toys wins'. Indeed, Nizan begins the novel with Bloyé's death (and then proceeds to recount his life in flashback), as if to emphasise the importance of death in defining this mode of life. By contrast, peasants and other manual labourers (such as the parents Bloyé leaves behind), like the captains of industry who control Bloyé's fate from distant Paris, simply are where they are, where they always have been, where they always will be, throughout their whole lives: their mode of life charges death with no special significance regarding their relative social position at the moment of their demise.

Equally as important as what the 'slowly-rising curve' of petty-bour-geois existence *leads to*, however, is what it leads *away from*; the theme of separation echoes throughout the novel, as the price paid for fixation on regular advancement. Social and literary critics such as Lukács and Benjamin have long claimed that in a society dominated by market exchange, social relations become a pure means to individual ends, radically divorcing the individual from communion and community. Nizan's work shows that it is precisely such alienation that makes the individual's death a matter of anguish: thrown back on the self, the dying individual has no community, no common project through which to live on after death. *Antoine Bloyé* makes the agony of this long process of separation palpable: Bloyé abandons his parents, and then his classmates; he forsakes his fellow workers in order to become management; he forsakes Marcelle, his working-class lover, to 'marry up', by wedding the petty-bourgeois daughter of a railroad functionary higher on the social ladder than he: each move devoted to the advancement of his career, each step up the social hierarchy, leaves him emptier and more isolated than the last.

Finally, what Bloyé forgoes in following such a trajectory is not just the possibility of solidarity with a group larger than himself, as important as that is, but also the chance to expend energy freely or devote it to a cause that doesn't serve only his own advancement. Examples of missed chances to expend energy this way abound in the novel: the thrill of extreme physical exertion as an express-locomotive engineer (even though it also serves the profit-maximisation imperatives of the company), which Bloyé gives up for a series of desk jobs; the time and energy wasted gloriously in long evenings of pleasure with Marcelle; the communion with fellow workers trying to bring off a strike for their common good; the hopeless yet heroic attempt to save the life of his terminally-ill daughter – the one moment that brings him close to his convention-bound wife. Ultimately, it may be the impossibility of making good on such missed chances, as much or more than death itself, that Bloyé fears when the end of his life draws near:

> It was no longer bodily death that he feared but the shapeless image of his whole life, that defeated image of himself, that headless being that walked in the ashes of time with hurrying steps, aimlessly and chaotically. [. . .] No one had ever called his attention to the fact that he had no head. It was too late. The whole time he had been living his own death. (248–9)

This motive for anxiety at the approach of death has little to do with ideology or economic infrastructure, and much more to do with what an exact contemporary of Nizan's, Georges Bataille, called 'expenditure'[4] – and more precisely with capitalist society's distinctive compulsion to subordinate expenditure to accumulation, even the pettiest form of accumulation represented by the 'slowly-rising curve' of Antoine Bloyé's career. For Bataille, as for Nizan, refusing to acknowledge and embrace the necessity of expenditure means refusing to face the risk of death, being 'a party to the conspiracy in favour of . . . that life that was not life', as Nizan puts it (224).

I have invoked Bataille not just because he was a contemporary of Nizan, but also because his notion of expenditure lies at an intersection of Marxist and Nietzschean lines of thought that Deleuze and Guattari later develop under the rubric of 'anti-production' (see Deleuze and Guattari 1983; see also Holland 1999: 69ff). What distinguishes capitalism from all previous social forms, Deleuze and Guattari agree with Bataille, is that it subordinates expenditure and anti-production to production, ends to means, instead of the other way around. As the term implies, anti-production is the opposite of production; but it involves something other or more than life-enhancing or reproductive consumption alone: it designates especially *wasteful* consumption, expenditure and dilapidation, debt and the risk of death.

Drawing directly on Bataille's *The Accursed Share* (and to that extent departing significantly from orthodox Marxism), Deleuze and Guattari insist that no social formation is determined by production alone; social formations are determined by relations and forces of production *and* anti-production. In primitive society, the relations of anti-production entail a mobile patchwork of temporary and reciprocal debts and obligations cruelly enforced by local custom and social consensus; refusing this patchwork signifies ostracism and the risk of death. In despotic society, by contrast, all debts and obligations align on the despot himself; and instead of being mobile and temporary, they have become permanent and in a sense infinite. Primitive debts can always be discharged or renegotiated, partly because even while you owe something to clan x, clan y owes you something else that will enable you to repay clan x, and so on in a vast horizontal circuit or patchwork of exchanges. But the debt to the despot can never be discharged or renegotiated: he represents a transcendent instance of power to which everyone owes everything – even their very lives as his subjects. The mere risk of death due to social ostracism in primitive society becomes under despotism a permanent threat of death at the hands of the despot; he commands obedience to his Law and reigns by terror rather than by primitive cruelty arising from consensus. And, as Foucault has shown, such a reign of terror entails and may even depend on very public, ritual displays of capital punishment and torture sponsored by the despot to assert and maintain his sovereign power.

Modern, civilised power is not exercised in this way. In Deleuze and Guattari's account (here again following Bataille), civilised society is unique in that anti-production is subordinated to production, instead of the other way around. The production and continuous accumulation of surplus henceforth take priority over anti-production. Glorious waste and expenditure are seen to contradict the modern principle of rational efficiency and utility; they are able to survive only in a pale, privatised form, having lost their erstwhile social functions, or in grotesque, morbid forms of surplus-realisation such as war and the nuclear arms race. (Deleuze and Guattari also mention 'advertising, civil government, militarism, and imperialism' as instances of anti-production subordinated to surplus-realisation (Deleuze and Guattari: 1983: 235).)

In modern civilisation, then, anti-production loses primacy and all emphasis is placed on enhancing 'productivity' and what we might call by analogy 'reproductivity': power no longer wields death as a means of punishment. Its aim is instead to increase the forces of life and the forces of production as much as possible: to inflict death under this regime would be counter-productive, inefficient. To put the point of the comparison another way, there is a sense in which, although sovereigns have the power of life and death over their subjects, they only ever owe them their death (if they disobey), not their life; the subjects of civilisation, by contrast, owe capital their lives, and rather than 'taking' those lives, capital exercises power to keep them alive and make them as productive and reproductive as possible. Conceived of in this way, of course, Deleuze-Guattari's notion of 'civilisation' corresponds closely to what the Foucault of *The History of Sexuality* (1978) and *Discipline and Punish* (1977), called 'bio-technico-power' (Dreyfus and Rabinow 1982: 128).[5] Normalising sexuality and disciplining the body serve to increase techno-productivity and bio-reproductivity alike, whether the ultimate end is considered to be furthering the accumulation of capital or the power of the State. (Foucault would presumably disagree with Deleuze- and Guattari on where to put the emphasis here.)

We are now in a position, I think, to consider what Deleuze and Guattari refer to as the 'becoming-instinct' of death in relation to the subordination of anti-production, expenditure and death in modern civilisation. Their reading of the death-instinct in Freud – as of so much else in the psychoanalytic corpus – is critical without being dismissive: just as he didn't describe the Oedipus complex incorrectly, but didn't understand its historical foundations either, Deleuze and Guattari argue that Freud didn't describe the death-instinct incorrectly, but failed to historicise it adequately. The death-instinct, in Freud's account, is 'silent', not given in experience (except when already combined with Eros). But death only becomes an instinct, gets internalised or privatised and falls silent, Deleuze and Guattari insist, when it is deprived of its social functions – as happens under capitalism. Death is not silent under sovereign despotism: it is on the contrary very noisy, visible, dramatic – and terrifying. But once social value in the modern regime of bio-technico-power is assigned to continually enhanced production and reproduction to the exclusion of death, waste, expenditure and deviance, then death must fall silent, must become instinctual. This instinctualisation amounts to a modern perversion of death that subordinates it, along with expenditure in general, to the principles of rational utility, efficiency and productivity and to the mechanisms of surplus-production and -accumulation characteristic of capitalist civilisation.

As we have seen, *Antoine Bloyé* shows how completely the capitalist subordination of expenditure shapes the death and life of a first-generation petty-bourgeois functionary. This question of the relations between life to death returns in the sequel to *Antoine Bloyé*, the autobiographical novel dealing with Antoine's son Pierre Bloyé, entitled *The Trojan Horse*. Here, instead of focusing on a single class, Nizan undertakes a comparative diagnosis of two classes, proletariat and petty bourgeoisie, examining their modes of existence and relations to death. And the diagnostic force of the sequel has not gone unfelt, either. As Allan Stoekl has noted in 'Nizan . . . and the Question of Death' (1988: 117–45), *The Trojan Horse* raises such issues as, 'How . . . the apparently purely negative experience of death [can] be seen in a positive light' and 'How can a sacrificial death have value in itself but also have a positive social role?' (1988: 118). Like *Antoine Bloyé*, which seeks both to appropriate and critique existentialism from a class perspective, *The Trojan Horse*, too, sets itself a double task: one is 'to present a model of social growth (and [of] Revolution) through a positive sacrifice', as Stoekl puts it, while the other involves 'confronting and disproving the avant-garde model of sacrifice' in which death would be strictly useless and meaningless, or to adopt the existentialist term, absurd (118, but see also 119). As I have already suggested, the main characters, Bloyé and Lange, can be understood to portray the positions of Nizan and Sartre. For Nizan/Bloyé, the world we inhabit is scandalous and needs to be transformed; such is the aim of revolutionary activism and of *littérature engagée*. For Sartre/Lange, Being itself is scandalous in whatever world we might inhabit: language and Being are incommensurable; essence and existence never match – and so any attempt to address and redress the particular scandals of this world would be misguided and hopeless. And each has a corresponding view of violence and death: for Bloyé, violence and death can be meaningful if they constitute a positive sacrifice for the revolutionary cause; for Lange, violence is absolutely pointless – like the truly surrealist act imagined by Breton in the *Second Manifesto*, which would involve firing at random into a crowd. And this is in effect what happens in the novel: at one point, Lange inadvertently fires into a crowd; this gratuitous act touches off a shoot-out in which one of Bloyé's comrades is killed, this sacrificial death then provides Bloyé with a rallying-point for further revolutionary mobilisation and action. The novel clearly endorses Bloyé's meaningful, constructive attitude towards death over Lange's senseless and purely destructive one – and furthermore reinforces the notion illustrated in *Antoine Bloyé* that it is devotion to social causes larger than the self – even to the point of death – that can make human existence fulfilling.

But Stoekl's strategy (like Suleiman's) is to find a passage in the text that for him casts doubt on such a diagnosis, by raising the question: what happens to the meaning of death 'after the revolution' (123)? 'People will die anyway,' says a minor character at one point, 'They'll always end up in a hole in the ground' (*Trojan Horse*, p. 250; quoted in Stoekl, p. 123). Bloyé answers the question by making an 'implicit comparison' (123) between dying for a social cause and dying of natural causes. But Stoekl finds Bloyé's answer 'unconvincing' and concludes that Bloyé and Lange are symmetrical mirror-opposites (127): Bloyé denies (or 'represses', as Stoekl puts it) the potential meaninglessness of violence and death after the Revolution, just as Lange denies (or 'represses') the potential meaningfulness of violence and death in the service of the Revolution.

But Bloyé's implicit comparison between natural and social causes of death (between dying from illness and dying from torture) has more merit than Stoekl is willing to recognise: death from cancer is strictly fortuitous and in a sense unavoidable (it arises haphazardly and 'from within', as Deleuze might say),[6] whereas death from torture is strictly intentional and unnecessary, and is imposed 'from without' by and for others. After the Revolution, Bloyé suggests,

> [W]e shall be able to put an end to all unjust, preventable causes for death. Then, once we have finished with all forms of death for which human beings are responsible, we shall have to give death a new significance. (250)

There is, then, a substantial difference between these two kinds of death. And the difference can be summed up in one word: justice. The difference between a fortuitous death from within and one imposed by others from without is that the category of justice applies to the one and not the other (unless one subscribes to some notion of divine intervention whereby cancer – or AIDS – would be visited as punishment on the wicked). In this light, Bloyé's and Lange's positions don't appear symmetrical at all. (And it is only fair to point out in this connection that Derrida has distinguished himself in crucial ways from his North American epigones by insisting on the centrality of justice to his version of deconstruction.)

There is, in fact, an important asymmetry in their respective relations to death that prevents Bloyé and Lange from comprising an undecidable 'aporia' in the way Stoekl's reading strategy would demand. Change in Lange's relation to death is unimaginable: society is always everywhere the same; Being is always everywhere the same scandal; the conditions of human existence are always everywhere the same – including or especially their relation to death. Bloyé's relation to death, by contrast, *is* subject to change. After the elimination of preventable injustice as a cause of death, the significance of death will be different. For one thing, and as we saw in *Antoine Bloyé*, the (re-)connection of human life with collective activity will itself diminish the anguish attributed to individual death: the individual lives on in the common project. Perhaps more important, the centrality of sacrifice as the principal meaning of death before or during the Revolution is shown by the novel to be a meaning *imposed* on life by the alienated conditions of class warfare; in a classless society, the conditions of existence would link individuals with a range of group activities in the context of which individual death would lose this meaning – and perhaps even lose meaning altogether. Far from 'repressing' the potential meaninglessness of death after the Revolution, the views expressed in Nizan's novel are at least compatible with the Bataillian endorsement of the sacrifice of meaning,[7] yet locate this sacrifice precisely in the period 'after the Revolution' when injustice and class warfare no longer imposes sacrificial meaning on individual death.

I want to conclude, then, that Nizan's diagnosis of existentialism and its relation to the conditions of petty-bourgeois existence holds up rather well, despite readings in a deconstructive vein that would seek to disrupt or destabilise it. Furthermore, there is an important sense in which Nizan's novels diagnose the very kind of reading Suleiman and Stoekl are proposing.[8] For there is a hidden continuity and point of agreement linking the Heideggerian and Sartrean existentialism Nizan explicitly addresses with structuralism and neo-Derridean deconstruction: that Being and language are incommensurable, that language offers us no purchase on the world (as in the pervasive mistranslation of Derrida's 'il n'y a pas de hors-texte' as 'there is nothing outside the text' (instead of 'there is no outside to textuality')), that literature is beset by undecidable aporias and is thus constitutionally unable to proffer diagnoses of social ills. Despite all that he shares with Derrida, Deleuze departs strikingly from this dominant line of thinking about language. If, for Deleuze, there is 'no outside to textuality', it is because the world is itself composed of signs – and if we're deft and fortunate, the signs we emit and those of the world line up in illuminating and productive ways (see Deleuze 1990a, 1990b and 1972). With this understanding of language use and textuality, it should be clear that literary works are no more subject to the unavoidable reiteration of semantic or grammatical aporias than they are to the unconscious expression of perversions – and that they may be able to offer compelling diagnoses of ourselves and our world after all.

Notes

1. See Felman's introduction in Felman 1982.
2. For Nietzsche's analogous view of the philosopher, see especially 'The Philosopher as Cultural Physician', in Nietzsche 1979: 67–76. See also Deleuze 1981.
3. See his 'The Symbolic Inference; or, Kenneth Burke and Ideological Analysis', (Jameson 1988: 137–52). Jameson there defines a strategy of containment as a process of 'substitution designed to arrest the movement of ideological analysis before it can begin to draw in the social, historical, and political parameters that are the ultimate horizon of every cultural artifact' (147–7); here, I am suggesting, the strategy of containment is designed to arrest the diagnostic force of the novel itself.
4. See especially Georges Bataille 1988; but also his earlier essay, 'The Notion of Expenditure' (Bataille 1985: 116–29).
5. For a discussion, see Dreyfus and Rabinow 1982: 128 and passim.
6. On the death that arises from within, see Deleuze and Guattari 1983: 262, 330–7.
7. See especially Bataille's remarks on poetry in 'The Notion of Expenditure' (1985: 120 and passim).
8. Perhaps this is why they of all critics should be so sensitive to the diagnostic force of the novels. Stoekl discusses at some length the profound effect on Sartre of Nizan's diagnosis of his position; see Stoekl 1988: 143–4, n. 10 and 11.

Bibliography

Bataille, Georges (1985), *Vision of Excess*, trans. Allan Stoekl, Minneapolis: University of Minnesota Press.

Bataille, Georges (1988), *The Accursed Share: An Essay on General Economy: Consumption*, trans. Robert Hurley, New York: Zone.

Deleuze, Gilles (1972), *Proust and Signs*, trans. Richard Howard, New York: George Braziller.

Deleuze, Gilles (1981), *Nietzsche and Philosophy*, trans. Hugh Tomlinson, New York: Columbia University Press.

Deleuze, Gilles (1989), *Masochism*, trans. Jean McNeil, New York: Zone.

Deleuze, Gilles (1990a), *Expressionism in Philosophy: Spinoza*, trans. Martin Joughin, New York: Zone.

Deleuze, Gilles (1990b), *The Logic of Sense*, trans. Constantin Boundas, Charles Stivale and Mark Lester, New York: Columbia University Press.

Deleuze, Gilles (1997), *Essays Critical and Clinical*, trans. D. Smith and M. Greco, Minneapolis: University of Minnesota Press.

Deleuze, Gilles and Guattari, Félix (1983), *Anti-Oedipus*, trans. Robert Hurley, Mark Seem and Helen R. Lane, Minneapolis: University of Minnesota Press.

Dreyfus, Hubert and Rabinow, Paul (1982), *Michel Foucault: Beyond Structuralism and Hermeneutics*, Chicago: University of Chicago Press.

Felman, Shoshana (ed.) (1982), *Literature and Psychoanalysis: The Question of Reading Otherwise*, Baltimore: John Hopkins University Press.

Foucault, Michel (1977), *Discipline and Punish*, trans. Alan Sheridan, New York: Pantheon.

Foucault, Michel (1978), *The History of Sexuality: Volume 1*, trans. Robert Hurley, New York: Pantheon.

Holland, Eugene (1999), *Deleuze and Guattari's Anti-Oedipus*, London: Routledge.

Ishaghpour, Youssef (1980), *Paul Nizan*, Paris: Le Sycomore.

Jameson, Fredric (1988), *The Ideologies of Theory: Essays 1971–1986, Volume One, Situations of Theory*, Minneapolis, University of Minnesota Press.

Nietzsche, Friedrich (1979), *Philosophy and Truth: Selections from Nietzsche's Notebooks of the early 1870's*, trans. and ed., with an intro, and notes, by Daniel Brezeale, with a foreword by Walter Kaufmann, Atlantic Highlands, NJ: Humanities Press.

Nizan, Paul (1973), *Antoine Bloyé*, trans. E. Stevens, New York: Monthly Review Press.

Nizan, Paul (1975), *The Trojan Horse*, New York: Howard Fertig.

Stoekl, Allan (1988), 'Nizan, Drieu, and the Question of Death', *Representations*, vol. 21, Winter, pp. 117–45.

Suleiman, Susan Rubin (1983), *Authoritarian Fictions: The Ideological Novel as a Literary Genre*, New York: Columbia University Press.

Chapter 11

I and My Deleuze

Tom Conley

Ian Buchanan, in an array of articles appearing in Australian journals, has shown that the work of Gilles Deleuze wages new stakes for literary and cultural studies.[1] For Buchanan the work is in itself what its author calls 'multiple lines of flight' that move multifariously, cutting through contexts and issues far from an ostensive origin. For the reader located north of the Equator the Deleuze he fashions in antipodean lands, far from rival camps and cabalas of devoted theorists in Paris, attests to a strength and mobility that also crosses disciplinary barriers. Such is the context of this volume, in which the philosophical writings are drawn through the context of literature. As Buchanan has also insisted, Deleuze's *oeuvre* invites movement and migration all over the world-map, at once in its different orientations, in the scope of its topics found, and the problems undertaken within its own borders.

To think of Deleuze *and* literature is tantamount to engaging his concepts of difference *and* repetition, of intercession, of spiritual automata, of the creation of minoritarian practices, of a politics of sensation but, above all, of styles *and* ways of doing things. Wherever a reader enters in the philosophical opus he or she will find works of literature intervening. Literature might thus be the difference that sustains the recurring issues of philosophy. It might intercede, like an uninvited dinner guest or a Socratian sosie in convivia in the style of *The Symposium*, who arrives late and brings inebriate wit to the company. It could be the 'other' of the philosopher who returns from the margins of knowledge to reconfigure their boundaries before disappearing again. Literature would bring, in its strange ways of constructing images, new flashes of sensation and pleasure that logicians would be hard put to create in the filigree of reason. Because literature is the domain of comparative styles of handling and playing language, it would be a practice or way of doing that the philosopher could only admire or better, by ruse and guile, deploy with artful cunning.

Even if it succeeded in locating how Deleuze crafts a reading of Proust on the grounds of Bergson's studies of intutition and memory, or in finding what and how different poets, authors, genres, and canons recur in the sum of his writings, the topic of Deleuze *and* literature might amount to an exercise in difference itself. It would resemble what he calls the 'method of AND,' of 'this and then that', by which, '[b]etween two actions, between two affections, between two perceptions, between two visual images, between two sound images, between sound and image,' something indiscernible irrupts. It would be what he calls the 'and' constitutive of things and images (1985: 235).[2] *And* would deny the overarching impression that as a whole Deleuze's work is *of* and *about* literature. And it would show how in fact the work is driven by the creative tactics of the very writers he so often calls forward to serve, convey, but also to embody his concepts. There is no way of getting around the fact that to consider his corpus in the light of literature means that he has to be read *as* literature, and that time and again the reader must work through the writing with the eye of an artist and the ear of a poet.

Yet, as he notes at the end of *Proust et les signes* (*Proust and Signs*), a body of work of consequence needs to be esteemed at once in its detail and in its sum. Parts and wholes need to be articulated wherever philosophers and writers create universes of their own fashion and signature that rival with the world whence they are derived. 'Over and again the problem of the work of art is that of a unity and of a totality that would be neither logical nor organic, in other words, that would be neither presupposed by the parts as a lost unity or a fragmented totality, nor formed or prefigured by them in the course of a logical development or of an organic evolution' (1979: 179). The remark falls in the context of Proust's affinity for Leibniz's paradox of communication that takes place within the closed shape of monads (parts) that have opaque windows giving on to a same world (a whole). As a result each unit possesses 'a clear region of expression, distinct from the others, all thus being different points of view on the same world in which God enveloped them' (1979: 196). The total work of art, literature and philosophy, such as that of *In Search of Lost Time*, finds its origins in Balzac, who had the mendacious talent of making his readers believe that he had plotted and gridded the placement and the content of each of the individual novels in *The Human Comedy* prior to or in the midst of writing them. With Leibniz, Proust and Balzac there results an *effect* that is neither in the detail nor in the illusion of a self-contained sum. No groundplan precedes the result; no set of concepts or themes serves as a point of reference.

The observation can be directed towards the whole of Deleuze's *oeuvre*. A finite sum of texts accumulates in the lists of 'works of the same author' opposite the title-pages of each successive book in his opus. Like a reader of Proust or Balzac who is apt to identify in a turn of phrase a geographical place and movement in the work at large (a reader seeing in a single locution 'une espèce de fumier philosophique auquel rien ne manquait' (a kind of philosophical manure-heap in which nothing lacked) immediately recalls the beginning of *La peau de chagrin*, but might – as it might not – apply to the entire work. An unsettling effect is manifest; it derives from the realisation that it is impossible to make a minimal expression reflect, as might a microcosm, the reassuring closure of a total and pregiven macrocosm. A turn of phrase in *Proust et les signes*, such as what is given on point of view and style, explains why.

> Le style ici ne se propose pas de décrire ni de suggérer: comme chez Balzac, il est explicatif, il explique avec des images. Il est non-style, parce qu'il se confond avec 'l'interpréter' pur et sans sujet, et multiplie les points de vue sur la phrase, à l'intérieur de la phrase. Celle-ci est donc comme le fleuve qui apparaît 'entièrement disloqué, étalé ici en lac, aminci là en filet, rompu ailleurs par l'interposition d'une colline'. Le style est l'explication des signes, à des vitesses de développement différentes, en suivant les chaînes associatives propres à chacun d'eux, en atteignant pour chacun d'eux le point de rupture de l'essence comme Point de vue (1979: 199)
>
> [Here style is not given either to describe or to suggest: as in Balzac, it tends to explain. It explains with images. It is non-style because it gets confused with the pure and unattached drive 'to interpret', and it multiplies points of view on the sentence, inside of the sentence. What is thus like the great river that appears 'entirely dislocated, here extended as a lake, there shrunken into a thread, elsewhere broken by the interposition of a hill.' Style is the explication of signs, at different speeds of development, that follow the associative links belonging to each and every one of them, in attaining for both the point of rupture of essence as Point of view]

Here and elsewhere fragments of Deleuze's work come into view and, no sooner, vanish. A text that 'explains with images' becomes the topic of his study of Beckett, 'L'épuisé' (The Spent) that follows *Quad* (1992). It applies to his attraction to Godard, in *L'image-temps* (The Time-Image) (1985: 263ff). It informs and articulates his words on Rossellini about films being organised around disparate images, frail and forceful convergences of form that constitute film-events, at the beginning of the same work or at the end of *L'image-mouvement* (The Movement-Image) (1983: 285–7). What he intuits of the multiplication of points of view runs through *Le pli: Leibniz et le Baroque* (The Fold: Leibniz and the

Baroque) (1988: 27–9) and also, when point of view 'is divided into a thousand diverse and incommunicating points of view' (1988: 199), the process inspires the writing of *Mille plateaux* (A Thousand Plateaus) (Deleuze and Guattari 1980). When one work is added to another we witness a thought that 'swarms' and moves in all directions at once. Deleuze's preferred verb to convey the effect is *fourmiller*, that recalls the world of ants (*fourmis*), but that multiplies *four* by a thousand (*mille*) across two different idioms, but also arches towards his praise of American literature, that moves towards Henry Miller (Deleuze and Guattari 1980: 233 and *passim*) and Herman Melville.

The transverse dimension of writing, which in *Proust et les signes* he defines as style, and that in the books on cinema Deleuze will call 'a way of doing things', is said to be what moves across a single sentence or a sonata, and that ties Proust's own book to those its author so admired, such as Nerval, Chateaubriand and Balzac. The time of the narrator, he concludes, has the virtue of being the sum of all the parts of the book without totalising them, and the unity the part without unifying them. The conclusion that follows begins as a new critical episode in his literary study. 'Présence et fonction de la folie l' Araignée' (Presence and Function of Madness the Spider), a fragment adjoined to the third edition of *Proust et les signes* (1979), like its title that bears a run-on noun, signalling a deviance or a twist. The apparent folly of the narrator of *In Search of Lost Time* results from what might roughly be called an 'interpretation deficiency syndrome'. But not that the narrator lacks attention enough to decipher what happens around him: rather, he discovers in the sexual valence of the signs circulating in his midst a 'schizoid universe of hermetic boxes, of cloistered space, in which contiguity itself is a distance' (1979: 210). He discovers them in what in *Mille plateaux* Deleuze and Félix Guattari will later call *visagéité*, 'faceness', by the 'ultimately uncanny world of signs and boxes, of signs packed and unpacked' (1979: 211) that are both seen in the shine of Charlus' eyes and heard in the proximity of his lips. Eyes and lips are discovered when the stalking narrator casts his gaze upon Albertine's face, 'a mobile array' (1979: 211) of signs. He stares at her beauty spot which 'shines like a singular point' before he jumps to another point, ultimately in a movement through which he discovers, while losing the use of his own lips, eyes and nose, in the midst of all these 'execrable signs' that 'he is making love with the desired object' (1979: 212).

By way of the encounter with these perplexing faces Proust's narrator attains a 'vegetal innocence in decomposition', in which madness is assigned an absolving function 'in a world where boxes explode and close upon one another' (1979: 213), where crime and sequestration comprise 'the human comedy' à la Proust, where a mad power is born, that of the Search itself, in which are reunited 'the cop and the madman, the spy and the merchant, the interpreter and the protester' (1979: 213). Telescoping Deleuze's concluding argument, we can observe that it moves towards two conceptual forms that run through the work on philosophy and on literature. First, the narrator's discovery of an elementary madness in all relations leads to the perception that he himself is a machine. He is not a figure in control of, or defined by, 'his' subjectivity, or a private spatiality that would be defined by the signs emanating from his body. The redemptive discovery of madness is not controlled by a point of view that looks on to it or that is in a position, as a reader of Balzac might be led to believe through the bogus voice of his omniscient narrators, to identify what it describes. 'There is less a narrator than a machine of the Search, and less a hero than the workings in which the machine functions in one configuration or another, according to a given use, or for a given production' (1979: 217).[3] The narrator observes human folly from a point that disallows any ethical qualifications.[4]

Second, and as a consequence that bears on literature in general, the narrator is assimilated into what Deleuze calls a *corps sans organes*, a body without organs, a mass of protoplasm sensitive to everything in its midst, without needing to use an appendage for any practical function. He is an ambient sensibility in a permanent state of psychogenesis, and one that never regresses to an ancestral condition in the accepted biology of the evolution of species. The body is a sensitive surface that registers sensation but does not distinguish seeing from hearing or touching from tasting. In explaining the concept further, responding to his own didactic question, Deleuze appeals to the spider, one of many species in his gallery of fauna:

Mais qu'est-ce que c'est, un corps sans organes? L'araignée non plus ne voit rien, ne perçoit rien, ne se souvinet de rien. Seulement, à un bout de sa toile, elle recueille la moindre vibration qui se propage à son corps en onde intensive, et qui la fait bondir à l'endroit nécessaire. Sans yeux, sans nez, sans bouche, elle répond uniquement aux signes, est pénétrée du moindre signe qui traverse son corps comme une onde et la fait sauter sur sa proie. La Recherche n'est pas bâtie comme une cathédrale ni comme une robe, mais comme une toile. Le Narrateur-araignée, dont la toile même est la Recherche en train de se faire, de se tisser avec chaque fil remué par tel ou tel signe: la toile et l'araignée, la toile et le corps sont une seule et même machine. (1979: 218)

[But what is it, a body without organs? Neither does a spider see anything, perceive anything, remember anything. Only at the edge of its web does it gather the slightest vibration that propagates to its body in an intensive wave, and that makes it jump upon its prey. The Search is built neither like a cathedral nor a dress, but like a cobweb. The Narrator-spider, whose very web is the Search as it is being made, being woven, each strand stirred by one sign or another: the web and the spider, the web and the body are a single and unique machine.]

Located at the end of *Proust et les signes*, the comparison and assimilation of the narrator to the spider might be part of an emblem and a stratagem that apply to Deleuze and his work in general. At the time of its writing it was a webbing constructed so as to respond to the signs in its midst and, thereby, in a supremely modern literary tactic, to include in its own purview its observations about its form as process.

The difficult pleasure of following the work as literature may owe to its failure to separate its conclusions from its style. This means that the work is a tenuous webbing of philosophical fragments, impressions and reflections continually moving in the flow and the rifts of its form. If a metaphor can be extended – like the pigments on the reverse of the canvas of the paintings of a Morris Louis – one work drips or bleeds into the tissue of the others. They suggest lines separating and confusing thought taken to be chromatic in at once musical, metallic and visual senses. And further, when Deleuze's writing is taken to be a problem, that is, a subject that begs scrutiny of its composition at the same time its lines of reasoning are being followed, when its creative strategies, or its invitations to make interrelated connections and discern different strata and riftlines in its overall mass, are viewed in the crux of the statements, it asks for extensive speculation on the part of those of us who are *not* philosophers.[5]

On these grounds I should like to ascertain how the work moves across hemispheric boundaries and how it can inform the reading of the literatures, beginning with the sustained study of Proust, to which it tends only to refer or, in passing, invite its reader to recall. Time and again, in the *Pourparlers, 1972–1990* (Negotiations, 1971–1990) in his *Dialogues* (Dialogues) with Claire Parnet, and in *Mille plateaux* (A Thousand Plateaus) Deleuze argues that American literature offers open vistas and new spaces that are lacking in the French canon. But no sustained study of either tradition exists within Deleuze's work. Outside of his essay on Proust, the presence of Artaud in *Logique du sens* (Logic of Sense) or occasional articles on Jarry, Zola and Renoir, Deleuze's appreciation of the French canon is highly selective. He casts his eyes towards Anglo-American writing to counter what he takes to be the sterility of the very style that Proust also admonished. French literature, he and Guattari affirm,

> is too taken up with measuring walls, even with building them, in sounding black holes, in composing faces. The French novel is profoundly pessimistic, idealistic, 'a critique of life rather than a creation of life.' It stuffs its characters into the hole, it makes them bounce off the wall. It can only conceive of organized travels and of salvation through art. It's still a Catholic salvation, in other words, a salvation through eternity. It spends its time making points instead of drawing lines, active lines of fight or of positive deterritorialization. Entirely other is the Anglo-American novel. (1980: 228)

Readers weaned on the French tradition wonder immediately if a politics is not informing the position being taken. In America – at least in the postwar years and in the decade from the early 1960s up to 1980, the halcyon days of theory in which Deleuze's writing emerged and became visible to Anglo-American readers – French writing served to displace a tradition in which the American and British novel served didactic and homiletic ends. High-school and college students plodded through Thackeray, Austen, and Trollope to be shown that by dint of the endurance required to read each of their monuments they too would be edified. Students were told to heed the virtue of being 'athletes dying young' by memorising the forgettable verse of A. E. Housman (in the line of 'Malt can do more than Milton can/To justify God's ways to man,' impelling them not to look into the pewter pot to see the world as 'the world's not', and so on).[6] Undergraduate classes on Hawthorne and James served the purpose of showing students that, before such complex crafts of fiction, they would be subjects eternally subservient to a new and great tradition.

Melville stood as the genius of enigma and the author of a novel, *Moby-Dick*, that was an 'American' epic to be revered and fetishised but not read in any close or critical way. By contrast, students who worked along a diagonal axis used Balzac and Proust to liberate themselves from the moral yoke of common sense and pragmatism. Zola, Maupassant and Vallès shaped worlds for reader daring to leave the miasm and paranoia of the Cold War and so-called communist menace. What the French tradition of analysis, with its *explication de textes*, brought to articulating parts and wholes and to careful treatment of the torsions of discourse, led students astray from the edifying roads of Anglo-American traditions. Thus the foreign reader of French who follows Deleuze's turn away from France, deliberately aimed at defying an established canon by going back to the British Isles and the New World, takes part in a folding process or, more likely, a sudden and new point of view, or perception of a condition of variation that amounts to a discovery of what has always been obvious but invisible.[7]

With Deleuze the Anglo-American reader of French returns to native idioms of literature to find them estranging whatever goes without saying, acquiring a vastly different look from what was given in their representation in pragmatic traditions. They no longer bear the label of formative texts or works attesting to the new ground of a national experience, grown in the soil of 'our own' subjectivity and signature. Already the two leitmotivs of Deleuze's occasional work on literature – in which great authors write in foreign or estranging idioms in the fabric of their work, and in which the same figures are forever minoritarian because their public needs to be invented, not written for – displace all geographical and historical claims for national traditions. Works that had been framed in manuals, whether in France or elsewhere, begin thus to mingle and circulate among each other.

'I and My Chimney', a short story that Herman Melville published in *Putnam's Magazine* in 1856, would seem to be a case study. It never figures in Deleuze's allusions to Melville that stud the dialogues, recorded conversations or the rhapsodies of *A Thousand Plateaus*. Nor is it mentioned in 'Bartleby, ou la formule' (in 1993: 89–114), the philosopher's single article on the writer he elsewhere cites as often as any other in his canon. The story might stand as a test for what Deleuze can 'make' or 'do' with literature when the work is set on an axis that moves back and forth across geographical boundaries. On cursory glance the tale tells of immobility, of the self-defensive retreat of an 'I' into a loving relation with the chimney of his New England abode.

A tale in the first person tells of nothing more than the narrator's identification with and protection of his pyramidally-shaped chimney from the attack of family or community who might want to destroy the structure. It resembles 'Bartleby' by being a study of self-immurement, or of bodily assimilation into a walled space of enclosure. It recalls the 'boxes' Deleuze uses to describe the maddening compartmentalisation of the late Proust, but also a regime of abstraction in which characters or gendered subjects, identified by a psychology given in the signs displayed on their faces, dissolve into a relation of language to its own multilateral movements. The story relates how the 'I', the sovereign sign of subjectivity, is not individuated by dint of telling of his mad love with his architectural object.

The configuration somewhat resembles Deleuze's allegory of the

Baroque House in which a thinking inhabitant is located in an upper storey that is dark and closed off from the world whence he or she receives sensations emanating from a quasi-public space below.[8] In this sense the tale also rehearses the origins of modern philosophy by setting itself in an insulated thermal zone where an 'I' can think as a result of the parallelism of one part of a couple 'smoking' its pipe in a preestablished concord or in parallel with the other. It would be a faintly Spinozist remodelling of the Cartesian space of thinking in the *poêle*, where the slow warming of the closed space animates the brain and slowly heats matter enough to prime cogitation. In this story 'I and my chimney still smoke our pipes' (Melville 1987: 375). The subject and the object or predicate fold over and upon each other.

The narrating self occupies his home less than he lives in a relation with it. From the first sentence, 'I and my chimney, two gray-headed old smokers, reside in the country' (1987: 352), to the beginning of the last paragraph, '[i]t is now some seven years since I have stirred from home. My city friends all wonder why I don't come to see them, as in former times' (1987: 377) nothing really happens.[9] The chimney is described in a way that it dissolves into an *oiko-nomia*, a household economy in and of the world at large. The narrator relates how his erstwhile and pragmatic spouse and two daughters do their best to have it 'razeed' in a campaign of home improvement when abetted by an architectural planner named Hiram Scribe. The narrator 'more than even now . . . suspected a plot' (1987: 374) when Scribe, armed with a crowbar, returns to the domicile to see if a secret space might hold within the stone a mummified treasure. The self-defending 'I' imagines the family's ruse to destroy the cherished object in the name of a dig while he speculates on what he thinks might be an Egyptian archaeology displaced into New England. A miniature pyramid could be the subject of a post-Napoleonic excavation, the squat shape of the chimney suggesting that it might have been designed, if not to conceal a treasure, at least to encrypt a secret.

At the same time the lines of the story begin to configure a hieroglyph. As an enigma the chimney resists the transcriptive mission of language. The paginal surface is connoted to be a dumb and mute wall of stone, the objectal mass of the latter become an impediment to any nominative appropriation. The object itself is akin to what Deleuze perceives in the similarity of the *wall* of the street of that name in the emblem of 'Bartleby the Scrivener' and the great white *whale* (wall, or 'whal') of resistance that the crew of the *Pequod* seeks as their quarry. In its form then, in its image of a 'whitewashed wall' (1987: 366) on which it is written, 'I and My Chimney' would count among the many obsessive shapes in the *oeuvre* –

cetaceans, islands, stone masonry, and even the *oeuvre* itself – that resist reduction to nomination. That the chimney pierces the roof as might 'an anvil-headed whale, through the crest of a billow' (1987: 355) of the sea indicates an affinity with the other work.

The text constantly brings into view its printed surface as if it were a hieroglyph translating its plot into strings of verbal images that accrete and hide meaning when they are seen describing the very space of their narration. The form of expression is indissociable from the story in the same way that the narrator himself is inseparable from the object he describes with reverence. There results a 'perverse magic, I a thousand times think' (1987: 364) of proliferations of lines of meaning radiating at points where the form of the printed characters is set in play with that of the content they would appear to be transcribing. The chimney becomes more and less than an enigma because it translates into the sign of a path born of a parallel reflection of smoking pipes; a *cheminée* in Melville's French, or a passage skyward; a weave of lines of smoke that move through a containing tunnel; and a forge, a *caminus*, in which the industry of the creation takes place in the site described, *semper ardente camino*. The chimney seems to be an aggregate of minimal but selectively decisive marks, each one in itself insignificant, that generates force by dint of recombination. When passing travellers laugh at the squat form of its apex over the roof of his abode, he notes,

> But what cared I? The same travelers would travel across the sea to view Kenilworth peeling away, and for a very good reason; that of all artists of the picturesque, decay wears the palm – I would say, the ivy. In fact, I've often thought that the proper place for my old chimney is ivied old England.
>
> In vain my wife – with what probably ulterior intent will, ere long, appear – solemnly warned me, that unless something were done, and speedily, we should be burnt to the ground, owing to the holes crumbling through the aforesaid blotchy parts, where the chimney joined the roof. (1987: 356–7)

Summoned with irony are romantic tropes of ruin, extending from nineteenth-century taste for Du Bellay's Rome to Tintern Abbey or, westward, to the land of Hawthorne 'and his mosses'. The resulting itinerary implied by the critique of the romantic era is one of picturesque sublimity flattened or mapped on to two dimensions.

'I' grows into the '*i*-vy' of what '*I*'ve' felt to be the ideal site of the chimney in 'ivied' old England, in something of a painting in the mode of Constable or the Barbizon School. But the images is in *New* England, not the nature about Salisbury or Fontainebleau. 'In vain' his wife burns to destroy his beloved object. *I-v*: the ivy tale of the *I* in his upstate abode adjoins the *v* such that a 'four', an *iv*, or a four-square glyph emerges in the syntax so often reiterating the same formula. But in French, an oven or a furnace, a *four*, is cognate with the act of what the narrator seems to be celebrating, the act of making a chimney, that what will be both success and failure, as it will *faire four*. Ivy four: the invention of the space for the tale is made coextensive with the areas where it will be received in the 'ivy league' implied by Melville's tourniquet, a group of four Latinising New England schools that became associated with the climbing weed when the Roman numeral, when linked to their initial sum, was read as *i-v*, or eye-vee.

At this point in the narrative the 'I' is transformed or estranged into a parasitical vine that lends a bogus aura to the old stones that its tendrils seem to lick and grasp. In a general vein it might be said that the ivied I becomes floral or aspires to a condition other than a subject-position or a self-arrogated agency that comes with the utterance of the *I*. The narrator of this story embodies what happens to the 'I' before it gains autonomy or self-identity. Here, in miniature, in the ricochets of three or four letters in the description of an English country house displaced into postrevolutionary America, in the narrative picture of the story the 'I' 'becomes chimney'. A molecular entity becomes molar, and vice versa. In the implied atomism the smoke that breathes through the narrator and his chimney would be an essence composed of rock, mortar, brick and protoplasm. The atmospheric quality of Melville's text sets the movement of its signifying matter in play with what would otherwise be the sedimented matter of the episodes of a plot.

The unmitigated egocentrism of the narrator dissolves exactly where it is edified. The ostensive subjectivity of a character who might dare say 'I' is sublated in the text literally and, as it were, *avant la lettre*. It is conveyed by a surfeit of pronominal markers betraying a vacillating position in the midst of what seems to be an obdurate and stubborn self-defensiveness. No single figure prevails as much as 'I'. In a flurry we read: 'What I am about to add . . . I would say . . . "Wife," said I . . . "Of one thing, however, I am proud . . ." I've often thought . . . Am I bound to supply [a traveller] with a sweet taste?' (1987: 356). The repetition causes the I, like the phantasm of the chimney being a pyramid, to turn into a mute calligram that confers the letter with the orthogonal shape of a chimney.[10] 'I' turns into a cipher determining a perspective on variation. In other words, it does not mark a subject-position that would assure a speaker's place or existential agency in the world, but only a token sign or a relational trait. The overweaning narcissism of the narrator betrayed by a surfeit of 'I' turns into a perception where visibility takes place, that is, where visibility is seen becoming visible, thanks to the fact that the staccato repetition of the subject pronoun 'I' eradicates an implied presence of a face or body of a narrator. Underscored in the aural register is a visual configuration that betrays or translates a dimension other than that which is being spoken or described. The eye is the I that swarms in the text. If Deleuze's lexicon applies to the effect of the shifter in the story, the 'I' becomes imperceptible because it bleeds, as a vowel and drawn line, into the surrounding verbal texture of other lines.

If anything is encrypted in the pyramid-chimney-world of the story, it might be that which most often meets the eye – the I. But if we consider Deleuze's concept of the *celibatarian machine* that characterizes Proust's Marcel and Melville's Ishmael, it is worth examining how the tale encrypts the beloved other, the *wife* (a variant on *I*, *v*, *v*, and *e*, a four letters of *fiwe* to the *iv* in the ciphering of the sentences) in the space being created. She inhabits the area in a fashion not unrelated to the calculation of the square plan of the chimney (an 'adequate conception of the magnitude of this chimney is only to be got at by a sort of process in the higher mathematics, by a method somewhat akin to those whereby the surprising distances of fixed stars are computed' (1987: 358)). Like 'I', 'she' is ciphered and compassed.

Biographical critics of Melville might affirm that the misogyny of the work owes to the writer plotting a 'room of one's own' by writing a nasty piece of fiction in the course of a life spent in insecurity and shrewishness.[11] 'Wife' becomes a field of energy countering what is emitted by 'this chimney less as a pile of masonry than as a personage' (1987: 357). If the description of his characters seems directed towards a centre or a vanishing point, the wife can be seen to be of a measure similar to the architectural plan of the house and its fireplace. She is almost squinched into the space. 'And here, respectfully craving her permission, I must say a few words about this enterprising wife of mine' (1987: 360). The wife brims with 'vitality' that rhymes with life while he, passive, although not death, remains a figure of living ashes. A philosopher, he enjoys 'sitting in the comfortable shadow of my chimney, with ashes not unwelcome at my feet, and ashes not unwelcome all but in my mouth' (1987: 372). His salient trait is ashen, his colour is assimilated to the spent forces and the 'pipes' that are at once his innards, the burnt bowl of the clay bottom of his smoking instrument 'we sons of clay, that is my pipe and I . . .' (1987: 370)) and the threshold of the chimney. When fearful of a conspiracy spawned among his spouse, Biddy, he projects the three of them hiring

Hiram Scribe to destroy the chimney in guise of searching for a concealed treasure. He appeals to synecdoche – the figure of a part for a whole – to conflate the secret space of the building that surrounds the chimney, his wife's body, and her being. 'Secret ash-hole wife, why don't you have it? Yes, I dare say there is a secret ash-hole in the chimney; for where do all the ashes go that we drop down the queer hole yonder?' (1987: 372).

An abstraction of a group of bodies without organs emerges from the lower orifice of the chimney and the odd 'hole yonder' at the center of the narrator's gaze. That he mocks her for crawling into the chimney's ash-hole implies that the bodies are surfaces with orifices that cannot be distinguished by phases of sexual evolution.[12] He follows his wife's entry into the inner walls of the strange womb, but all the while he describes the chimney as if it were something bearing zonal intensities, miniature pocks or manifold erotic sites, 'out-of-the-way cupboards and closets, of all sorts and sizes, clinging here and there, like nests in the crotches of some old oak' (1987: 373). The anal drive of Melville's story seems only apparent; at best, it is facetiously occulted. An expression of orificial intensity collapses official hierarchies of eyes, ears, nose, mouth and anus.

'Car enfin l'anus aussi exprime une intensité, ici le rapprochement de zéro de la distance qui ne se décompose pas que les éléments ne changent de nature. Champ d'anus, tout comme meute de loups. [. . .] Devenir trou, c'est se déterritorialiser' (Deleuze and Guattari 1980: 45) (In the last analysis the anus is expressive of an intensity, here the meeting at degree-zero of the distance that decomposes only if the elements change in nature. The field of the anus just like a pack of wolves. (. . .) To become a hole means being deterritorialised).[13] Although Deleuze and Guattari take Freud to task for seeking to correct the perversion of an anal phantasm in *The Wolf-Man*, and although they conflate the wolf (*loup*) and the anus (*trou*), they also deterritorialize what they elsewhere thematise in sidelong glances at Melville's *oeuvre* in *A Thousand Plateaus* (1980: 231). A drive to nestle into holes serves to locate where the 'I', as pure point of view, is related not to 'scopophilia', or some sinful malady of ocular pleasure, but to a totalising process.

The Wolf-Man, they note, 'pense: et mon cul, c'est pas un loup?' (thinks: and isn't my asshole a wolf?). In the translinguistic register they share with Melville, the thought that an anus may be a wolf is tied to its presence as a monocular magnifying glass, a *loupe*, heard in the Anglo-American pronunciation of *loup*. There is, too, the figure of a feedback *loop* of the kind that seems to move between the textual shape of 'I and My Chimney' and its imaginary field of reference. The printed discourse as an image or a field of intensive points feeds back to the plot and vice versa, such that different meanings are glimpsed in the aural or tran-scriptive register. *Mon cul* would thus seem to be one or two letters away from a *monocle*, that is *mon(o)cul(aire)* in the visual field insofar as it is celebrated in the anal phantasm. The process shatters the closure of a phobic reading that would underscore Melville's propensity for ash-holes. Pleasure begins to circulate all over the textual surface of the fiction.

One of the striking features of 'I and My Chimney' that intensifies Deleuze's reading of Proust is found in the absence of any discernible psychology that would owe to the taste for physiognomy so prevalent in contemporary fiction of the day (in the tradition of that name, that Balzac distorts in *La physionomie du marriage* and in the first section of *La fille aux yeux d'or*). This story is stuffed with architectural description, some sketches of romantic landscapes written with an ironic pen, and sardonic vignettes of domestic life, but hardly ever is attention paid to the visages of its characters. Every personage seems to be invisible. There are chimney-holes, but not faces; intensities, but neither psychology nor subjectivity. The narrator is faceless. He stands under – is almost sodomised by and sodomises – his chimney ('I bring up the rear of my chimney . . . and that too, both in fancy and fact. In brief, my chimney is my superior' (1987: 352)). It and 'I' are defined positionally. Husband and wife are likened to arboreal shapes, not integral human beings. Where she is 'straight as a pine' he, with his sciatica, is 'sometimes crippled up as any old apple tree' (1987: 360).

In Deleuze and Guattari's reading of *Un amour de Swann* in *Mille plateaux* Odette de Crécy's face is recalled having 'wide or yellow cheeks, and eyes like black holes [*trous noirs*]' (1980: 227). For Swann her face always recalls something else, often a painting, one of its details, or else a musical phrase. It is a 'white wall' pocked with black holes. On a second level, 'Odette's face moves on a line that goes toward a single black hole,' which is that of Swann's passion, a 'catatonic hole about which all the lines of music and the landscapes seem to turn' (1980: 228). Then, at a third echelon, when Swann falls out of love, he perceives at social gatherings the faces of the domestics and guests '*decomposed* into autonomous aesthetic traits, as if the line of picturality were recovering an independence *at once beyond the wall and outside of the black hole*' (1980: 228; emphasis mine). The same process marks the incident of the *madeleine*, when the narrator 'chews on' (*mâchouille*) the pastry when there suddenly appears an involuntary memory of a black hole, out of which, we later learn, he will exit by means of art and of art alone.

The unity of fragments and shards of signs, argued Deleuze in his work on *A la recherche du temps perdu*, are destined for failure. Therein also the writer's success. The book that Proust wanted to compare to the synthetic and scholastic integrity of a French cathedral in the high-gothic style could not find analogies in which textual elements would be the proper homologues to arcades, glazed triforia, clerestoreys; bays, side-aisles, transepts, choirs, ambulatories, chevets; flying buttresses, ogival ribs, transverse arches, or tas-de-charge: however seductive had been the transcending holism of Emile Mâle's iconographical studies of medieval art and architecture, in which the viewer of a detail on any surface could relate the part to the entire edifice, the commanding architectural metaphor had to be jettisoned. Now Melville would be of similar allure in the utterly logical but also ill-fit figure of a chimney that would be at once the self-and-other, the part-and-whole, or the figure-and-ground, if not of a narrator vying to become the obdurate matter of a stone hearth and its pipe, then of a writer seeking to produce a literary 'monument' that resists the wear and tear of time. To those desires 'I and My Chimney' says *no*. The care with which the tale of an apparently inept man in love with a stone pipe is crafted infers the presence of a drive that 'would prefer not to' eternise a signature. The story can be esteemed both for what it seeks not to do and also for its pulverisation of the individuated self.

The story is thus reflective more of a magnificent obsession than of a schematic design. In its parts that do not connect to wholes the tale becomes, in Deleuze's terms, a minoritarian work. It invents itself with its own pieces and, in doing so, fails to appeal to a sum of established formulas or a tested public of readers. The third sentence of the story inaugurates the sense of a mosaic of fragments. 'Though I always say, *I and my chimney*, as Cardinal Wolsey used to say, *I and my King*, yet this egotistic way of speaking, wherein I take precedence of my chimney, is hardly borne out by the facts; in everything, except the above phrase, my chimney taking precedence of me' (1987: 352). Allusion to Cardinal Wolsey, advisor to Henry VIII, also the most powerful figure in English domestic and foreign policy in the early sixteenth century, invokes both a world past and an inaugural movement of *translatio studii*. The 'I' who settles into the American earth is and is not so imperious as the Cardinal. It strives to obtain a mastery of its own insular space, its 'house', an isle and a kingdom in a western hemisphere. The narrator defends an I-land that resists European dominion. Yet, as the tale unfolds, the comparison itself seems to erode as the space encloses upon itself. The plot of the tale tells of a retreat from a whole and a drive towards metamorphosis by which the human becomes inorganic matter. A self-pulverising or self-triturating effect accompanies the move from a world-historical scene to another, of more modest measure, of self-dissemination.

'The world', notes Deleuze in an essay on Walt Whitman, can be seen 'as an array of heterogenous parts: an infinite patchwork, or a limitless wall of dried stones (a cemented wall, or the pieces of a puzzle recomposing a totality)' (1993: 76). In this light the confusion of Proust and Melville seems almost patent when Deleuze, or Deleuze and Guattari, conflate the 'white whale' of language with the 'white wall' of Odette de Crécy's face. Responding to the question about how to get out of the black hole or how to cut a chink in the stone and mortar, Deleuze and Guattari observe that the French novel measures walls, sounds the depths of black holes, and takes pleasure in describing faces. The Anglo-American novel, they retort, shows how difficult it is to climb out of the 'black hole of subjectivity' (1980: 229). A wall is breached, and a face undone or left aside when a personage can 'become-flower' or 'become-rock' (1980: 229). Crystallising their words, they say that 'decomposing the face is the same as piercing the wall of the signifier, climbing out of the black hole of subjectivity' (1980: 230).

No short story offers a better exit from the 'ash-hole' of subjectivity than 'I and My Chimney'. Faces that would be wholes disappear from the very beginning, and the 'becoming-rock' of the narrator appears to be what distinguishes the 'black hole' of the chimney itself when the narrator is assimilated into its stone, brick and mortar. The I is the part separated from and melded into its whole, in its world-figure that is economy – the household of the *oikos*, of habitation at large, an arena of activity cast as a total social fact. It would seem that the New Englander who defends his decomposed relation with his chimney bears more than a passing resemblance to what Deleuze and Guattari discern in the confusion of Proust and Melville in respect to cream-coloured faces, black orifices, white walls and parts of worlds:

C'est seulement dans le trou noir de la conscience et de la passion subjective qu'on découvrira les particules capturées, échauffées, transformées qu'il faut relancer pour un amour vivant, non subjectif, où chacun se connecte aux espaces inconnus de l'autre sans y entrer ni les conquérir, où les lignes se composent comme des lignes brisées. C'est seulement au sein du visage, du fond de son trou noir et sur son mur blanc, qu'on pourra libérer les traits de visagéité, comme des oiseaux, non pas revenir à une tête primitive, mais inventer les combinaisons où les traits se connectent à des traits de picturalité, de musicalité, eux-mêmes libérés de leurs codes respectifs. (232)

[Only in the black hole of consciousness and of subjective passion do we discover captured, heated, transformed particles that must be thrown over and again for a live, non-subjective love, in which each one is connected to the unknown spaces of the other without entering into or conquering them, in which lines are composed like broken lines. Only in the heart of the face, from the depth of the black hole and on its white wall can the traits of faceness be bred, like birds, not to return to a primordial head, but to invent combinations in which these traits are connected to the traits of the sense of landscape, to traits of picturality, of musicality, themselves liberated from their respective codes.]

The enthusiast of literature or theorist who dares say 'I' can use his or her own Deleuze as might Melville's narrator his chimney. By way of conclusion, we might say that, first, Deleuze confuses a preferred body of literature, mostly of Anglo-American origin, but one riddled by other languages passing through its signifiers, with his own tactics of writing. Different works have different styles and modes of composition. In *Proust et les signes* the author vies to make the sensibility of the narrator equivalent to his own reading of the 'signs' of *A la recherche du temps perdu* that inspire the pursuit of other signs. In *Mille plateaux* a cinematic and emblematic composition of images and texts comprises a glossalia, in which multiple itineraries are woven into a novel and a summa that bear no resemblance to any other work of his or Félix Guattari's signature. Other books are the results of other tactics.

But it is clear that, second, Deleuze's work *as* literature, *and* literature, informs, by way of its own identity with them, works of a personal and difficult signature. Melville figures strongly in his pantheon, and the *oeuvre* is often conflated with Proust and the Anglo-American novel in general. But third, and most important, when seen as an effect and a mosaic of many enamelled fragments, the work informs other and many productively estranging readings on the basis of its own process. Such is Deleuze and his Melville and such too, as each diligent reader might be likely to say, I and my Deleuze.

Notes

1. The work is assembled in his *Deleuzism: A Metacommentary* (2000).
2. Here and elsewhere reference is made to French editions of the writings of Deleuze and of Deleuze and Félix Guattari as listed in the bibliography. English translations are mine.
3. A reader referring to the French original quickly notes that, contrary to the rules of English usage, Deleuze rarely uses conjunctions to link one clause to another.

Each proposition is separated by commas. The resulting syntax seems faithful in style to the fragmentary quality of the impressions of the narrator's discoveries at the end of *La recherche*.

4. Anglo-American readers may have first encountered explanation of this effect in Germaine Brée (1969), *Du temps perdu au Temps retrouvé: Introduction à l'oeuvre de Marcel Proust* (1950 and 1969), in which she notes that the narrator is *never* given to passing any moral judgement on what he or she observes and describes. In respect to the 'great tradition' of the nineteenth- and early twentieth-century novel, that was said by Stendhal to be a mirror held above a road along which it strolled, Proust's 'machine-narrator' stands as a culmination and realisation.

5. We can thank Jean-Louis Leutrat for opening the *oeuvre* to creative rereading. He advocates that the 'users' of Deleuze first of all be familiar with the sum of the writing, and that they use the same stratagems with which Deleuze crafts his work as creative form. 'When Deleuze declares that in his view concepts are like personages, he must be read as might a novelist, or as a poet,' in 'L'horloge et la momie,' in Leutrat (1997): 407. Leutrat adds that to *apply* Deleuze to a given work means missing the relational quality that inspires reflection moving diagonally from Deleuze through and about issues of cinema, philosophy, poetics, and the like.

6. In his *Invention of Love* (performed in London, winter 1999) Tom Stoppard offers a keen perspective on the Victorian bard who edified generations of students in his wake. In that play Housman's athlete would be a flunky *erotomane* who cannot drive desire through language and sensation. He would be the poet who scales his verse to stave off what its Latin origins might otherwise cause it to move. Stoppard's play offers a keen analysis of the history of a repression that might, on the other side of the Channel, be seen in the institution of Sainte-Beuve and his followers.

7. Deleuze's westward glance is not unique. It partakes of a general reorientation of the French artist and writer *away* from the 'academy' of his or her own country. From the middle of the sixteenth century Rome had been the site for the formation of the French writer, scholar, artist, and tourist. After the Second World War the Americas replaced Rome. Consciousness of American commodities had been piqued. Intellectuals saw in American cinema and in the novel, on first view, a refreshing *absence* of tradition that bespoke, as Marcel Mauss and Claude Lévi-Strauss discovered, the presence of many other, indigenous cultures of different type of history. In 'Où les Amériques commencent à faire histoire' Michel Butor sums up the elements of a decisive shift in focus on the part of French intellectuals (1998: 249ff).

8. 'The floor above, blind and closed, but in contrast resonating, like a chamber that would translate into sounds the musical movements from below,' in *Le pli: Leibniz et le Baroque* (Deleuze: 1988: 6)

9. Herman Melville (1987), *The Piazza Tales and Other Proses Pieces, 1839–1860,* in *The Writings of Herman Melville*. All reference will be made to the text of this edition.

10. In a study of the ideogrammatic dimension of Paul Claudel's poetry Henri Meschonnic (1993) notes how the poet saw the word 'toit' as a household made visible to the eye: each surrounding 't' comprised a wall seen in profile, while the 'o' is the woman at the table by the chimney of the 'i' marked by the dot of smoke that rises from the vertical end of its form. Yet, he argues, the conception of language is not entirely built on nature or cratylism; its craft undoes convention. Anglo-American readers will note Deleuze's attraction to Walt Whitman, a poet of grist similar to Claudel, in *Critique et clinique*. 'It's as if the syntax that

composes the sentence, and that makes it a totality capable of turning upon itself, were tending to disappear by liberating an infinite *asyntactic* sentence, which is extended or pushes with hyphens as if they were spatio-temporal intervals' (1993: 77). He calls Whitman's sentence 'an almost mad sentence, with its shifts of direction, its bifurcations, its ruptures and its jumps, its extensions, its burgeonings, its parentheses' (77). The calligram or letter-image inserted into the text would be cause for these effects that in the study of Whitman Deleuze quickly compares to Melville, who is noted for praising how Americans need not write in a British (or, it is implied, a much more controlled and surveiled) style.

11. Editor Warner Berthoff reports that '[p]articularly in the tales of 1853–56 there appears to be, first of all, a fairly constant burden of autobiographical statement. Nearly all remind us somewhere that they are the work of a writer whose literary career seemed by 1853 to have fallen on evil days' (1969: 15).

12. Leo Bersani notes that the motley crew of the *Pequod* seems to be of implacably indifferent origin, all having sprouted from the 'ash-holes' of the earth in *The Culture of Redemption* (1990: 148). He compellingly asserts that 'the homoeroticism itself is merely the secondary expression of a comically anarchic sensuality' (145).

13. More extensive treatment of this passage is taken up in 'From Multiplicities to Folds: On Style and Form in Deleuze', (Conley 1997): 629–46, especially 634–5.

Bibliography

Bersani, Leo (1990), *The Culture of Redemption*, Cambridge, MA: Harvard University Press.

Berthoff, Warner (ed.) (1969), *Great Short Works of Herman Melville*. New York: Harper and Row.

Brée, Germaine (1969), *Du temps perdu au temps retrouvé: Introduction à l'oeuvre de Marcel Proust*, 2nd edn, Paris: Les Belles Lettres.

Buchanan, Ian (2000), *Deleuzism: A Metacommentary*, Durham, NC: Duke University Press.

Butor, Michel (1998), 'Où les Amériques commencent à faire histoire', in Mireille Calle-Gruber (ed.), *Butor et les Amériques*, Paris: l'Harmattan, pp. 249–65.

Conley, Tom (1997), 'From Multiplicities to Folds: On Style and Form in Deleuze', *The South Atlantic Quarterly* 96.3, pp. 629–46.

Deleuze, Gilles (1969), *Logique de sens*, Paris: Éditions de Minuit.

Deleuze, Gilles (1979 [1965]), *Proust et le signes*, 3rd edn, Paris: Presses Universitaires de France.

Deleuze, Gilles (1983), *Cinéma 1: L'image-mouvement*, Paris: Éditions de Minuit.

Deleuze, Gilles (1985), *Cinéma 2: L'image-temps*, Paris: Éditions de Minuit.

Deleuze, Gilles (1988), *Le pli: Leibniz et le Baroque*, Paris: Éditions de Minuit.

Deleuze, Gilles (1990), *Pourparlers*, 1972–1990, Paris: Éditions de Minuit.

Deleuze, Gilles (1992), 'L'epuisé', afterword to Samuel Beckett, *Quad*, Paris: Éditions de Minuit.

Deleuze, Gilles (1993), *Critique et clinique*, Paris: Éditions de Minuit.

Deleuze, Gilles and Guattari Félix (1980), *Capitalisme et schizophrénie 2: Mille plateaux*, Paris: Éditions de Minuit.

Deleuze, Gilles and Parnet Claire, (1977), *Dialogues*, Paris: Flammarion.

Leutrat, Jean-Louis (1997), 'L'horloge et la momie', in Oliver Fahle and Lorenz, Engell, (eds), *Der Film bei Deleuze/Le cinéma selon Deleuze*, Weimar/Paris: Verlag des Hauhaus-Universität Weimar/Presses de la Sorbonne Nouvelle, pp. 407–25.

Melville, Herman (1987), *The Piazza Tales and Other Prose Pieces, 1839–1860*. In *The Writings of Herman Melville 9*, The Northwestern-Newberry Edition, Evanston and Chicago, IL: Northwestern University Press and The Newberry Library.
Meschonnic, Henri (1993), 'Calligraphies de Claudel', in Gisèle Mathieu-Castellani, (ed), *La pensée de l'image*, Paris: Presses de l'Université de Paris-VIII, pp. 35–56.

Notes on Contributors

Bruce Baugh
Associate Professor of Philosophy at the University College of the Cariboo (Canada). He has published articles on Deleuze, Sartre, Heidegger and the aesthetics of rock music.

Ian Buchanan
Assistant Professor in the School of English and European Languages and Literatures at the University of Tasmania. He is the author of *Deleuzism: A Metacommentary* (Edinburgh University Press, 2000) and *Michel de Certeau: Cultural Theorist* (Sage, 2000).

Claire Colebrook
Teaches in English Studies at Stirling University. She is the author of *New Literary Histories* (1997), *Ethics and Representation* (Edinburgh University Press, 1999) and the co-editor, with Ian Buchanan, of *Deleuze and Feminist Theory* (Edinburgh University Press, 2000). She has published a number of articles on Blake, Feminist Theory, Ethics and Contemporary European Philosophy. She has completed a book on irony, to be published in 2001, and is now writing a book on happiness.

André Pierre Colombat
Associate Professor of French at Loyola College in Maryland. He is the author of *Deleuze et la littérature* (1990) and *The Holocaust in French Film*.

Tom Conley
Teaches in the Department of Romance Languages and Literatures at Harvard University. He has translated *The Fold: Leibniz and the Baroque*

and written book-chapters on Deleuze in *Le Cinéma chez Deleuze, La pensée de l'image*, and *The Brain is the Screen*. Articles on similar topics have appeared in *Iris, Discourse*, and *The South Atlantic Quarterly*.

T. Hugh Crawford
Associate Professor in the Science, Technology and Culture program at the Georgia Institute of Technology. He is author of *Modernism, Medicine, and William Carlos Williams* and is editor of *Configurations*, a journal of science and technology studies published by the Johns Hopkins University Press. He is currently writing a book on Melville, Foucault and Deleuze.

Marlene Goldman
Teaches Canadian literature at the University of Toronto. She is the author of, *Paths of Desire: Images of Exploration and Mapping in Canadian Women's Writing* (University of Toronto Press, 1997). She has published numerous articles on Canadian fiction and women's writing. She is currently completing a study of apocalyptic discourse in Canadian fiction.

Eugene W. Holland
Associate Professor of French and Comparative Studies at the Ohio State University. In addition to articles on modern French literature and theory, he has published *Baudelaire and Schizoanalysis: The Sociopoetics of Modernism* (Cambridge University Press, 1993) and *Deleuze and Guattari's Anti-Oedipus: Introduction to Schizoanalysis* (Routledge, 1999).

Gregg Lambert
Assistant Professor of English and Textual Studies, Syracuse University, New York. His numerous essays and articles on Deleuze and Guattari have appeared in the United States and the UK, a selection of which will be included in a forthcoming volume on Deleuze and the philosophy of expression.

John Marks
Reader in French in the Department of Modern Languages at The Nottingham Trent University. Recent publications include *Gilles Deleuze: Vitalism and Multiplicity* (Pluto Press, 1998). He is currently working on an edited collection dealing with contemporary French Cultural Debates.

Timothy S. Murphy
Assistant Professor of English at the University of Oklahoma in Norman. He is the author of *Wising Up the Marks: The Amodern William Burroughs* (University of California Press, 1997) and general editor of *Genre: Forms of Discourse and Culture*.

Kenneth Surin
Teaches in the Literature Program at Duke University.

Index